AMERICAN INDIANS:
THE FIRST OF THIS LAND

THE POPULATION OF THE UNITED STATES IN THE 1980s

A Census Monograph Series

AMERICAN INDIANS:
THE FIRST OF THIS LAND

C. Matthew Snipp

for the
National Committee for Research
on the 1980 Census

RUSSELL SAGE FOUNDATION / NEW YORK

The Russell Sage Foundation

The Russell Sage Foundation, one of the oldest of America's general purpose foundations, was established in 1907 by Mrs. Margaret Olivia Sage for "the improvement of social and living conditions in the United States." The Foundation seeks to fulfill the mandate by fostering the development and dissemination of knowledge about the political, social, and economic problems of America. It conducts research in the social sciences and public policy, and publishes books and pamphlets that derive from this research.

The Board of Trustees is responsible for oversight and the general policies of the Foundation, while administrative direction of the program and staff is vested in the President, assisted by the officers and staff. The President bears final responsibility for the decision to publish a manuscript as a Russell Sage Foundation book. In reaching a judgment on the competence, accuracy, and objectivity of each study, the President is advised by the staff and selected expert readers. The conclusions and interpretations in Russell Sage Foundation publications are those of the authors and not of the Foundation, its Trustees, or its staff. Publication by the Foundation, therefore, does not imply endorsement of the contents of the study.

Library of Congress Cataloging-in-Publication Data

Snipp, C. Matthew.
   American Indians : the first of this land / C. Matthew Snipp.
      p.   cm. — (The Population of the United States in the 1980s)
   "For the National Committee for Research on the 1980 Census."
   Bibliography: p.
   Includes index.
   ISBN 0-87154-822-4
   ISBN 0-87154-823-2 (pbk)
   1. Indians of North America—Census, 1980. I. National Committee
for Research on the 1980 Census. II. Title. III. Series.
E98.C3S65   1989
304.6'08997—dc20   89-6445
                                                 CIP

First Paperback Edition 1991

The National Committee for Research on the 1980 Census

The committee is sponsored by the Social Science Research Council, the Russell Sage Foundation, and the Alfred P. Sloan Foundation, in collaboration with the U.S. Bureau of the Census. The opinions, findings, and conclusions or recommendations expressed in the monographs supported by the committee are those of the author(s) and do not necessarily reflect the views of the committee or its sponsors.

Foreword

American Indians: The First of This Land is one of an ambitious series of volumes aimed at converting the vast statistical yield of the 1980 census into authoritative analyses of major changes and trends in American life. This series, "The Population of the United States in the 1980s," represents an important episode in social science research and revives a long tradition of independent census analysis. First in 1930, and then again in 1950 and 1960, teams of social scientists worked with the U.S. Bureau of the Census to investigate significant social, economic, and demographic developments revealed by the decennial censuses. These census projects produced three landmark series of studies, providing a firm foundation and setting a high standard for our present undertaking.

There is, in fact, more than a theoretical continuity between those earlier census projects and the present one. Like those previous efforts, this new census project has benefited from close cooperation between the Census Bureau and a distinguished, interdisciplinary group of scholars. Like the 1950 and 1960 research projects, research on the 1980 census was initiated by the Social Science Research Council and the Russell Sage Foundation. In deciding once again to promote a coordinated program of census analysis, Russell Sage and the Council were mindful not only of the severe budgetary restrictions imposed on the Census Bureau's own publishing and dissemination activities in the 1980s, but also of the extraordinary changes that have occurred in so many dimensions of American life over the past two decades.

The studies constituting "The Population of the United States in the 1980s" were planned, commissioned, and monitored by the National Committee for Research on the 1980 Census, a special committee appointed by the Social Science Research Council and sponsored by the Council, the Russell Sage Foundation, and the Alfred P. Sloan Foundation, with the collaboration of the U.S. Bureau of the Census. This committee includes leading social scientists from a broad range of fields—demography, economics, education, geography, history, political science, sociology, and statistics. It has been the committee's task to select the main topics for research, obtain highly qualified specialists to carry out that research, and provide the structure necessary to facilitate coordination among researchers and with the Census Bureau.

The topics treated in this series span virtually all the major features of American society—ethnic groups (blacks, Hispanics, foreign-born); spatial dimensions (migration, neighborhoods, housing, regional and metropolitan growth and decline); and status groups (income levels, families and households, women). Authors were encouraged to draw not only on the 1980 census but also on previous censuses and on subsequent national data. Each individual research project was assigned a special advisory panel made up of one committee member, one member nominated by the Census Bureau, one nominated by the National Science Foundation, and one or two other experts. These advisory panels were responsible for project liaison and review and for recommendations to the National Committee regarding the readiness of each manuscript for publication. With the final approval of the chairman of the National Committee, each report was released to the Russell Sage Foundation for publication and distribution.

The debts of gratitude incurred by a project of such scope and organizational complexity are necessarily large and numerous. The committee must thank, first, its sponsors—the Social Science Research Council, the Russell Sage Foundation, and the Alfred P. Sloan Foundation. The long-range vision and day-to-day persistence of these organizations and individuals sustained this research program over many years. The active and willing cooperation of the Bureau of the Census was clearly invaluable at all stages of this project, and the extra commitment of time and effort made by Bureau economist James R. Wetzel must be singled out for special recognition. A special tribute is also due to David L. Sills of the Social Science Research Council, staff member of the committee, whose organizational, administrative, and diplomatic skills kept this complicated project running smoothly.

The committee also wishes to thank those organizations that contributed additional funding to the 1980 census report—the Ford Foundation and its deputy vice president, Louis Winnick, the National Science Foundation, the National Institute on Aging, and the National Institute of Child Health and Human Development. Their support of the research program in general and of several particular studies is gratefully acknowledged.

The ultimate goal of the National Committee and its sponsors has been to produce a definitive, accurate, and comprehensive picture of the

U.S. population in the 1980s, a picture that would be primarily descriptive but also enriched by a historical perspective and a sense of the challenges for the future inherent in the trends of today. We hope our readers will agree that the present volume takes a significant step toward achieving that goal.

CHARLES F. WESTOFF

Chairman and Executive Director
National Committee for Research
on the 1980 Census

For my parents, Roland and Ozella

Acknowledgements

An undertaking such as this is possible only with support and guidance from many quarters. Research support was provided by the National Committee for Research on the 1980 Census sponsored by the Social Science Research Council, the Russell Sage Foundation, and the Alfred P. Sloan Foundation. Additional support was provided by the University of Maryland's Computer Science Center. This project was completed while I was on the faculty of the Department of Sociology at the University of Maryland–College Park.

There are many individuals to whom I owe a debt of gratitude for their contributions. Reynolds Farley and Suzanne Bianchi first encouraged me to consider preparing a census monograph on American Indians. Subsequent to the funding of this work, Professors James Sweet and Glenn Fuguitt of the University of Wisconsin graciously assisted me with the acquisition of data. Clarence Talley carried out the many extensive file construction and data analytic programming tasks. Research assistance also was provided by Regina Dibbiwayan and Isik Aytac. Kelly Zanin and Carol Jones provided excellent clerical and bibliographic assistance.

I owe an expecially large debt to my colleagues who read and commented on all or parts of manuscript drafts. Nancy Breen, Fred Eggan, Kenneth C. W. Kammeyer, and Gene F. Summers gave many helpful comments on selected chapters. Joane Nagel, Gary Sandefur, Alan Sorkin, and Russell Thornton read and commented on the manuscript in its entirety. I thank Charles F. Westoff and David L. Sills for their guidance and encouragement. Professor Westoff read and commented on the entire manuscript—the chapter on family and household structure benefited greatly from his suggestions, though I bear responsibility for any remaining flaws. David Sills was important for his advice and encouragement that I should be mindful of the historical context of my subject matter. Last but not least, Priscilla Lewis, Charlotte Shelby, and their staff at Russell Sage deserve special praise for their patience and expert editorial work on this volume—it is much better for their efforts. Needless to say, I bear full responsibility for all opinions and for any errors that appear in this book.

Not much is known in detail about the living conditions and demography of the contemporary American Indian population. The individuals and organizations named above deserve credit for helping make possible what I believe is a unprecedented source of information about American Indians. It is my hope that others will use this information in ways that will eventually benefit the people to whom this book is devoted.

C. Matthew Snipp
University of Wisconsin–Madison

Contents

List of Tables

List of Figures

List of Maps

AMERICAN INDIAN DEMOGRAPHY
IN HISTORIC PERSPECTIVE

It is my land, my home, my father's land to which I now ask to be allowed to return. . . . If this could be I might die in peace, feeling that my people, placed in their native homes, would increase in numbers, rather than diminish as at present, and that our name would not become extinct.

Geronimo, 1877

WHEN COLUMBUS first encountered the original inhabitants of the Americas, people he later described as "Indios," nothing was known about their numbers, where they lived, or the characteristics of their social structure. Three hundred years later Thomas Malthus published his *Essay on the Principle of Population* and launched demography, the scientific study of populations. Since Malthus, Western society has amassed a wealth of information about the immigrants and their descendants who settled in North America. Yet compared with what is known about these newcomers, Western society knows little more about the original inhabitants of this continent than Columbus did 500 years ago.

This book is about the demography of the first Americans. It deals with the number, distribution, and social characteristics of American Indians and Alaska Natives. These dimensions of the Native American population reveal more than basic demographic information. They also

1

chart the position of this group within the larger complex of American society.

In 1980 American Indians and Alaska Natives numbered 1,423,043, or a little more than one half of 1 percent of the total U.S. population. About one half live in rural areas, many of which are remote and inaccessible. In most urban centers Indians do not reside in sufficient numbers and density to form outwardly recognizable communities, as do blacks, Hispanics, Asians, and other ethnic groups. Compared with larger ethnic groups, Native Americans are not numerous enough to swing elections, contribute significantly to the Gross National Product, affect unemployment figures, or otherwise attract the attention of academics or the mass media.

Given the smallness of the Native American population, why should this group concern the rest of American society? First, American Indians and Alaska Natives are the first inhabitants of the land known today as the United States of America, which makes knowledge about them essential for a complete view of American society.

Second, American Indians, like other economically disadvantaged groups such as blacks, Hispanics, and women, are important because their experiences in the labor market contradict institutionalized ideals about equal opportunities regardless of race, color, or creed. The hardships of these groups make a profound statement about the actual conditions of American society, suggesting unmet needs, unachieved goals, and areas for further improvement. Historically, Indians represent the low end of the U.S. socioeconomic spectrum. American Indian reservations have been consistently among the poorest areas in the United States. The standard of living on many reservations, in terms of sanitary conditions, running water, paved roads, and other public facilities, is not very different from that in Third World countries.[1] Compared with other minority groups, American Indians, rural and urban, are still among the most poorly housed, poorly nourished, least educated, unhealthiest, and most unemployed. For example, data from the 1980 census show that 44 percent had less than 12 years of schooling, 13 percent were unemployed, and 30 percent were below the official poverty line. In the same year, 6.5 percent of the American population as a whole were unemployed, 12.4 percent were below the poverty line, and 67.5 percent had a high school education.

Third, American Indians have played a continuing role in the development and expansion of American society from the earliest days of European discovery and exploration. The presence, contributions, and even opposition of Indian people helped shape the history of the United

---

[1]Lorraine Turner Ruffing, "Navajo Economic Development: A Dual Perspective," in Sam Stanley, ed., *American Indian Economic Development* (The Hague: Mouton, 1978).

States. Perhaps no other minority group is as deeply embedded in the common culture as are American Indians. In American folklore, they are as central as the immigrant pioneers who settled the western plains. In American art, literature, and popular culture Indians are often portrayed as either cunning and untrustworthy savages or spiritual beings living in ethereal harmony with nature: in reality, they are neither.[2]

Fourth, the bureaucratic institutions of American society have been no less influenced. At the federal level, a specialized branch of law and legal study is devoted to Indian issues; an entire volume of the Code of Federal Regulations outlines the scope of Indian law; a special agency, the Bureau of Indian Affairs (BIA), administers federal policies and legislation affecting Indians; and American Indians are the only ethnic minority specifically mentioned in the Constitution.

Fifth, because traditional American Indian culture and lifestyles are a unique form of non-Western social organization and because contemporary American Indians have adapted to Western society by amalgamating old traditions with new innovations from American culture,[3] anthropologists and other social scientists have a major interest in studying them.

Finally, a less obvious but no less valid reason that American Indians deserve special attention is related to the popular interest in the diffuse ancestry of the American people. The links between American Indians and the balance of the U.S. population are perhaps far more extensive than might be expected from simply examining population statistics. Indians are a relatively small group, but a sizable number of Americans (nearly 7 million) include at least one Indian among their ancestors. Regarding themselves as the distant or not-so-distant relatives of contemporary Indians, many Americans have more than a passing interest in the present status of American Indians.

Several abiding themes frame the content of this book. A foremost objective is to chronicle the position of American Indians within the larger context of American society. The 1980 decennial Census of Population and Housing constitutes a major source of information for this task for two reasons. One is that studies of modern Indian demography are virtually nonexistent, except for a few studies of specific tribes.[4]

---

[2]For a discussion of racial stereotypes about American Indians, readers should consult Robert F. Berkhofer, Jr., *The White Man's Indian* (New York: Vintage Books, 1978).

[3]Joan Ablon, "Relocated American Indians in the San Francisco Bay Area: Social Interactions and Indian Identity," *Human Organization* 23(1964):296–304.

[4]Robert A. Hackenberg and C. Roderick Wilson, "Reluctant Emigrants: The Role of Migration in Papago Indian Adaptation," *Human Organization* 31(1972):171–186; Julie M. Uhlmann, "The Impact of Modernization of Papago Indian Fertility," *Human Organization* 31 (1972):149–161; Henry F. Dobyns, *Native American Historical Demography: A Critical Bibliography* (Bloomington: Indiana University Press, 1976).

Most of what is known about American Indian demography is for historical populations based on centuries-old documentary evidence such as the diaries of explorers and archaeological discoveries. There is a need to know something about currently living populations of American Indians in terms of their size, location, and social characteristics.

Another reason is that the U.S. Bureau of the Census went to great lengths to obtain high-quality data for the Indian population. The scope of the Census Bureau's efforts to accurately enumerate Indians in the 1980 census was unprecedented. As a result, the quality of the data, although not perfect, is better than that of earlier enumerations. Since so little is known about contemporary Indian demography, this information presents an extraordinary opportunity for significantly advancing the current state of knowledge.

The information collected in the 1980 census is especially useful for highlighting two other objectives related to the status of Indians in American society. One is to portray the diversity and uniqueness of the whole Indian population: American Indian tribes, Eskimos, and Aleuts. The diversity among these groups is staggering and should not be discounted: Some tribes are very large and others are very small; some Indians live in highly urbanized areas while others reside in remote wilderness areas; some Indians are relatively well off economically while many others live in desperate poverty.

A second objective is to show the influence of the federal government in shaping the social profile of the Indian population. Federal authorities in the Bureau of Indian Affairs and numerous other agencies exercise a pervasive influence on the lives of many Indians, especially those residing on federally administered reservations.[5]

Unlike other minority groups, Native Americans vary profoundly in terms of having different languages, cultures, and historical backgrounds. For example, American Indians of the East Coast have little in common with Indians of the Plains, and these groups have even less in common with Indians in California. The differences between Alaska Natives, Eskimos and Aleuts, and American Indians in the lower 48 states are especially striking. As Thornton explains, the anthropological differences are sufficiently great that Alaska Natives are rightly considered Native Americans, but they *are not* American Indians, that is, the original inhabitants of the lower 48 states.[6]

However, a growing number of American Indians and Alaska Natives are not comfortable with the term "Native American" because it

[5]Sar A. Levitan, and William B. Johnston, *Indian Giving: Federal Programs for Native Americans* (Baltimore: Johns Hopkins University Press, 1975).

[6]Russell Thornton, *American Indian Holocaust and Survival: A Population History Since 1492* (Norman: University of Oklahoma Press, 1987).

creates even greater confusion than the term it was once proposed to replace—namely, American Indian.[7] American Indians are easily distinguished from Asian Indians by a single locational adjective, but "Native Americans" include Hawaiian natives and the descendants of immigrants from all nations, along with American Indians, Eskimos, and Aleuts. A casual survey of recently published books and articles indicates that the term "Native American" is falling into disuse and that "American Indian" is preferable. Given this nomenclature, readers should note that much of the data presented in this book is not reported separately for American Indians, Eskimos, and Aleuts because the Census Bureau usually does not make these data available. However, for the sake of convenience and unless otherwise specified, the term "American Indian" will be used as a shorthand expression for the longer and more cumbersome "American Indians, Eskimos, and Aleuts."

The Demography of Pre-Contact American Indian Populations

As an introduction to the demography of contemporary American Indians, estimates of the size and distribution of pre-Contact populations provide a background for understanding modern demographic conditions. Estimates of the Indian population before 1492 have been a subject of great interest to a small group of scholars, primarily anthropologists and historians, for over 50 years and continue to generate sharp controversies. Understanding these debates over the pre-Columbian population is useful because they offer insight into the discrepancies among widely differing population estimates and because they offer alternative views of the nature of North American Indian social organization before the arrival of Europeans. The original inhabitants of North America did not leave a written legacy to be studied by modern scholars, and consequently most of what is known is speculative and inferential. Surveying the literature dealing with historic Indian populations exposes markedly different images of the culture and social organization of these people. Alternative views of fifteenth century Indian societies deeply influence contemporary assessments of how much and in what fashion the native population has changed since Columbus. Insights about the character of pre-Contact populations serve as a benchmark for judging the implications of modern population estimates.

[7]Joyotpaul Chaudhuri, "American Indian Policy: An Overview," in Vine Deloria, Jr., ed., *American Indian Policy in the Twentieth Century* (Norman: University of Oklahoma Press, 1985), p. 20.

The estimates of pre-Contact populations, the manner in which they are derived, and their implications are relevant to the modern demography of American Indians because they provide a benchmark for recently gathered statistics. (An extensive literature is available on American Indian historical demography, and there are numerous books and annotated bibliographies better suited for readers specifically interested in pre-Contact populations.)[8]

Early Population Estimates

In some ways the vast range of estimates for the size of the pre-Columbian Indian population is as interesting as the actual estimates. Fifteenth century population estimates typically describe population sizes in the last pre-Contact years preceding the arrival of Columbus. Unless otherwise specified, most of these figures are for population size in 1492. These estimates of the population in the region of North America above the Rio Grande river range from a low of 900,000 to a high of 18 million.

The earliest available estimates for the North American Indian population are provided by individuals who had the opportunity to observe firsthand American Indian settlements. In many instances, explorers, missionaries, and, later, Indian agents were the first to visit Indian villages and make reports about the numbers of inhabitants. These eyewitness accounts are the nearest facsimile to objective data about early village populations. As estimates of the pre-Columbian North American population, these recollections are not especially useful, and there are many reasons for doubting their validity.

Among the shortcomings of these figures is that they are necessarily impressionistic and limited to a single tribe, or to a few villages or tribes within a relatively small geographic area familiar to the authors of these accounts. Systematic estimates of the complete North American population are unavailable in these early descriptions. Apart from military purposes, European explorers had little serious interest in the exact size of native villages, and as a result their reports are sketchy. Many of these early estimates are for the number of warriors defending a particular location or the number of "houses." Dobyns also suggests

---

[8]Dobyns (1976); Alfred W. Crosby, Jr., *The Columbian Exchange: Biological and Cultural Consequences of 1492* (Westport, CT: Greenwood, 1972); Sherburne F. Cook and Woodrow W. Borah, *Essays in Population History: Mexico and the Caribbean*, vol. 1 (Berkeley: University of California Press, 1971); Sherburne F. Cook and Woodrow W. Borah, *Essays in Population History: Mexico and the Caribbean*, vol. 2 (Berkeley: University of California Press, 1974).

that most of these figures are for populations already reduced by epidemics that spread across the continent following the arrival of Europeans.[9] For example, the Pilgrims arrived at Plymouth in the aftermath of an epidemic that depopulated the area in which they settled.[10]

Systematic estimates of the sixteenth century population in North America were not developed until James Mooney's work in the early twentieth century, and few individuals equal his importance in the development of American Indian historical demography. Mooney was an anthropologist employed by the Bureau of American Ethnology of the Smithsonian Institution. In his time, the Bureau of Ethnology was engaged in an intensive effort to document information about American Indian lifestyles that were rapidly changing, if not headed toward extinction. Mooney's contribution to this effort involved studying and recording the size and location of Indian tribes and settlements at the time of contact with Europeans. His work in this area represented a pioneer attempt to produce the first scholarly estimates of the pre-Contact native population in North America. In 1910 Mooney published a brief article in a Bureau of Ethnology Bulletin wherein he reported that by his reckoning the North American Indian population numbered 1.15 million in 1600.

Mooney's work established the study of pre-Contact American Indian demography as a subject of scientific inquiry, but in his lifetime he did not publish detailed tribal estimates. After Mooney's death, a colleague at the Bureau of American Ethnology, John Swanton, had the opportunity to review Mooney's notes and unpublished work. Swanton found that Mooney had completed population estimates for all major tribal groups, and in 1928 he published Mooney's work posthumously. Swanton was unable to ascertain Mooney's exact resources, but in prefacing these materials he encouraged readers to accept their accuracy because of Mooney's reputation for careful and meticulous research.[11] The 1928 publication reported that the North American aboriginal population numbered 1,152,950 at the time of European contact. MacLeod and Willcox[12] published studies at approximately the same time as

[9]Henry F. Dobyns, *Their Number Become Thinned: Native American Population Dynamics in Eastern North America* (Knoxville: University of Tennessee Press, 1983).

[10]Thornton (1987).

[11]John Reed Swanton, "Preface," in James Mooney, *The Aboriginal Population of America North of Mexico*, Smithsonian Miscellaneous Collections, vol. 80, no. 7 (Washington, DC: Smithsonian Institution, 1928).

[12]Walter F. Willcox, "Increase in the Population of the Earth and of the Continents since 1650," in Walter F. Willcox, ed., *International Migrations*, vol. 2 (New York: National Bureau of Economic Research, 1931); William C. MacLeod, *The American Indian Frontier* (New York: Knopf, 1928).

Mooney's posthumous work appeared, but they did not seriously dispute Mooney's estimate.

The population estimates published by Swanton were highly influential, and they went unchallenged for over a decade. In 1939 Kroeber reviewed these figures and concluded that Mooney's estimate for the total population was too high, especially for the California area. He substituted his own estimates for California and reduced Mooney's estimate for the total population by 152,000, to 1.0 million. On the basis of his findings for the prehistoric California population, Kroeber observed that the correct figure for the pre-Contact North American population was probably closer to 900,000. Nevertheless, he did not raise major objections to Mooney's other estimates and endorsed them as essentially correct.[13]

Kroeber's acceptance of Mooney's estimates added to their influence, and they continue to be a frequently cited source of information.[14] In 1959 Aschmann published a substantially higher number of 2.2 million for the North American population, twice the estimates of Mooney and Kroeber.[15] Dobyns offered in 1966 one of the most controversial challenges to the Mooney and Kroeber data,[16] criticizing their work as excessively conservative. Applying newly developed techniques to historic and archaeological data, Dobyns obtained an estimate of 9.8 million to over 12.0 million. This remains one of the highest estimates in the published literature.

Dobyns's work was a breakthrough because it raised scholarly interests in American Indian historical demography by seriously challenging the long-established work of Mooney and Kroeber. Since their publication, Dobyns's estimates have stimulated a flurry of publications. Aspects of his work, especially some of his methodological assumptions, have been harshly criticized.[17] Driver modified some of the more objectionable assumptions in Dobyns's methodology and re-estimated

[13]Alfred L. Kroeber, "Native American Population," *American Anthropologist* 36 (1934):1–25; Alfred L. Kroeber, "Cultural and Natural Areas of Native North America," *American Archaeology and Ethnology,* no. 38(Berkeley: University of California Press, 1939).

[14]John Upton Terrell, *American Indian Almanac* (New York and Cleveland: World, 1971), uses Mooney's figures for example.

[15]Homer Aschmann, *The Central Desert of Baja California: Demography and Ecology* (Riverside, CA: Manessier, 1967 [1959]).

[16]Henry F. Dobyns, "Estimating Aboriginal American Population: An Appraisal of Techniques with a New Hemispheric Estimate," *Current Anthropology* 7(1966):395–416; and "Reply," *Current Anthropology* 7(1966):440–444.

[17]Harold E. Driver, *Indians of North America* (Chicago and London: University of Chicago Press, 1969); William M. Denevan, "Introduction," in William M. Denevan, ed., *The Native Population of the Americas in 1492* (Madison: University of Wisconsin Press, 1976); Russell Thornton, "But How Thick Were They?" *Contemporary Sociology* 31 (1984):149–150.

his population figures to obtain a much more conservative estimate of 3.5 million, but still substantially higher than the estimates of Mooney and Kroeber.

More recently, Ubelaker reviewed a series of updated population estimates for tribes included in Mooney's original figures.[18] Combining these newer figures with Mooney's original estimates, Ubelaker surmises that Mooney would have obtained a number twice as large if he had had access to better data. Adjusting Mooney's data, Ubelaker reports a projection of 2.2 million instead of 1.15 million. Viewing Ubelaker's adjustment of Mooney's figures in light of the work of other researchers, Denevan believes that the pre-Columbian North American population was probably nearer to 4.4 million.[19] Thornton and Marsh-Thornton obtain a slightly higher estimate of 5.13 million by adjusting the data used by Dobyns.[20]

Among the recent contributions to this literature, Dobyns subsequently presented estimates which he admits will be controversial well into the future.[21] He reviews a variety of documentary and archaeological data to conclude that the aboriginal population north of meso-America numbered as many as 18.0 million, nearly doubling his 1966 estimate. This figure represents the largest credible estimate published.

Dobyns's estimate of 18 million North American natives is four to five times greater than most of the appraisals submitted by other experts on pre-Contact populations. A sampling of the better-known estimates are shown in Table 1.1. The definitive estimate of the North American pre-Contact population size has not been established, and there is much work to be done before this is achieved. However, these figures unequivocally demonstrate the enormous problems in constructing meaningful estimates of pre-Contact population sizes.

How Many Indians?

There is probably no single figure that can be accepted as the "best" estimate of the late fifteenth century North American population, especially given the wide range of numbers from which to choose. For

---

[18]Douglas H. Ubelaker, "The Sources and Methodology for Mooney's Estimates of North American Indian Populations," in William M. Denevan, ed., *The Native Population of the Americas in 1492* (Madison: University of Wisconsin Press, 1976).

[19]Denevan (1976), p. 291.

[20]Russell Thornton and Joan Marsh-Thornton, "Estimating Prehistoric American Indian Population Size for United States Area: Implications of the Nineteenth Century Population Decline and Nadir," *American Journal of Physical Anthropology* 55(1981):47–53.

[21]Dobyns (1983).

TABLE 1.1

Estimates of the North American Native Population, Circa 1492

	Publication Date	Population Estimate
Mooney	1910, 1928*	1,152,950
Sapper	1924	2.5–3.5 million
MacLeod	1928	1.0 million
Willcox	1931	1,002,000
Kroeber	1939	900,000
Rosenblatt	1954	1.0 million
Aschmann	1959	2.24 million
Dobyns	1966	9.8 million
Driver	1969	3.5 million
Ubelaker	1976	2.2 million
Denevan	1976	4.4 million
Thornton and Marsh-Thornton	1981	1.8–5.13 million
Dobyns	1984	18 million

*Published posthumously by Swanton.

decades the Mooney-Kroeber figures stood unchallenged, but most contemporary studies reject them for being overly conservative. The available evidence suggests that the pre-Columbian population was substantially larger than the approximately 1 million advocated by Mooney and Kroeber. In view of recently obtained data from archaeological and other sources, a conservative estimate is that at least 2 million natives inhabited the North American continent at the time of Columbus's arrival. As Ubelaker shows, updating Mooney's conservatively inclined data with recently obtained information yields a population size exceeding 2 million. Thornton and Marsh-Thornton extrapolate the Indian population decline from 1800 to 1880 backward to 1492 and find that 2 million is a reasonable estimate based on this linear trend alone. In all likelihood, the pre-Columbian American population was much larger.

If 2 million constitutes an acceptable lower bound for the range of aboriginal population estimates, the upper bound is much more difficult to ascertain. Dobyns's work clearly suggests that a much higher number is conceivable, if not highly plausible. A liberal upper bound includes the estimates of a majority of researchers, and most estimates do not exceed 5 million. This approach yields a range for the pre-Columbian North American population size of 2 million to 5 million. This range reflects a consensus across a wide spectrum of scholars. It is higher than the Mooney-Kroeber figures, which demonstrably underestimate the population. It is much lower than the number Dobyns proposes; but as

Dobyns admits and Thornton[22] emphasizes, it is unlikely that a plurality of scientific experts will accept a number as high as 18 million in the near future.

Techniques for Estimating Pre-Contact Populations

Variation in population estimates can be understood as partly the result of differences in the techniques used to calculate estimates, and especially the consequence of different assumptions embedded in these methods. Understanding the manner in which population estimates are derived reveals much about the sources of differences in these figures.

At the outset, it should be realized that the very nature of the problem denies prehistoric demography much of the exacting scientific rigor found in demographic studies of modern populations. A large part of pre-Contact American Indian demography is speculative, indirect, and inferential, as written records seldom exist, and by definition careful enumerations are unavailable. Dobyns addresses this problem succinctly, noting that "demographers accustomed to analyzing census data will be little satisfied with the quality of information necessarily utilized in the historical demography of the New World. . . . One either uses such data as may be available and learns something, however inadequate, or abjures such data and learns nothing."[23]

The data for pre-Contact population estimates are primarily derived from two basic sources. Archaeological data in a variety of forms are extremely important, especially as technological advances have made reliable dating possible. Archaeologists are now able to make remarkably accurate determinations of the age of artifacts. These artifacts provide a great deal of information about the lifestyles and settlement patterns of early populations, and they can be used for estimating settlement sizes and population densities for prehistoric areas. For example, prehistoric middens reveal dietary habits and consumption patterns. Comparing this information with other data about environmental conditions reveals the likely number of inhabitants sustained by environmental resources. Areas with bountiful protein sources have predictably larger prehistoric populations than areas with limited access to food and fiber.

Another important source of data is extracted from the written records left by the few literate Europeans who first encountered the native

[22]Thornton (1984).
[23]Dobyns (1976), p. 7.

population. As mentioned, there are many reasons to question this information. In some instances the entries in diaries, reports, and letters appear reliable, and in others the information is clearly distorted. Dobyns discounts this evidence as overly conservative and untrustworthy. At the very least, this is an important source of information as the only written records of early Indian populations. It is corroborating information for archaeological data, and the more reputable documentary sources offer important primary data for generating area population estimates.

Archaeological and documentary data are used in all of the major techniques for estimating prehistoric populations. Two major methodological strategies are found in the literature and reflect varying degrees of technical sophistication and scientific rigor. They also embrace certain assumptions that heavily influence the magnitude of prehistoric population estimates.

The "dead reckoning" method is the oldest and least exacting in its application of technical information. Mooney's population estimates are the best-known examples of this method. The exact sources of many of these figures are lost to history, and Ubelaker is responsible for most of what is known about Mooney's original sources. The estimates Mooney published in 1910 and the tribal figures posthumously published by Swanton were based primarily on the records of literate colonials. For example, many of Mooney's estimates for tribes of the South Atlantic states in 1600 are based on the writings of Captain John Smith. Mooney's technique is dead reckoning because for each tribe he relied on educated guesswork to determine the accuracy of colonial reports. He raised or lowered the estimates to counter understated or exaggerated colonial documents. In other cases, he reckoned population size by choosing the most apparently reliable figure among conflicting reports of tribal size or selecting a compromise estimate.

More rigorous than dead reckoning, "depopulation ratios" and various sorts of projection methods are other tools used to estimate pre-Contract populations.[24] Area projection, for example, takes the population densities known for one area and obtains a population estimate for another unknown area by assuming similar population densities in the known and unknown areas. Other projection methods extrapolate total population numbers from fragmentary sources such as partial information about age-sex distributions, the numbers of warriors, or the number of dwellings and their likely number of inhabitants. These projection techniques rely heavily on corroborating evidence such as information about agricultural practices, the complexity of social structures, environmental resources, and skeletal remains.

[24]Denevan (1976), pp. 7–12.

Depopulation ratios are an especially important tool used to estimate prehistoric populations. From the arrival of Columbus until 1890 the native North American population experienced an almost genocidal reduction. The largest population losses resulted from the introduction of European diseases to a population with little immunity and no experience in treating these afflictions. Smallpox heads a list of maladies that nearly annihilated the aboriginal populations in North America and South America. Scholars generally agree on these facts but disagree on the magnitude of depopulation and the details of constructing depopulation ratios.

Depopulation ratios are constructed by estimating maximum and minimum population sizes for one or more well-known areas. These ratios are then applied to larger or less well known geographic areas. Minimum populations are relatively undisputed because frequently they can be obtained from recent historical sources such as ethnographies or actual enumerations. For example, the North American Indian population minimum was cited as approximately 228,000 in 1890. In contrast, establishing a population maximum is much more problematic, and it is usually derived indirectly from archaeological and/or corroborating documentary data.

Once maximum and minimum populations are established for one or more known areas, a "standard" depopulation ratio can be computed and applied to lesser known regions for the purpose of obtaining complete population estimates. In his 1966 article, Dobyns reviews data for several areas and obtains a standard depopulation ratio for North America of 20 or 25 to 1. This ratio means that peak populations were 20 to 25 times larger than their smallest size. Dobyns applies this ratio to the 1930 census estimate of American Indians to arrive at a figure of 6.6 million for the continental United States (and 9.5 million for the entire North American region). Thornton and Marsh-Thornton point out that the American Indian population reached its nadir 40 years earlier than Dobyns's 1930 estimate. They find that the 1890 nadir yields a peak population estimate one half as large as Dobyns's estimate. Driver also criticizes Dobyns's depopulation ratio of 20:1 as unnecessarily high. Driver favors a lower depopulation ratio of 10:1, and applying this to the 1890 minimum population he obtains an estimate of 2.5 million. However, as the Thorntons point out, Driver uses an estimate of the minimum population that is too high.

Another technique for estimating early American Indian populations is linear extrapolation. This method is less widely used than depopulation ratios but is equally, if not more, rigorous. Depopulation ratios use data for two extreme points in time, while linear extrapolation employs trend line data for known periods to project backward into history. Thornton and Marsh-Thornton argue that American Indian population declines from 1800 to 1880 approximate a linear trend and use this information to project population estimates backward to 1490. They conclude that the Indian population of North America was about 2.5 million when Columbus arrived. This technique assumes that population declines are constant across long historical periods and does not allow for precipitous decreases in size resulting from widespread epidemics.

However, assuming linear, monotonic population declines and neglecting the profound impact of epidemic disease are at variance with much of what is known about demographic events after 1500. There were steep declines in the native population after 1500, and by 1700 numerous tribes were nearly extinct or already vanished. Figure 1.1 compares population estimates based on Dobyns's depopulation ratios and Thornton and Marsh-Thornton's linear trend. As this illustrates, the depopulation ratios reflect the massive drop in population while the linear trend does not. This figure also forcefully demonstrates how methodological assumptions influence population estimates.

FIGURE 1.1

Pre-European American Indian Population Estimates for the United States Area Minus Alaska and Hawaii, by Mooney, the Thorntons, and Dobyns (adjusted), and Their Likely Patterns of Decline from 1492 to 1890

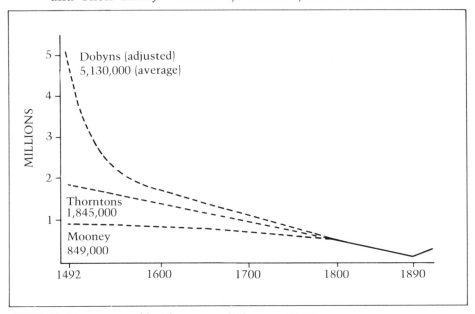

SOURCE: Figure prepared by Thornton and Thornton (1981).

Implications of Pre-Columbian Population Estimates

The Magnitude of Depopulation

Estimates of the pre-Columbian native population have profound implications about the nature of these societies, the impact of Western society, and the outcomes of contact between fundamentally different cultures.[25] These implications are closely tied to the magnitude of depopulation after 1500.

It is generally agreed that native populations declined precipitously in North America and South America after 1500. Numerous factors were responsible for population declines that continued well into the nineteenth century. Military action, genocide, slavery, and famine are commonly cited agents of depopulation, but these factors played a relatively small role for most tribes compared with the extraordinarily lethal influence of European diseases. Natural selection and repeated exposure to strains of communicable diseases helped the European population develop resistance to illnesses such as smallpox and cholera. North American populations were free of these Old World diseases until the early 1500s. Because they possessed no resistance to the most virulent and lethal symptoms of these diseases, exposure meant almost certain death to American Indians and decimated the aboriginal population. Smallpox headed a list of communicable diseases, including cholera, diphtheria, bubonic plague, influenza, typhus, typhoid, measles, and scarlet fever, which annihilated Indian people.

Crosby notes that the first 100 years of contact with Europeans and Africans were accompanied by a spectacular rate of mortality among Indians.[26] In Denevan's words, "the discovery of America was followed by possibly the greatest demographic disaster in the history of the world."[27] Europeans were awestruck at the rate at which the natives succumbed to diseases that were not nearly as virulent among their own people. Undoubtedly this reinforced beliefs about the natural inferiority of the Indian population. A German missionary wrote in 1699 that "the Indians die so easily that the bane look and smell of a Spaniard causes them to give up the ghost."[28]

Without an exact estimate of the pre-Columbian population, it is impossible to determine precisely the magnitude of depopulation among

[25]Woodrow Wilson Borah, "The Historical Demography of Aboriginal and Colonial America: An Attempt at Perspective," in Denevan (1976), and Dobyns (1983, essay 7), provide a review of the implications of different population estimates for understanding the impact of depopulation.

[26]Crosby (1972).

[27]Denevan (1976), p. 7.

[28]Quoted in Crosby (1972).

American Indians. Conservatively, on the North American continent Indian population declined by 1.75 million to 4.75 million between 1500 and 1890. If the figures of scholars such as Dobyns are acceptable, the population decline for the same period is massive: 9.75 million to 17.75 million. The latter figures indicate that the Indian population declined at an average rate of 500,000 to 850,000 in each 20-year generation after 1500.

The extent of depopulation from disease and other factors is perhaps most significant because it shapes the image of American Indian social structure and culture prior to 1492. Borah identifies two conflicting views of Indian social organization before depopulation.[29] One view portrays Indian social structure as lacking the social and cultural amenities found in the more highly developed societies of the period; in primitive societies economic production is limited, surpluses are small, and exchange between groups is relatively uncommon. Another perspective argues that early native societies were highly complex and engaged in widespread economic exchanges with one another.

The relative merits of these opposing views of pre-Columbian social structure are heavily influenced by estimates of pre-1500 population sizes and the extent of sixteenth century depopulation. Highly complex social structures are most likely given large, densely settled populations. Adherents of this perspective argue that the American continent was heavily populated before the arrival of Columbus, equaling or exceeding the population of Europe. They are inclined to describe Indian depopulation in terms of a holocaust that lingered into the nineteenth century. In contrast, proponents of low population estimates generally believe that pre-Columbian social structures were relatively simple, with thinly scattered groups of natives living in Stone Age conditions. These competing views portray the impact of European discovery as either relatively slight or tragically significant.

Civilizations Lost

The proposition that large, densely settled populations are conducive to elaborate political and economic systems is well supported by historical data. The Incas, Mayas, and Aztecs developed highly complex societies in terms of their economic and political structures. They also achieved high levels of artistic and architectural sophistication. These societies are well known because they were intact at the time of European arrival. Complex societies also developed in North America, al-

[29]In Denevan (1976).

though much less is known about them because many disappeared before directly meeting with Europeans. The Mississippi and Ohio river valleys were the center of development for two major cultures.

The Hopewell civilization emerged about 300 B.C. and lasted nearly 1,000 years, until A.D. 700. The Hopewell people settled throughout Illinois, Ohio, eastern Missouri, and the upper Mississippi valley.[30] Traces of Hopewell cultural influence spread as far as the Mid-Atlantic region. The artifacts of this culture are rich in intricate carvings and pottery resembling meso-American art forms. Archaeological sites indicate that Hopewell villages were stable settlements, organized around regional "capitals" in which major social events such as religious ceremonies were observed. Burial mounds and other types of spectacular earthworks are evidence that the Hopewell were sufficiently well organized to carry out large-scale "public works" and probably developed a rich spiritual and ceremonial repertoire. Very little is known about why this civilization declined. Archaeologists speculate that climatic changes, agricultural innovations, and protracted warfare with surrounding tribes may have dispersed the Hopewell.[31] Disease does not appear to be responsible for their disappearance.

The Hopewell were succeeded by another civilization known as the Mississippian culture.[32] Like the Hopewell, these people were scattered throughout the Ohio and Mississippi valleys, although there is some evidence that the Mississippian culture exercised a greater influence over the Southeast than their predecessors. The Mississippian culture developed around large settlements characterized by the construction of large temple mounds. Modern urban development has destroyed many of these sites. Cahokia, outside East St. Louis, is the largest known Mississippian settlement, and it is also the site of the largest known earthwork. Monk's mound is nearly 100 feet high and measures 600 by 900 feet at the base. Temples, the chief's home, and other important public buildings were located on this and other mounds. Mississippian artwork incorporated exotic materials such as conch shells and included finely detailed pottery and carvings. There is evidence suggesting that these people controlled an extensive trading network ranging from Wisconsin to Georgia.

The disappearance of the Mississippian culture is nearly as mysterious as the Hopewell decline. Some archaeologists rule out disease as a

---

[30]Gordon R. Willey, *An Introduction to American Archaeology* (Englewood Cliffs, NJ: Prentice-Hall, 1966); Robert L. Hall, "An Interpretation of the Two-Climax Model of Illinois Prehistory," in David L. Browman, ed., *Early Native Americans: Prehistoric Demography, Economy, and Technology* (The Hague: Mouton, 1980).

[31]Browman (1980).

[32]Willey (1966); Hall (1980).

cause; there are signs that some villages were abandoned much earlier than 1500.[33] However, the weight of circumstantial evidence is sufficiently great that disease cannot be easily discounted as a cause of Mississippian decline. The most compelling evidence links the disappearance of the Mississippians with the aftermath of epidemics documented by Dobyns and others. The Mississippian culture reached its peak influence between 1400 and 1500. In the wake of diseases that spread across North America after 1500, the Mississippians disappeared entirely by 1700. Archaeologists speculate that the Mississippian people dispersed throughout the Midwest and Southeast, dissolving into smaller, more primitive settlements after being decimated by disease. Many of the tribes encountered by early explorers—the Natchez, for example—were remnants of this culture.

The Hopewell and Mississippian cultures were not the only complex societies to develop in North America. Sophisticated towns and villages were carved out of the walls of mesas in the Southwest by the Anasazi people. In the centuries preceding Columbus, the Anasazi developed techniques for manufacturing pottery and agricultural practices for the arid southwestern climate. The Hokoham, Patayan, and Mogollon cultures joined the Anasazi to make the Southwest an important population center in pre-Columbian America. The Anasazi endured longer than most other southwestern cultures, surviving the massive pandemics of the seventeenth century, but frequent hostile encounters with Spanish military expeditions eventually dispersed this vigorous population by 1700. Descendants of the Anasazi are living in pueblo settlements throughout Arizona and New Mexico. Other large populations were not as successful in escaping the ravages of disease and military force. For example, Dobyns claims that 1.25 million inhabited the area of Florida. Of this number, 750,000 belonged to the now-extinct Timucuan tribe.

The welter of information produced by archaeologists and historical demographers leads to several conclusions about the native populations of North America. There are few doubts that these populations were much larger than once believed by researchers such as Mooney and Kroeber. Large populations imply that these cultures were also more highly developed than some have argued. The opinion that pre-Columbian populations consisted mostly of small disorganized groups roaming a deserted territory and foraging a Stone Age subsistence is not consistent with available data. A more likely scenario is that well-organized population centers developed throughout North America and South America. The greatest and most well known attainments belong to the

[33]Hall (1980).

Aztecs, Incas, and Mayas of Central America and South America, and the achievements of these cultures were mirrored on a smaller scale by the cultures of North America. In the decades preceding European discovery, North America was, as one anthropologist observed, "civilization aborning."[34]

The Impact of Depopulation

The presence of large native populations with complex social structures dramatizes the destructive forces of epidemic disease and warfare. In nightmarish proportions, the sixteenth century depopulation of America rivals the plagues of medieval Europe. The words of a Maya Indian describe the ghastly virulence of an epidemic.

> Great was the stench of the dead. After our fathers and grandfathers succumbed, half of the people fled to the fields. The dogs and vultures devoured the bodies. The mortality was terrible. Your grandfathers died, and with them died the son of the king and his brothers and kinsmen. So it was that we became orphans, oh, my sons! So we became when we were young. All of us were thus. We were born to die![35]

Massive depopulation had a pervasive impact on the culture and social organization of American Indians. Pre-Columbian Indian social life was irrevocably changed by the upheaval of large-scale population losses.[36]

Depopulation forced a massive reorganization of village settlement patterns. Villages in areas poorly endowed with food and fiber resources were abandoned in favor of more productive locations because of less competition for scarce environmental resources. As the survivors of epidemics relocated to more prosperous areas, they became incorporated into existing settlements, resulting in the gradual amalgamation of villages. In some instances, the process of village amalgamation facilitated changes in language, tribal and ethnic distinctions, and a smaller number of tribal polities. Indians also responded to the spread of disease by relocating entire villages. There is evidence of widespread migratory behavior and redistribution of population centers throughout North America in the sixteenth century.

Perhaps the most profound changes resulted from the cultural response to depopulation. Village amalgamation and territorial resettlement stimulated one set of adjustments by promoting contact between

---

[34]Hall (1980), p. 402.
[35]Quoted in Crosby (1972), p. 58.
[36]Dobyns (1983) discusses these changes at length.

tribal cultures. Declining populations adapting to conditions of depopulated and sparsely settled areas displayed another set of changes: namely, less complex social structures and more rudimentary economic systems. Smaller populations spent more time securing the food and fiber necessary for survival. They devoted less energy to manufacturing surpluses such as fine crafts for exchange. Depopulation disrupted trade networks and further reduced the demand for nonessential economic goods. Smaller populations and declining economic change downgraded Indian economic systems into progressively lower levels of specialization characterized by rudimentary forms of technology.[37] Despecialization is particularly responsible for the primitive economic systems and production technologies witnessed by early colonial settlers. Low levels of economic complexity were matched by uncomplicated systems of social organization. Elaborate systems of organization require large investments in personnel and other resources and are unnecessary for coordinating the activities of smaller populations.

The response of native populations to disease and depopulation created lasting impressions of American Indians that still influence modern ideas. Many of these ideas are increasingly questionable in light of findings from recent studies in historical demography. One enduring misconception, a popular myth in American culture, is that Europeans discovered a territory sparsely settled by nomadic Stone Age primitives. Implicit in this view is that American Indian populations were so small and poorly organized, and their culture so technologically inferior, that they were swept away by their first contact with non-Indians. A more likely explanation is that the debilitating effects of infectious diseases advancing ahead of European settlers disorganized and dispersed native populations, leaving only the remnants of tribal societies to be overcome by European settlers. Disease, as much as technical superiority, was responsible for the success of early European settlers in acquiring new territory. Conquistadors such as Cortez and DeSoto were assisted by the lethal effects of smallpox in their military exploits.[38]

Tribal amalgamation and territorial resettlement led early colonists to view the land as virgin territory, untouched and ripe for settlement. In reality, abandonment was often a very large factor in making land available to colonial settlers. The Pilgrims and other early colonists from England were among the beneficiaries of land given up by disease-stricken tribes. The Massachusetts Indians, numbering several thousand, lived along the coastal region bearing their name. Shortly before the Pilgrims arrived at Plymouth Rock, this tribe was conveniently dis-

[37]Dobyns (1983).
[38]Crosby (1972).

persed by a series of epidemics, most likely smallpox. Captain John Smith observed 11 towns along the coast in 1614. Three years later, most of these localities were depopulated, just three years before the Pilgrims landed in 1620.[39]

Concluding Remarks

The number and distribution of American natives can only be guessed from fragmentary, painstakingly collected data. However, there is a growing consensus that the Americas were inhabited by a much larger population than experts once believed. As new data become available and as estimation procedures become more sophisticated, an upward trend is evident in the estimate of pre-Columbian population size. The significance of this trend is that new developments in historical demography may produce widely accepted population estimates that exceed the 2 million to 5 million figure for North America circulating among contemporary scholars.

The significance of higher population estimates is directly related to the magnitude of depopulation resulting from disease and warfare. Among the numerous infectious diseases that periodically raged in the sixteenth century, smallpox had the most devastating effects. Disease arrested the military power of the native population and opened the land for European settlement. A less-appreciated fact is that epidemic disease was a massive shock to pre-Columbian culture and social structure as these populations adapted to the spread of mysterious illnesses and dwindling communities.

The full impact of depopulation on American Indians will never be known. Uncountable details are lost to history, and the cultural changes are immeasurable. Following the arrival of explorers in the Caribbean basin, disease spread rapidly outward and farther away in North America; its deadly influence arrived years ahead of the earliest European settlers. Table 1.2 is a chronology of known smallpox outbreaks that began with a massive pandemic in 1520–1524 and resulted in a precipitous decline in the indigenous population. Similar chronologies can be constructed for a host of other diseases.[40]

For most North American Indians, the earliest ethnographic records were prepared by observers who arrived in the aftermath of the early pandemics. Dobyns insightfully argues that most of these early accounts

[39]Ubelaker (1976).
[40]Dobyns (1983), pp. 8–32.

TABLE 1.2

*Probable Smallpox Epidemics Among North American Indians,
1520–1797*

Date	Areas of Outbreak
1520–1524	Total Geographic Area Unknown; Possibly from Chile Across Present United States
1592–1593	Central Mexico to Sinaloa; Southern New England; Eastern Great Lakes
1602	Sinaloa and Northward
1639	French and British Northeastern North America
1646–1648	New Spain North to Nuevo Leon, Western Sierra Madre to Florida
1649–1650	Northeastern United States, Florida
1655	Florida
1662–1663	Mid-Atlantic, Northeast, Canada
1665–1667	Florida to Virginia
1669–1670	United States and Canada
1674–1675	Texas, Northeastern New Spain
1677–1679	Northeast in New France and British Territory
1687–1691	Northeast in French and British Frontiers; Texas
1696–1699	Southeastern and Gulf Coast
1701–1703	Northeastern to Illinois
1706	Texas and Northeastern New Spain
1715–1721	Northeast to Texas
1729–1733	New England; California Tribes; Southeast
1738–1739	Southeast to Hudson Bay; Texas Peoples
1746	New York, New England; New Spain
1750–1752	Texas to Great Lakes
1755–1760	From Canada and New England and Great Lakes to Virginia, Carolinas, and Texas
1762–1766	From Central Mexico through Texas and the Southeast to Great Lakes; Northwest Coast
1779–1783	From Central Mexico across all of North America
1785–1787	Alaskan coast across northern Canada
1788	New Mexico Pueblos
1793–1797	New Spain

SOURCE: Henry F. Dobyns, *Their Number Become Thinned: Native American Population Dynamics in Eastern North America* (Knoxville, TN: University of Tennessee Press, 1983) pp. 15–16.

record native culture in the wake of depopulation. By the time they were written, traditional pre-Columbian cultures had collapsed under the burden of rapidly declining populations. By the time white explorers arrived, the "traditional" forms of social organization that existed before 1492 had disappeared forever. The standard belief that early settlers witnessed pristine lifestyles and social systems unaffected by the presence of Europeans is misleading. More commonly, the early colonists observed the survivors of European pathogens practicing newly adapted lifestyles in response to their sharply reduced populations. As Dobyns points out, many tribal practices witnessed at the time of first contact are mistakenly associated with centuries-old traditions.[41] These practices were probably recent adaptations of an earlier way of life and are not "traditional" in the usual sense of the term. The physical arrival of Europeans did not contaminate ancient Indian societies; European diseases had forced dramatic social changes years earlier.

Spelling out the likely extent of social change that resulted from depopulation is far beyond the scope of this brief survey of American Indian historical demography. The following chapters deal exclusively with modern demography. In closing, it is important to realize what the findings of historical demography mean for contemporary American Indians. One significant point is that today's American Indians are experiencing a demographic resurgence that is relatively recent in origin. American Indians almost disappeared from American society. By 1890 there were so few Indians left in America that it was widely believed that they would eventually disappear. The Bureau of Ethnology in the Smithsonian Institution proceeded to copiously document Indian culture for posterity. Gradually improved living conditions, especially in health care and nutrition, and the cessation of military hostilities helped American Indians make a demographic comeback. Instead of disappearing, their number has grown steadily, and for the first time in over two centuries their population exceeded 1 million in 1980.

Modern American Indians descended from people who coped with extreme adversity and who were nearly pushed into extinction. Their survival depended on their ability to change and adapt their lifestyle to changing conditions in the environment. The dynamic quality of American Indian cultures results from combining old and new ways, saving some practices, and discarding others. Since the arrival of Columbus, if not before, American Indian social life has been continuously changing. After 1500 many of these changes were forced by the appearance of large numbers of foreign populations with new technologies, deadly maladies, and warlike predispositions. The ever-changing quality of American Indian culture is routinely ignored by two popular views of Indian people.

A highly romanticized view of traditional American Indian culture creates an image of people living in perfect harmony with nature and untouched by the afflictions of Western civilization, especially those en-

---

[41]See Dobyns's 1983 discussion of the methodological implications of cultural discontinuity resulting from epidemics. See also Julian H. Steward, "Theory and Application in Social Science," *Ethnology* 2(1955):292–302.

demic to modern industrial society. This image of traditional American Indians is perpetrated in literary classics such as Longfellow's "Hiawatha" and more recently in not-so-classic works such as Ruth Hill's *Hanta Yo*. If American Indians ever lived as they are described in romantic literature, it was only for a brief moment in history.

The romantic image of American Indians is based on highly stylized perceptions of eighteenth and nineteenth century Indian culture, which itself evolved from lifestyles of earlier eras. American Indians of the eighteenth and nineteenth centuries did not live as their ancestors did in the sixteenth and seventeenth centuries, and Indians of the sixteenth and seventeenth centuries were undoubtedly different from their ancestors of, say, the twelfth century. Weaving and sheep herding among the Navajos and buffalo hunting from horseback among the Sioux did not become traditional activities for these tribes until the Spanish introduced domestic sheep and horses to the Americas in the sixteenth and seventeenth centuries. To speak meaningfully of "traditional" Indian culture, it is imperative to specify a particular historical period. Omitting a reference point conjures a static image of Indian culture, lifeless and divorced from the reality of social change.

Social scientists frequently subscribe to another view of American Indians which is not unlike the stereotypes of romantic literature. Social science images of Indian social behavior are derived from ethnographic reports written in the eighteenth, nineteenth, and even the twentieth centuries. Early reports consisted of eyewitness descriptions, but later studies systematically collected data by soliciting recollections of eighteenth and nineteenth century social life. Dobyns attacks this approach for confusing lifestyles peculiar to the nineteenth century with centuries-old customs. As a source of information about ancient traditions, ethnographies are especially misleading because they seldom recognize the widespread social and cultural changes resulting from earlier population declines. Dobyns compares ethnographic images of traditional Indian social life to "paintings of extinct birds based on hearsay and on the artist's imagination."[42]

The distortions built into this view of traditional Indian culture are significant because they influence thinking about contemporary American Indians. Until recently, population declines and highly stylized images of traditional Indian social life led many social scientists to conclude that American Indians were about to disappear from American society. Observing that fewer Indians practice lifestyles once common among "traditional" nineteenth century Indian tribes, and that modern Indians have adopted many of the trappings of Western society, social

[42]Dobyns (1983), p. 26.

scientists predicted that American Indians would soon fade into history. Evidence of changing lifestyles signaled that American Indians were slowly giving up their ethnicity and joining the American mainstream. This perspective contends that social change is eroding the core of Indian ethnicity, implying that American Indians will retain their place in society only by living as their ancestors did in the nineteenth century.

Few Indians faithfully follow the lifestyles of their ancestors; neither do most Americans, including those who claim membership in an ethnic group. Most American Indians live in houses, drive cars, participate in recreational activities, and earn a livelihood, like most other Americans. Unlike most Americans, they may belong to the Native American Church and use ritual peyote, speak a native language, participate in special social activities such as tribal ceremonies and pow-wows, live under the authority of tribal governments and the Bureau of Indian Affairs, and learn as a part of their heritage about the Trail of Tears or how the coyote stole the moon.

Indians are different from most Americans because they live in enclaves that were intentionally established away from the American mainstream. They have a complex relationship with the federal government that is different from that of any other segment of society. In the most fundamental sense, the many differences that set American Indians apart from other Americans are underscored by a single, self-evident fact: They share a common identity and heritage with their fellow tribesmen and with every other descendant of the original inhabitants of this continent. The boundaries of the American Indian population are set by this identity. Understanding how these population boundaries are drawn in empirical data is one of the fundamental problems for the study of American Indian demography.

2

WHO ARE AMERICAN INDIANS?

B EFORE THE arrival of Columbus, there could be no mistake about who was an Indian: Everyone qualified for the appellation. Since 1492 distinguishing Indians from non-Indians has become increasingly complicated, and there are few reliable guides for identifying American Indians amid the diversity of the American population. Historically, the federal government has had a significant role in defining the American Indian and Alaska Native population, a complex problem for reasons to be explained shortly. The purpose of this chapter is to discuss several alternative definitions for the Indian population and to explain how American Indians are defined and classified in subsequent chapters of this book.

A basic source of ambiguity about who is an American Indian stems from the popular stereotypes of American Indians that attribute to them physical characteristics such as well-defined cheekbones, reddish-brown complexions, straight black hair, almond-shaped eyes, and very little male facial hair. It is true that many American Indians have one or more of these characteristics. It is also true that some American Indians have none of these features, and in any event characteristics such as straight black hair and high cheekbones are not found exclusively in the American Indian population. Obviously, physical appearance is a wholly inappropriate criterion for deciding who is and is not an American Indian or Alaska Native.

Physical tests designed to measure pre-Columbian genetic traits also are not reliable guides for identifying members of the American Indian population. Over the centuries the pure genotype of the aboriginal pre-Columbian population succumbed to repeated exposures to infectious diseases and from sexual relations with non-Indians. The extent of genetic change cannot be measured precisely, but for modern American Indians "pure" genetic ancestry dating back to the fifteenth century is an unlikely prospect. A "pure" genotype of American Indian ancestry would involve a large and complex lineage spanning 15 to 20 generations in which not a single individual was non-Indian. Such lineages are not impossible, but in view of four centuries of contact with Africans and Europeans they are most likely rare.

Thus, the boundaries of the American Indian population are best defined in social terms. Delineating the social boundaries is complicated by ideas about American Indians that shift from one context to another. For example, the federal government has a large stake in defining who is an Indian or an Alaska Native, but different agencies with different missions employ a variety of different definitions. In studying federal policies, the American Indian Policy Review Commission (AIPRC) uncovered so many different definitions for the American Indian population that it declined to propose a single statement that might be widely acceptable.[1]

Explicit and consistently applied definitions are vital for social scientific research. An absence of well-understood definitions results in chaotically organized statistical data that are virtually meaningless and useless for making important policy decisions. Commenting on the problems posed by numerous definitions of American Indians, AIPRC warned that "if simply defining who is an Indian presents problems, compiling other vital statistics about Indians and Indian affairs presents almost insurmountable problems."[2]

Demographers typically classify the Indian population as either a racial or an ethnic group, or sometimes both. The criteria for defining who is an Indian are derived from theoretical concepts about race and ethnicity which are seldom stated explicitly. These concepts are closely related, and it is not always easy to distinguish racial definitions from ethnic definitions. The strategy of classifying American Indians as a race *and* as an ethnicity is somewhat unusual because many different ethnic groups are frequently subsumed within a single race; for example, the "white" race includes Germans, Poles, Sicilians, and many other differ-

[1] American Indian Policy Review Commission (AIPRC), *Final Report of the American Indian Policy Review Commission* (Washington, DC: U.S. Government Printing Office, 1977).

[2] AIPRC (1977), p. 89.

ent ethnic groups. By the same token, most ethnic groups do not include members with significantly different racial backgrounds. Furthermore, definitions based on different concepts of race and ethnicity produce remarkably different results in demographic research. In particular, differences in racial and ethnic definitions in the 1980 census generate surprisingly different statistics about the Indian population.

Racial Definitions for Native Americans

Concepts of Race

Using racial characteristics to define the boundaries of the Native American population presupposes that the concept of race is itself well known and clearly defined. On the contrary, few concepts are as misunderstood as race. In their influential textbook on race relations, Simpson and Yinger divide racial definitions into three types, which they label mystical, biological, and administrative.[3] All three types of definitions have been applied to American Indians.

Mystical definitions of race are easily the most pernicious and far removed from reality. They typically assert that modern racial groups are descended from mysterious ancient populations. Drawing on overly romanticized, if not altogether fictional, images of the past, this type of definition has been invoked to support beliefs about racial superiority. The Nazis invented the mythology of the Aryan race to press their claims of superiority; southern racists in the United States used similar ideas to oppose civil rights for blacks.

Biological definitions commonly view race as representative of a homogeneous gene pool within a relatively closed population. Scientists use a variety of genetic indicators such as blood type, earwax texture, and other anatomical characteristics to distinguish racial groups. The number of biological races identified by physical scientists varies considerably. The most well known classification[4] divides the human species into four basic varieties: australoid, caucasoid, mongoloid, and negroid. However, within these major categories, Goldsby[5] further identifies 26 distinct varieties, or races, of human beings.

Administrative definitions of race are promulgated by bureaucratic and political institutions and are designed to serve their particular ad-

[3]George Eaton Simpson and J. Milton Yinger, *Racial and Cultural Minorities*, 3rd ed. (New York: Harper & Row, 1965).

[4]M. F. Ashley Montagu, *An Introduction to Physical Anthropology*, 3rd ed. (New York: Columbia University Press, 1960).

[5]Richard A. Goldsby, *Race and Races* (New York: Macmillan, 1971).

ministrative needs and political agenda. Bureaucratic institutions rarely divulge the reasoning behind their definitions of race, and there is a large amount of variation in these definitions. The 1980 census identifies 13 racial groups, including separate categories for Asian nationalities such as Vietnamese and Japanese and a residual category for "other." In contrast, many universities, for affirmative action policies, classify their students and employees into five categories of American Indian, Asian, black, Hispanic, white, and other.

Mystical Views of American Indians

Highly romanticized, mystical views of American Indian racial characteristics are deeply embedded in American culture. Mystical ideas about the racial features of American Indians and Alaska Natives are evident in the writings of early European settlers and persist today in the mass media and other outlets of popular culture. The origins of mystical beliefs about American Indians in particular and the historical forces that have shaped their development are exceedingly complex. In a study of the history of popular images of American Indians, Berkhofer argues convincingly that these views are closely tied to the development of intellectual and moral thinking in Western culture.[6] Namely, the way in which non-Indians have viewed American Indians has been influenced more by Western philosophical trends than by an objective understanding of American Indians.

Berkhofer suggests that white society's concept of American Indians is marked by two sharply contrasting views that evolved from a single idea. Unifying the disparate range of mystical white conceptions about American Indians is the consistent belief that the American Indian personifies traits and characteristics believed missing in white society; American Indians are everything that non-Indians are not. According to Berkhofer, American Indians are an alter ego for the cultural psyche of white society.

Critics of Western culture employ a concept of American Indians in which the most disagreeable conditions in white society are absent; the lack of Western influence on American Indian lifestyles is a genuine virtue. To these critics, American Indians are praiseworthy because they represent an ideal to which non-Indians should strive. If Western culture is corrupt, avaricious, treacherous, and earthbound, then American In-

[6]Robert F. Berkhofer, Jr., *The White Man's Indian* (New York: Vintage Books, 1978). Most of the discussion about mystical definitions of American Indians is based on Berkhofer's argument.

dians are noble savages, unsullied by the white world; they are loyal, generous, trustworthy, and spiritual, living in harmony with the natural rhythms of the universe. Western civilization is shamed for victimizing a race of innocent primitives.

An opposing concept of American Indians views their lack of Western manners as a vice and as evidence of moral and intellectual inferiority. Ethnocentric ideas about the superiority of Western culture define American Indians in unsavory terms. Compared with the high levels of intellectual, artistic, and moral development of Europeans, the lowest instincts in human beings are attributed to American Indians. If Western culture is humane and civilized, then by definition American Indians are immoral and barbaric. For example, early settlers believed that Indians were the agents of Satan, and the smallpox epidemics that raged among the East Coast tribes were the result of divine intervention.[7]

Genetic Characteristics of Native Americans

Compared with the vague and conflicting mystical definitions in popular culture, biological definitions of American Indians are relatively straightforward. These definitions originated with the development of physical anthropology and advances in the biological sciences. In relation to the four broad racial groups mentioned earlier, physical anthropologists ordinarily classify Native Americans as a variety within the Mongoloid race. This judgment is based on physical appearances and theories about the Asiatic origins of American Indians and Alaska Natives. Although Native Americans and Asians share similar genetic characteristics, these same genetic indicators also reveal a number of differences. For this reason, some physical anthropologists believe that Native Americans constitute a separate race within the larger, polyglot category of Mongoloid.[8]

Numerous genetic characteristics can be used to identify members of the American Indian race. The five most common measures include earwax texture, organic compounds in urine, blood types and Rh factor, fingerprint patterns, and the ability to taste a slightly bitter test chemical called phenylthiocarbamide (PTC). American Indians and Asians are

---

[7]Berkhofer (1978); see also Henry F. Dobyns, *Native American Historical Demography: A Critical Bibliography* (Bloomington: Indiana University Press, 1976), and the discussion in the preceding chapter. Another excellent source is Lee Eldridge Huddleston, *Origins of the American Indians: European Concepts, 1492–1729* (Austin: University of Texas Press, 1967).

[8]Goldsby (1971).

more likely to have dry, crumbly earwax than Europeans or other races. They also are more likely to be able to detect the bitter taste of PTC than other races. Urine analysis, however, reveals a slight difference between Asians and American Indians. Asians frequently have high levels of a compound called beta-amino-isobutyric (BAIB) acid in their urine. This is uncommon in other racial groups, including some groups of American Indians. That is, some groups of American Indians are similar to Asians in having high levels of BAIB in their urine, while other groups of Indians do not share this trait.

American Indians and Asians are most different in their fingerprint patterns and blood types. Studies show that there is very little variation in blood types for American Indians, and most have blood type O. Similarly, very few have negative Rh factors. Asians and all other races are less likely than American Indians to have type O blood and more likely to have negative Rh factors. Asians have about equal numbers of loops and whorls in their fingerprint patterns, but American Indians usually have more loops than whorls. Indian patterns are similar to white patterns.

The presence of distinct genetic characteristics such as blood types and the ability to taste PTC among American Indians should not be misunderstood as evidence of a pure genotype. For reasons already mentioned, American Indians as a pure genotype probably disappeared sometime after the beginning of the sixteenth century. The genetic indicators that identify members of the American Indian race do not consistently identify the descendants of pre-Columbian populations, and these characteristics can be found in members of other races. It is misleading to suggest that a handful of biological characteristics can meaningfully define the bounds of the American Indian and Alaska Native population. Goldsby offers a note of warning about the inconclusiveness of genetic tests:

> Man is a single species, and so, when the opportunity presents itself, members of different races often interbreed and sometimes even intermarry. The frequent failure to exchange marital vows has not prevented populations from exchanging genes. . . . It is for this reason that descriptions of the race of man are at best *general idealizations* to which one must match groups of real men. We must understand that the assignment of men to racial categories, even though it is a real and possible exercise in judgment, is in many cases only an approximate one.[9]

[9]Goldsby (1971); Harold E. Driver, *Indians of North America* (Chicago and London: University of Chicago Press, 1969), also discusses controversies about whether American Indians constitute one or several genetic stocks; see pp. 5–6.

Bureaucratic Views of Native Americans

Demographers who work with government data seldom have the luxury (or burden) of using their own definitions of race. Instead, most definitions affecting the collection of public data are established by government agencies seeking information for guiding the administration of public affairs. Of necessity, the statistical data provided in later chapters of this book are based on the administrative definition of the American Indian race employed by the U.S. Bureau of the Census. Census and other types of administrative definitions are the subject of intensive debate and negotiation because they must satisfy countervailing political interests, meet numerous bureaucratic needs, and occasionally lend themselves to scientific work. Over the years, defining who is an Indian or Alaska Native has been exceedingly problematic for many agencies of the federal government, including the Census Bureau. This problem has caused a proliferation of administrative definitions at all levels of government.

Blood Quantum

Historically, "blood quantum" has been a central concept in administrative definitions of Native Americans. In the nineteenth century scientists believed that blood was the carrier of genetic material and cultural traits. The mixing of racial characteristics was equivalent to mixing blood types. One of the founders of modern anthropology, Lewis Henry Morgan, was a leading proponent of this view, and it constituted a central tenet in the eugenics movement of the late nineteenth century.[10] According to this view of racial inheritance, each race possessed a unique blood type which determined its physical appearances *and* social behavior. Cultural differences, no less than physical differences, were the result of different blood types.

This reasoning led to the belief that the amount of blood that a person possessed from a particular race governed the degree to which that individual would resemble and behave like other persons of similar racial background. For example, full-blood Indians possessed the full measure of preconceived physical and social characteristics ascribed to the Indian population. On the other hand, individuals with mixed par-

[10]Berkhofer, (1978), pt. 2; Robert E. Bieder, "Scientific Attitudes Toward Indian Mixed-Bloods in Early Nineteenth Century America," *Journal of Ethnic Studies* 8 (1980):17–30; Robert E. Bieder, *Science Encounters the Indian, 1820–1880: The Early Years of American Ethnology* (Norman: University of Oklahoma Press, 1986).

entage—one white and the other Indian, for instance—were expected to have one half of the preconceived physical and social characteristics from each parent; thus, the term "half-breed" was coined. Morgan believed, for example, that habits of dress, such as wearing loincloths or sleeping in the nude, along with forms of music, dance, language, and family organization were biologically determined through the inheritance of blood types. To hasten the assimilation of American Indians, Morgan advocated a program of selective breeding.[11]

For many years, blood quantum was the single most important criterion used by the federal government, especially the Bureau of Indian Affairs (BIA), for identifying members of the American Indian population. Congress also resorted to blood quantum definitions for legislative purposes. When it was first used by federal authorities, blood quantum was meant to measure the amount of Indian blood possessed by an individual. Because racial blood types could not be observed directly, Indian blood quantum was inferred from the racial backgrounds of parents. If both parents were reputed to have "unadulterated" Indian blood, then the blood quantum of their children was fixed at 100 percent. For children of racially mixed parents, their Indian blood quantum might be some fractional amount such as 3/4, 1/2, or 1/8. This test was intended to reflect the extent to which a person would have the appearance and culture of Indians, thereby establishing membership in the Indian population, white population, or some other racial group.

Implementing a blood quantum definition required a benchmark for ascertaining the distribution of racial blood types in the Indian population. It was, and still is, impossible to designate a person as 3/4 blood quantum without knowing the blood types of his or her parents, grandparents, great-grandparents, and even earlier ancestors. The federal government settled this problem by documenting the blood quantums of Indians belonging to tribes under the jurisdiction of federal authorities. In the late nineteenth and early twentieth centuries, BIA agents were responsible for developing and maintaining records documenting the blood quantums of tribal populations. These records of tribal enrollments, called tribal rolls, were assembled for tribes recognized by the BIA. Federal agents enumerated Indian households and recorded the number of adults and children and the racial blood quantum of each person. At the time when these rolls were constructed, blood quantum was determined on the basis of subjective judgments by Indian agents, the reports of household members about their parentage, and information supplied by neighbors, friends, and relatives. Since tribal rolls were established, blood quantum has usually been determined by tracing ge-

[11]Bieder (1986), chap. 6.

nealogical histories back to these early records. Traditionally, tribal rolls have served as a basic reference point for most administrative definitions of American Indians.

The use of blood quantum to define the modern Indian population poses enormous conceptual and practical problems. Conceptually, the development of modern genetics and environmentalism in the social sciences dispelled the validity of eugenics and undermined the intellectual credibility of blood quantum racial definitions. Over time, eugenics came to be viewed as intellectually veiled racism. Confronted by legal challenges, federal authorities were forced to concede that blood quantum definitions cannot be legally enforced for most purposes.[12] Furthermore, the blood quantum information haphazardly collected in the early rolls is at best unsystematic, if not altogether unreliable.

Besides the doubtful reliability of early tribal rolls, an even larger problem arises from how to use blood quantum to distinguish Indians from non-Indians. Genealogical bloodlines do not clearly signal who is a member of the Indian population and who is not. There is no sound rationale for setting a blood quantum below which an individual is no longer an Indian; small differences in blood quantum are equally meaningless.

Nevertheless, the BIA, for example, uses 1/4 blood quantum as a minimum requirement for entitlement to certain government services. In 1986 the Department of Health and Human Services proposed that 1/4 blood quantum should be a criterion for receiving medical service at Indian Health Service clinics.[13] Furthermore, a large number of tribal governments use blood quantum criteria ranging from 1/16 to 1/2 for determining tribal membership. American Indians are the only group in American society for whom pedigreed bloodlines have the same economic importance as they do for show animals and race horses.

Many tribes follow the BIA practice and use the 1/4 blood quantum criterion. This standard requires an individual to have at least one enrolled full-blooded Indian grandparent. Other combinations of ancestry are also permissible as long as the 1/4 blood quantum requirement is satisfied. Nevertheless, there is little justification for believing that someone who is 15/64 blood quantum is decidedly "less Indian" than someone who is 1/4 blood quantum. Individual differences as small as 1/64 blood quantum can result from one person having one more full-blooded great-great-great-great-grandparent than another.

Blood quantum is an archaic concept that is gradually disappearing

[12]See *Whiting* v. *United States*, 201 US 117 (1975); see also AIPRC (1977), chap. 3.
[13]Spencer Rich, "HHS Proposes to Curb Indian Health Benefits," *Washington Post*, June 29, 1986, p. A8.

from administrative use. In its place the federal government has tried several different approaches. For example, in 1950 the Census Bureau relied on the visual acuity of its enumerators to identify members of the American Indian race. Census enumerators were instructed to record the race of each person by observing physical characteristics. If enumerators were uncertain as to whether a person was Indian, they were instructed to inquire if the person was enrolled, claimed 1/4 blood quantum, or was recognized by the community as an Indian. The Census Bureau did not establish the exact conditions that constitute community recognition, but it is not the only agency to use this criterion. The principle of "community recognition" appears repeatedly in bureaucratic regulations and congressional actions. By this standard the testimony of one's neighbors is sufficient to establish membership in the Indian population. In practice, this often means that if tribal authorities are willing to extend tribal membership to an individual, this is sufficient to establish membership in the Indian population—regardless of genealogy.

Indians Taxed

The earliest enumerations of American Indians by the Census Bureau distinguished between "Indians Taxed" and "Indians Not Taxed." In the 1870 census marshals were instructed that *Indians taxed* were "Indians out of their tribal relations and exercising the rights of citizens under State or Territorial laws. . . ."[14] The determination of whether Indians were out of their tribal relations or enjoying the rights of citizenship was left to the marshals taking the census. However, Indians taxed were most likely persons who had settled in white communities and intended to assimilate. Such individuals were not reservation residents and most likely were not practicing a traditional lifestyle, especially if they had once belonged to the nomadic Plains tribes. On the other hand, marshals were instructed that *Indians not taxed* "are not to be enumerated on schedule 1. Although no provision is made for the enumeration of 'Indians not taxed,' it is highly desirable, for statistical purposes, that the number of such persons not living upon reservations should be known. Assistant Marshals are therefore requested . . . [to make] a special report to the census office."[15]

It is important to realize that this definition of who is an Indian in

[14]U.S. Bureau of the Census, *Twenty Censuses: Population and Housing Questions, 1790–1980* (Washington, DC: U.S. Government Printing Office, 1979), p. 19.
[15]U.S. Bureau of the Census (1979), p. 19.

the census is based on political status. American Indians practicing their traditional culture and living under the sovereignty of their tribal leaders were not U.S. citizens, not taxed, and therefore not subject to "official enumeration" by the census, though efforts were made to count them. After the Allotment Acts (1887), the number of Indians taxed increased markedly because each Indian receiving an allotment of land was also granted citizenship. Eventually, the distinction between Indians taxed and those not taxed became obsolete with the passage of the Indian Citizenship Act of 1924, which extended the rights of citizenship to all American Indians, regardless of residence or lifestyle.[16]

Indian Self-Identification

Recognizing the limitations of blood quantum definitions and the ambiguities of community recognition, Congress has tried to avoid the problem altogether by simply defining "Indians" as members of Indian tribes.[17] Congress has never passed a general, all-purpose definition for the Indian population, and this most recent definition leaves the question of who is an Indian to be settled by tribal governments and federal bureaucrats. Conceding the impossibility of developing an acceptable all-purpose administrative definition, many agencies of the federal government, including the Census Bureau, rely on self-identification to define the Indian population. That is, the boundaries of the American Indian population include all persons who declare their race as American Indian.

The primary advantage of a minimal definition based on self-identification is that it imposes virtually no prior assumptions about the concept of race. Unlike blood quantum definitions, there are no implicit genetic theories linked to racial self-identification. Self-identification does not require special tests, genealogical investigations, or other complex conditions for ascertaining racial membership. The use of self-identification means that the concept of race probably varies greatly from one person to another since individuals are given the discretion to develop their own personal ideas about race and to decide which information will be relevant for classifying themselves into one or another racial category.

The absence of strong prior assumptions is a strength of self-identification, but it is also one of its major liabilities. For social research,

---

[16]Harold E. Fey and D'Arcy McNickle, *Indians and Other Americans: Two Ways of Life Meet* (New York: Harper & Brothers, 1959), p. 93.

[17]AIPRC (1977).

this is a serious problem because there is no way of knowing precisely what is meant when someone identifies himself or herself as an Indian. Demographers also do not know how the concept of race varies across the population or the kinds of factors that are important for shaping racial identification. In sum, demographers know virtually nothing about the highly complex calculus involved in racial self-identification.

American Indian Ethnicity

Concepts of Ethnicity

The concept of ethnicity is not as emotionally charged as the concept of race and is perhaps subject to less confusion.

Broadly construed, an ethnic group, as defined by De Vos, is a "self-perceived group of people who hold in common a set of traditions not shared by the others with whom they are in contact."[18] Barth also shares this view and argues that "ethnic groups are categories of ascription and identification by the actors themselves, and thus have the characteristic of organizing interaction between people."[19] These definitions suggest that there are two dimensions of ethnicity. First, there are the objective, observable social characteristics that distinguish an ethnic group from other segments of society. Second, there is a subjective sense of belonging and personal identification which ethnic group members share in common with each other.

Knowledge about the most significant social characteristics used by groups to define themselves and their boundaries is essential for understanding the concept of ethnicity. One of the major tasks facing scholars of ethnicity has been to identify those factors that are most salient in defining the uniqueness of ethnic groups. Petersen argues that at the very least, race, language, and geographic region are consistently associated with ethnic group identity and therefore represent the fundamental domains of ethnicity.[20] Minimally, members of ethnic groups belong to a common gene pool and have a similar physical appearance, communicate with each other in a common language, and live in close proximity to one another in a specific geographic area.

[18]George De Vos, "Ethnic Pluralism: Conflict and Accommodation," in George De Vos and Lola Romanucci-Ross, eds., *Ethnic Identity: Cultural Continuities and Change* (Palo Alto: Mayfield, 1975), p. 9.

[19]Fredrik Barth, "Introduction," in Fredrik Barth, ed., *Ethnic Groups and Boundaries* (Boston: Little, Brown, 1969).

[20]William Petersen, "Concepts of Ethnicity," in Stephan Thernstrom, ed., *Harvard Encyclopedia of American Ethnic Groups* (Cambridge, MA: Harvard University Press, 1980).

Barth proposed a definition of ethnic groups which is very similar to Petersen's ideas. Barth agrees that ethnic groups are biologically self-perpetuating and share a common language. However, he adds that ethnic groups share fundamental cultural values and, most notably, they also form the basis of self-identification by group members.[21] This perspective is noteworthy because it explicitly focuses on self-identification as one of the hallmarks of ethnic group boundaries. De Vos agrees with Barth and Petersen in his review of ethnic group characteristics, but he also includes a number of characteristics not listed by the others.[22] Besides race, culture, territory, and language, De Vos states that ethnic groups often have unique religious practices and frequently occupy special niches within the larger economy. Specialized niches develop in the larger economy when members of ethnic groups develop skills in specialized occupations. For example, the Mohawk Indians of upstate New York have an almost legendary reputation for their skills in the high steel construction industry.[23]

Undoubtedly motivated by a desire to be comprehensive, the *Harvard Encyclopedia of American Ethnic Groups* contains a long inventory of characteristics that define ethnic group boundaries.[24] According to this list, the ways in which ethnic group members are similar include the following:

1. Common geographic origins
2. Migratory status
3. Race
4. Language or dialect
5. Religious faith or faiths
6. Ties that transcend kinship, neighborhood, or community barriers
7. Shared traditions, values, and symbols
8. Literature, folklore, and music
9. Food preferences
10. Settlement and employment patterns
11. Special interests in regard to politics in the homeland and in the United States

[21]Barth (1969).

[22]De Vos (1975).

[23]Ruth Blumenfeld, "Mohawks: Round Trip to the High Steel," *Transaction* 3 (1965):19–22.

[24]Stephan Thernstrom, Ann Orlov, and Oscar Handlin, "Introduction," in Thernstrom (1980).

12. Institutions that specifically serve and maintain the group
13. An internal sense of distinctiveness
14. An external perception of distinctiveness

Most of these characteristics are self-explanatory; shared traditions, values, folklore, literature, religion, and food preferences are the basic elements of a common culture. Transcendental ties and internal and external perceptions of distinctiveness mirror ethnic self-identification and the outwardly apparent differences of ethnic groups. This list also reflects the fact that with the exception of American Indians and Alaska Natives, American ethnic groups migrated to this country more or less together during specific periods of U.S. history. The Harvard list is most significant because, unlike many other definitions, it recognizes that politics are an important feature of ethnic groups. Ethnic groups have specialized political interests that are directly related to the well-being of the group. These interests are frequently served by organizations identified with specific ethnic groups—for example, the B'nai B'rith, the Sons of Italy, and the National Congress of American Indians.

A Single Ethnic Group?

By any definition or set of criteria one might choose, there can be little doubt that American Indians are a bona fide ethnic group. The authenticity of American Indian ethnicity is widely recognized by social scientists. However, the criteria that ordinarily define the boundaries of ethnic populations raise a serious doubt about whether American Indians can be legitimately regarded as a single, relatively homogeneous ethnic group. Likewise, there are a number of reasons why it is reasonable to think about American Indians and Alaska Natives as a multi-ethnic population. But if the American Indian population is really a hodge-podge of different ethnic groups, how should this population be subdivided to reflect the basic social and cultural differences that exist among the various tribal groups across the United States?

In many respects, the groups included in the American Indian population are extremely diverse. American Indians in the Pacific Northwest have little in common with Indians of the Southwest or Southeast. Members of the Salish tribe (a Pacific Northwest tribe) are as different from members of the Papago tribe (a Southwest tribe) as Italians are different from Norwegians. Norwegians and Italians are both of the Caucasian race, and both originate in western Europe, but except for these commonalities there are more differences than similarities. The same logic applies to American Indians and Alaska Natives. In fact, Alaska Natives have very little in common with the tribal cultures found in the lower 48 states. Evidence of the cultural diversity within the American Indian population is abundant in Driver's survey of North American tribes.

Driver's work shows that with the possible exception of physical appearance,[25] the common characteristics that would justify viewing American Indians as a single ethnic group are very few. American Indian tribes are characterized by significant differences in their lifestyles and cultural practices. Sizable geographic distances separate many tribes, and the number of distinct Indian languages is immense. According to sources reported by Driver, there are 221 different Indian languages known today, but before the arrival of Columbus the number could have been much higher, perhaps as many as 2,000. Driver describes different traditions in music and folklore, different types of religious practices, different types of family organization, different craft specializations, and even different dietary habits. For example, fish is a staple of Coastal Indians but it is not common in the diets of Plains Indians.

It is impossible to cover completely the spectrum of differences that exist among American Indians. However, amid these differences the single unifying tie that binds American Indians and Alaska Natives together is their singular willingness to identify themselves as descendants of the original inhabitants of North America.[26] Furthermore, viewing American Indians as a multi-ethnic population does not discount the similarities that exist among many tribes. Nevertheless, a multi-ethnic view of the Indian population poses a particularly difficult conceptual problem: namely, how many ethnic subgroups are contained in the Indian population and what criteria should be used to identify them?

Culture Areas

Although anthropologists do not often describe American Indians as a multi-ethnic population, they have not been blind to the cultural differences that exist among tribes. To describe these differences, the concepts of American Indian cultural groups and culture areas are important in the anthropological literature. Cultural groups include one or

[25]Driver (1969).

[26]Sam Stanley and Robert K. Thomas, "Current Demographic and Social Trends Among North American Indians," *Annals* 436(1978):111–120; Bruce A. Chadwick and Joseph H. Stauss, "The Assimilation of American Indians in Urban Society: The Seattle Case," *Human Organization* 34(1975):359–369.

more tribes with similar cultural practices, and culture areas are geographic regions presently or formerly occupied by a cultural group. Culture areas are useful because they lend themselves to thinking about American Indians as a multi-ethnic population. They subdivide the Indian population into smaller, more culturally homogeneous groups with similar language, lifestyles, and art. In other words, they define the major ethnic divisions in the American Indian population. For example, the culture areas that Driver presents reflect a high degree of cultural homogeneity. Culture areas typically overlap the geographic location of major Indian groups, predictably showing that the geographic distribution of cultural practices and linguistic patterns are closely related.

Culture areas highlight important cultural divisions, but these areas are plagued with two major problems that limit their usefulness in the research dealing with the contemporary American Indian population. One problem is that most published work on culture areas circumscribes the location of tribal cultures in earlier historical periods; the literature does not deal with the cultural divisions among modern American Indians but describes Indians as they were organized and situated generations ago. For example, Driver's discussion divides North America into areas in which one or another cultural group prevailed in about 1600.

A related problem is that maps for 1600 or earlier are not useful for modern Indians because they do not reflect the massive redistribution of Indian tribes during the nineteenth century. Beginning in the early 1800s, the federal government used military force to uproot many tribes from their traditional settlement areas and resettled them in distant regions. The Cherokee, Choctaw, Creek, Seminole, and Chickasaw tribes were moved from the southeastern United States and resettled in Oklahoma. The Oneida and Mahican were moved from upstate New York to Wisconsin, while the Winnebago were moved from Wisconsin to Nebraska. Furthermore, the literature on culture areas does not consider migration behavior among American Indians in the twentieth century. Modern Indians are considerably more mobile than were their ancestors (see Chapter 9). As a result of this mobility, urban Indian populations are typically a diverse blend of tribal groups. In view of these problems, it is nearly impossible to use sixteenth century culture areas to describe American Indians and Alaska Natives in the late twentieth century.

Despite these limitations, culture areas are still useful for calling attention to ethnic divisions that still exist within the Indian population, though not as they existed 400 years ago. Loosely speaking, culture areas represent a map of the "old country" for American Indians. Just as Polish Americans can trace their ethnicity to a geographic location in eastern Europe, tribes of American Indians can trace their origins back to regions of the United States. Because regional origins are an important dimension of ethnicity, maps of American Indian culture areas are useful guides to the major ethnic groups within the Indian population, just as European regions are associated with the history of other American ethnic groups.

Map 2.1 (see foldout following page 36) is adapted from Driver and Massey's map of American Indian culture areas and shows the major culture areas in the North American continent. Map 2.2 (following page 36) provides further details about the tribes located in the contiguous 48 states. These areas represent, in an admittedly imprecise manner, the major ethnic subdivisions within the American Indian population. For example, tribes from the Southeast have much more in common with one another culturally than they do with tribes from, say, the Plains area. The Oklahoma Cherokee are originally from the Southeast, and they have more in common with other tribes from states such as Georgia and Alabama than with tribes native to the eastern Oklahoma area, such as the Osage or Wichita.

Needless to say, there is little correspondence between tribal culture areas and modern civil divisions such as states and counties. The U.S. Bureau of the Census routinely reports data for a variety of civil divisions, but in regard to American Indians the Census Bureau does not report data for cultural subdivisions within the Indian population. In policy and practice the Census Bureau recognizes American Indians only as a single ethnic group and has never formally addressed the issue of whether Indians are a bona fide multi-ethnic population. As a result, it is difficult to use published census data to identify cultural subgroups within the Indian population. However, it is possible to compare culture areas with state boundaries and the major geographic areas for which the Census Bureau reports data.

Table 2.1 lists the states included in the culture areas of Map 2.1. Together Map 2.1 and Table 2.1 link modern state boundaries with settlement areas belonging to different Indian ethnic groups in an earlier historical period. Again, the present location of many tribes is not the location they occupied prior to the nineteenth century. The overlap between culture areas and state boundaries is variable as well. For example, the culture areas for the Plateau and Northwest tribes are not well matched by state boundaries. The Plateau culture region includes only Idaho, but it would more closely approximate the Plateau culture area by including eastern Washington and Oregon and parts of western Montana. West of the Plateau Indians, the northwestern tribes were concentrated along the coast of Oregon, Washington, and British Columbia and continue to live in this area today. In contrast, the southeastern and eastern Woodland culture areas are relatively well defined by state

TABLE 2.1

*Culture Regions Based on Modern State Boundaries
and Major Culture Areas in 1600*

Eastern Woodland	Southeast	Prairies
Connecticut	Alabama	Arkansas
Indiana	Delaware	Illinois
Maine	Florida	Iowa
Massachusetts	Georgia	Minnesota
Michigan	Kentucky	Missouri
New Hampshire	Louisiana	Wisconsin
New Jersey	Maryland	
New York	Mississippi	
Ohio	North Carolina	
Pennsylvania	South Carolina	
Rhode Island	Tennessee	
Vermont	Virginia	
	West Virginia	
Plains	Great Basin	Plateau
Colorado	Nevada	Idaho
Kansas	Utah	
Nebraska		
North Dakota		
Oklahoma		
South Dakota		
Texas		
Wyoming		
Northwest	Southwest	California
Washington	Arizona	California
Oregon	New Mexico	
Arctic and Subarctic		
Alaska		

boundaries. For instance, Map 2.1 and Table 2.1 show that in the six-teenth century, eastern Woodland tribes were the dominant ethnic group settled in the area now occupied by the states of Michigan, Ohio, and Indiana, eastward to the New England states. It also should be mentioned that many eastern Woodland and southeastern tribes were removed to areas farther west in the nineteenth century, and many disappeared in the wake of disease and warfare.

Culture areas are most useful because they highlight the major cultural divisions that make American Indians a multi-ethnic population. Conventional ethnic classifications do not readily acknowledge the diversity among tribes or tribal groups. As a result, ethnic differences among American Indians and Alaska Natives are routinely obscured and discounted. Cultural differentiation is certainly not a new idea, but in the framework of American Indian demography it changes the question of who is an Indian to who is *what kind* of an Indian.

One obvious problem with the multi-ethnic view of the American Indian population is that it is unmanageable insofar as it implies a need to make exceedingly fine distinctions within a relatively small population. Indeed, the tribal population estimates listed in Appendix 1 show that many tribes have very small memberships.

At this level of detail, numbers smaller than a few hundred are not uncommon. Despite the diversity among tribes, it is not always possible to differentiate explicitly among the many distinct cultural groups within the Indian population. In most instances, the level of required detail is simply too overwhelming to manage, and the data are not readily available. Treating each tribe as a separate cultural entity demands a large investment of time and resources[27] and necessarily limits the scope of any analysis to only a few tribes. Indeed, this has been a limitation on most past research dealing with American Indians. For these reasons the research reported in this volume concerns the entire U.S. Indian population, and the subsequent chapters necessarily focus on only broad geographic areas such as census divisions and places of residence such as metropolitan, nonmetropolitan, reservation, and nonreservation areas.

The analytic problems posed by cultural differences and the methodologies for dealing with these problems are controversial matters that are far from resolution. In the absence of simple, well-defined solutions, concepts such as culture areas and regions should make users of demographic data aware of the intricate composition of the Indian population and wary of the dangers of overgeneralization.

Race and Ethnicity in American Indian Identity
Measuring Race and Ethnicity

Without doubt, the question of who is an Indian is as crucial for understanding the results of demographic studies as it is complex. The numerous ways in which American Indians can be defined in terms of

---

[27]William C. Sturtevant, ed., *Handbook of North American Indians* (Washington, DC: U.S. Government Printing Office, 1981), a multivolume work. Some volumes are still being prepared by the Smithsonian Institution, which reflects the magnitude of detail necessary in scholarly work dealing with a group as culturally diverse as American Indians.

race or ethnicity, or as a collection of ethnicities, means that the answer to this question depends on how it is posed.

When population boundaries are based on personal reports of race and ethnicity, otherwise objectively measured demographic data are sensitive to the elusive processes that influence self-perceptions. Disregarding these subtleties poses a serious risk of misunderstanding data for American Indians. For this reason, it is useful to examine statistical estimates of population characteristics based on alternative definitions of who belongs to the Indian population to see how different definitions affect the interpretation of American Indian data.

Race: The Census Bureau collects data primarily for the needs of the federal government, and predictably it uses a narrowly construed, administrative definition of race. As a tool of public administration, the racial classification developed by the Census Bureau bears little resemblance to classifications based on biological characteristics. Census documents emphasize this point by clearly stating that "the concept of race as used by the Census Bureau reflects self-identification by respondents; it does not denote any clear-cut scientific definition of biological stock."[28]

A facsimile of the item used in the 1980 census to obtain information about the racial composition of American households is displayed at the top of Figure 2.1. The race item shows that the Census Bureau recognizes 15 different racial groups, including a residual category for "other" races. Whites, blacks, and nine other types of Asian and Pacific Islanders are represented in this classification. Hispanic groups are usually assigned to the categories of white, black or "other" races, but they are specifically identified by the question about Hispanic origins, shown in the middle of Figure 2.1. In fact, about 7.1 percent of the American Indian population (101,529 persons) reported Hispanic origins. Finally, three categories are allotted to the native North American population, allowing American Indians, Eskimos, and Aleuts to identify themselves in separate racial categories. American Indians are also asked to disclose their tribal background.

An important characteristic of this classification is that the categories are mutually exclusive so that respondents cannot report that they are multiracial. For instance, individuals cannot respond that their race is Indian *and* white. They are either Indian or white, but not both. Information from persons who reported more than one race on their census questionnaire was handled with special procedures. In some cases, individuals giving multiracial responses were assigned the race of their

---

[28]U.S. Bureau of the Census, *Public-Use Microdata Samples Technical Documentation* (Washington, DC: U.S. Department of Commerce, 1983), p. K-37.

FIGURE 2.1

Facsimiles of Race and Ethnicity Questions in the 1980 Census

---

Facsimile of questionnaire item 4.

| 4. Is this person—

Fill one circle | ○ White   ○ Asian Indian
○ Black or Negro   ○ Hawaiian
○ Japanese   ○ Guamanian
○ Chinese   ○ Samoan
○ Filipino   ○ Eskimo
○ Korean   ○ Aleut
○ Vietnamese   ○ Other—*Specify*
                            ↓
○ Indian (Amer.)
  Print
  tribe → - - - - - - - - - - - - - - - - - - - |

Facsimile of questionnaire item 7.

| 7. Is this person of Spanish/Hispanic
   origin or descent?

Fill one circle | ○ No (not Spanish/Hispanic)
○ Yes, Mexican. Mexican-Amer.,
   Chicano
○ Yes, Puerto Rican
○ Yes, Cuban   ■
○ Yes, other Spanish/Hispanic |

Facsimile of questionnaire item 14.

| 14. What is this person's ancestry? *If uncertain about*
    how to report ancestry, see instruction guide.

- -

(For example: Afro-Amer., English, French, German,
Honduran, Hungarian, Irish, Italian, Jamaican,
Korean, Lebanese, Mexican, Nigerian, Polish,
Ukrainian, Venezuelan, etc.) |

Facsimile of instructions to the respondent for questionnaire item 14.

| 14. Print the ancestry group with which the person *identifies*. ancestry (or origin or descent) may be viewed as the nationality group, the lineage, or the country in which the person or the person's parents or ancestors were born before their arrival in the United States. Persons who are of more than one origin and who cannot identify with a single group should print their multiple ancestry (for example, German-Irish).
Be specific: for example, if ancestry is 'Indian', specify whether American Indian, Asian Indian, or West Indian. Distinguish Cape Verdean from Portuguese, and French Canadian from Canadian. A religious group should not be reported as a person's ancestry. |

mother, when it was possible to ascertain the mother's race. This was possible only when the mothers of multiracial offspring resided in the same household as their children, which was most likely to be true for younger individuals. In some cases, when the mother's race could not be ascertained, multiracial individuals were assigned the first race of their multiple response. Persons reporting their race as "Indian-White" were counted as Indians, and those reporting their race as "White-Indian" were counted as whites.

Ethnicity: American Indians, Aleuts, and Eskimos were also designated categories of ethnicity in the 1980 census. Information about ethnicity was obtained with the item appearing at the bottom of Figure 2.1. This item has two significant features: (1) The census uses *ancestry* as the operational definition of ethnicity. Persons are asked to report the nationality, lineage, or national origin of themselves *or* their ancestors. In other words, individuals are asked to identify their ethnic origins in terms of their personal and/or ancestral heritage. (2) Respondents are not asked to choose among a set of predetermined categories, as they do for the race item. Instead, respondents are permitted to freely report as many different ancestries as they please.

For data processing purposes, the Census Bureau used only the first two responses of individuals who gave several ancestries. In most cases, the census ignored the third and subsequent ancestries. Individuals who reported that their ancestry was "Irish-French-Indian" were counted as "Irish-French." Persons who reported a single ancestry such as "Indian" were counted as "Indian." Similarly, double ancestries were not changed, so that responses such as "Irish-Indian" or "Irish-German" were recorded exactly as they appeared on the completed census questionnaires. Census procedures also recognized a few cases of frequently reported triple ancestries. Four triple ancestries were frequently reported for American Indians: Indian-English-French, Indian-English-German, Indian-English-Irish, Indian-German-Irish.

The Intersection of Race and Ethnicity

The race and ancestry questions used in the 1980 census uncovered two sharply discrepant boundaries for the Indian population. Table 2.2 shows sex-specific estimates of the Indian population based on race and ethnic ancestry definitions. Using race to define population boundaries results in an estimate of approximately 1.5 million American Indians and Alaska Natives. Ethnic ancestry produces a dramatically different figure. Including everyone who reports any American Indian ancestry

TABLE 2.2

Sex-Specific Population Estimates of American Indians*
Classified by Categories of Race and Ancestry

	Persons Reporting American Indian Race	Persons Reporting American Indian Ancestry
Male	760,520 (49%)	3,259,600 (48%)
Female	779,300 (51%)	3,495,200 (52%)
Total	1,539,820 (100%)	6,754,800 (100%)

SOURCES: Estimates for persons reporting Indian race are based on a 5 percent sample of the 1980 census (5 percent PUMS). Estimates for persons reporting Indian ancestry are based on a 1 percent sample of the 1980 census (20 percent sample of 5 percent PUMS). Sampling errors cause these estimates to differ slightly from the published estimates of the U.S. Bureau of the Census.

*Includes Eskimos and Aleuts.

yields a population estimate of 6.8 million, a number 4.4 times larger than the estimate based on racially defined population boundaries. The sheer magnitude of this difference makes it difficult to reconcile these numbers.

Conventionally, the racial composition of ethnic groups tends to be fairly homogeneous. This is clearly not true for those who indicate that their ancestry includes American Indians. Table 2.3 shows the racial profile of all individuals who reported American Indian ancestry in the 1980 census. Of the nearly 6.8 million persons who reported American Indian ancestry, almost 5.2 million (77 percent) identified their race as white. A much smaller group, slightly over 1.2 million (18 percent), also reported their race as Indian. Blacks and other races made up the small remaining balance (5 percent) of persons reporting Indian ancestry. Of course, the most significant finding in this table is that the vast majority of persons claiming Indian ancestry do not consider their race as Indian; most regard themselves as white.

Using the same format as Table 2.3, a parallel analysis can be made of the distribution of ethnic ancestry among persons reporting American Indian as their race. Table 2.4 presents a profile of the ancestries reported by persons of American Indian race. This profile is based on "first" ancestries, meaning that they are the first of a series of ancestries for persons of multi-ethnic background or they are the only ancestry of persons reporting a single ethnic background. Table 2.4 shows that of the 1.5 million people identifying their race as Indian, only about 11

TABLE 2.3
Race of Persons Reporting American Indian Ancestry

Race	Male	Female	Total
American Indian	599,200 (18%)	618,000 (18%)	1,217,200 (18%)
Blacks	108,000 (3%)	148,700 (4%)	256,700 (4%)
Whites	2,497,100 (77%)	2,676,400 (77%)	5,173,500 (77%)
Hispanics and Others	38,200 (1%)	37,400 (1%)	75,600 (1%)
Asians	17,100 (1%)	14,700 (0%)	31,800 (0%)
Total	3,259,600 (100%)	3,495,200 (100%)	6,754,800 (100%)

SOURCE: One percent sample of 1980 census data (20 percent sample of 5 percent Public-Use Microdata Sample, A File).

percent indicated a European group as their first or only ethnic ancestry. Although their race is Indian, this group consists of persons who identify their ethnic ancestry in terms such as Irish-Indian, German-Indian, English-Indian, Italian-Indian; or simply as Irish, German, French, English, or Italian; or include any one of a large number of other European

TABLE 2.4
First Ancestry of Persons Reporting American Indian Race

Ancestry	Male	Female	Total
American Indian	554,680 (73%)	572,080 (73%)	1,126,760 (73%)
African	1,700 (0%)	1,340 (0%)	3,040 (0%)
European	79,380 (10%)	82,260 (11%)	161,640 (11%)
Hispanic	25,840 (3%)	24,980 (3%)	50,820 (3%)
Asian and Pacific Islanders	2,440 (0%)	2,540 (0%)	4,980 (0%)
Other U.S.	22,880 (3%)	23,440 (3%)	46,320 (3%)
Ancestry Not Reported	73,600 (10%)	72,660 (9%)	146,260 (9%)

SOURCE: Public-Use Microdata Sample, 5 percent A File.

ethnic groups. However, most people (73 percent) who identify their race as American Indian also report that their ancestry is American Indian. About 6 percent report Hispanic, African, and other ethnic ancestries. Persons who did not report an ancestry constitute the third most common response category; one possible reason is that once they reported their race, they viewed the question about ancestry as redundant and did not bother to respond.

Several conclusions are suggested by Tables 2.3 and 2.4. One is that among American Indians there is a significant amount of overlap between race and ethnic background. This is not unusual; the linkage between race and ethnicity is frequently noted by social scientists. A more unexpected finding is the heterogeneity among persons citing an American Indian ethnic background; the racial composition of this group is highly diverse. This is unusual because the racial composition of most ethnic groups is commonly believed to be relatively homogeneous. Even more striking, the race of most persons reporting Indian ancestry is *white* and not Indian. In contrast, the composition of ethnic backgrounds within the American Indian race, tribal differences notwithstanding, is relatively homogeneous. Most persons who report that their race is American Indian also report that their ethnic background is American Indian. Given that a person has an American Indian ethnic ancestry, the odds *against* that person identifying his or her race as Indian are almost 5 to 1. On the other hand, given that a person reports Indian as his or her race, the odds *favoring* an Indian ancestry for the same individual are almost 3 to 1. Most persons who claim Indian ancestry do not consider their race as Indian, but most persons who identify their race as Indian also claim Indian ancestry.

Categories of American Indian Identity

These findings highlight the fact that there are several different ways to claim membership in the Indian population. This is an extremely important point because it means that several different categories of American Indian identity have been captured in the 1980 census. These categories are based on several different patterns of self-identified race and ethnic background which depend, of course, on personal perceptions of race and ethnicity.

The first category of American Indian identity includes persons who disclose their race and ethnic background as American Indian, leaving no doubt that they are members of this population. For the remainder of this chapter, this group will be referred to simply as "American Indians" because the consistency of their responses makes them the core

TABLE 2.5

Population Estimates for Categories of American Indian Identity

Identity	Male	Female	Total
American Indian	466,100	481,400	947,500
	(14.3%)	(13.8%)	(14.0%)
American Indian of	133,100	136,600	269,700
Multiple Ancestry	(4.1%)	(3.9%)	(4.0%)
American of	2,660,400	2,877,200	5,537,600
Indian Descent	(81.6%)	(82.3%)	(82.0%)
Total	3,259,600	3,495,200	6,754,800
	(100.0%)	(100.0%)	(100.0%)

SOURCE: One percent sample of 1980 census data (20 percent sample of 5 percent PUMS data).

group within the Indian population. A second category of Indian identity includes persons who report their race as Indian but include non-Indian ancestry in their ethnic background. Using the outdated jargon of blood quantum definitions, such persons would be known as "mixed bloods" or in some cases "half-breeds." "American Indians of Multiple Ancestry" is a more accurate designation for these individuals. A third category of American Indian identity contains persons who cite a non-Indian race yet claim Indian ancestry for their ethnic background. Borrowing a term from Yinger and Simpson,[29] these individuals should be known as "Americans of Indian Descent."

Each of these American Indian identities defines a distinct population, and Table 2.5 displays the population estimates for each group. In 1980, 6.8 million persons reported that their race and/or ethnic ancestry was Indian, and out of this group 82 percent were Americans of Indian Descent. American Indians and American Indians of Multiple Ancestry constitute the second and third largest groups, respectively. By construction, the American Indian identity is racially and ethnically homogeneous, making it unlike the other two categories. The racial and ethnic diversity of Americans of Indian Descent and American Indians of Multiple Ancestry is shown in Tables 2.6 and 2.7. Table 2.6 shows the primary, or first, ethnic ancestry for American Indians of Multiple Ancestry. These figures indicate that 63 percent of the persons reporting a non-Indian ancestry still cite American Indian as their primary ethnic background. These individuals give responses such as Indian-Irish or In-

[29]J. Milton Yinger and George Eaton Simpson, "The Integration of Americans of Indian Descent," *Annals* 436(1978):137–151.

TABLE 2.6

First Ancestry of American Indians of Multiple Ancestry

Ancestry	Male	Female	Total
African	600	400	1,000
	(0%)	(0%)	(0%)
European	38,400	36,800	72,200
	(29%)	(27%)	(28%)
Hispanic	7,100	7,100	14,200
	(3%)	(3%)	(5%)
Asian and	700	700	1,400
Pacific Islander	(1%)	(1%)	(1%)
Other U.S.	4,000	4,800	8,800
	(3%)	(4%)	(3%)
American Indian	82,300	86,800	179,100
	(62%)	(63%)	(63%)

SOURCE: One percent sample of 1980 census data (20 percent sample of 5 percent Public-Use Microdata Sample, A File).

dian-French. A much smaller group, 28 percent of all American Indians of Multiple Ancestry, prefix their ethnic background with European ancestries, such as French-Indian or English-Indian. Notably, only about 9 percent identify their primary ethnic ancestry as something other than Indian or European.

Table 2.7 shows that Americans of Indian Descent are most homogeneous with respect to ethnic ancestry. An overwhelming majority of Americans of Indian Descent are concentrated in a single racial category: 93 percent of this group identify their race as white, leaving relatively small percentages in other racial categories.

TABLE 2.7

Race of Americans of Indian Descent

Race	Male	Female	Total
Black	108,000	148,700	256,700
	(4%)	(5%)	(5%)
White	2,497,100	2,676,400	5,173,500
	(94%)	(93%)	(93%)
Hispanic	38,200	37,400	75,600
	(1%)	(1%)	(1%)
Asian	17,100	14,700	31,800
	(0%)	(0%)	(0%)

SOURCE: One percent sample of 1980 census data (20 percent sample of 5 percent Public-Use Microdata Sample, A File).

Identity and Social Characteristics

Demonstrating that three types of American Indian identity can be found in census data has serious implications for the way in which the Indian population is defined. These categories circumscribe a set of distinctive and mutually exclusive populations. For studies of the Indian population, which of these groups should analysts choose, or is it acceptable to disregard these different identities and pool them? The gravity of these questions should not be discounted because their impact on empirical work is considerable. For instance, population estimates will be less than 1.0 million if studies are restricted to persons consistently identifying their race and ethnicity as Indian or over 7.5 million if all three identities are pooled. A critical consideration is the degree to which these groups have different compositions. The way people identify their race and ethnicity takes on added meaning insofar as different Indian identities describe markedly different populations in terms of social characteristics. In this regard, the observation that most Americans of Indian Descent identify their race as white is revealing because it foretells other compositional differences.

Education and Earnings: Socioeconomic status is a key dimension of population composition. Differences in socioeconomic status mark divisions between populations, indicating differential access to economic opportunity, material well-being, and overall quality of life in terms of health and comfort. Education and earnings are two measures of socioeconomic status, and they are shown for each Indian identity in Table 2.8. Of the three groups, American Indians have the lowest mean

TABLE 2.8

*Mean Education and Earnings
for Householders of American Indian Background,
and United States Total for Householders of All Races*

Identity	Years of Education	1979 Earnings
American Indian	10.7	$8,307
Indian of Multiple Ancestry	12.3	10,680
American of Indian Descent	11.5	10,742
Total	12.1	10,929

SOURCE: One percent sample of 1980 census data (20 percent sample of 5 percent Public-Use Microdata Sample, A File; 1-1000 Public-Use Microdata Sample).

education and earnings, 10.7 years and $8,307 in 1979. American Indians earned $2,373 less than Indians of Multiple Ancestry and $2,435 less than Americans of Indian Descent. American Indians also have between 0.8 and 1.6 fewer years of schooling, which partly accounts for their low earnings. Another way of viewing the relative standing of these groups is in terms of the gross economic returns to education, or earnings per year of education. Other factors notwithstanding, Americans of Indian Descent receive the highest returns, $934 per year of education ($10,742/11.5), and American Indians receive the least, $776.

Poverty: Poverty status is another measure of socioeconomic conditions within categories of the Indian population. Poverty status is based on official standards employed by the federal government, which reflect the minimum income levels needed to ensure adequate housing, nutrition, health, and other material needs. Persons living below the poverty line are probably living in substandard housing, have poor nutrition, and endure other kinds of hardship harmful to their health and well-being. Poverty status depends on income and family size, and in 1979 it ranged between $7,412 for a family of four to $3,686 for single individuals. Table 2.9 shows the number of persons living above and below the poverty line for each type of Indian identity. The differences in education and earnings among these groups appear in the distribution of poverty. About 15 percent of all Americans of Indian Descent live below the poverty line, while the figure is nearly double, 29 percent, for American Indians. Indians of Multiple Ancestry are between these

TABLE 2.9

*Percent Distribution of Poverty
Among Householders of American Indian Background in 1979,
and United States Total for Householders of All Races*

Percentage Below and Above Poverty	American Indians	Indians of Multiple Ancestry	Americans of Indian Descent	United States Total
Below the Poverty Line	29.0	17.2	15.1	12.7
1.0–1.49 Above	14.3	11.8	11.1	10.0
1.5–1.99 Above	12.9	10.5	11.2	9.5
2.0 and More Above	43.8	60.5	62.6	67.8
Total	100.0	100.0	100.0	100.0

SOURCE: One percent sample 1980 census data (20 percent sample of 5 percent Public-Use Microdata Sample, A File; 1-1000 Public-Use Microdata Sample).

groups, but in relation to poverty they closely resemble Americans of Indian Descent. American Indians also have a much smaller share of householders living well above the poverty line. Only 44 percent of American Indian householders have incomes twice the minimum standard, compared with 63 percent of Americans of Indian Descent.

Employment: Patterns of labor force participation are important because they help explain differences in poverty, income, earnings, and the economic returns on years of schooling. The differences in indicators of socioeconomic status should be reflected in differences in labor force participation, unemployment, and/or concentration in low-wage occupations. Table 2.10 profiles the labor force participation patterns for different types of American Indian householders. Consistent with other indicators of socioeconomic status, Americans of Indian Descent have an unemployment rate 2 to 3 percent lower than the other Indian populations and an employment rate almost 12 percent higher than that of American Indians. The proportion not in the labor force is 11 percent higher for American Indians than for Americans of Indian Descent, which is significant because persons not in the labor force include the hard-core unemployed and discouraged workers who have given up seeking work.

Language: There are unmistakable differences in the socioeconomic status of persons reporting different types of American Indian identity. Americans of Indian Descent consistently appear better off than their

TABLE 2.10

Percent Distribution of Labor Force Participation
Among Householders of American Indian Background,
and United States Total for Householders of All Races

Identity	Employed	Unemployed	Not in Labor Force	Military and N/A*	Total
American Indian	61.6	6.7	30.5	1.2	100.0
Indian of Multiple Ancestry	68.1	8.1	21.6	2.2	100.0
American of Indian Descent	73.4	5.1	19.9	1.6	100.0
Total	66.4	3.4	27.7	2.5	100.0

SOURCE: One percent sample of 1980 census data (20 sample of 5 percent Public-Use Microdata Sample, A File; 1-1000 Public-Use Microdata Sample).

*N/A includes householders who are under age 16 who are not in the labor force by definition, regardless of their labor force activity.

American Indian counterparts; in some instances the differences between these groups are large. The socioeconomic status of Indians of Multiple Ancestry is midway between these populations, although in some cases Indians of Multiple Ancestry are not far behind Americans of Indian Descent. The data collected by the Census Bureau make it easy to document socioeconomic conditions, but other dimensions of population composition are not as accessible. The discussion in this chapter has frequently referred to Indian culture, and an underlying implication of this reference is that different types of Indian identities will be linked to weaker or stronger attachment to Indian cultural practices. It would also be valuable to know if there are systematic cultural differences between these groups.

The available census data approach the subject of cultural behavior obliquely, at best. Information about language use is the single possible exception to this rule. It is widely agreed that language is a basic form of cultural expression and that the use of a different language sets ethnic groups apart from the dominant culture. The 1980 census included several questions about language use, and one of these items asked about the language used at home. Table 2.11 shows that English is the most commonly used language by all persons of Indian background, but there are large differences between groups. Nearly one third of American Indian householders regularly speak another language, presumably Indian, at home; less than one tenth of American Indians of Multiple Ancestry use another language at home; and Americans of Indian Descent speak English at home almost exclusively. These findings indicate that American Indians are by far the most likely to be active practitioners of traditional Indian culture, certainly in terms of language use.

TABLE 2.11

Percent Distribution of Language Used at Home
by Householders of American Indian Background,
and United States Total for Householders of All Races

	American Indians	Indians of Multiple Ancestry	Americans of Indian Descent	United States Total
Language Other than English	31.2	9.0	3.9	10.6
English Only	68.8	91.0	96.1	89.4
Total	100.0	100.0	100.0	100.0

SOURCE: One percent sample of 1980 census data (20 percent sample of 5 percent Public-Use Microdata Sample, A file; 1-1000 Public-Use Microdata Sample).

Distinctions Among Identities

The differences in socioeconomic status and patterns of language use lead to several conclusions about the populations associated with each type of Indian identity. Americans of Indian Descent, as their name implies, are like most other middle-class Americans. They are mostly white, speak no other language than English, and are relatively well off in material terms. Members of this group probably do not think of themselves as part of a disadvantaged minority population because in most respects they are not. These individuals differ from other segments of mainstream American society mainly by virtue of recollecting an Indian ancestor in their family background.

In any case, Americans of Indian Descent do not conform to the common perception of American Indians as a culturally distinct population of economically disadvantaged individuals. This perception is better applied to persons who consistently identify their race and ethnic background as American Indian. This group is more likely composed of persons residing on reservations or participating in urban Indian communities—it is the core of the Indian population. As reflected in their socioeconomic status, this group also suffers obvious economic hardships.

American Indians of Multiple Ancestry probably are a diverse collection of individuals. Certainly, some are Indians who recall non-Indian ancestors but in every other respect are fully recognized as Indians and belong as much to their Indian community and population as persons who do not recall a non-Indian ancestor. Other Indians of Multiple Ancestry are likely "new" Indians,[30] individuals who in an earlier era of American history would have "passed" unrecognized into white society. They are "new" Indians in the sense that the ethnic pride movements of the 1970s motivated them to rediscover their ethnic heritage and to identify themselves as American Indian. The degree to which these individuals are recognized by other members of the Indian population, and the degree to which they are involved in the community life of the Indian population, is difficult to assess.

An Operational View of American Indians

Given the different ways in which individuals can identify themselves as American Indian or Alaska Native, it is extremely important to be explicit about the population with whom this book is concerned.

[30]Stan Steiner, *The New Indians* (New York: Dell, 1968).

For the record, the *statistical data presented in subsequent chapters of this book pertain only to persons who identified their race as American Indian, Eskimo, or Aleut in the 1980 census,* regardless of how they described their ethnic ancestry. This means that the coverage of this book includes persons described earlier as "American Indians" *and* "American Indians of Multiple Ancestry," but it *excludes* "Americans of Indian Descent."

There are several reasons for adopting this definition of the American Indian and Alaska Native population. Most important, this approach is consistent with the procedures of the Census Bureau. Using a different definition would make it impossible to compare the figures in this book with the data published by the Census Bureau. Using race instead of ethnic ancestry to define population boundaries is most consistent with the ways in which the Census Bureau has approached this problem in past censuses. The concept of ethnic ancestry was first introduced in the 1980 census, and as a result it has little comparability with data from earlier decennial censuses. Another closely related reason is that individuals identified as Americans of Indian Descent in 1980 most likely were not identified as American Indians in 1970 or earlier censuses. As a result, it makes little sense to compare the characteristics of this group with the characteristics of American Indians in earlier censuses as a way of describing changes over time.

A Note on Indian States

Another approach to defining the American Indian population focuses on persons who identify their race as American Indian *and* reside in one of 19 states identified as "Indian States."[31] The discussion in the next chapter deals with the quality of census data for American Indians and suggests that the most accurate enumerations of American Indians occurred in the so-called Indian states. Despite this fact, there are good reasons for not restricting research on American Indians to these places.

An especially important reason for not focusing exclusively on the so-called Indian states is that this approach poses a serious risk of producing a highly biased view of American Indians. The most apparent source of bias is that the list of Indian states includes only a few states with significant urban Indian populations, though it is well known that sizable communities of American Indians can be found in urban areas.

For example, California is not considered an Indian state; and al-

[31]See Jeffrey S. Passel and Patricia A. Berman, "Quality of 1980 Census Data for American Indians," *Social Biology* 33(1986):163–182.

though there are reasons for this omission, neglecting California means excluding the state with the largest (227,757) and most heavily urbanized Indian population in the country. Since World War II, Los Angeles and the San Francisco Bay area have had very large urban Indian populations by dint of being among a preselected set of destination cities for participants in the Bureau of Indian Affairs relocation programs. Indeed, nearly two thirds of the California urban Indian population reside in these two metropolitan areas. Similarly, Illinois and Colorado are not considered Indian states despite the fact that Chicago and Denver have large urban Indian populations.

On the other hand, American Indians residing in Indian states are most heavily concentrated in nonmetropolitan areas: 36 percent of American Indians in Indian states resided in metropolitan places in 1980 compared with 49 percent of the total American Indian population residing in metropolitan places. This discrepancy is most troubling because it means that a strong nonmetropolitan bias will be associated with demographic characteristics that vary by place of residence.

Nonmetropolitan residents, Indians and non-Indians alike, are generally poorer and less educated, have larger families, and face greater economic hardships than city dwellers. This means that an analysis restricted to Indian states is almost certain to produce an image of American Indians tilted toward a group that is poorer and more disadvantaged. Stated another way, American Indian states are composed of a select cross-section of the American Indian population, but by no means does this cross-section constitute a representative sample of persons identifying themselves as American Indian. Because of this bias, this book is based on the total population of American Indians rather than limited to those residing in "Indian states."

Concluding Remarks

The matter of who is an Indian is an exceedingly complex question for which there is no simple answer. It depends on how the population is defined, and an almost endless number of different definitions are possible. Race and ethnicity, however, represent two very general conceptual frameworks for defining the boundaries of the Indian population. Several different types of racial definitions have been used in various contexts to describe the Indian population, but administrative definitions are the most common as they have proliferated to serve the bureaucratic needs of public administration. Early administrative definitions developed around the concept of blood quantum, but in recent years the intellectual and legal integrity of this concept has been seriously challenged. In its place, administrative definitions typically rely on self-identification.

The criteria normally used to define ethnic group boundaries do not necessarily sustain a unified image of the Indian population. Instead, these criteria make it possible to view American Indians as a truly multi-ethnic population composed of many different tribal cultures. A multi-ethnic model of the Indian population highlights the social and cultural diversity among American Indians, but its chief limitation is that relatively little work has been done to identify the major cultural divisions within the contemporary Indian population. Although dated for a much earlier period in history, the concepts of culture areas and culture regions are helpful guides for locating the diverse cultures within the Indian population.

The relationship between race and ethnicity also is an important consideration. Hypothetically, it is possible to have many different ethnic groups within a single category of race and, conversely, ethnic groups should be racially homogeneous. In a loosely defined sense, it is possible to consider the Indian race as consisting of numerous ethnic groups, namely, tribal cultures. The data on race and ethnic ancestry show how three unique types of Indian identity emerge from the relationship between race and ethnicity. American Indians, American Indians of Multiple Ancestry, and Americans of Indian Descent are distinctive not only in terms of Indian identity but also in terms of social characteristics. For example, these groups have very different socioeconomic statuses and very different population sizes. This reinforces the exceptional importance of clearly understood definitions of population boundaries.

Confronted by the many ways in which the Indian population can be defined, most analysts are bound to wonder which approach is best for deciding who is an Indian. As a practical matter self-identification is a thoroughly flawed procedure, but it is also the lesser evil among many worse alternatives. Blood quantum tests have fallen into disrepute, and training objective observers to recognize Indians on sight alone is impossible. Biological definitions would require physical tests such as blood, urine, or earwax analysis. These tests would undoubtedly be controversial, if not an outright violation of privacy and civil rights. In any event, biological tests are not infallible and they ignore the uniquely social content of race and ethnicity. Ideally, racial and ethnic self-identification should be fortified with supplementary information about membership in the Indian population. Details about involvement with the Indian community such as social and cultural activities are further evidence of membership in the Indian population. Until there is a major revolution in the way race and ethnicity are conceived and measured, self-identification, supported by additional validating data, is likely to remain the best method for locating the Indian population.

A second recommendation is specifically directed at users of census data for the American Indian population. The data that showed that three distinct populations are associated with different types of Indian identity should be taken seriously. The most important lesson from a methodological standpoint is that the ethnic ancestry data should be handled with caution. The group reporting American Indian ethnic ancestry includes bona fide members of the Indian population and non-Indians who recall having an American Indian ancestor. In comparison, persons who identify their race and ancestry as Indian appear to have social characteristics, in terms of socioeconomic status and language use, that are more consistent with intuitive concepts about who is an Indian. However, for many applications, requiring consistent race and ancestry responses is overly stringent. It is most undesirable because it discounts intermarriage and is certain to underestimate the true size of the Indian population. In other words, ethnic ancestry alone includes too many non-Indians, and insisting on consistent race and ancestry reports excludes too many true Indians. Therefore, defining the Indian population as all persons who report their race as Indian is recommended as a compromise solution to those who use census data to study the Indian population.

3

DIMENSIONS OF THE
AMERICAN INDIAN POPULATION

IN THE PAST, detailed information about the demographic characteristics of the Indian population was not widely available. The 1970
Census of Housing and Population, and especially the special subject report on American Indians,[1] was a quantum leap forward: It presented a wealth of data not only about the size and distribution of the
population but also about many detailed characteristics such as socioeconomic status, labor force participation, and fertility. Unfortunately,
the 1970 census was marred by a well-documented undercount[2] that
became the basis for attacks on the quality of the data.[3] Although far
from perfect, the quality of the 1980 census information is a marked
improvement over the 1970 enumeration and provides the opportunity, for the first time, to closely examine the demographic conditions
of American Indians.

This chapter outlines the size and distribution of the American Indian and Alaska Native population. Subsequent chapters will examine

[1]U.S. Bureau of the Census, "American Indians," *1970 Census of Housing and Population, Subject Report* (Washington, DC: U.S. Government Printing Office, 1973).
[2]Jeffrey S. Passel, "Provisional Evaluation of the 1970 Census Count of American
Indians," *Demography* 13(1976):397–409.
[3]American Indian Policy Review Commission (AIPRC), *Final Report of the American
Indian Policy Review Commission* (Washington, DC: U.S. Government Printing Office,
1977).

in detail the composition of the Indian population. To place these population dimensions in perspective, comparisons are made with the white and black populations. Comparisons with the white population show how Indians stand in relation to the bearers of the dominant U.S. culture, former rivals, and a segment of the population ordinarily considered more privileged.

Comparisons with the black population illustrate how Indians fare relative to another disadvantaged minority population. Other minority groups could have been chosen—Hispanics, for example—but comparisons with the black population are especially important because blacks are the largest and, historically, most widely recognized disadvantaged minority group in the United States. Trends over time are also important, but in most instances comparisons are possible only between 1970 and 1980. Very little information is available for years before 1970, and the limited quality of the data, even for 1970, means that generalizations about trends can be no more than limited approximations.

There are a vast number of interesting "facts" available in census data. Out of necessity, this information requires sifting and winnowing to glean the most significant demographic characteristics of the Indian population. The general orientation of this information also means that it is not possible to present highly detailed data for individual tribes. At most, population estimates by tribe are available in Appendix 1. While the absence of detailed tribal data will not trouble most demographers, it will sorely disappoint the Indian readers of this book.

Population Growth Since 1890

In the historical demography literature reviewed in the first chapter, several important conclusions emerged about the size of the Indian population in about 1492. (1) Recent estimates of the fifteenth century Indian population place their number near 2.0 million to 5.0 million. However, the Indian population could have been much larger, 10.0 to 12.0 million, or even larger. (2) The Indian population declined sharply from epidemics and warfare after the arrival of Europeans. This decline was precipitous in the early years of European settlement but continued into the late nineteenth century. Since then, the Indian population has staged a remarkable comeback.

As a race, American Indians declined to their smallest number in 1890; their population was about 228,000. From this low point, the population has grown throughout the twentieth century. Figure 3.1 charts the growth of the Indian population from 1900 to 1980. It shows that

FIGURE 3.1

American Indian Population Growth, 1900–1980

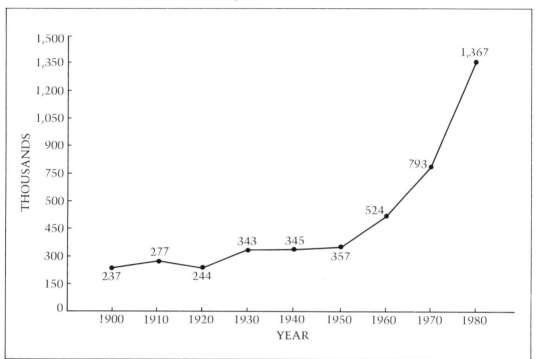

SOURCE: U.S. Bureau of the Census.

historically most of the growth in the population has occurred in the second half of the twentieth century: From 1900 to 1950 the number of Indians increased by about 46 percent, while from 1950 to 1980 the number increased by 282 percent.

Among the factors contributing to the growth of the Indian population since 1950, medical innovations, greater access to health care, and improvements in housing and sanitation have undoubtedly resulted in better health, greater longevity, and, most important, lower infant mortality. However, increases in the number of American Indians identified by the Census Bureau also are attributable to other factors. Procedural changes have improved the quality of enumerations, and changing habits in racial self-identification have increased the number of American Indians who have chosen to identify themselves as American Indians. Unfortunately, data are not available to assess the extent of these changes.

As the data indicate, the growth of the Indian population has not been uniform throughout the twentieth century. From 1890 to 1910 the population increased slightly by about 50,000, or an increase of 21 percent over 20 years. This is a growth rate of a little more than 1 percent per year, and if this trend had continued the modern Indian population would number less than 600,000 today. However, the growth that began in 1890 was curtailed between 1910 and 1920. In this period the Indian population declined to 88 percent of its 1910 peak, probably the result of an influenza epidemic that swept the United States in 1918. Specific figures for American Indians are not available, but statistics for the causes of death among nonwhites are helpful in understanding what precipitated the 1910–1920 population downturn. In 1917, 19 nonwhite deaths in 100,000 were due to influenza, but in the wake of the 1918 flu outbreak death by influenza accounted for over 300 nonwhite deaths in 100,000. Death rates for influenza-related diseases such as pneumonia and whooping cough also rose sharply for nonwhites.[4]

The 1920 census showed the the Indian population had not recovered from the mortality of the 1918 epidemic, but it rebounded strongly between 1920 and 1930. By 1930 the Indian population exceeded its 1920 post-epidemic level by 41 percent and managed to surpass the pre-epidemic 1910 level by 24 percent. This rapid growth rate was not sustained. After 1930 population growth remained relatively level and increased only 4 percent between 1930 and 1950. Establishing beyond doubt the causes of this slowdown in population growth is not possible; however, the Great Depression of the 1930s and World War II slowed growth in all segments of the U.S. population. This suggests, though not conclusively, that the social and cultural isolation ordinarily ascribed to the Indian population did not shield it from the historical events that slowed fertility and accelerated mortality in the rest of the American population.

American Indians also were not exempt from rapid rises in population growth in the postwar years; they were as much a part of the "baby boom" as other Americans. Between 1950 and 1960 births outnumbered deaths so greatly that the Indian population increased by 47 percent. In the following decade it increased by 51 percent and continued to climb through the 1970s. In fact, the rapid and sustained growth through the 1950s and 1960s was relatively slow compared with the remarkable and unprecedented growth in the 1970s. By 1980 the Indian population had increased by 72 percent over its 1970 level. If the Indian population continues to grow as it did in the 1970s, it will exceed 4 million by the end

---

[4]U.S. Bureau of the Census, *Vital Statistics Rates in the United States, 1900–1940* (Washington, DC: U.S. Government Printing Office, 1943), pp. 278–279.

of the century. These figures are historically significant. For the first time in almost 300 years, the 1980 Indian population exceeded 1 million.[5] By 2000 the contemporary American Indian population could reach numbers approximating pre-Columbian levels, but it is an open question whether the growth rates of the 1970s can be sustained until or exceeded by 2000.

Factors Affecting Population Growth

Public Policy

Major changes in the relationship between Indians and whites have promoted Indian population growth in the twentieth century. Some of the most important changes have been in the form of public policy toward Indians. Prior to 1900 fear and hostility prevailed in attitudes toward American Indians. These sentiments were probably best expressed in the apocryphal statement attributed to President Ulysses S. Grant that "the only good Indian is a dead Indian." Indian resistance was met with military force, and docile Indians, such as many of the California bands, were hunted like animals. Hostile public policy supported by a hostile American public took a heavy toll on the Indian population through frequent wars and wholesale removals. By 1900 Indians had been subdued as military threats, and a rapidly urbanizing America turned its attention to developing cities instead of settling frontiers. This shift in public interest meant that the Indian population enjoyed a measure of safety from the mortality inflicted by wars and other genocidal threats common in the nineteenth century.

Health Care

Another factor that stimulated expansion of the Indian population was the introduction of Western medicine and especially medical advances in the mid twentieth century. Just as wars and other violent acts hastened the decline of the Indian population in the 1800s, modern medicine has undoubtedly had an important role in the population

[5]Russell Thornton and Joan Marsh-Thornton, "Estimating Prehistoric American Indian Population Size for United States Area: Implications of the Nineteenth Century Population Decline and Nadir," *American Journal of Physical Anthropology* 55(1981):47–53, estimate that the 1690 Indian population was about 1 million and dropped below this number in 1700.

growth of this century. Developments that improved the health of the American population likewise improved the health of Indians. Vaccines and antibiotics for infectious diseases, along with measures for lessening maternal and infant mortality, have played a major role in reducing Indian mortality rates. Treatments for diseases such as tuberculosis and diabetes have been especially important because these illnesses have a high incidence rate among Indians.

The Indian Health Service has been instrumental in bringing about improved health care for American Indians. Funds for Indian health care were first allocated by Congress as early as 1832. Yet by 1880 Indian health services offered by the Bureau of Indian Affairs amounted to four hospitals and 75 physicians for the entire Indian population. Commenting on the development of Indian health care, Sorkin writes that "during the next seventy-five years [after 1880] the number of health facilities and personnel employed by the BIA gradually expanded, but because of limited appropriations the level of services was not adequate."[6] In 1955 responsibility for Indian health care was transferred to the Public Health Service in the Department of Health, Education, and Welfare. For a variety of reasons, appropriations for Indian health care tripled between 1955 and 1965. Sorkin argues that this increase led to a marked improvement in the health of the Indian population.[7] For example, between 1955 and 1967 deaths of Indian infants dropped from 61 per 1,000 live births to 30 per 1,000 live births. For all races, infant deaths declined from 26 to 22 per 1,000 live births in the same period. Deaths from tuberculosis also fell sharply. In 1955 Indian deaths from TB were 41 per 100,000 population compared with 9 per 100,000 for all races. By 1967 Indian deaths from TB had fallen 66 percent to 17 deaths per 100,000 population compared with 4 deaths per 100,000 for all races in the same year.[8] Additional information about American Indian mortality is provided in Appendix 3.

Changes in Life Expectancy

Advances in medical technology and greater access to health care services were most likely responsible for significant gains in the life expectancy of the American Indian population. These gains are illustrated in Table 3.1 for selected birth cohorts. As this table shows, the

[6]Alan L. Sorkin, *American Indians and Federal Aid* (Washington, DC: Brookings Institution, 1971), p. 51.
[7]Sorkin (1971).
[8]Sorkin (1971), p. 53.

TABLE 3.1

Life Expectancy at Birth, by Race, Gender, and Year

Race and Gender	1940	1950	1960	1970	1980
American Indian and Alaska Native					
Male	51.3	58.1	60.0	60.7	67.1
Female	51.9	62.2	65.7	71.2	75.1
Total	51.6	60.0	61.7	65.1	71.1
Black and Other					
Male	51.5	59.1	61.1	61.3	65.3
Female	54.9	62.9	66.3	69.4	73.6
Total	53.1	60.8	63.6	65.3	69.5
White					
Male	62.1	66.5	67.4	68.0	70.7
Female	66.6	72.2	74.1	75.6	78.1
Total	64.2	69.1	70.6	71.1	74.4

SOURCES: Indian Health Service, *Chart Series Book*, April 1987; and U.S. Bureau of the Census, *Statistical Abstract of the United States: 1985*. American Indian and Alaska Native life expectancy based upon three years of mortality experience and centered in the decennial census year.

life expectancy for Indian men and women born before midcentury was a relatively brief 51.6 years. Unlike later cohorts, women born about 1940 do not possess a significant advantage over men in terms of life expectancy.

Medical achievements such as the development of antibiotics were probably a major factor in the large increases in life expectancy that followed after 1940. For men born about 1950 life expectancy had increased by slightly over 13 percent. Women enjoyed an even larger gain of nearly 20 percent and developed an advantage over men that has persisted into recent years. Gains in life expectancy during the 1950s were much less dramatic than the gains of the 1940s. By 1960 male life expectancy had increased only about 3 percent over the preceding 10 years. Although small, the gains for women outstripped those for men. The greatest differences in life expectancy between Indian men and women were accrued during the 1960s. Life expectancy for men born in 1970 remained virtually the same as that for men born in 1960. In contrast, Indian women experienced a significant increase from 65.7 to 71.2 years, an 8.4 percent increase.

It is impossible to link directly Indian Health Service expenditures with the longevity of the Indian population. Yet whatever effect improved health care delivery has on population mortality, the massive buildup of the Indian Health Service that Sorkin describes evidently had great impact on female longevity and almost no effect on male longevity. Between 1970 and 1980 Indian men enjoyed a significant lengthening of their life expectancy that reduced the gap between them and Indian women. Unfortunately, the data necessary to further explore this increase are not available. Female life expectancy also increased in this decade. Indian women born in 1980 can reasonably expect to witness the year 2055, an average lifetime of 75 years.

It is clear that American Indians do not live as long as whites. This was just as true in 1980 as it was in 1940, although the longevity gap closed considerably in the four decades between these years. In 1940 the longevity of whites exceeded that of American Indians by over 24 percent, or nearly 13 years. Forty years later the life expectancies of whites were 5 percent, or a little over 3 years, longer than the life expectancies of American Indians.

Until 1970 the life expectancies of blacks and American Indians were very similar, though black women tended to live slightly longer than American Indian women. However, between 1970 and 1980 American Indian life expectancies overtook those of blacks, and by 1980 American Indians enjoyed a small advantage in longevity. These gains in longevity are not necessarily the result of changes in racial self-identification (see Chapter 2 and subsequent discussion in this chapter) because the agencies that prepared these data, the National Center for Health Statistics (NCHS) and the Indian Health Service (IHS), use racial classification procedures that are different from those employed by the Census Bureau; that is, they rely on methods other than self-identification.

Recent Increases in Birthrates

Throughout the twentieth century, the American Indian population has grown rapidly. Much of this growth could be anticipated from twentieth century scientific developments and from the rapid growth of the U.S. population as a whole. However, growth in the Indian population between 1970 and 1980 greatly exceeded increases in any previous era and outstripped the growth of the U.S. population for the same period.

Table 3.2 shows births, deaths, and projected annual population size for each year beginning with 1970. The difference between births and deaths indicates, in absolute numbers, growth in the Indian population

TABLE 3.2

Annual Estimates of American Indian and Alaska Native Population Size and Components of Change, 1970–1980

Year of Period	Population (January 1 or Census Date)	Births[a] (Calendar Year)	Deaths (Calendar Year)	Natural Increase[b]
1970 Census	827,268	26,784	5,675	21,109
1971	843,100	26,899	5,951	20,948
1972	864,048	26,717	5,934	20,783
1973	884,831	26,882	6,381	20,501
1974	905,332	27,248	6,141	21,107
1975	926,439	28,598	6,166	22,432
1976	948,871	30,097	6,301	23,796
1977	942,667	31,177	6,455	24,722
1978	997,389	33,843	6,959	26,884
1979	1,024,273	35,094	6,728	28,366
1980	1,052,639	37,726	6,923	30,803
1980 (April 1)	1,060,340	N/A	N/A	N/A
Intercensal Period	N/A	296,075	63,003	233,072
1980 Census	1,423,043			

SOURCES: Unpublished tabulations, Indian Health Service; and U.S. Bureau of the Census, *1980 Supplementary Report, American Indian Areas and Alaska Native Villages.*

[a]Births corrected for underregistration, see Passel (1976) and Passel and Berman (1987).
[b]Difference between births and deaths.

for each year. During the first half of the decade the balance between births and deaths remained fairly stable. In fact, between 1970 and 1973 the number of Indians added to the population dipped slightly each year. In 1970 births exceeded deaths by 21,109 compared with 20,501 more births than deaths in 1973. This trend was reversed in 1974 by a slight increase in births (see Chapter 5) and an equally small decline in deaths. Trends in the second half of the decade showed more consistency. In absolute numbers, deaths continued to increase by an average of 2 percent each year. There was, however, a visible increase in 1978, which was offset by a decline the following year. In contrast, births increased sharply in 1975, especially compared with increases in previous years. Beginning in 1975 the average yearly increase in births was nearly 6 percent, exceeding the average annual increase in previous years (0.1 percent for 1970 to 1973). At the end of the decade, births exceeded deaths by well over five to one.

Several factors might be responsible for the especially rapid increase in births. The large increase in births which began in 1975 may indicate changing procedures, better record management, and fewer classification errors in identifying Indian babies. The mid 1970s were also years of heightened awareness about American Indians, with armed occupations of Wounded Knee, South Dakota, and the Bureau of Indian Affairs in Washington, D.C., and a series of other actions widely publicized in the mass media. Heightened awareness may be involved in actual shifts of self-identification among mothers, resulting in more babies identified as Indian at birth. Also, the timing of these increases coincides with the Indian baby boom generation reaching childbearing age. In 1975, the year of the first major increase, young women born in 1960 were turning 15. The oldest members of the baby boom generation born in 1950 or earlier were not much older than 25. The data in Table 3.2 suggest that the first ripple of an echo boom resulting from post–World War II population growth appeared in 1975 and was sustained through the reminder of the decade.

Changes in Racial Self-Identification

Before 1960 census enumerators were responsible for reporting race, and as a result some individuals were misclassified as black or white instead of as American Indian.[9] Since the adoption of racial self-identification in 1960, changing popular attitudes about race and corresponding changes in racial self-identification have undoubtedly played a significant role in the growth of the American Indian population between 1960 and 1970, and especially between 1970 and 1980. In his analysis of data for the 1970 census, Passel also observed that the growth in the Indian population from 1960 to 1970 could not be attributed to natural processes alone.[10] His explanation of this growth was that changes in racial self-identification, and especially the developing "ethnic pride" movements, resulted in greater numbers of persons identifying their race as American Indian. Passel and Berman found even more pronounced evidence that changes in racial self-identification were responsible for population growth between 1970 and 1980.[11] Documenting behavior such as changes in the personal identification of race is virtually impossible, yet it seems likely that this is one of the leading sources of growth in the American Indian population since 1960.

In Table 3.2 the impact of changing self-identification on population growth can be seen by comparing the census numbers based on self-

[9]However, as Chapter 2 documents, self-identification is a far from perfect solution.
[10]Passel (1976).

[11]Jeffrey S. Passel and Patricia A. Berman, "Quality of 1980 Census Data for American Indians," *Social Biology* 33(1986):163–182.

reports with the projected numbers of American Indians based on natural increase alone. In 1980, 1,423,043 persons identified themselves as American Indian or Alaska Native, which represents a 72 percent gain from the 1970 census that counted 827,268 American Indians and Alaska Natives. However, the population size projected from natural increase is substantially less—1,060,340 persons. Based on the excess of births over deaths between 1970 and 1980, the American Indian and Alaska Native population would have grown by 28 percent instead of the 72 percent counted by the Census Bureau. This means that for the total increase in the numbers of American Indians and Alaska Natives, about 39 percent was due to natural processes and nearly 61 percent was due to changes in self-identification and other factors.

Are persons who change their self-identification less than bona fide Indians (by whatever criterion)? To answer this question requires precise criteria about who is and is not a "real" Indian. As the discussion in Chapter 2 indicated, there are many criteria for deciding who is a "real" Indian and none are demonstrably unambiguous. Consequently, even if the necessary data were available, it would be impossible to determine conclusively how many persons who changed their self-identification to American Indian were indeed not qualified for the appellation. Furthermore, it is impossible to identify those individuals who changed their racial self-identification between 1970 and 1980.

There are two other considerations worth noting about the meaning of changing self-identification. One is that such changes are not necessarily reporting "errors"; they may, in fact, be reporting "corrections." Again, it is impossible to sort errors from corrections, but in the past American Indians seeking to avoid the stigma of racial discrimination were reluctant to disclose their racial background, choosing instead to pass as white Americans.[12] For these individuals to identify their race as American Indian represents an improvement, not a decline, in the quality of data for American Indians.

Finally, besides natural increase and changes in self-identification, data production procedures also affect the discrepancy between the observed and predicted population counts. Improvements in enumeration and processing have already been mentioned. Passel and Berman suggest that the "best" data for American Indians were collected in places where the Indian population was large—in the Southwest, for example.[13] Ironically, the evaluation of data for American Indians in the 1940 census

---

[12]Nancy O. Lurie, "The Enduring Indian," *Natural History* 75(1966):10–22. Lurie argues that the spread of pan-Indianism has increased the viability of American Indian ethnic identity by encouraging persons who once would have "passed" into white society to retain their American Indian identity.

[13]Passel and Berman (1986).

reached the same conclusion.[14] Also, the data for births and deaths used to estimate natural increase are not infallible. As a result, the true (and unknown) excess of births over deaths may be larger, or smaller, than the figures in Table 3.2.

The upshot of these issues is that the true meaning of changes in racial self-identification is difficult to assess. But in no way do such changes invalidate the usefulness of census data for American Indians. Without knowing what kinds of individuals changed their identity, comparisons across time must be made with caution, but for other purposes the 1980 census is a useful gauge of the Indian population in the late twentieth century.

The Geographic Distribution of American Indians

Before the arrival of Columbus, American Indians were not evenly distributed across the North American continent, and they are not evenly distributed across the United States today. In earlier times, American Indians were most densely settled in areas abundant with the environmental resources necessary for physical survival. Many of the largest pre-Columbian settlements were located near rivers or other sites where fish and game were plentiful. Today, the distribution of American Indians does not reflect ecological pressures but instead represents the outcomes of particular historical developments. Some of these are diffuse processes such as industrialization and urbanization, which have an impact on all segments of American society. Other developments stem from the confrontations between American Indians and European settlers, which set events in motion that ultimately led to a complete resettlement of the American Indian population.

Historically, one of the most far-reaching federal initiatives affecting American Indian settlement patterns was enacted 150 years before the 1980 census. As Europeans streamed to America, pressures grew to open more land in the name of "manifest destiny." As a political doctrine, manifest destiny prevailed in federal Indian policy and was a major impetus for the passage of the Indian Removal Bill. This legislation was signed into law by Andrew Jackson on June 30, 1830, and it called for the removal of all Indians from lands east of the Mississippi River to the territories west of the Mississippi. Most of the Indians scheduled for removal were to be settled in the Indian Territory of what is now Oklahoma.

[14]U.S. Bureau of the Census, *Special Reports: Nonwhite Population by Race* (Washington, DC: U.S. Government Printing Office, 1953), p. 3B-5.

The passage of the removal legislation spurred nearly a decade of resistance in courtrooms and military confrontations. The Choctaw were among the first to resettle in Indian territory, moving from Mississippi in 1831 and 1832.[15] In contrast, the Seminole of Florida actively resisted removal, causing the U.S. government to lose more than 1,500 soldiers and $20 million in a campaign that resulted in only partial removal.[16] The Cherokee resorted to legal action to prevent their removal, which resulted in precedent-setting court cases, but eventually they were removed in October 1838. Accompanied by a military escort, 13,000 Cherokee set out for Oklahoma on an 800-mile journey still known as the "Trail of Tears" because over 4,000 of the tribe died before reaching their destination.[17]

Regional Distribution

America's continuing westward expansion, as well as the removal laws, gradually pushed many tribes westward also. Although this westward push ended when the American frontier closed about 100 years ago, the resettlement of American Indians in the nineteenth century is still evident in modern demographic data. The impact of western settlement and the removal laws can be seen in Table 3.3, which shows the distribution of American Indians across official census regions and divisions of the United States. The areas east of the Mississippi River include the entire Northeast region and the East North Central, South Atlantic, and East South Central divisions. As history suggests, there are relatively few Indians living in this area—about 365,000, or 23 percent of the total U.S. Indian population. In contrast, this area is home for nearly 63 percent of the total U.S. population. About 77 percent of the Indian population reside in the West division and in the West South Central and West North Central divisions.

Obviously the removal acts were far from completely successful, and American Indians were not pushed inexorably toward the Pacific coast. Some Indians were able to escape removal by giving up claims to

---

[15]Arthur H. DeRosier, *The Removal of the Choctaw Indians* (Knoxville: University of Tennessee Press, 1970).

[16]Francis Paul Prucha, *The Great Father: The United States Government and the American Indians* (Lincoln: University of Nebraska Press, 1984).

[17]See Grant Foreman, *Indian Removal* (Norman: University of Oklahoma Press, 1932), for detailed history of the removal. The population losses among the Cherokee were probably much higher. Thornton estimates that the total population losses accruing to the Trail of Tears were probably close to 8,000. Readers should consult Russell Thornton, "Cherokee Population Losses During the Trail of Tears: A New Perspective and a New Estimate," *Ethnohistory* 31(1984):289–300.

TABLE 3.3

Regional Distribution of the American Indian and Alaska Native Population, 1970–1980 (percentage of totals in parentheses)

Region and Division	1970	1980	Percent Change
Northeast Region	45,720 (5.8)	79,038 (5.6)	72.9
New England	10,362 (1.3)	21,597 (1.5)	108.4
Mid-Atlantic	35,358 (4.5)	57,441 (4.0)	62.5
North Central Region	144,254 (18.2)	248,413 (17.5)	72.2
East North Central	54,578 (6.9)	105,927 (7.4)	94.1
West North Central	89,676 (11.3)	142,486 (10.0)	58.9
South Region	194,406 (24.5)	372,825 (26.2)	91.8
South Atlantic	65,367 (8.2)	118,938 (8.4)	82.0
East South Central	8,708 (1.1)	22,477 (1.6)	158.1
West South Central	120,331 (15.2)	231,410 (16.3)	92.3
West Region	408,350 (51.5)	722,769 (50.8)	77.0
Mountain	229,669 (29.0)	366,291 (25.7)	59.5
Pacific	178,681 (22.5)	356,478 (25.1)	99.5
U.S. Total	792,730	1,423,045	79.5

SOURCES: U.S. Bureau of the Census, *1980 Census of Population, General Social and Economic Statistics, United States Summary; American Indian Areas and Alaskan Native Villages;* and *1980, Supplementary Report.*

their land and retreating to isolated areas where they could live undetected by authorities. Others were removed, only to return to their original homes. For example, the Winnebago tribe was relocated from Wisconsin to Nebraska. Some Winnebagos escaped, but others refused to remain in Nebraska and returned to Wisconsin at their first opportunity.

The data in Table 3.3 also show the geographic location of the greatest changes in population size.[18] In absolute numbers, the largest increase occurred in the West, where the Indian population increased by over 300,000. Within the West, the Pacific division grew most rapidly. However, in proportional terms, the areas that grew fastest also had the least number of Indians: The New England division doubled its Indian population, and the equally small East South Central division nearly trebled its Indian population. The location of these gains brings up an earlier point about changes in self-identification as a source of population growth. Again, it is impossible to explain fully the nature of this

[18]This population total includes 1.36 million Indians plus another 60,000 Alaska Natives, for a total of 1.42 million in 1980.

process, but it appears very likely that these are the sites of significantly changed perceptions of racial identity.

In Maine one of the largest Indian land claim settlements in history received national publicity in the mid 1970s. This settlement may have encouraged some individuals to take an active interest in their racial background and others to change their racial identity in anticipation of potential benefits from the land claim. For whatever reasons, the Indian population grew rapidly in every state of New England. Maine and the neighboring states of New Hampshire and Vermont experienced the largest proportional gains in population, ranging from 117 percent in Maine (1,832 in 1970 to 4,097 in 1980) to nearly 400 percent in Vermont (204 in 1970 to 968 in 1980). Large increases in the South, as in the Northeast, may mark changing attitudes about race and racial self-iden-tification. In earlier years most persons with Indian heritage who could pass for white in the South probably preferred to be recognized as such. Again, changing attitudes about race in the 1960s and 1970s made "In-dian" a distinctive, if not "respectable," alternative to being known as white in this part of the United States.

State Populations

The population estimates in Table 3.4 are for states with 15,000 or more American Indians and Alaska Natives in 1980. Map 3.1 shows the distribution of the Indian population in all 50 states. These data provide a more detailed and somewhat different perspective on the regional dis-tribution of American Indians and Alaska Natives shown in Table 3.3. In terms of state distribution, the Indian population is relatively concen-trated. Predictably, all but six (or nearly three quarters) of these states are located west of the Mississippi River. Only four states have Indian populations larger than 100,000 and all are western states: California, Oklahoma, Arizona, and New Mexico.

Several important changes occurred between 1970 and 1980. One is that the concentration of the Indian population in these states declined slightly, from 88 percent to 86 percent of the total U.S. Indian popula-tion. Despite this small decline, a number of these states experienced sharp growth in their Indian populations. Florida registered a massive increase exceeding 200 percent. Smaller but consequential gains also oc-curred in Michigan, Texas, California, Colorado, and Oregon. The In-dian populations in all of these states more than doubled during the 1970s. Factors such as migration and natural increase explain part of this growth, but again the magnitude of growth suggests that these states are locations where basic changes in racial self-identification oc-

TABLE 3.4

States with American Indian and Alaska Native Populations Larger than 15,000 in 1980

State	1970	1980	Percent Change
California	88,263	201,489	128.3
Oklahoma	96,803	169,459	75.1
Arizona	94,310	152,745	62.0
New Mexico	71,582	107,483	50.2
North Carolina	44,195	64,652	46.3
Alaska	45,216	64,103	41.8
Washington	30,824	60,804	97.3
South Dakota	31,043	44,968	44.9
Texas	16,921	40,440	139.0
Michigan	16,012	40,070	150.2
New York	25,560	39,582	54.9
Montana	26,385	37,715	42.9
Minnesota	22,322	35,016	56.9
Wisconsin	18,776	29,499	57.1
Oregon	13,210	27,314	106.8
North Dakota	13,565	20,158	48.6
Florida	6,392	19,469	204.6
Utah	10,551	19,256	82.5
Colorado	8,002	18,068	125.8
Illinois	10,304	16,283	58.0
Kansas	8,261	15,373	86.1
Percent of Total Indian Population	88.1	86.0	

SOURCES: U.S. Bureau of the Census, *1980 Census of Population, General Social and Economic Statistics, United States Summary; American Indian Areas and Alaskan Native Villages;* and *1980, Supplementary Report.*

curred during the 1970s. This is especially true for states not ordinarily identified with large Indian populations such as Texas and Michigan. In 1970 these states ranked 13th and 14th in numbers of Indians, but their rapid growth moved them ahead of other states, and by 1980 they were host to the 9th and 10th largest American Indian populations.

California also jumped ahead, with an increase of 128 percent, surpassing Arizona and Oklahoma to move from third to first place. In 1980 California boasted the largest Indian population of any state, with 14 percent of the total U.S. Indian and Alaska Native population, nearly 20 percent larger than the next largest population in Oklahoma. Although California's growth is not the largest percentage increase, it is especially symbolic. Since the nineteenth century, the Oklahoma area

MAP 3.1

Distribution of American Indians and Alaska Natives, 1980

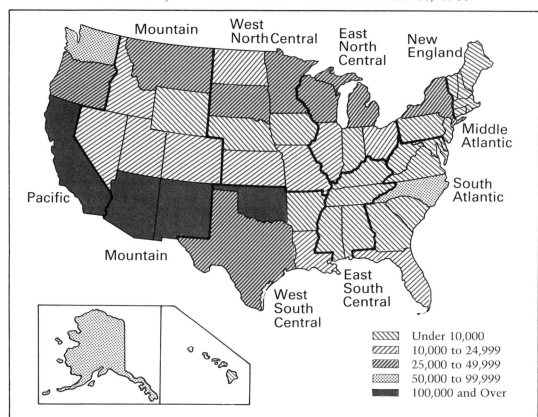

traditionally has been home to large numbers of Indians because it was originally set aside as the official "Indian Territory"; the large Indian population of this area was largely the result of removal policies that brought tribes from the eastern United States west to Oklahoma. The Indian population of California, however, declined precipitously, falling from 150,000 in 1845 to 35,000 in 1860, and by 1900 the native population of California was almost extinct.[19] In view of these differences, the fact that the Indian population of California now exceeds the Indian population of the old Indian territory is remarkable.

The resurgence of the California Indian population is probably the

[19]Robert M. Utley, *The Indian Frontier of the American West, 1846–1890* (Albuquerque: University of New Mexico Press, 1984).

result of several factors, for which there is little documentary evidence. A number of these, such as advances in medicine, natural processes, and changing self-identity, have already been discussed at length, and undoubtedly these factors were as important for population growth in California as for anywhere else in the United States. Paralleling Oklahoma, much of California's Indian population growth can also be ascribed to migration, but unlike Oklahoma the Indian migration to California was voluntary and relatively recent in origin.

In a detailed study of the Los Angeles area, Price identifies two major waves of Indian migrants which helped restore the Indian population of southern California.[20] The first wave came primarily from nonreservation areas outside California, mainly from Oklahoma in the 1930s and from diverse areas of the United States in the 1940s and 1950s. This pattern of migration paralleled non-Indian migration streams into California, beginning with the dust bowl "Okies" from Oklahoma and Texas in the 1930s and continuing with California's rapid population growth after World War II. In the nineteenth century Indians were forcibly pushed westward by non-Indians, but by the mid twentieth century Indians and non-Indians alike were carried along in the same migration streams.

The Bureau of Indian Affairs Direct Employment ("Relocation") Program also stimulated Indian migration to a select group of cities during the 1950s and 1960s. Beginning in the early 1950s, relocation programs attempted to reduce reservation unemployment and hasten Indian assimilation by encouraging reservation residents to resettle voluntarily in urban areas designated as relocation centers. BIA relocation assistance included job training, counseling, and a temporary stipend, with the expectation that program participants would find jobs and become integrated into the American mainstream. Between 1952 and 1972 the BIA resettled more than 100,000 reservation Indians, most of whom were processed through centers in Chicago, Cleveland, Dallas, Denver, Los Angeles, Oakland, San Francisco, San Jose, Seattle, Tulsa, and Oklahoma City.[21]

One of the largest BIA relocation centers was located in Los Angeles.[22] Price cites this program as the main cause of the second major wave of migration to Los Angeles; reaching its peak about 1961, it was three times larger than earlier prewar migrations to southern California.

[20]John A. Price, "The Migration and Adaptation of American Indians to Los Angeles," *Human Organization* 27(1968):168–175.

[21]Alan L. Sorkin, *The Urban American Indian* (Lexington, MA: Heath, 1978).

[22]James E. Officer, "The American Indian and Federal Policy," in Jack O. Waddell and O. Michael Watson, eds., *The American Indian in Urban Society* (Boston: Little, Brown, 1971), pp. 9–63.

During the early 1960s the Los Angeles BIA office was helping resettle almost 1,300 Indians annually, most from outside California.[23] As a result, the American Indian population of Los Angeles contains a relatively small number of persons belonging to native California tribes. For example, near the peak of the Los Angeles relocation program in 1960, 25 percent of all Los Angeles Indians were from Oklahoma.

The impact of the BIA relocation programs on Los Angeles and other cities where Indians were resettled underscores a basic and seldom recognized fact about geographic distribution of American Indians—namely, that migration patterns played a major role in making California and Oklahoma the states with the first and second largest Indian populations; over one fourth of all American Indians and Alaska natives reside in these two states.

Urban Populations

Under these circumstances, the distribution of the urban Indian population is not surprising. Table 3.5 shows the population estimates for cities with 10,000 or more American Indian or Alaska Native residents. Only three of these cities—New York, Chicago, and Detroit—are located east of the Mississippi, and predictably 6 of the 17 metropolitan areas with 10,000 or more Indians are in California. In 1970 these cities contained 62 percent of the California Indian population, declining slightly to 60 percent in 1980. Similarly, the two largest metropolitan areas in Oklahoma—Tulsa and Oklahoma City—are also home to the second and fourth largest urban Indian populations. Of the 11 major relocation centers, 8 have Indian populations exceeding 10,000, and only Cleveland, Denver, and San Jose (located near San Francisco) are missing; 8,973 Indians reside in Denver, 8,312 in San Jose, and 1,958 in Cleveland.

Table 3.5 also shows the percentage of growth in the Indian population and the percentage of the population aged 5 and over that reported living in a different county in 1975. Consistent with state and regional patterns, population growth in these urban areas is strikingly large.[24] The growth rate between 1970 and 1980 for these cities averaged 116 percent, and three localities—Anaheim, Albuquerque, and Sacra-

---

[23]Price (1968); Estelle Fuchs and Robert J. Havighurst, *To Live on This Earth: American Indian Education* (New York: Doubleday, 1972); Sorkin (1978).

[24]Some of this growth may be due to expanding SMSA boundaries between 1970 and 1980, but it is difficult to determine precisely how much this affected urban Indian population growth. In all likelihood, the impact of changing boundaries was probably negligible.

TABLE 3.5

Migration and Population Change in Standard Metropolitan Statistical Areas (SMSAs) with 10,000 or more American Indians, 1970–1980

SMSA	1970	1980	Percent Change	Percent Living in Another County, 1975
Los Angeles–				
Long Beach CA	23,908	47,234	97.6	13.1
Tulsa, OK	15,183	38,463	153.3	26.1
Phoenix, AZ	19.996	27,788	39.0	24.5
Oklahoma City, OK	12,951	24,695	90.7	27.0
Albuquerque, NM	5,822	20,721	255.9	20.9
San Francisco–				
Oakland, CA	12,041	17,546	45.7	24.5
Riverside–				
San Bernadino–				
Ontario, CA	5,941	17,107	187.9	35.6
Minneapolis–				
St. Paul, MN	9,911	15,831	59.7	23.3
Seattle–				
Everett, WA	8,814	15,162	72.0	27.6
Tucson, AZ	8,704	14,880	71.0	12.1
San Diego, CA	6,007	14,355	139.0	27.3
New York, NY	9,984	13,440	34.6	16.6
Anaheim–Santa Ana–				
Garden Grove, CA	3,664	12,782	248.9	25.5
Detroit, MI	5,203	12,372	137.8	15.5
Dallas–				
Ft. Worth , TX	5,500	11,076	101.4	30.3
Sacramento, CA	3,548	10,944	208.5	27.8
Chicago, IL	8,203	10,415	27.0	15.8
Total in SMSAs	165,380	324,811		
Percentage of Total U.S.				
Indian Population	20.7	23.8		

SOURCES: U.S. Bureau of the Census, *1980 General Population Characteristics, United States Summary; General Social and Economic Characteristics, State Reports, 1980;* and "American Indians," *1970 Census of Population, Subject Report.*

mento—trebled their Indian population in this period. Although an imperfect measure of migration, the percentage of the population living in a different county in 1975 reflects the share of population growth due to resettlement. In the 17 largest urban Indian populations, 77 percent, on average, lived in their current county residence five years or more— ranging from 64 percent of the Riverside–San Bernadino–Ontario, California, population to 88 percent of the Tucson population.

Readers who wish to compare these figures with other studies, especially anthropological research on urban Indian populations, should be cautious. First, the metropolitan areas in Table 3.5 are Standard Metropolitan Statistical Areas (SMSAs), which are geographic units defined by the Census Bureau according to a strict set of specific criteria. SMSAs are intended to reflect urban areas, but they do not always correspond closely to city limits, county boundaries, or other more intuitive notions about the boundaries of urban localities. As a result, the geographic territory included in official SMSA boundaries does not always correspond to the territory covered in studies of urban communities done by individual researchers.

Second, Indians may be particularly undercounted in urban areas. Away from reservations, Indians can be difficult to identify. In appearance they blend with other ethnic groups, and the Indian transient population may be especially difficult to locate; most urban Indian populations are too small to form an identifiable enclave. Thus, census counts of urban Indian populations are usually much lower than studies show for specific urban locations; the Chicago Indian population is a good example. Sol Tax harshly criticizes 1960 and 1970 census statistics and quotes studies of the Chicago Indian population which number it between 12,000 and 20,000. Census figures are much smaller and estimate the Indian population as 8,203 in 1970 and 10,415 in 1980.[25] Most field studies of urban Indian populations use population estimates based on indirect evidence such as social service or school records, or simply impressionistic judgments. Probably little can be done to reconcile the discrepancies between field studies of urban Indian populations and census figures, except to recognize their existence and to exercise caution in making comparisons.

The 17 cities in Table 3.5 include about 24 percent of the total Indian population in 1980, up from 20 percent in 1970. This is significant because American Indians are relative newcomers to urban environments; and, again, it is not accidental that the largest urban Indian populations include the sites of former BIA relocation centers.

While over half the U.S. population resided in urban areas by 1930, it was estimated that in 1926 fewer than 10,000 Indians lived in cities, most in urban localities near reservations.[26] Thirty years later the Census Bureau estimated that about 160,000 American Indians lived in urban areas. This number doubled in 10 years to raise the 1970 urban Indian population to over 340,000.

[25]Sol Tax, "The Impact of Urbanization on American Indians," *Annals* 436 (1978):121–135.
[26]Meriam Report, quoted in Fuchs and Havighurst (1972), p. 273.

Between 1960 and 1970 the urban Indian population increased from 30 to 45 percent of the total population. The downscaling of relocation programs and efforts to upgrade economic opportunity on reservations in the 1970s have apparently slowed the flow of Indians to urban areas. Between 1970 and 1980 there was a substantial reduction in the rural-urban migration of American Indians. The percentage of the Indian population in urban areas increased to 49 percent, up only four points for the decade; thus, a majority of Indians still reside in nonmetropolitan areas. This characteristic of American Indians makes them unique among other segments of the U.S. population. The residential distribution of American Indians is compared with other racial and ethnic groups in Table 3.6.

Only one fourth of the total U.S. population resides in nonmetropolitan areas compared with over one half of all American Indians. American Indians are also the most rural of the major American ethnic minority groups. Blacks and Hispanics traditionally have been identified with agricultural production through sharecropping and migrant labor. In spite of this connection, the share of the black and Hispanic population residing in rural areas is much smaller than that of the Indian population. No more than one tenth to one fifth of all Asians, blacks, and Hispanics are settled in nonmetropolitan areas. In metropolitan areas

TABLE 3.6

Residential Distribution of the American Population,
by Race and Spanish Origin, 1980

| Race | Inside SMSAs | | Inside SMSAs % | Outside SMSAs % | Inside and Outside SMSAs % |
	Inside Central Cities %	Outside Central Cities %			
American Indian and Alaska Native	20.9	28.1	49.0	51.0	100.0
Asian and Pacific Islander	46.0	45.4	91.4	8.6	100.0
Black	57.2	23.9	81.1	19.9	100.0
Hispanic[a]	48.8	38.8	87.6	12.4	100.0
White	24.6	48.7	73.3	26.7	100.0
Total U.S. Population	29.6	45.2	74.8	25.2	100.0

SOURCE: *1980 General Population Characteristics, United States Summary.*
[a]Hispanic persons may belong to any race.

American Indian settlement patterns also do not resemble those of other ethnic minority groups. Asians, Hispanics, and especially blacks tend to be concentrated in inner city areas. Perhaps because of their rural background, American Indians, particularly former reservation residents, prefer to remain outside densely populated inner cities. The settlement patterns of urban Indians resemble the settlement patterns of the general population; over 57 percent of the metropolitan Indian population and about 60 percent of the total U.S. metropolitan population resides outside central cities.

American Indians will probably remain concentrated in nonmetropolitan areas for the foreseeable future. They will certainly remain much more rural than any other ethnic minority group. The reason is that, unlike other segments of American society, many American Indians are strongly attached to localities outside urban centers—that is, reservations. Not all reservations are located in remote, rural areas; for example, the Puyallup reservation is located in the Tacoma, Washington, SMSA. However, the overwhelming majority of reservations are located in traditionally rural places in the West.

Reservation Residence

The reservation system is an important factor in explaining why American Indians are heavily concentrated in rural areas and are likely to remain a rural population. In many respects, reservations offer a type of social life that is impossible in urban settings. Most reservations enjoy a form of limited political authority in which elected tribal leaders have much the same status as state legislators or governors. By virtue of treaties and other agreements, reservations also provide certain types of services and opportunities not available to urban Indians. Life on the reservation means for most Indians an opportunity for self-government and social services such as health care at a level unattainable in urban localities. Proximity to family, friends, religious ceremonies, and community celebrations also make reservations attractive.

However, reservations are not without problems. Political factionalism, lack of economic opportunity, and violence related to drug and alcohol abuse are frequently cited reasons why many Indians emigrate from reservations. There are, in sum, a large number of factors that push and pull Indians between urban and reservation life. Hodge compiled a list of conditions that influence members of the Navajo tribe to stay on or leave the reservation.[27] Many of these factors apply equally well to

[27]William H. Hodge, "Navajo Urban Migration: An Analysis from the Perspective of the Family," in Waddell and Watson (1971).

TABLE 3.7

Incentives and Disincentives to Reservation Emigration

Incentives	Disincentives
Poverty	Congenial Family Ties
Friction with Relatives	Relaxed Lifestyle
BIA Schooling Influences	Obligations to Kinsmen
Non-Indian Spouse	Language Barriers
Disputes with Tribal Leaders	Dissatisfaction with Urban Life
Military Service	Access to Community Services
Job Opportunities	Religious Practices
Low Material Standard of Living	Indian Spouse
Urban Preference of, or for, Children	Availability of Medical Care
Dissatisfaction with Reservation Lifestyle	Low Standard of Living in City
	Relocation Costs
Dissatisfaction with Indian Health Service	Access to Community Events
	Low-Cost Housing
	Proximity to Natural Resources such as Hunting and Fishing

SOURCE: Adapted from William H. Hodge, "Navajo Urban Migration: An Analysis from the Perspective of the Family," in Jack O. Waddell and O. Michael Watson, eds., *The American Indian in Urban Society* (Boston: Little, Brown, 1971), chap. 9.

other tribes and other reservations. Hodge's list is presented in Table 3.7, and Figure 3.2 shows the distribution of the Indian population on and off reservation lands.

Figure 3.2 shows that 53 percent of American Indians live on or near Indian lands.[28] Indian lands include a number of different areas which are differentiated primarily by their legal or historical status. Reservation lands, on which 25 percent of all Indians reside, are probably most familiar. Legally, reservations are tracts of land set aside by treaties or other agreements. Reservations are owned, in principle, by a tribe in common, but in fact the federal government holds the title to reservation land through a complex trust relationship. Tribal trust lands have a somewhat different legal status than reservations, but for most purposes these are lands located on, adjacent to, or near reservation lands. Like reservations, tribal trust lands are under the control of tribal and BIA authorities, but generally they are relatively small areas compared with reservations; only about 2 percent of the Indian population lives on this type of land.

[28]The term "living near a reservation" is defined as residence within a cluster of counties (which the Census Bureau designates a "county group") in which at least one reservation is located. Maps and descriptions of these county groups are available in the Public-Use Microdata Sample Technical Documentation. This documentation does not, however, give a listing of reservations located in these county groups.

FIGURE 3.2

*Percent Distribution of American Indians and Alaska Natives
Residing on Native Lands, 1980*

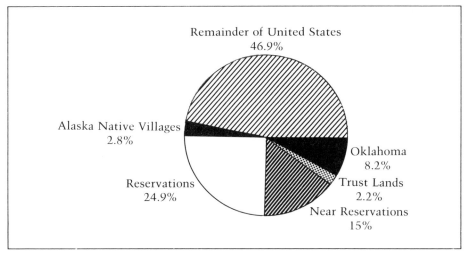

SOURCE: U.S. Bureau of the Census.

Historic Areas of Oklahoma are important because they formed the
Indian Territory of Oklahoma before statehood in 1907. Unlike reservation and tribal trust lands, the Oklahoma counties designated as Historic Areas (see Appendix 6) are not under tribal or BIA supervision. A
significant number of American Indians (117,000) reside in Historic
Areas of Oklahoma, in areas which many Indians still consider Indian
land. Alaska Native Villages are a relatively new category of land created in the early 1970s by the Alaska Native Claims Settlement Act
(Public Law 92-203); 80 percent of the inhabitants are Eskimos and
Aleuts and the remainder are American Indians.

Reservations are important to American Indians in the same way
that "hometowns" or neighborhoods are important to non-Indians. Established groups such as Italians, Poles, Chinese, and Hispanics often
attach a special meaning to their respective ethnic enclaves, and many
American Indians attach great social and cultural significance to their
reservations. Reservations are as different as the tribes that inhabit
them; they can be as large as the Navajo nation, which crosses three
states and covers hundreds of thousands of acres, or as small as the few-
acre rancherias of southern California. It can be as difficult to identify
reservation boundaries as it is to recognize state or county lines without
signs.

TABLE 3.8

Population Sizes of the 16 Largest American Indian Reservations

Reservation	1970	1980	Percent Change
Navajo (AZ, NM, UT)	56,949	104,968	84.3
Pine Ridge (SD)	8,280	11,882	43.5
Gila River (AZ)	4,573	7,067	54.5
Papago (AZ)	4,879	6,959	42.6
Fort Apache (AZ)	5,903	6,880	16.6
Hopi (AZ)	7,726	6,601	*
Zuni Pueblo (NM)	4,736	5,988	26.4
San Carlos (AZ)	4,525	5,872	29.8
Rosebud (SD)	5,656	5,688	0.6
Blackfeet (MT)	4,757	5,080	6.8
Yakima (WA)	2,509	4,983	98.6
Eastern Cherokee (NC)	3,455	4,844	40.2
Standing Rock (ND, SD)	2,925	4,800	60.8
Osage (OK)	†	4,749	†
Fort Peck (MT)	3,182	4,273	34.3
Wind River (WY)	3,319	4,150	25.0
Total of 16 Reservations	123,374	194,784	
Percentage of U.S. Indian Population	16.2	14.3	

SOURCES: U.S. Bureau of the Census, *General Social and Economic Characteristics, 1980, United States Summary;* and "American Indians," *1970 Census of Population, Subject Report.*

*Figures for 1970 and 1980 are not comparable because of administrative changes in reservation boundaries.

†Not reported for 1970 and not included in reservation total.

Table 3.8 shows the population estimates for the 16 largest reservations; another 263 federal and state reservations and 209 Alaska Native villages are not listed. The locations of these reservations are shown in Map 3.2 (see foldout following page 36). In terms of both area and population, the Navajo reservation is easily the largest. It consists of 14,124,068 acres (about the size of West Virginia), overlapping the states of Arizona, New Mexico, and Utah.[29] The reservation population is nearly 10 times larger than the next largest reservation of the Pine Ridge Sioux in South Dakota. However, most reservations are not large, populous expanses. Of the 15 largest reservations, 13 have fewer than 10,000 persons. In fact, these largest reservations account for less than

[29]Lorraine Turner Ruffing, "Navajo Economic Development: A Dual Perspective," in Sam Stanley, ed., *American Indian Economic Development* (The Hague: Mouton, 1978), pp. 15–86.

a third of the total Indian reservation population—about 667,408. About two thirds of the Indian population living on reservations reside in communities smaller than 4,000. Some of these localities, such as the rancherias in California, number only a handful of residents.

Compared with urban growth, reservation growth was relatively restrained during the 1970s. The 17 largest metropolitan Indian populations (see Table 3.5) increased by an average 116 percent compared with an average 62 percent for reservations. Some reservations, such as the Rosebud Sioux and the Blackfeet, experienced virtually no growth, and no reservation succeeded in doubling its population, as did many urban areas. In view of the fact that the balance between rural and urban populations changed little in the 1970s, the differences between reservation and urban areas are surprisingly large. There are three possible reasons: (1) Reservations, unlike urban areas, have a relatively fixed growth potential; reservation territory can be increased only through the purchase of land. Reservation growth is further limited by the absence of physical infrastructure—roads, sewers, water—and economic activity necessary for sustaining larger concentrations of people. (2) In the 1970 census Indians in cities were less likely than those on reservations to identify their race as Indian. This may be especially true for the children of interracial couples. Consequently, changes in racial identification produced larger gains in urban areas than on reservations. (3) Not all reservations are located in rural areas, so that comparisons for rural and urban populations are not exactly the same as comparisons for reservation and urban populations.

Age-Sex Distributions

Another way of viewing the distribution of American Indians is in terms of age and sex. See Figures 3.3–3.7 for the American Indian, Alaska Native, and white age-sex distributions. Comparing Figures 3.3, 3.4, and 3.5 we see that the American Indian population is marked by a large concentration of young people and relatively small numbers of older individuals. For example, in 1970 49.2 percent of the American Indian population was under age 20. The age composition of the Indian population changed between 1970 and 1980, but not in a striking way; specifically, the proportion of the population under age 20 declined to 43.8 percent in 1980.

The pyramid-like shapes of Figures 3.3 and 3.4 are noteworthy because they indicate large numbers of persons in younger age groups and

FIGURE 3.3

Age-Sex Distribution of the American Indian Population, 1970

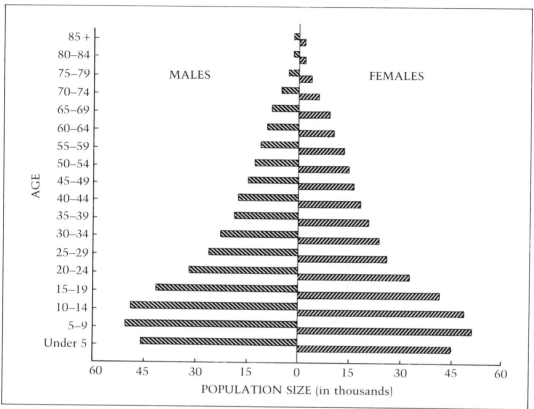

SOURCE: U.S. Bureau of the Census.

relatively small numbers in older age groups, denoting short life spans and high fertility; such conditions are prevalent in developing Third World nations. The white population age structure in Figure 3.5 resembles a pyramid much less than the American Indian and Alaska Native population, revealing that, not surprisingly, whites have lower fertility and live longer than American Indians. For instance, in 1980 the median age was 30.0 years for white males and 31.3 years for white females. In contrast, the median age for American Indian men and women in 1980 was 22.3 and 23.4 years, respectively.

Overall, American Indian women have significantly larger numbers of children (see Chapter 5) than white women, which has the effect of

FIGURE 3.4

Age-Sex Distribution of the American Indian and Alaska Native Population, 1980

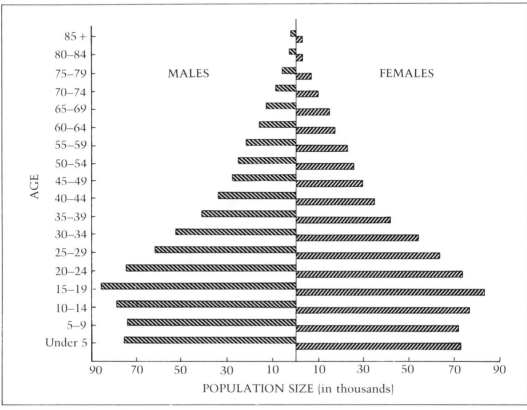

SOURCE: U.S. Bureau of the Census.

swelling the Indian population with relatively large numbers of young people and making it significantly younger than the white population. Differences in longevity between whites and American Indians play a relatively unimportant role in these distributions because the life expectancies of these populations are not particularly large (see Table 3.1).

Figures 3.6 and 3.7 show the differences in the age-sex distributions for American Indians residing in metropolitan and nonmetropolitan places. American Indians and Alaska Natives residing in metropolitan areas tend to have a larger number of older persons and a relatively

FIGURE 3.5

Age-Sex Distribution of the White American Population, 1980

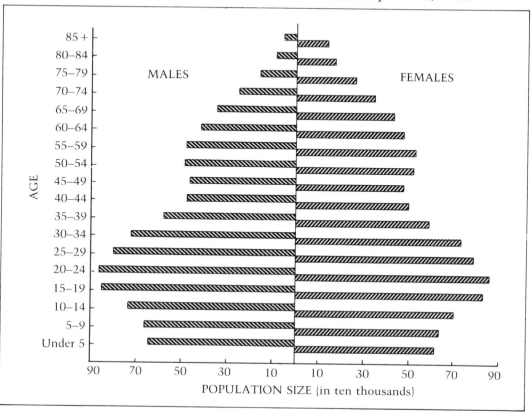

SOURCE: U.S. Bureau of the Census.

smaller number of young persons than their counterparts in nonmetropolitan areas. In metropolitan places, for instance, 40.0 percent of the Indian population is under age 20, while in nonmetropolitan locales 47.4 percent of the American Indian population is under age 20. Likewise, for metropolitan American Indians the median age is 24.4 years and for nonmetropolitan American Indians 21.2 years.

The most striking differences are evident between whites and Indians, with Indians clearly being a much more "youthful" population than whites. For readers desiring further details, the percentage distributions for the data in Figures 3.3–3.7 are provided in Tables 3.9 and 3.10.

FIGURE 3.6

Age-Sex Distribution of the American Indian and Alaska Native Population Residing in Metropolitan Places, 1980

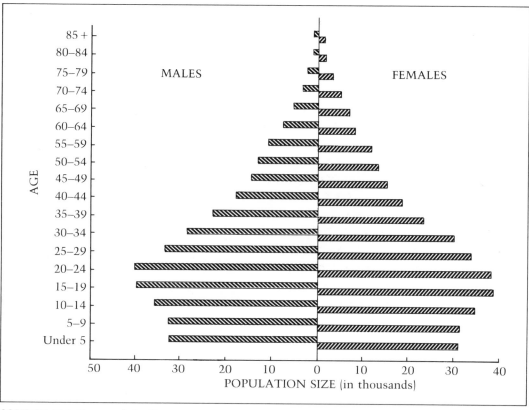

SOURCE: U.S. Bureau of the Census.

Concluding Remarks

The demographic dimensions of any population are defined by its size, distribution, composition, and rates of change. This chapter has described in detail Indian population growth since its turn-of-the-century resurgence, the spatial distribution of American Indians, and a few basic population characteristics. The data presented in this chapter sketch a general outline of the demography of American Indians, but as with any sketch many details are omitted. It would be a mistake to apply the broad generalizations of this chapter to all tribes of American Indians in urban and rural places; that is, to view Indians as a homogeneous population.

FIGURE 3.7

Age-Sex Distribution of the American Indian and Alaska Native Population Residing in Nonmetropolitan Places, 1980

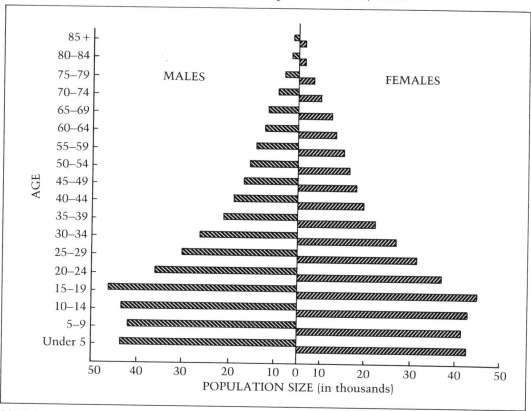

SOURCE: U.S. Bureau of the Census.

Some points are important to remember about the size of the Indian population: (1) Its growth is a relatively new phenomenon. While other ethnic groups have grown almost continually since their arrival in North America, Indians declined, and this trend was not halted until the twentieth century. (2) The Indian population has grown rapidly in the past 80 years. High fertility, developments in science and technology, and sympathetic public policies have been major contributors to this growth. Nevertheless, American Indian population growth in the decade of the 1970s was remarkable, and it cannot be fully attributed to natural increase alone. Fully isolating the causes of this expansion is not possible, but a definite shift in racial self-identification is an obvious source.

TABLE 3.9

Percent Distribution of Age and Sex of American Indians and Alaska Natives, 1970 and 1980, and Whites, 1980

Age	American Indians, 1970		American Indians and Alaska Natives, 1980		Whites, 1980	
	Males	Females	Males	Females	Males	Females
85+	0.4	0.5	0.3	0.5	0.7	1.5
80–84	0.5	0.6	0.4	0.6	1.0	1.8
75–79	0.9	1.0	0.9	1.1	1.8	2.8
70–74	1.4	1.5	1.3	1.5	2.8	3.7
65–69	2.2	2.3	1.8	2.2	3.8	4.5
60–64	2.6	2.7	2.3	2.5	4.6	5.0
55–59	3.1	3.4	3.1	3.3	5.3	5.6
50–54	3.5	3.8	3.6	3.7	5.4	5.4
45–49	4.1	4.3	4.0	4.2	5.1	5.0
40–44	4.7	4.8	4.8	5.0	5.3	5.2
35–39	5.0	5.3	5.9	6.0	6.4	6.0
30–34	6.0	6.2	7.5	7.6	8.0	7.6
25–29	6.8	6.8	8.8	8.8	8.7	8.2
20–24	8.5	8.6	10.7	10.4	9.5	8.9
15–19	11.2	10.9	12.2	11.7	9.4	8.6
10–14	13.1	12.6	11.2	10.7	8.0	7.2
5–9	13.6	13.2	10.6	10.1	7.2	6.6
Under 5	12.4	11.5	10.6	10.1	7.0	6.4
Total	100.0	100.0	100.0	100.0	100.0	100.0
Population Size	375,384	388,210	702,228	718,172	91,685,333	96,686,289
Median Age	19.9	20.9	22.3	23.4	30.0	31.3

SOURCES: *1980 Census of Population, General Population Characteristics, United States Summary;* and "American Indians," *1970 Census of Population, Subject Report.*

Historical events are also important for understanding Indians' spatial distribution. During the early nineteenth century, American Indians east of the Mississippi River were removed en masse to areas in the West, primarily to the area that is now Oklahoma. Testimony to the success of these measures is that most contemporary Indians live west of the Mississippi, and the size of the Indian population in Oklahoma is exceeded only by the Indian population in California. The large Indian population in California is relatively new, and its growth is concentrated in urban areas. By tradition, American Indians are a rural population, and the majority still live in nonmetropolitan areas. However, after World War II cities such as Los Angeles, Seattle, and Denver hosted a large influx of Indians because of federal programs that encouraged

TABLE 3.10

Percent Distribution of Age and Sex
of American Indians and Alaska Natives
Residing Inside and Outside Metropolitan Areas, 1980

Age	Metropolitan Areas		Nonmetropolitan Areas	
	Males	Females	Males	Females
85 +	0.3	0.5	0.4	0.5
80–84	0.3	0.6	0.5	0.6
75–79	0.7	1.0	1.0	1.2
70–74	1.1	1.5	1.5	1.6
65–69	1.6	2.0	2.0	2.3
60–64	2.2	2.5	2.3	2.5
55–59	3.2	3.4	2.9	3.2
50–54	3.8	3.9	3.3	3.5
45–49	4.3	4.4	3.7	4.0
40–44	5.2	5.4	4.4	4.6
35–39	6.6	6.7	5.1	5.3
30–34	8.3	8.5	6.6	6.7
25–29	9.7	9.6	7.9	8.0
20–24	11.7	11.0	9.7	9.7
15–19	11.6	11.2	13.0	12.2
10–14	10.4	9.9	12.0	11.5
5–9	9.5	9.0	11.6	11.1
Under 5	9.5	8.9	12.1	11.5
Total	100.0	100.0	100.0	100.0
Population Size	343,960	352,164	358,268	366,008
Median Age	23.8	25.0	20.6	21.8

SOURCE: *1980 Census of Population, General Population Characteristics, United States Summary.*

Indians to move to these areas. Federal relocation programs have had a profound impact on the distribution of American Indians, forcing the nineteenth century westward movement and offering incentives for urbanization in the twentieth century.

The resurgence of the American Indian population in this century has been facilitated by relatively high rates of fertility but slowed by relatively short life spans. The combined effect of these conditions is an age distribution within the American Indian population which most closely resembles the age distributions of impoverished populations in Third World countries and bears little resemblance to the age distribution of the largely middle-class white population. Significantly, this finding foretells the precarious socioeconomic standing of American Indians and Alaska Natives in the U.S. economy.

4

HOUSING

THIS CHAPTER describes the housing of American Indians from the perspectives of quantity, quality, and cost.[1] These characteristics form a basic framework for addressing questions concerning the kind of housing utilized by American Indians, its adequacy for providing minimum levels of personal comfort, and its cost, especially in relation to household incomes.

At the outset it is important to emphasize that the structural design of housing inhabited by most American Indians is not unique. Except for occasional ornamental embellishments, the quarters in which Amer-

[1]For the purposes of this chapter, Indian housing is defined in two ways: (1) The Census Bureau identifies Indian housing as dwellings occupied by an Indian householder. This highly restricted definition excludes housing occupied by the Indian spouses of non-Indian householders and the adopted children of non-Indian parents—both of which can be thought of legitimately as Indian-occupied housing. Regardless, this definition must be adhered to for the sake of using published sources of information. (2) A less restrictive definition identifies Indian housing as dwellings occupied by one or more persons reporting their race as American Indian. It is possible to apply this definition to machine readable microdata also distributed by the Census Bureau. An especially desirable feature of this definition is that it does not exclude the housing of Indian spouses and non-Indian householders. The definition used in published data includes Indian householders and spouses and Indian householders and non-Indian spouses. A small disadvantage of using two somewhat different definitions of Indian housing is that figures from published sources cannot be compared with figures obtained from machine readable data. Some readers may wish to compare tables to gain a sense of the differences created by alternative definitions; they are not large.

ican Indians reside resemble those of other segments of American society, especially low-income groups. Most dwellings occupied by American Indians are constructed from conventional materials such as brick, wood, and stucco. Indians no longer live in wigwams, longhouses, tipis, or hogans. There are, however, exceptions such as traditional Navajos who refuse to give up their hogan. Otherwise, most traditional forms of Indian housing are built mainly for ceremonial purposes, such as tipis at pow-wows, and they are seldom used for year-round residence. This is a relatively recent development.[2]

Changes in housing styles occurred in two ways. In some cases, the change was gradual and voluntarily adopted; for example, some southeastern tribes such as the Cherokees were living in log cabins at the turn of the century. In other cases, European tastes in housing were abruptly forced on tribes after they settled on reservations. Describing the confrontations between the Sioux and federal authorities in the late 1800s, Utley noted that "at first the reservation Indians lived in their traditional dwellings but later, responding to official pressures to adopt white ways, moved into dark, unhealthful cabins."[3] The Sioux holy man Black Elk sadly observed that "all our people now were settling down in square gray houses, scattered here and there across this hungry land."[4]

The urbanization of America—particularly technological developments such as large-scale waste disposal systems, electrification, indoor plumbing, and heating and cooling systems, as well as the implementation of building codes—was responsible for significant improvements in the housing of most Americans. However, for Indians outside the urban American mainstream and too poor for luxuries such as pressurized water systems, housing conditions improved very little during the first half of this century. For example, in 1959 a medical team visiting Cherokee homes in eastern Oklahoma observed:

> The houses were made of unpainted irregular slabs, sometimes partially covered with tarpaper. Almost all homes had kitchens and sinks although some depended on hand pumps for water. Where there was no well, water was often brought in buckets from a nearby brook or spring and stored by the kitchen sink. . . . A typical Cherokee family consisted of one or more young women in their twenties, perhaps an elderly woman, many children and infants, and the husbands of the young women.[5]

[2]See Harold E. Driver, *Indians of North America* (Chicago and London: University of Chicago Press, 1969), for discussion of traditional Indian housing (chap. 8).

[3]Robert M. Utley, *The Indian Frontier of the American West, 1846–1890* (Albuquerque: University of New Mexico Press, 1984), p. 230.

[4]Quoted in Utley (1984), p. 230.

[5]Quoted in William A. Brophy and Sophie D. Aberle, *The Indian: America's Unfinished Business* (Norman: University of Oklahoma Press, 1966), p. 166.

TABLE 4.1

Indian Housing Needs in 1980

	Number	Percent
Families in Standard Condition Housing	76,800	46.5
Families in Housing Suitable for Renovation	30,200	18.3
Families Needing New Housing (in housing unsuitable for renovation)	58,000	35.2
Total BIA Service Population (families)	165,000	100.0

SOURCE: Theodore W. Taylor, *The Bureau of Indian Affairs* (Boulder, CO: Westview Press, 1984), pp. 58–59.

These arrangements were considered relatively good compared with conditions on reservations elsewhere.

In the early 1960s the federal government stepped in to help improve housing conditions on reservations. Urban Indians were eligible for housing assistance through programs for low-income families. However, the first program specifically targeted at reservation housing was launched in 1961 through a cooperative effort involving tribal governments, the BIA, and the Public Housing Administration. It was a self-help program in which eligible families donated their land and labor as downpayment on their homes, and by 1965 over 300 homes were completed.[6] Since this program, the federal government, usually through the auspices of the BIA and the Department of Housing and Urban Development, has sponsored continuing efforts to upgrade Indian housing, especially in rural and reservation areas.[7] In 1980 a survey of Indian housing needs reported the results shown in Table 4.1. Excluding most off-reservation Indians, these figures include only families in the BIA service population, yet they reflect the scale of housing needs of American Indians. Of 165,000 families, over half reside in substandard housing. Most of these families live in dwellings dilapidated beyond renovation. Nearly two thirds of the 88,200 families needing housing assistance live in housing too deteriorated to be repaired.

[6]Brophy and Aberle (1966), p. 169.

[7]For a detailed discussion of these efforts, see C. Matthew Snipp and Alan L. Sorkin, "American Indian Housing: An Overview of Conditions and Public Policy," in Jamshid A. Momeni, ed., *Race, Ethnicity, and Housing in the United States* (Westport, CT: Greenwood Press, 1986).

These statistics are most striking because in 1982 the Reagan administration discontinued Indian housing assistance programs,[8] and in all likelihood the need for better housing has not diminished. Unlike housing surveys, the data available from census sources do not include measures of structural deficiencies or identify housing suitable for renovation. Nevertheless, census data provide a reasonably clear picture of the quantity, quality, and cost of housing, and especially the condition of housing for Indians compared with that for other groups in American society.

Housing Availability

The decade between 1970 and 1980 is an especially crucial period because of federal efforts to upgrade Indian housing. It is not possible to say with certainty that all improvements (if any) during this time are the result of housing programs, but it is true that these programs played an important role. Unfortunately, only limited comparisons can be made between 1970 and 1980 because very few data are available about Indian housing in 1970, and the 1970 and 1980 census data are not particularly comparable. The most serious limitation is that the available Indian housing data from 1970 are based on states with 10,000 or more Indians while the 1980 data are based on all 50 states and include in most instances Alaska Natives.

Home Ownership

Even with the shortcomings of the 1970 and 1980 data, it is still possible to get a general idea of changes in housing across the decade. Owner-occupied housing measures the amount of shelter belonging to the Indian population, and it represents a major source of economic collateral. In contrast, renter-occupied housing reflects the degree to which the Indian population must rely on housing belonging to others, exposed to the risks and uncertainties of rental housing markets. Needless to say, renters are exposed to greater risk from escalating rents, eviction actions, and inability to find suitable housing. The figures in Table 4.2 show changes in tenure between 1970 and 1980 and the standing of American Indians relative to blacks and whites. Between 1970 and 1980

[8]Theodore W. Taylor, *The Bureau of Indian Affairs* (Boulder, Co: Westview Press, 1984).

TABLE 4.2

Home Ownership and Mobile Home Residency
Among American Indian, Black, and White Householders, 1970–1980

Household	Percentage in Owner-Occupied Housing		Percentage in Mobile Homes
	1970	1980	1980
American Indian	49.8	53.2	8.6
Black	41.6	44.4	2.2
White	65.4	67.8	5.2

SOURCES: *1970 Census of Housing, General Housing Characteristics, United States Summary; 1970 Census of Population, Subject Report "American Indians," and 1980 Census of Housing, General Housing Characteristics, United States Summary.*

NOTES: Figures for American Indians do not include Alaska Natives; 1970 American Indian data are based on states with 10,000 or more Indians. Mobile home figures are for owners and renters.

the proportion of owner-occupied housing increased for all three groups. This is not surprising because during the 1970s housing programs assisted low- to moderate-income families in home ownership, and inflation rapidly increased the cost of housing and made home ownership highly attractive as a way of stabilizing shelter costs and as a personal investment. Despite these benefits, the increases in home ownership are relatively small, and the differences among these groups, in terms of change, are almost nonexistent. American Indians enjoyed the greatest percentage increase in ownership. About 3.4 percent more housing units were owned by Indians in 1980 than in 1970, but this is only 1.0 percent more than the whites' increase and less than 1.0 percent more than the blacks' increase. Furthermore, American Indians are 15 percent behind whites in home ownership and about 8 percent ahead of blacks, perhaps because blacks are a traditionally landless and recently urban population—urban environments and the absence of land are conducive to renting. Indians, in contrast, are traditionally landed and concentrated in rural areas.

A unique characteristic of Indian housing is the relatively extensive use of temporary shelter in the form of mobile homes. Nearly 9 percent of the homes occupied by Indian householders are not permanent dwellings compared with 5 percent of white homes and 2 percent of black homes. Although proportionally more Indian than black householders occupy single-family dwellings, Indians are substantially more likely than blacks to reside in mobile homes. Comparable information for mobile home use in 1970 is not available, so it is impossible to ascertain whether temporary housing among American Indians has increased or decreased. However, the growing commercial availability of this type of shelter and subsidies for mobile home purchases from government and tribal programs suggest that this type of housing probably increased during the 1970s.

Living Space

Home ownership is an important measure of the housing supply for the American Indian population, but it reveals very little about the actual living space available. In this regard, two important measures of this space are the median rooms per individual housing unit and the percentage of housing units with three or fewer rooms. Median rooms per unit measures the average number of rooms available, while housing with fewer than three rooms indexes the prevalence of housing with minimum or below minimum living areas. A typical housing unit with three rooms would probably include a single bedroom, a kitchen, and a common living area.

Of course, housing units with three rooms or fewer are not necessarily crowded; a single college student in a dormitory room or one-room studio apartment is not necessarily living in crowded quarters. As a measure of inventory, housing units with three or fewer rooms are relatively small units, by most standards, and this is closely related but distinct from crowded housing. Overcrowding represents another dimension of housing for which data will be presented later in this chapter.

Table 4.3 shows the percentage of dwellings with three or fewer rooms and the median rooms per housing unit for the housing of black, white, and American Indian householders. The typical number of rooms per housing unit is not dramatically different among whites, blacks, and American Indians. Although Indians are more likely than blacks to live in single-family homes, the average size of these homes tends to be smaller than the housing of blacks or whites. This pattern persisted through the 1970s, and by 1980 the relative differences between these groups showed little change, though the average number of rooms occupied by each group increased slightly for the decade.

The differences between these groups and across time are more evident in the distribution of small residences. In 1970, 33 percent of all Indian householders lived in housing units with three or fewer rooms compared with 23 and 15 percent for black and white householders, respectively. By 1980 the proportion of blacks and whites in housing units of three or fewer rooms declined a few points for each group, but American Indians experienced a precipitous decline in this type of housing,

TABLE 4.3

Percentage of Dwellings with Three or Fewer Rooms,
and Median Rooms per Housing Unit
Occupied by American Indian, Black, and White Householders

Household	1970		1980	
	Percentage with 3 or Fewer Rooms	Median Rooms	Percentage with 3 or Fewer Rooms	Median Rooms
American Indian	33.0	4.2	24.1	4.6
Black	23.0	4.6	20.8	4.8
White	15.0	4.8	11.5	5.3

SOURCES: *1970 Census of Housing, General Housing Characteristics, United States Summary;* "American Indians," *1970 Census of Population, Subject Report;* and *1980 Census of Housing, General Housing Characteristics, United States Summary.*

NOTES: Figures for American Indians do not include Alaska Natives; 1970 American Indian data are based on states with 10,000 or more Indians; and 1970 housing data for whites are based on nonblack housing units.

from 33 to 24 percent. In relative terms, Indians still lag behind blacks in this measure, and much behind whites, but the gap was smaller in 1980 than it was in 1970. The causes of the sharp decline are difficult to establish because the necessary data are not available. However, two plausible sources include the presence of federal Indian housing programs, especially those that built new housing, and fewer Indian householders living in traditional housing, such as one-room Navajo hogans.

Housing units with three or fewer rooms add another perspective on rates of home ownership. Owning a home and/or living in a single-family dwelling does not translate into larger housing units among American Indians. As the figures in Table 4.4 show, there is a great deal of variation between regions and between areas, and in general neither nonmetropolitan nor reservation areas consistently have larger or smaller houses than other areas. Around the East Coast (New England and Middle Atlantic states), for example, ownership rates are relatively low, but the percentage of Indian-occupied housing units with three or fewer rooms also is relatively low in most areas. Home ownership is more common among Indians in the Midwest and the South than in the Northeast, but the proportion of small housing units is, in most areas, lower than in New England or the Middle Atlantic states.

Although home ownership is most prevalent in the West, this does not translate into larger housing units. On the contrary, the lowest rate of housing units with three rooms or fewer in these regions is for off-reservation areas in the Mountain states; this figure is exceeded by few

TABLE 4.4

Percent Distribution Within Areas and Regions
of American Indian and Alaska Native Housing Units
with Three or Fewer Rooms

Census Division	Metropolitan	Nonmetropolitan	Off Reservation	On or Near Reservation
New England	14.5	16.6	16.4	11.3
Mid Atlantic	19.8	10.3	21.2	8.5
E. North Central	13.4	13.4	13.5	13.9
W. North Central	15.3	16.3	12.2	16.8
South Atlantic	11.9	8.6	10.5	13.2
E. South Central	13.8	10.2	12.8	10.6
W. South Central	13.2	11.1	12.9	10.7
Mountain	22.0	38.5	16.1	34.7
Pacific	18.8	27.3	20.2	21.3

SOURCE: Public-Use Microdata Sample, 5 percent A File.

NOTE: Estimates are based on housing units with at least one American Indian or Alaska Native resident.

other areas in the nation. The highest rates are for Indians in nonmetropolitan areas of the Mountain states, where over a third of Indian-occupied housing has three or fewer rooms. This is particularly noteworthy given the high rate of mobile home use in this area; nearly 15 percent of the housing units occupied by American Indians in the Mountain states in 1980 were mobile homes. Reservations in this region have relatively high rates of home ownership, but the housing units tend to be small. There are over twice as many Indian-occupied housing units with three or fewer rooms on or near reservations compared with Indian-occupied housing away from reservations.

Reservation Housing

On western reservations Indians were forced to give up their traditional housing for one-room shacks, and observers since the early twentieth century have commented on the housing conditions in these locales.[9] The availability of housing on the Navajo reservation and the 15 next largest reservations is displayed in Table 4.5. Their reliance on tra-

---

[9]Alan L. Sorkin, *American Indians and Federal Aid* (Washington, DC: Brookings Institution, 1971); Brophy and Aberle (1966); Sar A. Levitan and Barbara Hetrick, *Big Brother's Indian Programs: With Reservations* (New York: McGraw-Hill, 1971).

TABLE 4.5

Percentage of Owner-Occupied Housing and Median Rooms per Housing Unit on the 16 Largest Reservations in 1980

Reservation	Percentage in Owner-Occupied Housing		Median Rooms	
	1970	1980	1970	1980
Navajo (AZ, NM, UT)	61.5	67.7	2.0	2.7
Pine Ridge (SD)	62.2	44.8	3.3	4.3
Gila River (AZ)	78.1	65.7	2.8	3.9
Papago (AZ)	87.9	72.9	2.5	3.5
Fort Apache (AZ)	79.1	68.5	3.0	4.3
Hopi (AZ)	82.5	77.3	2.7	2.8
Zuni Pueblo (NM)	92.5	68.6	4.5	5.1
San Carlos (AZ)	88.0	74.9	2.8	3.8
Rosebud (SD)	68.2	52.2	3.9	4.4
Blackfeet (MT)	60.3	61.1	4.1	4.8
Yakima (WA)	53.8	60.0	4.8	4.8
Eastern Cherokee (NC)	80.6	83.8	4.2	5.0
Standing Rock (ND, SD)	61.2	35.8	3.3	4.5
Osage (OK)	—	72.5	—	5.2
Fort Peck (MT)	42.2	54.4	4.1	4.9
Wind River (WY)	75.3	67.4	4.0	4.8

SOURCES: *Census of Housing, General Housing Characteristics, United States Summary, 1980;* and "American Indians," *1970 Census of Population, Subject Report.*

NOTES: Osage reservation data are not available for 1970. Hopi and Navajo reservation data are not strictly comparable because of administrative changes in Navajo-Hopi joint use area during the 1970s.

ditional one-room hogans means that the Navajo reservation, followed by the Hopi (located inside the Navajo reservation), has a heavy concentration of one- and two-room structures. In 1970 the median number of rooms per unit was 2.0 and, with fewer hogans in year-round occupation, this figure increased to 2.7 in 1980.

As explained, access to housing is an important benefit of reservation residence, but changes in the structure of reservation housing are dramatically transforming tenure arrangements. One of the major innovations of the public housing programs for reservations during the 1960s and 1970s was the creation of "housing authorities" operated by the tribe, the BIA, or both. Tribal/BIA housing authorities supervised the construction of public housing for low-income families, and these authorities manage and maintain often extensive systems of rental housing.

The impact of these programs, especially in making low-cost rental housing available, is evident in Table 4.5. Between 1970 and 1980 on 10 of the 16 largest reservations, housing units increased while the number of owner-occupied homes remained about the same, which reduced the percentage of owner-occupied units. In some instances the decline was dramatic, such as the Zuni pueblo, which in 1970 had 546 Indian-owned units out of 590 Indian-occupied units. In 1980 there were 1,077 Indian-occupied units, of which 739 were owner-occupied. For the decade housing units increased on the Zuni pueblo by 83 percent while owner-occupied units grew by 35 percent. However, the gain in new units meant larger housing units as the median rooms per unit increased during this period. Because most programs for reservation housing have been terminated or sharply reduced, it is likely that the downward trends in owner-occupied housing will be stabilized at the expense of more and larger public housing.

Group Quarters

Before turning to other dimensions of Indian housing, it is worth noting that some Indians do not live in apartments or houses; instead, they reside in group quarters (see Table 4.6). More than 6 percent of all housing units occupied by Indians are group quarters, but less than 3 percent of the total Indian population reside in this type of housing. The differences between areas are relatively small, except that military quar-

TABLE 4.6

Percent Distribution Within Areas of American Indians and Alaska Natives Occupying Group Quarters, by Place of Residence and Type

Group Quarters	Metropolitan	Nonmetropolitan	Off Reservation	On or Near Reservation
Mental Hospital	4.1	3.4	3.7	4.1
Home for Aged	9.6	12.6	10.3	10.9
Correctional Facility	18.5	21.9	20.7	17.8
Other Institution	10.6	11.5	10.5	11.5
Military Quarters	20.8	5.3	17.7	12.7
College Dormitory	19.9	26.1	20.1	24.8
Rooming House	4.7	4.6	4.4	5.0
Other Group Quarters	12.0	14.6	12.6	13.2

SOURCE: Public-Use Microdata Sample, 5 percent A File.

NOTES: Estimates are based on American Indian and Alaska Native population in group quarters. Columns may not sum to 100.0 because of rounding errors.

ters tend to be located in metropolitan and/or nonreservation areas. A more meaningful statistic is that between 40 and 50 percent of Indian-occupied group quarters are in institutions such as correctional facilities, homes for the aged, and other facilities where regular care is required. A yet more telling commentary on the status of Indians in American society is that Indians occupy cells in correctional facilities in about the same proportions as they occupy college dormitory rooms.

Housing Quality

Housing quality is an elusive concept, and there is no single measure which best reflects the structural fitness of a dwelling, much less the comfort of its inhabitants. Ideally, housing units could be inspected and rated according to their dilapidation, but the enormity of such a project makes it impossible. As a result, the data bearing on housing quality from the 1980 census consist of no more than imprecise and general indicators. For example, the year a house is built may indicate that it is old and may need renovation or replacement. On the other hand, some structures built 50 years ago or earlier are more soundly constructed and hence in better shape today than some houses built less than 20 years ago.

Crowded Housing Conditions

Although difficult to measure, the quality of housing is important because, for obvious reasons, it is directly related to material comfort and well-being. Generally speaking, among Indians and non-Indians alike, the number of persons sharing a fixed amount of space is an important consideration. Crowded dwellings offer less privacy and less comfort than larger homes with fewer people. By this standard, a significant segment of the American Indian and Alaska Native population is not well housed. Evidence of this problem is displayed in Table 4.7.

As a rule of thumb, crowded housing conditions exist when there are more occupants than rooms in a dwelling. For example, a family of four occupying a small two-bedroom apartment with only a kitchen and a single common living room would have 1.00 persons per room. Whether such an arrangement could be considered crowded is debatable, but a family of five would certainly be crowded with 1.25 persons per room. Few would disagree that six or more persons in the same two-bedroom apartment, 1.50 or more persons per room, are living in crowded quarters. The columns in Table 4.7 compare uncrowded (1.00

TABLE 4.7

Percentage of Persons per Room in Housing Units
Occupied by American Indian, Black, and White Householders

Household	1.0 and Less		1.01 to 1.50		1.51 and Over	
	1970	1980	1970	1980	1970	1980
American Indian	68.8	82.4	13.8	9.2	17.4	8.4
Black	80.1	88.8	12.4	7.8	7.5	3.4
White	93.1	97.1	5.3	2.2	1.6	0.7

SOURCES: *1970 Census of Housing, General Housing Characteristics, United States Summary;* "American Indians," *1970 Census of Population, Subject Report;* and *1980 Census of Housing, General Housing Characteristics, United States Summary.*

NOTES: Figures for American Indians do not include Alaska Natives; 1970 American Indian data are based on states with 10,000 or more Indians. Figures for whites in 1970 are estimated from occupied units not occupied by blacks.

or fewer), moderately crowded (1.01 to 1.50), and very crowded (1.51 or more) housing conditions among American Indians, blacks, and whites.

American Indians, in 1970 and 1980, lived in the most densely occupied housing units. Although they were considerably more likely to own their homes and live in a detached single-family dwelling than blacks, they also were more likely to live in crowded conditions. Between 1970 and 1980 crowded conditions in Indian households improved substantially, along with conditions in the households of blacks and whites, but the relative status of these groups changed very little. In 1970, 68.8 percent of Indian-occupied housing units had 1.00 or fewer persons per room compared with 80.1 percent of black-occupied units and 93.1 percent of white-occupied units. In contrast, 17.4 percent of Indian-occupied houses had 1.51 or more persons per room compared with 1.6 percent of white-occupied houses. While all three groups resided in less crowded housing in 1980, 8.4 percent of Indian houses still were very crowded compared with 3.4 and 0.7 percent of black and white houses, respectively. American Indians also experienced the greatest gains in uncrowded houses: from 68.8 percent in 1970 to 82.4 percent in 1980, lagging behind blacks and whites by 6 and 14 points, respectively.

Some of the differences in housing quality between American Indians, blacks, and whites can be attributed to environmental factors such as rural-urban residence. The role of environmental factors and the benefits of reservation proximity where housing assistance is available are more evident in differences in Indian housing across residential areas and regions. Table 4.8 shows the distribution of crowded and uncrowded housing across divisions and by place of residence.

TABLE 4.8

Percentage of Persons per Room in Housing Units Occupied by American Indians and Alaska Natives, Within Regions and Areas, 1980

Census Division	Metropolitan			Nonmetropolitan		
	1.0 and Less	1.01 to 1.50	1.51 and More	1.0 and Less	1.01 to 1.50	1.51 and More
New England	91.8	7.1	1.1	90.8	8.3	0.9
Mid Atlantic	90.2	7.0	2.8	90.7	5.4	3.9
E. North Central	91.9	6.4	1.8	87.7	9.1	3.2
W. North Central	87.6	9.1	3.4	81.1	12.0	6.9
South Atlantic	92.2	6.1	1.7	87.5	10.2	2.3
E. South Central	92.9	4.4	2.7	86.8	8.1	5.1
W. South Central	90.5	7.0	2.5	89.7	7.6	2.7
Mountain	81.4	10.8	7.9	59.1	14.7	26.1
Pacific	90.1	6.4	3.5	78.5	10.4	11.1

SOURCE: Public-Use Microdata Sample, 5 percent A File.

NOTE: Estimates are based on housing units with at least one American Indian or Alaska Native resident.

Across metropolitan and nonmetropolitan areas, there is relatively little variation in the pervasiveness of crowded or uncrowded housing as measured by persons per room. Because of the large numbers of Indians in the Mountain region, it has relatively and absolutely more housing units with 1.51 or more persons per room and fewer with 1.0 or fewer persons per room than other regions. Somewhat larger differences exist between metropolitan and nonmetropolitan areas and between areas on or near reservations and areas away from reservation land, but in most regions these differences are negligible.

Indian housing conditions in the West are similar to housing conditions in the West North Central division. However, there are appreciable differences between metropolitan and nonmetropolitan areas, as well as between reservation and nonreservation areas. Metropolitan and nonreservation areas have the least crowded housing, about 90 percent occupied by 1.0 or fewer persons per room, while nonmetropolitan and reservation areas have the most crowded housing. For example, 26 per-

TABLE 4.8 *(continued)*

Census Division	Off Reservation			On or Near Reservation		
	1.0 and Less	1.01 to 1.50	1.51 and More	1.0 and Less	1.01 to 1.50	1.51 and More
New England	92.8	6.4	0.9	89.2	9.3	1.5
Mid Atlantic	89.5	7.1	3.4	93.4	5.4	1.2
E. North Central	91.8	6.3	1.8	86.7	10.1	3.2
W. North Central	91.1	7.0	2.0	76.3	14.9	8.8
South Atlantic	90.6	7.6	1.8	88.3	8.3	3.4
E. South Central	92.3	4.7	3.0	70.2	19.1	10.6
W. South Central	89.9	7.4	2.7	92.4	5.7	1.3
Mountain	90.3	7.2	2.5	64.0	14.2	21.7
Pacific	90.0	6.4	3.5	84.3	8.5	7.2

cent of the housing units in nonmetropolitan areas of the Mountain region contain 1.51 or more persons per room. This figure coincides with other indicators of low-quality housing in this region. Crowded housing suggests that housing is scarce, but it also may result from the prevalence of extended and other large families unable to afford more spacious housing.

Age of Structure

As already mentioned, the age of a house is not necessarily related to its condition but, as Table 4.1 indicates, the housing occupied by many American Indians is in need of renovation or dilapidated beyond repair; these houses are most likely older units. The age of housing occupied by American Indians, blacks, and whites is shown in Table 4.9; these figures are unadjusted for "cohort shifts." For example, housing units 11 to 20 years old in 1980 were 10 years old or less in 1970. These figures indicate, very crudely, how Indians, blacks, and whites are moving in and out of older or newer housing.

TABLE 4.9

Percentage of Housing Units
Occupied by American Indian, Black, and White Householders,
by Age of Structure

Age of Structure	American Indians		Blacks		Whites	
	1970	1980	1970	1980	1970	1980
10 Years or Less	25.2	32.3	15.8	17.9	26.0	26.1
11 to 20 Years	19.2	20.6	17.5	19.3	21.8	19.8
21 to 30 Years	14.9	15.5	18.1	18.6	12.5	17.1
31 Years or More	40.7	31.6	48.6	44.2	39.7	37.0
Total	100.0	100.0	100.0	100.0	100.0	100.0

SOURCES: *1970 Census of Housing, General Housing Characteristics, United States Summary;* "American Indians," *1970 Census of Population, Subject Report;* and *1980 Census of Housing, General Housing Characteristics, United States Summary.*

NOTES: Figures for American Indians do not include Alaska Natives; 1970 American Indian data are based on states with 10,000 or more Indians. Figures for whites in 1970 are estimated from year-round units not occupied by blacks.

The effects of World War II and postwar housing shortages were evident in 1970 and 1980 among all three races. American Indians, blacks, and whites lived in relatively new housing or in relatively old structures. In 1970 structures built after 1960 were "relatively new," and structures built before 1940 were relatively old. American Indians and whites occupied about the same proportion of units built 10 years or less before 1970, while blacks were considerably less likely to reside in newly built housing. Public housing programs were undoubtedly important for changes after 1970 as the proportion of Indians in new housing climbed to over 32 percent while the proportion for blacks and whites in new housing remained about the same. Paralleling these changes, the percentage of American Indian householders in units 31 years old or more declined from 41 percent in 1970 to 32 percent in 1980, while blacks and whites experienced much smaller changes.

In terms of shifts between old and new housing, American Indians resemble whites more than blacks. In 1970 about one fourth of white- and Indian-occupied units were less than 10 years old. As these units aged, reaching 11 to 20 years in 1980, the proportion of the units occupied by whites and Indians declined to 20 percent in favor of newer units, while the proportion of black-occupied units increased slightly. Among units 11 to 20 years old in 1970, the percentage of white and Indian householders also declined as this housing aged to 21 to 30 years, while the percentage of black householders remained nearly the same.

Just as it would be unwise to draw strong conclusions from these shifts, one would be equally mistaken to read too much into the similarities between whites and Indians. During the 1970s extremely low real interest rates and rapid inflation made real estate an excellent investment for developers and home owners alike. For economically advantaged whites, and for blacks and Indians to a lesser extent, the financial benefits of real estate offered a powerful incentive for new home purchases. For apartment dwellers, these conditions also made available newer, more attractive units for households that could afford them. However, among American Indians, public housing programs were probably as important as low interest rates. Although the housing needs on many reservations are still critical, public housing programs most likely were responsible for a portion of the significant increase in newly built units occupied by American Indians. Another important factor that should not be overlooked is that Indians are more likely than blacks to reside outside central cities, in suburban areas where newer housing stocks typically are more available.

Table 4.10 shows the age of housing occupied by American Indians across the United States, and juxtaposed with Table 4.8, it also shows that newer housing is not necessarily less crowded housing. About 44 percent of housing occupied by American Indians in the Mountain region was built in the 1970s, and about 19 percent of these units were built before 1950. In regions with fewer Indians and fewer reservations, American Indian housing tends to be older. For example, Indian housing in New England is relatively old; nearly 60 percent of Indian-occupied units were built before 1950. Also, there are almost no differences in the availability of older housing in this region, yet there is substantially more newer housing available in nonmetropolitan areas and in areas on or near reservation land. With few exceptions, there are 10 to 15 percent more Indian-occupied housing units less than 10 years old in nonmetropolitan locales and in areas on or near reservation land than in other areas. The most likely explanation for this difference is that tribal and government-sponsored programs were able to make newer, if not less crowded, housing available to reservation households. For Indians away from reservations, newer housing is usually more expensive housing, and units less than 10 years old are beyond the financial wherewithal of many nonreservation Indian households.

TABLE 4.10

*Percentage Distribution of Old and New Housing Units
Occupied by American Indians and Alaska Natives, 1980*

Census Division	Metropolitan		Nonmetropolitan	
	10 Years or Less	Over 30 Years	10 Years or Less	Over 30 Years
New England	16.7	61.5	32.1	45.0
Mid Atlantic	13.1	59.4	23.4	55.6
E. North Central	20.4	49.2	25.8	36.8
W. North Central	26.8	41.6	33.5	20.7
South Atlantic	34.8	21.2 ·	44.4	26.8
E. South Central	34.3	26.0	38.3	38.1
W. South Central	35.1	26.4	32.8	38.1
Mountain	37.2	23.9	45.9	17.3
Pacific	26.7	28.7	41.8	26.9

SOURCE: Public-Use Microdata Sample, 5 percent A File.

NOTE: Estimates are based on housing units with at least one American Indian or Alaska Native resident.

Amenities

Another facet of housing quality is reflected in the amenities available within a dwelling. Table 4.11 lists amenities that most middle-class urban households would consider essential for basic comfort, such as complete bathroom and kitchen facilities, air conditioning, and a telephone. The data for American Indians in 1970 are incomplete because the Census Bureau did not publish the same items for Indians as it did for blacks and whites.

Available data show that in 1970 dwellings occupied by American Indian householders were substantially more likely to lack a complete bathroom, public water, and public sewer than the housing of blacks and whites. Amenities such as public water, sewer, and to a lesser degree a complete bathroom are almost universally available in urban localities. Water and waste disposal are basic services available to virtually all urban residents with the possible exception of outlying

TABLE 4.10 *(continued)*

Census Division	Off Reservation		On or Near Reservation	
	10 Years or Less	Over 30 Years	10 Years or Less	Over 30 Years
New England	16.9	59.9	24.5	56.4
Mid Atlantic	13.2	60.2	19.3	53.8
E. North Central	20.0	50.4	29.6	44.5
W. North Central	23.0	46.4	38.6	30.3
South Atlantic	37.5	22.6	51.0	13.1
E. South Central	35.0	26.2	44.7	27.6
W. South Central	35.1	29.5	30.1	31.0
Mountain	35.9	27.3	43.6	18.6
Pacific	25.4	28.9	35.9	27.6

suburban homes with water wells and septic tanks. Incomplete bathrooms in urban areas are most common in tenements and transient hotels, where facilities are shared and public health laws forbid outdoor toilets. In contrast, Indians are more likely to reside in rural areas, so predictably they have less access to public sewer and water and may rely on privies more than urbanized white and black populations. Unlike water and waste disposal, air conditioning is not a public good. It is contingent on economic resources, and this is clearly evident in Table 4.11. In 1970 almost 38 percent of white-occupied dwellings had air conditioning, while only 19 and 18 percent, respectively, of American Indian and black dwellings had air conditioning.

The data for 1980 are more complete for American Indians and show marked increases in the availability of household amenities. Among the most dramatic improvements, complete bathrooms in American Indian housing increased from 72 to 90 percent. Although Indians still lag behind blacks by 3.6 percent and whites by 7.8 percent, the gap was considerably narrower in 1980 than it was in 1970. Indians registered smaller increases, about 10 percent, in gaining access to pub-

TABLE 4.11

Percentage of Housing Units with Selected Amenities
Occupied by American Indian, Black, and White Householders

Amenities	American Indians		Blacks		Whites	
	1970	1980	1970	1980	1970	1980
Complete Bathroom	72.0	90.0	82.4	93.6	94.7	97.8
Public Water	69.6	79.8	87.3	92.2	81.2	82.5
Public Sewer	57.7	67.0	80.7	86.3	70.3	72.4
Complete Kitchen	N/A	91.4	88.8	95.2	96.2	98.6
Telephone	N/A	73.1	69.5	83.9	88.9	94.5
Air Conditioning	19.3	40.3	18.0	42.7	37.5	58.1
Central Heating	N/A	39.8	23.2	35.3	45.5	51.2

SOURCES: *1970 Census of Housing, General Housing Characteristics, United States Summary;* "American Indians," *1970 Census of Population, Subject Report* and *1980 Census of Housing, General Housing Characteristics, U.S. Summary.*

NOTES: Figures for American Indians do not include Alaska Natives; 1970 American Indian data are based on states with 10,000 or more American Indians. Figures for whites in 1970 are estimated from year-round units not occupied by blacks.

lic water and sewage disposal, yet this growth exceeded proportional increases among blacks and whites. Several factors probably were responsible for these improvements in Indian housing. A larger share of the Indian population lived in or near urban areas in 1980 than in 1970 and, again, efforts were made by tribes, the BIA, and HUD throughout the 1970s to upgrade Indian housing and develop public services in Indian settlements. For other nonpublic amenities, Indians and blacks realized improvements, yet they still lag behind whites. For example, the gap in air conditioned homes was about 15 to 20 percent in 1980, just as it was in 1970. American Indians and blacks also lag far behind whites in the use of central heating. There are, however, much smaller differences in access to complete kitchens among these groups but, again, American Indians are least likely to have a fully equipped kitchen. Finally, there are particularly well defined differences in access to telephones among these groups: 27 percent of Indian housing units do not have a telephone compared with 16 percent of black units and 5 percent of white units. This may reflect a rural-urban difference. Telephones are more expensive in rural areas because long distance calls are required more often. Nevertheless, telephone service is an amenity to which American Indians have much less access than blacks and whites.

Differences in the utilization of public water and sewers are as much evidence of rural isolation as they are of low-quality housing. On many reservations community water and waste disposal systems developed in the 1960s and 1970s have narrowed the gap between reservation and nonreservation areas. The result is that the largest differences in these amenities exist between metropolitan and nonmetropolitan areas (see Table 4.12). Other kinds of amenities such as complete bathroom and kitchen facilities are less dependent on location, making the differences between areas more dramatic.

Complete bathroom and kitchen facilities are by most standards considered essential, but approximately 15 percent of housing units on or near reservation land do not have these facilities compared with about 4 percent in nonreservation areas. Similar, slightly smaller differences exist between rural and urban areas. Telephones, air conditioning, and central heating are items for which there are especially large differences between areas. About 30 percent of dwellings on or near reservation lands have some type of air conditioning compared with 50 percent in nonreservation areas, for example. Items such as air conditioning are less essential than, say, kitchen facilities, so they have lower rates of utilization and there is greater variation between areas.

TABLE 4.12

Percentage of Housing Units with Selected Amenities
Occupied by American Indians and Alaska Natives
Within Metropolitan and Nonmetropolitan Areas,
and Within Areas Off Reservations and Areas On or Near Reservations

Amenities	Metropolitan	Nonmetropolitan	Off Reservation	On or Near Reservation
Complete				
Bathroom	96.0	83.0	95.9	84.8
Public Water	87.1	67.1	82.7	84.8
Public Sewer	77.4	50.0	73.3	60.4
Air				
Conditioning	29.9	47.7	32.1	50.1
Central				
Heating	46.5	33.9	44.9	38.1
Complete				
Kitchen	97.0	84.8	97.0	86.3
Telephone	84.2	64.5	83.8	67.8

SOURCE: Public-Use Microdata Sample, 5 percent A File.

NOTE: Estimates are based on housing units with at least one American Indian or Alaska Native resident.

Regional differences also influence the use of some household amenities. For example, air conditioning and central heating are least used in New England, where the climate is relatively cool in the summer and wood is a primary source of heating fuel in the winter. Such differences are shown in Table 4.13, and most can be explained in geographic terms. Bathroom and kitchen facilities, for instance, are relatively independent of geography, and there is relatively little regional variation. Perhaps the most significant statistics in Table 4.13 are those that show, again, the poor quality of Indian housing in the Mountain region. By any standard, the dwellings in this region are the most rudimentary in the entire nation.

Housing on Reservations

Table 4.14 presents selected measures of housing quality for the 16 largest reservations in 1980. Compared with other American households (see Table 4.7), there is no question that housing on these reservations is crowded. Except for the Cherokee and Osage reservations, between 23 and 65 percent of dwellings have more than one person per room.[10] Although these figures indicate extraordinarily high rates of occupation, there was less crowded housing in 1980 than in 1970. Every reservation listed in Table 4.14 experienced a decline in crowded housing units between 1970 and 1980. The Zuni pueblo in New Mexico and the Eastern Cherokee in North Carolina registered the largest decreases of the decade—differences of 28 and 26 percent, respectively. In contrast, the Navajo and Hopi reservations had the smallest reductions, though both reservations began the 1970s with large percentages of crowded housing. The crowded housing conditions on these reservations coincide with the generally poor condition of housing in this region.

As noted, new housing units are not necessarily better in every respect, but they are less likely to be dilapidated than older units. The unit age data in Table 4.14 are not strictly comparable between 1970 and 1980; 1970 data are based on units with Indian householders, and 1980 data are based on all year-round units on the reservation, whether or not inhabited by an Indian householder. Unfortunately, more comparable data for all of the reservations in Table 4.14 are not available; however, this information provides a general, if imprecise view of changes between 1970 and 1980. The Rosebud Sioux reservation is particularly interesting because in 1970 it had the largest percentage of new housing units of the 16 largest reservations. It achieved this status with

[10]Data are not available for the Osage reservation in 1970.

TABLE 4.13

Percentage of Housing Units with Selected Amenities
Occupied by American Indians and Alaska Natives Within Regions

Census Division	Bathroom	Public Water	Public Sewer	Air Conditioning	Central Heating	Complete Kitchen	Telephone
New England	93.5	78.3	66.4	21.7	26.8	97.0	83.5
Mid Atlantic	92.8	80.9	73.0	30.8	33.3	96.4	85.1
E. North Central	95.8	76.3	73.7	34.0	61.5	97.7	85.0
W. North Central	93.5	78.1	71.9	40.7	54.4	94.3	75.7
South Atlantic	95.2	63.5	51.9	63.2	39.9	96.3	77.5
E. South Central	92.1	78.2	53.5	64.5	41.0	93.4	74.9
W. South Central	96.1	83.1	66.8	72.2	45.8	97.0	81.9
Mountain	78.3	79.8	61.4	29.8	40.0	79.5	56.3
Pacific	93.9	87.1	76.6	30.7	35.5	94.7	84.7

SOURCE: Public-Use Microdata Sample, 5 percent A File.

NOTE: Estimates are based on housing units with at least one American Indian or Alaska Native resident.

TABLE 4.14

Percentage of Housing Units with More Than 1.0 Persons per Room,
and Units 10 Years Old and Under
on the 16 Largest Reservations in 1980

Reservation	1.01 and More Persons per Room		Units 10 Years Old and Under	
	1970	1980	1970	1980
Navajo (AZ, NM, UT)	75.8	64.9	54.0	47.1
Pine Ridge (SD)	63.8	49.0	27.0	43.6
Gila River (AZ)	62.9	42.2	27.4	48.3
Papago (AZ)	68.8	49.4	19.0	47.8
Fort Apache (AZ)	69.6	48.2	42.6	50.0
Hopi (AZ)	65.8	58.0	9.2	33.1
Zuni Pueblo (NM)	70.5	42.2	28.8	42.8
San Carlos (AZ)	69.4	55.1	40.4	43.6
Rosebud (SD)	49.2	28.9	69.5	29.3
Blackfeet (MT)	49.6	25.9	38.0	28.2
Yakima (WA)	38.7	22.8	20.7	22.0
Eastern Cherokee (NC)	38.4	12.4	57.6	60.8
Standing Rock (ND, SD)	49.8	33.7	53.9	29.9
Osage (OK)	—	5.6	—	31.3
Fort Peck (MT)	36.9	24.0	32.6	27.7
Wind River (WY)	51.8	35.2	35.2	43.7

SOURCES: *Census of Housing, Detailed Housing Characteristics, and General Housing Characteristics, United States Summaries, 1980;* and "American Indians," *1970 Census of Population, Subject Report.*

NOTES: Osage reservation data are not available for 1970. Hopi and Navajo reservation data are not strictly comparable because of administrative changes in Navajo-Hopi joint use area in the 1970s.

a building boom that increased the number of new units built from 67 between 1960 and 1964 to 569 between 1965 and 1968.[11] Between 1969 and 1970, 92 units were built, more than were built in the entire first half of the decade. The Rosebud reservation also is one of the few reservations for which data reasonably comparable to 1970 are available. These figures indicate that the percentage of Indian-occupied housing 10 years old or less may be slightly higher than the percentage of *all* year-round housing units built on the reservation in the past 10 years. For example, 29 percent of all dwellings on the Rosebud reservation and 33 percent of those occupied by Indian householders were constructed after

[11]U.S. Bureau of the Census, *1980 Census of Housing, Detailed Housing Characteristics*, South Dakota state report. The figures for Todd County (see Table 96) are identical to reports for the Rosebud reservation.

1970. This also means that 24 percent fewer new units were constructed on the Rosebud reservation in the 1970s than in the 1960s, lending some credence to complaints that rapidly rising costs slowed Indian housing development in this period.[12] Nevertheless, from the standpoint of total year-round units, most of the largest reservations had larger percentages of recently built dwellings in 1980 than in 1970.

Housing Costs

Rents and Mortgages

The most obvious problem in comparing the costs of housing for American Indians across time and between areas stems from the high rate of inflation during the 1970s. Between 1970 and 1980 inflation increased the prices of all items by about 112 percent,[13] although not uniformly. For example, the costs associated with home purchases and home ownership increased more rapidly than the cost of renting. Home purchase prices increased 115 percent during the 1970s while rental housing prices increased 74 percent. These differences make time comparisons and cost comparisons of rental and mortgage housing difficult, though not impossible.

Inflation also varied between housing markets. The price of housing in some metropolitan areas exploded compared with price increases in other areas, especially nonmetropolitan localities. Conceivably, adjustments can be made to allow for different inflation rates in local housing markets, but for all practical purposes these adjustments are virtually impossible. Therefore, it is important to keep in mind these differences as a possible factor affecting housing prices from one area to another.

Table 4.15 contains estimates of median rents, mortgage payments, and the value of owner-occupied housing. The estimates of median rents distinguish contract from gross rent; contract rent is the amount paid by renters to landlords as stipulated in rental agreements, while gross rent is the total cost of rental housing including fuel and utility bills paid by either the renter or the landlord. As the figures show, the real cost of contract and gross rents increased during the 1970s, regardless of race. In 1970 American Indians and blacks paid about the same contract rent, but for reasons which are not altogether apparent the rents paid by

---

[12]David Stea, "Indian Reservation Housing: Progress Since the "Stanton Report," *American Indian Culture and Research Journal* 6:(1982)1–14.

[13]The Consumer Price Index published by the Commerce Department rose from 116.3 in 1970 to 246.8 in 1980.

TABLE 4.15

Median Rents, Value of Owner-Occupied Housing,
and Mortgage Payments for American Indian, Black, and White
Households (constant 1980 dollars)

	American Indians	Blacks	Whites
1970			
Contract Rent	$127	$124	$164
1980			
Contract Rent	171	156	208
1970			
Gross Rent	—	155	206
1980			
Gross Rent	224	208	251
1970			
Value	19,347	22,786	36,651
1980			
Value	34,400	27,200	48,600
1980			
Mortgage Payment	319	307	371

SOURCES: *1970 Census of Housing, General Housing Characteristics, United States Summary;* "American Indians," *1970 Census of Population, Subject Report; 1980 Census of Housing, General Housing Characteristics, United States Summary;* and *1980 Census of Housing, Detailed Housing Characteristics, United States Summary.*

NOTES: See text for descriptions of gross and contract rents; 1970 white medians are estimated from data for nonblack households. Gross rent figures are unavailable for American Indians in 1970, and mortgage payment data are unavailable for 1970. Mortgage payment figures include selected costs related to home ownership.

Indians increased by over one third while rents paid by blacks and whites increased by about one quarter. In 1980 contract rents paid by American Indians were roughly midway between black and white rental costs—about 10 percent more than black costs and about 22 percent less than white costs. Why this change occurred is difficult to ascertain. More Indians lived in high rent urban areas in 1980 than in 1970, and Indians may have experienced more economic progress than blacks during the 1970s, allowing them to rent more expensive housing. The median household incomes of Indian renters exceeded the median household incomes of black renters by almost 20 percent in 1980—$9,875 for Indians compared with $8,233 for blacks.

Changes similar to those in rental costs took place in the median value of owner-occupied housing. At the beginning of the decade American Indians occupied the least valued housing. However, as the value of black and white owner-occupied housing increased by 20 and 30 percent, the value of Indian-occupied housing increased by a surprising 78 percent, ahead of black-occupied housing but still markedly below the value of white-occupied housing. The relative value of housing owned by Indians, blacks, and whites is reflected in the median mortgage payments made by these groups. An equally surprising finding is that 1980 median household incomes of American Indian homeowners are less than those of black homeowners—$12,000 and $15, 506, respectively. In relation to monthly mortgage payments, this means that a typical, home-owning Indian household with a median income and median mortgage payment must allocate about 31 percent of its gross income for shelter, not including utilities, compared with 24 percent in a similar black household.

Location and Utilities

An indication of how housing costs depend on location is provided by the data in Table 4.16. The results are fairly predictable. Utility costs are relatively invariant with respect to location. Indian households living on or near reservation land typically pay about the same amount for utilities as Indian households in other areas. However, housing costs, either rents or mortgage payments, are more variable and they are lowest in nonmetropolitan areas. Median gross rents and mortgage payments are 36 and 48 percent higher inside SMSAs. Differences in housing costs are much smaller between reservation and nonreservation

TABLE 4.16

Selected Median Monthly Housing Costs
for American Indian and Alaska Native Households (1980 dollars)

Costs	Metropolitan	Nonmetropolitan	Off Reservation	On or Near Reservation
Gross Rent	$255	$188	$246	$220
Mortgage Payment	270	182	253	236
Electricity	33	35	35	32
Natural Gas	30	35	30	30
Other Fuel	21	21	21	21

SOURCE: Public-Use Microdata Sample, 5 percent A File

NOTES: Estimates are based on households with at least one American Indian or Alaska Native. Mortgage payments include selected costs related to home ownership.

areas. Median housing costs on or near reservation land also are slightly lower than costs in nonreservation areas.

In view of how reservation housing has been described, it may be surprising that housing on reservations is more expensive than housing in nonmetropolitan areas. However, reservation and metropolitan status are not mutually exclusive. Some reservations are inside metropolitan areas, and nonmetropolitan housing includes a sizable number of structures inside reservations. The mix of reservations inside and outside metropolitan areas has the net effect of reducing the gap in housing costs between Indian households living inside and outside reservations. This also implies that the rural location of many reservations is a major factor in the low cost of housing in these areas, and not simply their status as reservations.

Regional Differences in Housing Costs

The cost of housing, regardless of race, varies from one area to another depending on market conditions such as local supply and demand and local inflationary pressures. Climate also plays a role; it is less expensive to heat a house in the Southwest than in the Northeast. There are considerable differences in the cost of Indian housing across geographic areas, which are reflected in the median monthly housing costs displayed in Table 4.16.

In terms of gross rents, the West North Central division, which includes the Plains reservations, has the lowest median monthly costs. In contrast, costs in the Pacific are about 50 percent higher; Indians in the Pacific states paid a median $284 in rental costs. In all areas except two, the East North Central and West South Central, mortgage costs are higher than rental costs. Indians in the West South Central division have the lowest median mortgage payments, while those on the West Coast have the highest payments. However, the high cost of housing in the Pacific area is offset somewhat by the fact that Indian households in this area have slightly higher incomes than Indians in other areas of the nation.[14]

Energy costs are especially sensitive to geography because climatic conditions affect demand and because certain areas have access to cheap sources of energy such as hydroelectric power. American Indians in cold weather New England have the largest energy bills. Indians in this area are not heavy consumers of electricity or natural gas, but they apparently rely heavily on fuels such as coal, oil, wood, and kerosene. The cost of these fuels equals the cost of gas and electricity combined, and

[14]See the discussion of American Indian income in Chapter 8.

the total median monthly energy costs for Indians in New England are over $130. At the other extreme, Indians residing in the Pacific and Mountain areas have the lowest fuel-related expenses. Both of these areas have exceedingly low electric costs, which probably reflect the availability of hydroelectric power sources. Other fuel costs also are low in these areas, even in the Mountain states known for frigid winter weather. It is impossible to determine the extent to which Indians supplement their fuel purchases by gathering firewood, but this may partially explain why Indians in these areas have relatively low fuel bills.

Reservation Costs

Table 4.17 presents the limited amount of data available for housing costs on the 16 largest reservations. Housing costs on these reservations are exceedingly low, and much lower than the median costs shown in Table 4.16. However, these tables cannot be compared because of definitional differences concerning reservation status and rent types. The statistics in Table 4.17 reveal median contract rent and housing values for dwellings strictly within reservation boundaries. Data for gross rent are not available. For the 10 reservations with complete data for 1970 and 1980, most have experienced relatively small increases in the real cost of contract rent. In relative terms, 6 of the 10 experienced increases resulting in 17 to 34 percent higher rents in 1980 than in 1970. In contrast, 4 reservations (Pine Ridge, Blackfeet, Standing Rock, and Fort Peck) enjoyed decreases in real rent costs ranging from 10 to 27 percent. Why these declines occurred in a period of high inflation, and while other reservations experienced small increases, is not clear. Public housing programs may have induced these declines, but reporting errors also may be involved.

With a single exception, real housing values on all of the largest reservations increased during the 1970s. About half of these reservations experienced relatively small gains. The Navajo reservation, where the median value of housing was less than $7,000 in 1970 and did not exceed $10,000 in 1980, exemplifies a typical increase. Because exact housing values less than $10,000 are not reported, ascertaining exactly how small the increases are on these reservations is not possible. On reservations with housing values greater than $10,000, most of the increases were substantial. The Wind River reservation in Wyoming experienced the largest increase in the 1970s and by 1980 also reported the highest median housing value of the 16 largest reservations—$38,700 in 1980, up 169 percent from $14,402 in 1970. The Rosebud reservation in South Dakota is the only reservation where the real median value of housing declined. The spate of new housing built on the Rosebud reser-

TABLE 4.17

Median Contract Rent and Value of Owner-Occupied Units
on the 16 Largest Reservations (1980 constant dollars)

Reservation	Monthly Contract Rent		Value of Owner-Occupied Housing	
	1970	1980	1970	1980
Navajo (AZ, NM, UT)	82	96	6,664	LT 10,000
Pine Ridge (SD)	108	98	6,449	LT 10,000
Gila River (AZ)	—	54	6,664	LT 10,000
Papago (AZ)	—	69	6,449	LT 10,000
Fort Apache (AZ)	64	81	7,739	17,800
Hopi (AZ)	66	83	6,449	16,500
Zuni Pueblo (NM)	—	LT 50	13,327	21,800
San Carlos (AZ)	—	LT 50	6,449	LT 10,000
Rosebud (SD)	82	103	14,832	LT 10,000
Blackfeet (MT)	97	86	10,533	29,900
Yakima (WA)	88	118	20,636	31,000
Eastern Cherokee (NC)	—	92	13,972	34,900
Standing Rock (ND, SD)	92	79	6,019	LT 10,000
Osage (OK)	—	97	—	26,200
Fort Peck (MT)	113	89	12,253	21,600
Wind River (WY)	78	99	14,402	38,700

SOURCES: "American Indians, *1970 Census of Population, Subject Report;* and *1980 Census of Housing, General Housing Characteristics, United States Summary.*

NOTES: LT indicates "less than"; the 1980 census publications do not disclose exact rents less than $50 and housing valued less than $10,000. Osage reservation data are not available for 1970, and data for other reservations are missing because they were suppressed by the Census Bureau to protect confidentiality. Hopi and Navajo reservation data are not strictly comparable because of administrative changes in the Navajo-Hopi joint use area in the 1970s.

vation during the mid 1960s apparently is depreciating at a rapid rate as it ages and becomes less attractive. This is especially alarming because it may foretell a similar pattern of decline for much of the new housing built on reservations during the 1970s.

Concluding Remarks

This chapter has sought to describe the housing conditions of American Indians in terms of quantity, quality, and cost in different types of areas and in different locations. The housing of American Indians is not equal to the housing of whites, but in many respects it exceeds the quality of housing of blacks. This is different from 1970 when the housing of American Indians was, in almost every way, worse than the housing of blacks. Some of these gains can probably be attributed to the influence of public housing programs during the 1970s, particularly on reservations. Regrettably, the information necessary to determine this with certainty is not available.

Measures of the housing supply available to American Indians and Alaska Natives include home ownership and the number of rooms per unit. As a rule, American Indians are much more likely to own their homes than blacks, and only slightly less likely than whites. American Indians in rural and reservation areas are more likely to be homeowners than their counterparts in urbanized areas. In the same areas where home ownership is relatively concentrated, the largest percentages of housing with three or fewer rooms can also be found. Similarly, mobile home occupancy is relatively common in these areas.

Housing quality is a difficult concept to measure, but the age, crowdedness, and amenities available in a dwelling reflect, to a degree, the physical well-being of a structure and its inhabitants. The data indicate that American Indians in 1980 live in less crowded housing than they did 10 years earlier, but compared with blacks and whites they continue to occupy relatively crowded quarters. Crowded housing conditions are most common in nonmetropolitan and reservation areas and in the West in general. Ironically, newer housing, some of which presumably is the result of public housing programs, has not had much impact on crowding. Although Indians live in the most crowded housing, it is about as new as the housing of whites and markedly newer than the housing of blacks. In terms of amenities, American Indian housing improved in the 1970s. Public goods such as public sewers and water are less accessible to Indians than to other groups, probably because Indians are more densely concentrated in nonmetropolitan areas, where these facilities are not ordinarily available. Amenities that are not public goods, such as air conditioning, mirror the generally low incomes of most Indian households, especially in rural and reservation areas, where these amenities are less common than in other areas.

If the quality of housing occupied by many American Indians and Alaska Natives is not particularly high, neither is it particularly costly. This is mainly because the expense of better housing is beyond the reach of most American Indian households. American Indians pay less for housing in areas on or near reservations and in nonmetropolitan areas, but housing conditions are generally poorer in these places than in other areas. Other housing expenses, such as energy costs, are roughly the same regardless of location. Energy costs appear most influenced by climate. Unlike housing, the geographic location of energy consumption is much more important in determining costs than the type of areas in which it is consumed.

Out of necessity, this chapter has omitted many details about Indian housing. Nevertheless, the data presented here provide a general overview of Indian housing conditions. The significance of this information is that it represents a basic dimension of the material well-being of the Indian population. This well-being improved during the 1970s, but in most respects Indians still lag behind the mainstream of American society. This is true not only for housing but, as other chapters document, for most other aspects of socioeconomic standing as well.

5

FAMILY AND HOUSEHOLD
STRUCTURE

I
T WOULD NOT be very much of a generalization to state that the family is a pre-eminent institution in the organization of American Indian and Alaska Native cultures. In earlier times family ties made physical survival possible through economic cooperation and mutual defense in difficult and sometimes hostile environments. In such circumstances banishment from one's family could be equivalent to a death sentence. Among contemporary American Indians the family is no longer irreplaceable as an instrument of physical survival. Nevertheless, family networks continue to make up the fabric of tribal social organization. They are central in the day-to-day functions of child-rearing and in the economic lives of many, if not most, American Indians, and an important source of emotional support.

This chapter presents information about the structure and characteristics of American Indian families and about the fertility of Indian women. These issues routinely interest family demographers, but another subject especially pertinent for the American Indian population concerns the extent of intermarriage between Indians and non-Indians. Intermarriage is an important issue because of its implications about the genetic homogeneity of the Indian population and its potential implications for cultural assimilation.

It is important to take note of the precise meanings of terms that the Census Bureau uses to describe family and household characteristics. According to the Census Bureau, a family consists of "two or more persons, including the householder, who are related by birth, marriage, or adoption, and who live together as one household."[1] It also is important to note that not all households contain families and no household contains more than one family. For example, persons living alone or two or more unrelated individuals would constitute households without families. Furthermore, a second family in the household would not, by census definitions, be considered a family if these individuals were not related to the householder. Instead, these individuals are counted as "unrelated household members" despite the fact that they belong to a second family in the same household.

Family is defined strictly in terms of a relationship to the householder based on birth, marriage, or adoption. Recall that a householder is the person, or one of the persons, whose name is on the rental agreement or mortgage. In the absence of such persons, the householder can be any adult over age 15 who is not a boarder or paid employee. Although this definition is reasonably precise, it is worth noting its limitations, especially in the way that it affects information about American Indian families.

One of the most significant problems posed by this view of families is that it is constructed in such a way as to obscure the existence of extended family relationships. Extended families might be regarded as groups of individuals related by birth, marriage, or adoption who function as an economic unit by sharing economic resources such as rent or groceries. In cases where extended families reside in a single household, they would be enumerated as members of subfamilies related to the householder. However, extended families involving large numbers of individuals may not reside in a single household although they may reside in close proximity to one another. For example, an extended family which functions as a single economic unit might nonetheless reside in several separate dwellings, perhaps all within a few hundred yards of each other. Yet by census procedures, this family would not be recognized as a single entity but instead as independent households. Another perhaps more common instance is the situation where parents or grandparents reside in a dwelling such as a mobile home near children or grandchildren. Again, this type of family relationship would not be captured by census procedures.

Another potential problem arises from cultural conceptions of family relationships that differ in meaning from those intended by the Census Bureau. For example, an Indian "grandmother" may actually be a

[1] U.S. Bureau of the Census, *Public-Use Microdata Samples Technical Documentation* (Washington, DC: U.S. Department of Commerce, 1983), p. K-15.

child's aunt or grandaunt in the Anglo-Saxon use of the term. In another instance, extended families may form around complex kinship networks based on clan membership instead of birth, marriage, or adoption. The term "cousin" also may have a variable meaning not necessarily based on birth or marriage. To make these matters even more complex, definitions of family relationships vary from one tribal culture to another. The lesson to be taken from this variability is that the categories used by the Census Bureau to describe family relationships are not uniformly consistent and unambiguous when applied to the American Indian population. Consequently, these data should not be viewed as being precise representations of American Indian family relationships.[2] They are, however, useful approximations and the best data available for the American Indian population.

Household and Family Characteristics

Household Relationships

Table 5.1 shows the distribution of household relationships in the households occupied by blacks, whites, and American Indians. Nonfamily householders are persons who live alone or with persons with whom they have no family relationship, at least not in the sense that the Census Bureau uses the term. As the data in Table 5.1 show, nonfamily householders constitute a relatively small part of all three populations. In relation to their respective populations, white women are the largest group of nonfamily householders (5.9 percent) while Indian women are the smallest group (3.3 percent). Overall, the differences in the percentage of the population residing as nonfamily householders are small, but it is interesting to note that among blacks and whites the percentage of female nonfamily householders is slightly larger than the percentage of male nonfamily householders, while this pattern is reversed for American Indians. This suggests that American Indian men are probably less reluctant than Indian women to live away from their families, alone or with nonrelatives.

While whites have nearly 24 percent male family householders, American Indians and blacks have only 17 and 14 percent, respectively. On the other hand, Indians and blacks have noticeably higher percentages of female householders than whites. In terms of householders,

[2]Robert Staples and Alfredo Mirande, "Racial and Cultural Variations Among American Families: A Decennial Review of the Literature on Minority Families," *Journal of Marriage and the Family* 42(1980):887–903.

TABLE 5.1

Percent Distribution of Household Types and Family Relationships Among Blacks, Whites, and American Indians and Alaska Natives

Household Type and Relationship	Blacks	Whites	American Indians and Alaska Natives
Nonfamily Householder			
Male	4.2	4.1	3.5
Female	4.7	5.9	3.3
Family Householder			
Male	14.0	23.7	17.0
Female	9.8	3.8	6.0
Spouse	13.2	23.6	16.8
Child	41.1	33.1	41.5
Other Relative	9.5	3.3	7.6
Nonrelative	3.5	2.5	4.3
Total	100.0	100.0	100.0
Persons Per Household	3.05	2.68	3.30
Persons Per Family	3.69	3.19	3.83

SOURCE: *1980 Census of Population, General Social and Economic Characteristics, United States Summary.*

blacks and Indians have considerably more in common with each other than they do with whites.

The differences among American Indian, black, and white householders are the same among nonhouseholders. Predictably, American Indians and blacks have smaller percentages of persons as spouses, just as they have fewer male householders. In fact, the percentages of spouses and male householders are about the same for all three groups. Again, blacks and Indians are relatively similar and clearly different from whites. This is also true for children; Indian and black households have significantly more children than white households. Finally, blacks have a larger percentage of persons in "other" family roles than Indians, but Indians have more nonrelatives in their households. This may betray the existence of culturally defined family relationships which are outside the purview of census procedures.

The distribution of black and Indian household composition is similar in a number of ways, but there are some important differences. American Indians typically live in larger households and families than either blacks or whites, though blacks and Indians have almost the same percentages of children, and Indians have fewer of their number residing

TABLE 5.2

Percent Distribution of Marital Status and Median Age at First Marriage for Blacks, Whites, and American Indians and Alaska Natives Aged 15 and Over

Marital Status	Blacks		Whites		American Indians	
	Males	Females	Males	Females	Males	Females
Single	41.1	34.4	28.2	21.2	37.3	28.9
Married, Except Separated	42.6	35.1	62.5	57.4	49.6	48.0
Separated	6.1	8.6	1.4	1.8	2.9	4.1
Widowed	3.8	12.8	2.5	12.6	2.5	8.9
Divorced	6.4	9.1	5.4	7.0	7.7	10.1
Total	100.0	100.0	100.0	100.0	100.0	100.0
Median Age at First Marriage	23.3	20.7	23.2	20.8	22.3	19.7

SOURCES: *1980 Census of Population, General Population Characteristics, United States Summary;* and "Marital Characteristics," *1980 Census of Population, Subject Report.*

in households as "other" or nonrelatives. The most obvious explanation is that American Indians have larger percentages of male householders and spouses and smaller percentages of female householders who typically live in smaller households. This means that American Indians are more likely than blacks to live in intact family units, but with about the same number of children, relatives, and nonrelatives as black households.

The distribution of marital status among blacks, whites, and American Indians and Alaska Natives is shown in Table 5.2 For all of these groups women are more likely than men to be separated, widowed, or divorced. On average, Indians tend to get married about a year earlier than either blacks or whites, and Indians are more likely than blacks but less likely than whites to have been married. A particularly curious finding in Table 5.2 is that unlike black and white women, Indian women are more likely to exit their marriage through legal proceedings than through the death of their spouse.

Place of Residence and Household Relationship

Table 5.3 shows the distribution of persons in households by place of residence. Overall, the differences are remarkably small, and they are nearly nonexistent with respect to metropolitan and nonmetropolitan

TABLE 5.3

Percent Distribution of Household Type and Relationship, by Place of Residence

Household Type and Relationship	Metropolitan	Nonmetropolitan	Off Reservation	On or Near Reservation
In Households	96.9	97.1	97.3	95.9
Householder	33.3	31.9	33.8	30.7
Family Householder	28.8	24.8	24.0	23.4
Nonfamily Householder	9.5	7.1	9.8	7.3
Spouse	17.5	18.5	18.1	16.2
Child	35.1	36.3	34.3	38.1
Brother or Sister	0.9	1.3	0.9	1.1
Parent	0.5	0.7	0.5	0.6
Other Relatives	3.3	4.8	3.5	3.4
Nonrelatives	6.3	3.6	6.0	5.8
Group Quarters	3.1	2.9	2.7	4.1
Inmate	1.0	1.8	1.0	1.2
Other	2.2	1.1	1.7	2.9

SOURCE: Public-Use Microdata Sample, 5 percent A File.

areas: Only 1 percent more American Indians in nonmetropolitan areas are family householders or spouses than in metropolitan areas. Nonfamily householders, not surprisingly, are slightly more prevalent in metropolitan than in nonmetropolitan areas but only by a margin of 9.5 to 7.1 percent, respectively. The percentage of the nonmetropolitan Indian population who are children in households is greater than the percentage of the metropolitan population but, again, the difference is very small. In fact, the largest difference exists in the percentages of American Indians residing in households as nonrelatives: 6.3 percent in metropolitan areas and 3.6 percent in nonmetropolitan areas. Urban American Indians are apparently more inclined than Indians in other areas to share their residences. This most likely reflects roommate situations that defray the typically more costly housing expenses in metropolitan locations.

The differences between Indians in reservation and nonreservation areas are larger than those just described for metropolitan and nonmetropolitan places, though they are not dramatically larger. One interesting difference is that areas on or near reservations have a smaller percentage of persons in households and a larger percentage in group quarters than any other place of residence. There are many possible explanations for this finding, but the most likely is that Bureau of Indian Affairs (BIA) boarding schools are more common in the Southwest and Plains reservations.

As a percentage of the total population, householders are more common in metropolitan and nonreservation areas than in other locales, owing mainly to a larger percentage of nonfamily householders in these places—about 10 percent of the nonreservation Indian population and 7 percent of the reservation population are nonfamily householders. In contrast, the percentage of family householders is nearly the same in both areas. Although there is a substantial overlap between nonmetropolitan and reservation areas, the percentage of persons in households as unrelated individuals is larger on or near reservations, and barely different from nonreservation places. Indeed, the most significant difference between nonreservation places and those on or near reservations is that children make up a greater percentage of the population in the latter (about 38 percent) than in the former (about 34 percent).

The finding that reservation and nonmetropolitan places are hardly different from other places suggests that the composition of Indian households does not vary a great deal from one type of place to another. In particular, persons residing in households as nonrelatives or other relatives are fairly uncommon in places where they might be expected to be more common. Does this mean that the extended kinship networks which are an integral part of traditional Indian culture have all but disappeared? The answer to this question is no, not necessarily. Very clearly, American Indians do not reside in the same household with a large number of extended family members. However, because of the way census data are collected and households are defined, it is impossible to observe kinship ties extending outside the immediate household. As a result, it is not possible to determine the extent and importance of these networks outside the immediate household, or with other households which may be in close proximity.

Patterns of Marital Status

Patterns of marital status are displayed in Table 5.4 for each place of residence. Between metropolitan and nonmetropolitan areas, the differences are small in most instances. There are about 4 percent more single males in nonmetropolitan areas. This is one of the largest differences between metropolitan and nonmetropolitan areas, but it disappears among females. In contrast, nearly the same percentages of men are married in metropolitan and nonmetropolitan areas, but slightly more women who reside in nonmetropolitan areas are married than women who reside in metropolitan areas.

The explanation for this finding is that women marry younger and are less likely to remain single as long as men. Another factor is that

TABLE 5.4

*Percent Distribution of Marital Status
of American Indians and Alaska Natives Aged 15 and Over,
by Place of Residence and Sex*

Sex and Marital Status	Metropolitan	Nonmetropolitan	Off Reservation	On or Near Reservation
Male				
Single	33.8	37.7	32.5	39.0
Married, except separated	51.6	51.1	53.1	49.2
Separated	2.9	2.2	3.0	2.2
Widowed	2.2	2.8	2.2	2.8
Divorced	9.5	6.2	9.2	6.8
Total	100.0	100.0	100.0	100.0
Female				
Single	27.0	27.8	24.6	30.7
Married, except separated	48.8	50.7	50.5	48.4
Separated	4.3	3.4	4.3	3.4
Widowed	8.1	9.9	8.9	8.7
Divorced	11.8	8.2	11.7	8.8
Total	100.0	100.0	100.0	100.0

SOURCE: Public-Use Microdata Sample, 5 percent A File.

the marriage "gap" created by men who divorce and remarry and women who do not is less pronounced in nonmetropolitan areas than in metropolitan areas. Metropolitan places have a larger percentage of divorced Indian men and women than nonmetropolitan places. Indian women in metropolitan areas have the highest percentage of divorced persons, 11.8 percent, compared with 8.2 percent for women in nonmetropolitan areas and 9.5 percent for men in metropolitan areas. The result is that the gap between married Indian men and women is slightly larger in metropolitan locations.

The distribution of marital status in nonreservation and reservation areas is not much different from that in metropolitan and nonmetropolitan areas. The most apparent differences are in connection with the percentages for married and single persons. The relatively youthful population residing on or near reservations means that a substantial percentage of the population—39 percent of males and 31 percent of females—are single. This tends to reduce the percentage of the population currently married by a small amount because the distribution of marital disruptions, voluntary and involuntary, on or near reservations is comparable with other places. One interesting outcome of this situation is that the percentage of married women residing on or near a reservation is slightly smaller than the percentage of married women in nonreservation areas.

Household and Family Types

There are many different types of families and households.[3] It should be remembered, however, that all families reside in households but not all households include families. This discussion deals with a select but general set of family and household types. Specifically, these types are married couples, families that are headed by single males and females, and nonfamily households, namely, households of one or more unrelated individuals excluding persons residing in group quarters such as dormitories. Collectively, these family and household types represent over 95 percent of the households occupied by American Indians.

Comparisons with Blacks and Whites

Table 5.5 shows the distribution of family types among blacks, whites, and American Indians. White households are most likely to contain a married couple family (63.3 percent); in American Indian households 55.4 percent are married couples, while in black households only 41.4 percent are married couples. Similarly, American Indian households have a smaller percentage of single female householders than black households, 17.5 percent and 27.0 percent, respectively, and both of these groups are substantially above the 8.0 percent of white households with single female householders. American Indians occupy a position about midway between blacks and whites in terms of their propensity to live as married couples or as single female householders. About 23 percent of American Indian households consist of nonfamily units compared with approximately 27 percent of black and white households, suggesting that American Indians have a somewhat stronger tendency than blacks or whites to reside in a family environment, either as married couples or as single family householders.

[3]James A. Sweet, "Components of Change in the Number of Households, 1970–1980," *Demography* 21(1984):129–140.

TABLE 5.5

Percent Distribution of Households with Families and Nonfamilies Among Blacks, Whites, and American Indians and Alaska Natives

Household	Married Couples	Female Householders, Spouse Absent	Male Householders, Spouse Absent	Nonfamily Households	Total
Black	41.4	27.0	4.2	27.4	100.0
White	63.3	8.0	2.1	26.6	100.0
American Indian and Alaska Native	55.4	17.5	4.2	22.9	100.0

SOURCE: *1980 Census of Population, General Social and Economic Characteristics, United States Summary.*

Place of Residence and Household Type

The importance of family living arrangements in nonmetropolitan and reservation areas is apparent in Table 5.6. In these areas between 16 and 17 percent of households, respectively, are of the nonfamily type compared with about 20 percent in metropolitan and nonreservation areas. Alternatively, single female householders are most common in nonmetropolitan and reservation areas; in areas on or near a reservation 17 percent of households are occupied by a single female householder

TABLE 5.6

Percent Distribution of American Indian and Alaska Native Household Types, by Place of Residence

Household Type	Metropolitan	Nonmetropolitan	Off Reservation	On or Near Reservation
Married Couple	61.5	63.8	62.8	61.4
Female Householder, Spouse Absent	14.5	16.0	13.7	17.0
Male Householder, Spouse Absent	3.7	4.4	3.5	4.8
Nonfamily Household	20.3	15.8	20.0	16.8
Total	100.0	100.0	100.0	100.0

SOURCE: Public-Use Microdata Sample, 5 percent A File.

compared with about 14 percent in nonreservation areas. The gap is negligible between metropolitan and nonmetropolitan areas, and apart from
nonfamily households and single female householders the differences
associated with place of residence are minimal.

Children and Family Structure

One of the primary reasons for family formation is the care and
rearing of children. By the traditional norms of American society, children are best raised in the stable environment of a married couple
household. Rearing children in households where a spouse is absent is
considered undesirable for a number of reasons: (1) The absence of a
spouse deprives children of important role models necessary for their
socialization and development; (2) homes with a single parent provide a
less stable social environment for the upbringing of children; (3) single-
parent families, especially those of single females with young children,
are economically marginal and more likely to be subject to economic
hardships. Whether single-parent homes are intrinsically unstable or
whether absent role models cause lasting harm cannot be studied with
the demographic data available from the Census Bureau. However, the
economic status associated with different family types can be examined
in detail; a good place to begin is with data for the distribution and age
of children. Table 5.7 shows the presence and age of children for differ-

TABLE 5.7

Percent Distribution of the Presence and Age of Children
in American Indian and Alaska Native Households

Family Type	Married Couples	Female Householders, Spouse Absent	Male Householders, Spouse Absent
With Children Under Age 6 Only	16.1	15.4	18.0
With Children Aged 6–17	32.6	42.1	30.6
With Children Aged 0–17	16.6	14.3	7.2
Without Children	34.7	28.2	44.2
Total	100.0	100.0	100.0

SOURCE: Public-Use Microdata Sample, 5 percent A File.

ent types of families and households. Among married couples, about one third have children aged 6 to 17 while another third have no children in their households. This does not necessarily mean that these couples are childless but only that there are no children living with them. Among the remaining third, about half (16.1 percent) have young children under age 6, while the other half (16.6 percent) have children aged 0 to 17.

Single Female Householders

Single female householders are not very different from married couples in terms of the presence and age of children in their households, except in one very apparent way. These women are substantially more likely than other types of householders to have children aged 6 to 17 living with them—about 42 percent compared with about 31 percent for single male householders and 33 percent for married couples. This finding is undoubtedly the result of marital disruptions—divorce, separation—which occur within a few years after childbirth, combined with legal and social traditions which typically assign child custody to mothers. As one sociologist has noted, "the typical outcome of a marital break-up is that the man becomes single, while the woman becomes a single parent."[4] American Indians, it appears, are not very different from other parts of American society in this respect. This is consistent with the statistic showing that single female householders also are the *least* likely to be in a household without children.

The fact that nationwide about 18 percent of Indian households are headed by a single female householder (see Table 5.5) combined with the fact that over 70 percent of these women are caring for children under age 18 (Table 5.7) underscores the importance of information about the socioeconomic conditions of these households, especially in relation to other types of households. Table 5.8, showing the educational attainments of single female householders, indicates, in part, one of the factors involved with their marginal economic status.

Education: The figures in Table 5.8 show that about 48 percent of single female householders have less than 12 years of schooling. In contrast, 39 percent of the householders in married couple and 38 percent in nonfamily households have an equally low level of education. Especially significant is that about 24 percent of single female householders are high school dropouts with between 9 and 11 years of schooling. This

---

[4]Diana Pearce, "Women in Poverty," in Arthur Blaustein, ed., *The American Promise: Equal Justice and Economic Opportunity* (New Brunswick, NJ: Transaction Books, 1982), p. 12.

TABLE 5.8

*Percent Distribution of Educational Attainments
by American Indian and Alaska Native Householders,
by Household Type*

Years of Schooling	Married Couples	Female Householders, Spouse Absent	Male Householders, Spouse Absent	Nonfamily Households
0–8	21.0	23.9	27.3	23.0
9–11	17.9	23.7	18.2	15.4
12	32.2	29.1	31.6	27.5
13–15	19.1	18.6	17.2	22.0
16 and Over	9.8	4.7	5.7	12.1
Total	100.0	100.0	100.0	100.0

SOURCE: Public-Use Microdata Sample, 5 percent A File.

is significant because other data show that American Indians with 8 years or less of schooling tend to be older, while high school dropouts are younger (see Chapter 7). The implication of this observation is that younger single female householders with less than 12 years of schooling may have dropped out of school to become mothers.

Labor Force Participation: The limited education and child care responsibilities of single female householders predictably translate into a marginal attachment to the labor force for these women. As the data in Table 5.9 show, 47.2 percent of single female householders do not par-

TABLE 5.9

*Percent Distribution of Labor Force Participation
of Civilian American Indian and Alaska Native Householders,
by Household Type*

Labor Force Status	Married Couples	Female Householders, Spouse Absent	Male Householders, Spouse Absent	Nonfamily Households
Employed	72.0	46.1	64.0	54.8
Unemployed	7.3	6.7	9.5	7.0
Not in Labor Force	20.7	47.2	26.5	38.2
Total	100.0	100.0	100.0	100.0

SOURCE: Public-Use Microdata Sample, 5 percent A File.

ticipate in the labor force and 46.1 percent are employed. These figures are especially striking compared with the householders in married couples; 20.7 percent of this group are not in the labor force and 72.0 percent are employed. The only group that approaches the marginal labor force attachment of single female householders is householders in nonfamily households, with 38.2 percent of their number not in the labor force. However, many of these individuals are not in the labor force because, very likely, they are attending school—hence their high educational attainments.

Income: Table 5.10 shows the economic standing of households and householders as measured by poverty status and several different types of income. A clear indication of the marginal economic status of single female householders is that 33.5 percent of these women received public assistance income in 1979. In comparison, only 6.0 percent of married couple householders required public assistance. The differences between

TABLE 5.10

Characteristics of Income Received by American Indians
and Alaska Natives in 1979, by Household Type

	Married Couples	Female Householders, Spouse Absent	Male Householders, Spouse Absent	Nonfamily Households
Percentage of Householders Receiving Public Assistance	6.0	33.5	10.1	12.9
Percentage Below Poverty Line	16.7	47.3	22.5	31.3
Median Wages and Salaries of Householders	$12,005	6,005	10,005	8,505
Median Total Income of Householders	$11,165	5,005	9,005	6,305
Median Household Income	$18,005	8,610	15,095	8,845
Median Family Income	$17,870	7,710	13,105	*

SOURCE: Public-Use Microdata Sample, 5 percent A File.

*Not applicable.

these households are equally dramatic for the incidence of poverty; 16.7 percent of married couple householders reported incomes below the official poverty threshold in 1979. This figure is slightly higher than the poverty rate for the nation as a whole, but it is well below the figure for single female Indian householders. Among these women, 47.3 percent are poverty-stricken. This statistic is even more alarming when we recall that 71.8 percent (see Table 5.7) of these women have child care responsibilities.

In terms of other kinds of income, the situation of single female householders is no different, and married couple households are decisively ahead of other household types. Focusing on median family and household income, the gap between married couple householders and single female householders is substantial. For instance, the median family income of married householders ($18,005) is over twice the median family income of single female householders. The largest disparity between these household types is with respect to family income: The median incomes of the families of married couples is 2.3 times larger than the incomes of the families of single women. One reason why the gap between these households is slightly greater for family income than for household income is that single females may depend on sharing their residences with persons outside their immediate family for the purpose of generating additional income for household expenses, thereby raising their household income but not their family income.

Childbearing

Age-specific fertility and children ever born are two commonly used measures of childbearing behavior. Age-specific fertility measures current levels of fertility, while children ever born (also known as parity) reflects cumulative, lifetime fertility. This discussion begins with data for age-specific fertility but focuses mostly on children ever born. For obvious reasons, the number of children ever born to American Indian and Alaska Native women has a decisive role in the size of families and households. It also mirrors long-term processes such as changing norms regarding desirable family size and the use of contraceptives.[5]

[5]For additional descriptions of Indian fertility, see Frank D. Bean and John P. Marcum, "Differential Fertility and the Minority Group Status Hypothesis: An Assessment and Review," in Frank D. Bean and W. Parker Frisbie, eds., *The Demography of Racial and Ethnic Groups* (New York: Academic Press, 1978); and Stephen J. Kunitz, "Fertility, Mortality, and Social Organization," *Human Biology* 48(1976):361–377. See also Jamshid A. Momeni, *Demography of Racial and Ethnic Minorities in the United States: An Annotated Bibliography with a Review Essay* (Westport, CT: Greenwood Press, 1984).

Readers should be aware, however, that statistics for children ever born should be viewed carefully, especially for younger women who are still in their childbearing years. Nevertheless, comparisons of cumulative fertility among different groups of young women at a given age can provide useful insights into fertility-related behavior. Furthermore, details about the number of children ever born are the only American Indian fertility data available in census sources, and very little information about American Indian fertility exists elsewhere.

Age-Specific Fertility

The peak childbearing years of Indian women are shown in the age-specific fertility rates[6] of Table 5.11. Since 1965 Indian women aged 20–24 have been consistently the most fertile age group, though their fertility has declined in recent years. Beginning in 1965 Indian women aged 20–24 gave birth to approximately 2.2 children per woman in the five-year period ending in 1969. Ten years later, Indian women of the same age showed a marked reduction in their fertility by having only 1.6 children per woman between 1975 and 1979. The decline in fertility among these women of peak childbearing age is part of a decrease in fertility among all Indian women under age 45.

The steep reduction in American Indian fertility is easily seen in the figures for the total fertility of Indian women. Between 1965 and 1969 the total fertility was approximately 3.4 children. Ten years later, it dropped to about 2,400 children per 1,000 women, a reduction of 29 percent. The decline was not the result of uniform reductions in births by Indian women of all childbearing ages. Across time, the cohorts of Indian women over age 30 have most steeply curtailed their fertility with reductions ranging from 39 percent for women aged 30–34 to 50 percent for those aged 35–39. Under age 30 decreases in age-specific fertility were about 27 percent for women aged 20–29. Teen-age fertility declined least, by only 8 percent.

The decreases in age-specific American Indian fertility are part of a trend coinciding with the end of the postwar "baby boom." In an analysis of minority fertility patterns, Rindfuss and Sweet observed that total American Indian fertility declined 29 percent between 1957 and

[6]These figures were estimated by own children ever born to Indian women with techniques described in Robert D. Retherford and Lee-Jay Cho, "Age-Parity-Specific Birth Rates and Birth Probabilities from Census or Survey Data on Own Children," *Population Studies* 32(1978):567–581. Further details are available in Michael J. Levin and Nancy Breen, "Recent Fertility Trends Among American Indians in the United States," paper presented at the annual meeting of the Population Association of America, Chicago, 1987.

TABLE 5.11

Age-Specific Fertility Rates per 1,000 American Indian Women,
1965–1979

Age	1965–1969	1970–1974	1975–1979
15–19	92	89	85
20–24	216	177	160
25–29	168	133	122
30–34	113	84	69
35–39	66	44	33
40–44	25	19	13
45–49	6	5	5
Total Fertility Rate	3,423	2,751	2,427

SOURCE: U.S. Bureau of the Census, unpublished tabulations.

1969.[7] Most of this decline, 27 percent, occurred between 1963 and 1969, meaning that total fertility decreased only 2 percent between 1957 and 1963.[8] Rindfuss and Sweet attribute declines in fertility to changes in the composition of the Indian population arising from increasing numbers of persons declaring their race as Indian instead of white or some other race. They argue:

> The fact that the 1960 fertility measure based on persons enumerated as Indians at that time is so much higher than the 1970 measure based on persons reporting themselves as Indian in 1970 suggests that those persons who redefined themselves as Indian by 1970 had substantially lower fertility than those people who were defining themselves as Indian as of 1960. Our guess would be that the 1960 "Indian" population was predominantly a reservation population with low income and education.[9]

Rindfuss and Sweet are generally correct about the composition of the 1960 Indian population, but they do not provide any evidence supporting their conjecture that compositional changes stemming from changes in racial self-identification may have artificially lowered estimates of Indian fertility. However, the Indian Health Service (IHS), a major source of health care for reservation Indians, maintains fertility data for American Indians in the 32 states with reservations that it

[7]Ronald R. Rindfuss and James A. Sweet, *Postwar Fertility Trends and Differentials in the United States* (New York: Academic Press, 1977).

[8]Rindfuss and Sweet (1977), p. 91.

[9]Rindfuss and Sweet (1977), p. 101.

serves. IHS estimated 99.8 births per 1,000 Indian women aged 20–24 between 1980 and 1982.[10] It is difficult to compare this rate with the rates in Table 5.11 because it is obviously subsequent to the 1975–1979 period, and especially because it covers a three-year instead of five-year period.

However, assuming that the fertility of Indian women aged 20–24 between 1975 and 1979 is not dramatically different from their fertility between 1980 and 1982, it is possible to average the 99.8 per 1,000 estimate across three years and multiply it by 5 to obtain a five-year estimate. Doing this yields a fertility rate of 166 per 1,000 Indian women aged 20 to 24, which can be compared with the rate of 160 per 1,000 Indian women of the same age (see Table 5.11). Comparing IHS and census fertility estimates produces similar results for other age groups. While this comparison is imprecise, it implies that fertility estimates for the total U.S. Indian population based on census data are not dramatically different from IHS estimates based on populations with large concentrations of reservation residents. In short, the changes in racial self-identification noted by Rindfuss and Sweet may account for a small amount of the decline in Indian fertility, but they hardly explain the sharp drop in the age-specific fertility of American Indian women.

Racial Differences in Fertility

It is clear that the fertility of Indian women is greater than the fertility of white women. The total fertility rate of 2.4 is above the level needed for natural replacement and well above the 1.8 figure reported for white women in 1980.[11] White women also differ from Indian women by having their peak childbearing years throughout their 20s. In contrast, Indian women reach their maximum fertility in their early 20s, followed by reductions in the years thereafter. Not only do Indian women have more children than white women, but they also have them sooner.

To present a better view of these differences, Figures 5.1 and 5.2 show racial differences in fertility from two different perspectives. Figure 5.1 shows the crude fertility rates for American Indians and other groups between 1970 and 1983. Differences over time in crude birthrates can arise from a variety of sources besides real changes in fertility

[10] U.S. Office of Technology Assessment, *Indian Health Care* (Washington, DC: U.S. Government Printing Office, 1986), p. 76.

[11] Suzanne M. Bianchi and Daphne Spain, *American Women in Transition* (New York: Russell Sage Foundation, 1986), p. 48.

FIGURE 5.1

Birthrates per 1,000 American Indians and Alaska Natives,
All Races, and Nonwhites, 1970–1983

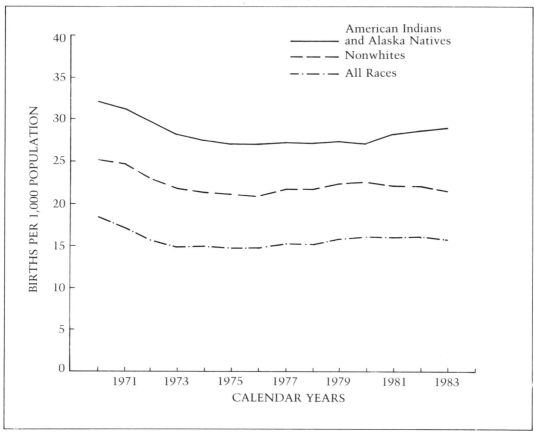

SOURCE: Indian Health Service Chart Series Book, April 1987.

behavior. Thus, one should not make too much of the details in Figure 5.1. All of these groups exhibited a small decline in their birthrates at the beginning of the 1970s. For the balance of this decade and into the 1980s, birthrates were relatively flat. This pattern is well known for blacks (who make up the largest group of "nonwhites") and for whites. This also appears to be true for American Indians and Alaska Natives. What is most remarkable about Figure 5.1 is that American Indian fertility has been, and continues to be, much higher than the fertility of either whites (the largest component of "all races") or nonwhite minority groups. In fact, the crude birthrates of the American Indian population are nearly twice the crude rates of the United States as a whole.

145

In Figure 5.2 the average (mean) number of children ever born to black, white, and American Indian and Alaska Native women is shown for women aged 15 and over in 1980. Most women complete their child-bearing before reaching age 45, and, as Figure 5.2 illustrates, black and American Indian women under this age have similar numbers of children ever born. Between ages 20 and 44, American Indian women have a slightly higher average number of children ever born than black women, but this difference is small. For example, American Indian women aged 35–39 have had an average of 3.27 children ever born,

FIGURE 5.2

Mean Number of Children Ever Born to Ever-Married Black, White, and American Indian and Alaska Native Women

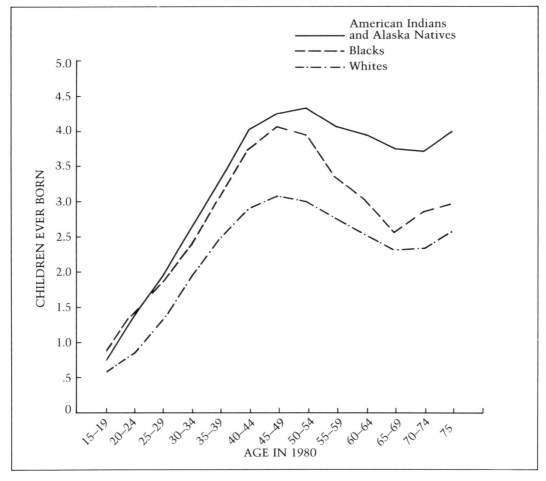

while black women have had 3.06 children and white women have had only 2.46 children.

Finally, the most striking differences in Figure 5.2 are for older women who have completed their fertility, say age 45 and over. Among blacks, whites, and American Indians and Alaska Natives, there are clear differences. Predictably, white women have the smallest number of children ever born, the average number ranging from about 3.1 for women aged 45–49 to about 2.3 for women aged 65–69. Black women have significantly higher fertility than white women, but American Indians have considerably more children ever born than either blacks or whites. On average, American Indian women over age 44 have 52 percent more children ever born than white women of the same ages, which means that the number of children ever born to American Indian women exceeds those born to white women by more than one child.

The number of children ever born to American Indian women, compared with black women and especially with white women, can be viewed from two different perspectives: the *social characteristics hypothesis* and the *minority group status hypothesis*.[12] The social characteristics hypothesis argues that blacks and other minorities have higher fertility than whites because minorities are poorer and less educated. As the socioeconomic characteristics of minorities become more similar to those of whites, the social characteristics hypothesis predicts a convergence in the fertility rates of these groups. In contrast, the minority group status hypothesis predicts that converging socioeconomic characteristics will not fully eradicate differences in fertility behavior. This perspective hypothesizes that minority groups, net of their economic position, maintain different values regarding the importance of children, ideal family size, contraceptive methods, and other ideas that impact on fertility. According to the minority group status hypothesis, such values are not fundamentally altered by changing socioecomomic status. As a result, minority groups will continue to have more, or fewer, children than is the norm for white couples, regardless of converging socioeconomic statuses.

Given the substantial differences that exist between American Indian and European cultures, and the large gap between white and American Indian fertility, the minority group status hypothesis is an appealing explanation. However, empirical support for this hypothesis, especially vis-à-vis the social characteristics hypothesis, is not unequivocal. The data supporting one or the other of these hypotheses provide

---

[12]Bean and Marcum (1978); also see Charles F. Westoff and Norman B. Ryder, "Contraceptive Practice Among Urban Blacks in the United States, 1965," *Milbank Memorial Fund Quarterly* 48(1970):215–233.

mixed assessments, and they are from studies of groups such as blacks or Catholics.[13] In a study of Canadian Indians, both hypotheses were supported.[14] This research found that improvements in socioeconomic status led to reductions in fertility, but net of these improvements it appeared that Canadian Indian fertility would remain higher than white fertility.

There is little consensus about these issues, and this discussion cannot begin to undertake their resolution. In subsequent tables it will be clear that lower levels of American Indian fertility, in the form of smaller numbers of children ever born, are associated with higher levels of socioeconomic status. However, it is not clear whether the complete socioeconomic assimilation of American Indians, in the unlikely event that this occurs, would necessarily result in fertility patterns identical to whites.

Geographic Differences in Fertility

Region: Geographic differences in fertility are interesting because regions such as census divisions can be associated, in a rough sense, with differences in tribal cultures. The tribal composition of the Mountain states area is very different from that of the East North Central area, for example. To the extent that there are significant tribal differences in fertility behavior, it might be possible to detect them in the geographic distribution of children ever born. At the very least, such information reveals where American Indian fertility tends to be highest and lowest and the degree of regional variation.

Table 5.12 shows the mean number of children ever born to Indian women throughout the United States. With a couple of exceptions, the distribution of children ever born is remarkably homogeneous. Younger women aged 15–24 have an average number of children ever born well below 2.0, ranging from 1.1 to 1.5. In contrast, the oldest cohort of Indian women varies widely from 4.0 to 5.3. In most areas, between two and three children seems to be the preferred number of offspring. These findings suggest that tribal variations in fertility behavior are not especially large or, equally plausible, that the regional classification in this table is not sufficiently sensitive to capture differences in tribal cultures.

[13]Calvin Goldscheider and Peter R. Uhlenberg, "Minority Group Status and Fertility," *American Journal of Sociology* 74(1969):361–372.
[14]Frank Trovato, "A Macrosociological Analysis of Native Indian Fertility in Canada: 1961, 1971, 1981," *Social Forces* 66(1987):463–485.

TABLE 5.12

*Geographic Distribution of Mean Number of Children Ever Born
to Ever-Married American Indian and Alaska Native Women
Aged 15–54 in 1980*

Census Division	Age				
	15–24	25–34	35–44	45–54	Total
New England	1.11	2.20	3.51	4.32	2.91
Mid Atlantic	1.29	2.18	3.58	3.99	2.85
E. North Central	1.11	2.27	3.52	4.25	2.80
W. North Central	1.27	2.61	4.14	4.88	3.20
South Atlantic	1.13	2.02	3.51	4.03	2.58
E. South Central	1.18	2.08	3.45	3.69	2.58
W. South Central	1.09	2.14	3.20	3.57	2.52
Mountain	1.49	2.51	4.24	5.34	3.30
Pacific	1.16	2.15	3.34	3.89	2.63

SOURCE: Public-Use Microdata Sample, 5 percent A File.

Two areas are markedly different from most other parts of the United States. These areas are exceptional by virtue of the high fertility of women residing in these places. For example, in the West North Central states the average number of children ever born ranges from 1.3 to 4.9 for the youngest and oldest cohorts of women, respectively. In the Mountain states the range is from 1.5 to 5.3 children ever born. It is hardly surprising that these areas also have the smallest percentages of childless women, less than 10 percent in both areas. The notably higher numbers of children ever born in these areas lend credence to Rindfuss and Sweet's suppositions about the high fertility of Indians residing on reservations, since many of the largest Indian reservations are located in these areas.

Residence: The relationship between cumulative fertility and place of residence, particularly reservation residence, can be observed directly in Table 5.13. Nonmetropolitan areas differ very little from reservation areas, reflecting the large overlap of reservation and nonmetropolitan Indian populations. Fertility is highest in nonmetropolitan and/or reservation locations, where American Indian women average 3.2 children ever born (compared with 2.6 children for women in metropolitan loca-

TABLE 5.13

*Place of Residence and Mean Number of Children Ever Born
to Ever-Married American Indian and Alaska Native Women
Aged 15–54 in 1980*

	Residence			
Age	Metropolitan	Nonmetropolitan	Off Reservation	On or Near Reservation
15–24	1.15	1.36	1.09	1.43
25–34	2.09	2.54	2.10	2.49
35–44	3.35	4.06	3.27	4.11
45–54	3.81	5.00	3.74	4.95
Total	2.59	3.20	2.55	3.20

SOURCE: Public-Use Microdata Sample, 5 percent A File.

tions). The numbers in this table show that Indian women in nonmetropolitan areas not only have more children by the time they finish childbearing, but they also have more children at younger ages.

One reason why American Indian women in nonmetropolitan and/or reservation areas have more children than women in other areas is that the traditional values of some tribes attach a premium to large families and that tribal culture is most likely to be strongest in rural and/or reservation communities. Another reason is that women residing in nonmetropolitan and reservation areas have less education and lower incomes than women in other places. The combination of these factors is responsible for the sizable differences in fertility associated with place of residence.

Age at First Marriage

The age at which American Indian women first marry is related to children ever born for the obvious reason that, like other women, most Indian women do not begin having children until after they are married. However, the prevalence of traditional "Indian marriages" and other kinds of common law arrangements introduces a considerable amount of slippage into what constitutes a marriage. Distinguishing simple cohabitation from longer term, established, and in some cases legally binding common law relationships is virtually impossible.

Nevertheless, Table 5.14 shows the association between age at first marriage and the number of children ever born to American Indian

TABLE 5.14

Mean Number of Children Ever Born and Age at First Marriage
of American Indian and Alaska Native Women Aged 15–54 in 1980

Age in 1980	Age at First Marriage		
	Under 20	20–24	25 and Over
15–24	1.33	0.96	*
25–34	2.57	2.02	1.55
35–44	4.05	3.27	2.76
45–54	4.77	3.97	3.48
Total	3.03	2.54	2.62[a]

SOURCE: Public-Use Microdata Sample, 5 percent A File.

*Not applicable.

[a]Includes only women aged 25–54 in 1980.

women. Overall, this table renders the not-too-surprising finding that Indian women, like other women, tend to have fewer children if they delay marriage than if they marry at a relatively young age.

Indian women who first married under age 20 had an average of 3.0 children ever born while women who delayed marriage until their early 20s had an average of 2.5 children. This pattern persists for all age groups in Table 5.14. Not surprisingly, however, the largest gap exists between women who have completed, or are about to complete, their childbearing years. Among these American Indian women, those who married in their teens had an average of 1.25 more children than women of the same ages who delayed marriage until their late 20s or later. In relative terms, older American Indian women who married in their teens had an average of 42 percent more children ever born than women of the same ages who delayed marriage.

Socioeconomic Status and Fertility

The next tables deal with the relationship between economic characteristics and children ever born. There is a well-known inverse relationship between socioeconomic status and fertility in which higher statuses are associated with fewer children.[15]

[15]Linda J. Waite and Glenna D. Spitze, "Young Women's Transition to Marriage," *Demography* 18(1976):681–694; and Lynne Smith-Lovin and Ann R. Tickamyer, "Nonrecursive Models of Labor Force Participation, Fertility Behavior, and Sex Role Attitudes," *American Sociological Review* 43(1978):541–556.

TABLE 5.15

*Educational Attainments and Mean Number of Children Ever Born
to Ever-Married American Indian and Alaska Native Women
Aged 15–54 in 1980*

Years of Schooling Completed	Age				
	15–24	25–34	35–44	45–54	Total
0–8	1.80	3.27	4.65	5.34	4.47
9–11	1.42	2.86	4.20	4.57	3.19
12	1.15	2.19	3.27	3.56	2.46
13–15	0.95	1.96	2.97	3.46	2.24
16 and Over	0.63	1.35	2.46	2.78	1.86

SOURCE: Public-Use Microdata Sample, 5 percent A File.

Education: Table 5.15 shows the inverse relationship between years of schooling completed and children ever born to American Indian and Alaska Native women. This relationship is most apparent in comparisons between poorly educated and well-educated women. For example, the least-educated women averaged 4.47 children ever born, while the most-educated women averaged 1.86 children. The mean number of children ever born varies across age groups, of course, but the inverse relationship between education and children ever born is consistently apparent among women regardless of age.

The inverse relationship between education and fertility has been observed and well documented for black and white women. Although this relationship has not been documented for Indian women, there are few reasons to expect that they are unique in terms of the ways fertility affects education and vice versa. For black and white women, and in all likelihood for American Indian women as well, there are several explanations for the inverse relationship between fertility and education.[16] One explanation is that education can alter preferences for children and that more educated couples are more successful in achieving desired family sizes. Among American Indians, this may mean that better-educated women are less wedded to traditional values about the importance of large families and are more inclined to limit their childbearing.

Another explanation is that the time spent pursuing an education tends to delay motherhood. Furthermore, well-educated women may

[16]Bianchi and Spain (1986).

152

TABLE 5.16

*Civilian Labor Force Participation and Mean Number of Children
Ever Born to Ever-Married American Indian
and Alaska Native Women Aged 15–54 in 1980*

Age	Employed	Unemployed	Not in Labor Force
15–24	0.99	1.24	1.44
25–34	1.98	2.24	2.63
35–44	3.32	3.90	3.97
45–54	3.92	4.77	4.54
Total	2.58	2.65	3.43

SOURCE: Public-Use Microdata Sample, 5 percent A File.

also limit their childbearing in order to pursue opportunities in the workplace.[17] Finally, there is some evidence that childbearing at early ages limits educational attainment.[18] Early marriages facilitate childbearing at younger ages, and data indicate that American Indian women tend to get married earlier than other women. For example, the median age at first marriage is 19.7, 20.7, and 20.8 years for American Indian, black, and white women, respectively.[19]

Work: Not surprisingly, labor force participation is another socioeconomic characteristic highly sensitive to fertility behavior. Perhaps no other event in a woman's life is more influential in decisions about joining or remaining a part of the work force than the event of childbirth. However, there is no consensus about whether women voluntarily withdraw from the labor force for childbirth and child-rearing activities or whether the event of childbirth necessarily curtails labor force participation. Regardless, the data in Table 5.16 show the inverse relationship between cumulative fertility and the labor force participation of American Indian women. Overall, these data show that women who are not in the labor force have the largest number of children ever born.

[17]Rindfuss and Sweet (1977); Ronald R. Rindfuss, Larry L. Bumpass, and Craig St. John, "Education and Fertility: Implications for the Roles Women Occupy," *American Sociological Review* 45(1980):431–437; Charles F. Westoff and Norman B. Ryder, *The Contraceptive Revolution* (Princeton, NJ: Princeton University Press, 1977).

[18]Linda J. Waite and Kirstin A. Moore, "The Impact of Early First Birth on Young Women's Educational Attainment," *Social Forces* 56(1978):845–865.

[19]U.S. Bureau of the Census, "Marital Characteristics," *1980 Census of Population, Subject Report,* PC80-2-4C (Washington, DC: U.S. Government Printing Office, 1985).

Among women who are in the labor force, employed women have slightly fewer children ever born than unemployed women.

There are two opposing explanations for the inverse relationship between fertility and labor force participation, both of which rest on the incompatibility of the roles associated with child-rearing and employment outside the home.[20] One explanation is that labor force participation is a function of fertility and not vice versa—that increasing child care responsibilities, in terms of the number of children and their ages, diminishes the likelihood that a woman will enter the labor force.[21] American Indian women are most likely to be employed while they are relatively young and then to leave the labor force as they grow older and enter their childbearing and child-rearing years.

A second explanation is that fertility is a function of labor force participation and that women may limit their childbearing in order to pursue opportunities in the labor market. From this viewpoint, poorly educated American Indian women with few job skills will have more children because they have fewer prospects in the labor force. Buttressing this argument is the often-made observation that for all races, American Indians included, increases in female labor force participation rates have been accompanied by decreases in fertility.[22]

Disentangling the causal relationship between fertility and labor force participation is likely to challenge social scientists for the foreseeable future. Bianchi and Spain summarize this best by noting that "the inherent chicken-and-egg nature of this debate may explain why it is so hard to resolve. And which comes first probably matters more to academic researchers than to the women actually involved. . . . [T]he best explanation for the negative correlation between employment and fertility seems to be that the role of mother often conflicts with the role of paid employee in our society."[23] Suffice it to say that however this debate is settled, American Indian women are not exceptional in being exempt from the endemic conflicts between working and parenting.

---

[20]Robert H. Weller, "The Employment of Wives, Role Incompatibility and Fertility," *Milbank Memorial Fund Quarterly* 46(1967):507–526; Larry L. Bumpass and Charles F. Westoff, *The Later Years of Childbearing* (Princeton, NJ: Princeton University Press, 1970); Bianchi and Spain (1986).

[21]Smith-Lovin and Tickamyer (1978); Bianchi and Spain (1986).

[22]Linda J. Waite and Ross M. Stolzenberg, "Intended Childbearing and Labor Force Participation of Young Women: Insights from Nonrecursive Models," *American Sociological Review* 41(1976):235–252; see also William Butz and Michael Ward, "The Emergence of Countercyclical U.S. Fertility," *American Economic Review* 69(1979):318–327; Richard A. Easterlin, *Birth and Fortune* (New York: Basic Books, 1980); and Bianchi and Spain (1986).

[23]Bianchi and Spain (1986), p. 224.

Family Income and Childbearing

The inverse relationship between cumulative fertility and charac-teristics such as education and labor force participation is relatively lin-ear, and most likely reciprocal: Greater numbers of children ever born result in lower levels of educational attainment and impede labor force participation. Similarly, well-educated women who are active in the la-bor force tend to have fewer children over the course of their lifetime. Despite the inverse relationship of cumulative fertility to other eco-nomic characteristics, the association between family income and fertil-ity is more complex in at least three ways.

Family income may be inversely related to children ever born be-cause American Indian families with relatively high incomes may re-flect the joint efforts of dual-earner couples, especially in view of the relatively low earnings of American Indian men.[24] Higher family in-comes depend on higher levels of female labor force participation, which in turn reduces the number of children ever born. By the same token, women may limit their fertility to facilitate labor force participation and thereby enhance their family income. Regardless, the upshot of these conditions is that cumulative fertility is negatively associated with family income because it also is negatively related to factors that are directly responsible for higher or lower levels of family income.

However, a plausible counterargument can be made that family in-come is positively related to fertility, particularly children ever born: As family income rises, the number of children desired and the number of children ever born increases.[25] Higher family income means that having additional children will pose a relatively small financial burden. In the extreme, families blessed with unlimited financial resources are also blessed with the privilege of having as many children as they wish, without the limits imposed by the financial costs of child-rearing. In this way, higher family income promotes higher fertility and the num-ber of children ever born, resulting in a positive association between them.

A third possibility is that the aforementioned contingencies offset one another with respect to raising or lowering the number of children ever born: namely, higher family incomes may promote higher fertility, but at the same time the conditions promoting higher family incomes—education and labor force participation—limit the number of children

[24]See Chapter 8 for further details about American Indian incomes.
[25]This idea is closely related to Easterlin's hypothesis about swings in fertility and the changing economic fortunes of men.

TABLE 5.17

*Family Income and Mean Number of Children Ever Born
to Ever-Married American Indian and Alaska Native Women
Aged 15–54 in 1980*

Family Income	15–24	25–34	35–44	45–54	Total
Under $2,500	1.24	1.86	3.11	3.45	2.42
2,500–4,999	1.38	2.81	4.20	4.90	3.22
5,000–7,499	1.48	2.70	4.38	4.94	3.15
7,500–9,999	1.33	2.49	4.12	4.59	2.95
10,000–12,499	1.31	2.48	4.14	4.83	3.00
12,500–14,999	1.19	2.35	3.84	4.54	2.77
15,000–17,499	1.13	2.36	3.63	4.46	2.77
17,500–19,999	1.09	2.27	3.40	5.03	2.79
20,000 and Over	1.03	2.00	3.30	4.01	2.76

SOURCE: Public-Use Microdata Sample, 5 percent A File.

that women are able to bear. It appears from the data in Table 5.17 that both contingencies are operative, with the result that there is virtually no apparent relationship between family income and the number of children ever born. The differences in the average number of children ever born are very small across income categories. Furthermore, the gap between the richest and the poorest families is not large.

American Indian women in the poorest families tend to have the least number of children, overall and within cohorts. Slightly higher incomes are associated with larger average numbers of children ever born. However, families with yet higher levels of income have slightly smaller numbers of children ever born. These results make it impossible to characterize easily the relationship between fertility and family income.

Racial Intermarriage

Needless to say, not all American Indians choose other American Indians as their spouses; they also marry persons with black, Asian, Hispanic, or white backgrounds. The racial characteristics of the spouses of American Indians are significant from at least two perspectives: (1) The extent to which American Indians are selected by non-Indians as marriage partners is an important indicator of racial discrimination; discriminatory practices and prejudicial beliefs reduce intermarriage by making members of particular racial or ethnic groups unacceptable as potential marriage partners. (2) Intermarriage represents an important form of cultural diffusion; Indians who marry non-Indians are more likely to enter mainstream American culture and, by the same token, some non-Indians who marry Indians will become incorporated into the tribal cultures of their spouses.

Racial Differences

Patterns of intermarriage are usually cast in terms of endogamy and exogamy. An endogamous marriage is between persons of the same race, and an exogamous marriage is between persons of different races. Table 5.18 shows patterns of racial endogamy and exogamy among blacks, whites, and American Indians and Alaska Natives. As the statistics in

TABLE 5.18

Percent Distribution of Racial Endogamy and Exogamy Among Blacks, Whites, and American Indians and Alaska Natives

Race	Whites	Blacks	American Indians and Alaska Natives
Wife's Race			
White	99.0	0.8	48.0
Black	0.2	98.8	2.1
American Indian	0.3	0.1	46.3
Asian[a]	0.1	0.0	0.3
Other	0.4	0.3	3.3
Total	100.0	100.0	100.0
Husband's Race			
White	98.9	2.6	48.3
Black	0.1	96.4	1.1
American Indian	0.3	0.2	47.6
Asian[a]	0.3	0.3	0.5
Other	0.4	0.5	2.5
Total	100.0	100.0	100.0

SOURCE: "Marital Characteristics," *1980 Census of Population, Subject Report.*
[a]Includes Japanese, Chinese, and Filipinos.

this table make amply clear, American Indians have high rates of exogamy compared with blacks or whites. Among married American Indian men and women, only about 47 percent are married to other Indians. In contrast, marital endogamy is about 98 percent among whites.

There are a number of possible explanations for why American Indians have such remarkably high rates of intermarriage. The most readily apparent reason is that American Indians are perceived, especially by whites, as more socially acceptable marriage partners than are blacks. Among American Indian men, 48.0 percent were married to white women. Similarly, 48.3 percent of Indian women were married to white men. Interestingly, Indian men resemble white men in being slightly more likely than their female counterparts to choose a black person as a spouse. About 1 percent of Indian women have black husbands, while 2 percent of Indian men have black wives.

Geographic Differences

Apart from racial preferences, another factor which probably contributes to the high rates of intermarriage for American Indians is their small population size. The fact that Indians are not shunned as marriage partners, especially by whites, means that the pool of potential partners is greatly enlarged by the prospect of intermarriage. From this perspective, intermarriage occurs simply because the pool of acceptable non-Indian partners vastly outnumbers the pool of potential mates among Indians.

If high rates of intermarriage are partially the result of greater opportunities to marry non-Indians than Indians, then areas with relatively small Indian populations should have significantly higher levels of exogamy than areas with relatively large American Indian populations. The data in Table 5.19 suggest that this is indeed the case in many areas of the United States. For example, the New England states have a very small Indian population, in absolute and relative numbers. As expected, this area also has the lowest percentage of racially endogamous Indian couples (9.4 percent) of any area in the United States. Indian men in this area seem especially predisposed to take non-Indian wives (49.0 percent), while Indian women seem somewhat less inclined to have non-Indian spouses (41.6 percent). Compared with New England, the Mountain states have a very large Indian population which is heavily concentrated on reservation lands. Predictably, these states have the highest proportion of racially endogamous American Indian couples

TABLE 5.19

Geographic Distribution of American Indian and Alaska Native
Racially Endogamous and Exogamous Married Couples

Census Division	American Indian Husband and Wife	Indian Husband, Non-Indian Wife	Non-Indian Husband, Indian Wife	Total
New England	9.4	49.0	41.6	100.0
Mid Atlantic	21.3	38.5	40.2	100.0
E. North Central	16.4	41.1	42.5	100.0
W. North Central	33.5	32.6	33.9	100.0
South Atlantic	35.1	34.2	30.7	100.0
E. South Central	21.9	36.8	41.3	100.0
W. South Central	23.0	38.4	38.6	100.0
Mountain	60.9	19.0	20.1	100.0
Pacific	21.6	37.3	41.1	100.0

SOURCE: Public-Use Microdata Sample, 5 percent A File.

(60.9 percent). The Pacific states, especially California, also have large numbers of American Indians, but they tend to be dispersed in large urban areas and consequently endogamous marriages are no more common than in the East South Central and Middle Atlantic states which have much smaller Indian populations.

The relatively high incidence of intermarriage between Indians and non-Indians in the Pacific states underscores the idea that absolute numbers alone are insufficient to promote endogamous relationships. Population concentrations and isolated areas where opportunities for choosing non-Indian spouses are limited also contribute to racial endogamy among American Indians. If this reasoning is correct, areas outside metropolitan localities and places on or near reservation lands should have fewer interracial marriages involving American Indians than other places. Support for this idea is provided by the data in Table 5.20. Couples in which both partners are American Indian are considerably more common in nonmetropolitan and/or reservation locales. For example, nearly 49 percent of nonmetropolitan American Indian married couples are racially endogamous compared with 21 percent of metropolitan couples.

TABLE 5.20

*Place of Residence for American Indian and Alaska Native
Racially Endogamous and Exogamous Married Couples*

Place of Residence	American Indian Husband and Wife	Indian Husband, Non-Indian Wife	Non-Indian Husband, Indian Wife	Total
Metropolitan	20.6	39.5	39.9	100.0
Nonmetropolitan	48.6	24.3	27.1	100.0
Off Reservation	20.6	39.5	39.9	100.0
On or Near Reservation	46.2	25.6	28.2	100.0

SOURCE: Public-Use Microdata Sample, 5 percent A File.

Fertility and Intermarriage

As mentioned, racial intermarriage is an important indicator of cultural assimilation. From this perspective, if traditional culture and values place a premium on large families, then less assimilated couples should have larger families than couples who are more assimilated into the dominant culture. In other words, racially endogamous couples are more likely to have larger families than racially exogamous couples, who are likely to be more assimilated. The data in Table 5.21 are consistent with this reasoning.

This finding notwithstanding, the figures in Table 5.21 are perhaps most significant because they indicate that women in exogamous couples, regardless of whether the husband or wife is Indian, seem to lower

TABLE 5.21

*Mean Number of Children Ever Born to Women in Married Couples
With at least One American Indian or Alaska Native Partner
Aged 15–54 in 1980*

Age	American Indian Husband and Wife	Indian Husband, Non-Indian Wife	Non-Indian Husband, Indian Wife
15–24	1.42	1.04	1.06
25–34	2.68	1.92	2.04
35–44	4.09	2.96	3.17
45–54	5.09	3.38	3.54
Total	3.35	2.23	2.42

SOURCE: Public-Use Microdata Sample, 5 percent A File.

160

their fertility. Among white women aged 15–44 the average number of children ever born is 1.85,[26] while among Indian women aged 15–44 married to non-Indians and the non-Indian wives of Indian men the average number of children ever born is 2.42 and 2.23, respectively. In comparison, women aged 15–44 in endogamous Indian couples average 3.35 ever born. This means that American Indians, when they marry non-Indians (most of whom are white), reduce their fertility instead of increasing the fertility of their partners.

Education and Intermarriage

Lower fertility is typically associated with higher levels of social and economic well-being. Furthermore, marriage to non-Indians may provide opportunities for upward social mobility or, alternatively, non-Indian spouses may reflect a measure of economic success for some Indians. By this logic, racially exogamous couples should be better educated and more economically advantaged than endogamous American Indian couples. The first evidence of systematic socioeconomic differences among these couples appears in Table 5.22. The percentages in this table clearly show that husbands and wives in endogamous marriages are less educated than those in exogamous marriages. They also show some interesting differences within the couples themselves.

Among endogamous American Indian couples, wives are slightly better educated than their husbands. About 30 percent of the men in these couples have less than 9 years of schooling compared with 26 percent of their wives. The women in these couples were more likely than their husbands to have completed high school or at least spent some time in secondary schooling. In contrast, there are virtually no differences between husbands and wives in terms of postsecondary education. This suggests that among Indians who marry other Indians relatively well-educated Indians probably seek equally well-educated spouses, but among the less educated it is typical for Indian women to have more schooling then their husbands.

The distribution of education among racially exogamous couples reflects a very different situation. The close resemblance of these couples suggests that which spouse is American Indian is not a decisive consideration in their well-being. However, the distribution of education among these couples is complex. Husbands are more likely than wives

---

[26]U.S. Bureau of the Census, *1980 Census of Population, General Social and Economic Characteristics, United States Summary* (Washington, DC: U.S. Government Printing Office, 1983).

TABLE 5.22

Percent Distribution of Educational Attainments of Persons
in Racially Endogamous and Exogamous Married Couples
With at least One American Indian or Alaska Native Partner

Years of Education	American Indian Husband and Wife		Indian Husband, Non-Indian Wife		Indian Wife, Non-Indian Husband	
	Husband	Wife	Husband	Wife	Husband	Wife
0–8	30.4	26.1	13.2	7.9	13.3	9.9
9–11	18.6	23.4	16.9	19.9	17.4	22.9
12	29.7	31.0	34.1	43.0	35.8	39.6
13–15	14.9	14.4	22.7	20.4	20.7	20.5
16 and Over	6.4	5.1	13.1	8.8	12.8	7.1
Total	100.0	100.0	100.0	100.0	100.0	100.0

SOURCE: Public-Use Microdata Sample, 5 percent A File.

to have very low levels of education. For example, about 13 percent of American Indian husbands had less than 9 years of schooling compared with 8 percent of the non-Indian wives in these marriages. Similarly, husbands are less likely than wives to be high school graduates but more likely to be college graduates; 13 percent of husbands in exogamous marriages, Indians and non-Indians alike, had 16 or more years of schooling compared with 7 and 9 percent of Indian and non-Indian wives, respectively. Overall, in racially exogamous couples, wives tend to complete their education through high school, and beyond this level their attainments fall below those of their husbands. On the other hand, the husbands in these marriages tend to have either very low or very high levels of education. If these husbands are well educated, they probably have more schooling than their wives but, conversely, if they are poorly educated, their school achievements are probably below those of their wives.

Work and Intermarriage

Labor force participation data in Table 5.23 offer a somewhat less complicated view of the differences between racially endogamous and exogamous couples than do educational attainments. However, these data are entirely consistent with the discussion of labor force participation in Chapter 7. For example, in every instance the labor force parti-

TABLE 5.23

Percent Distribution of Civilian Labor Force Participation
of Persons in Racially Endogamous and Exogamous Married Couples
With at least One American Indian or Alaska Native Partner

	Labor Force Participation				
	Employed	Unemployed	Not in Labor Force	Total	Unemployment Rate[a]
American Indian Husband and Wife					
Husband	66.6	8.0	25.4	100.0	10.7
Wife	41.5	4.6	53.9	100.0	10.0
Indian Husband, Non-Indian Wife					
Husband	77.7	7.0	15.3	100.0	8.3
Wife	48.6	4.6	46.8	100.0	8.6
Non-Indian Husband, Indian Wife					
Husband	78.5	6.1	15.5	100.0	7.2
Wife	45.5	4.6	49.9	100.0	9.2

SOURCE: Public-Use Microdata Sample, 5 percent A File.
[a]Percentage of civilian labor force unemployed.

cipation of husbands is higher than that of their wives. More important, racially exogamous couples have similar patterns of labor force participation, and their levels of participation are markedly higher than those of racially endogamous couples.

About 79 percent of the non-Indian husbands of Indian women are employed, but less than 67 percent of Indian husbands of Indian women are active jobholders. This finding also highlights the fact that in terms of labor force participation, non-Indians are uniformly ahead of Indians, regardless of which spouse is Indian. Among non-Indian women about 49 percent are employed, while among Indian women married to non-Indian men about 46 percent are employed. However, Indian women married to Indian men are the least likely to be employed—about 42 percent. Another interesting finding is that the differences in labor force participation are more pronounced among husbands than among wives; employment for wives ranges from 42 to 49 percent (for endogamous Indians and exogamous non-Indians, respectively), compared with 67 and 79 percent for endogamous Indian and exogamous non-Indian husbands, respectively.

Income and Poverty

Table 5.24 shows the income and poverty status for racially endogamous and exogamous couples. Again, racially exogamous couples are strikingly similar, and financially they are well ahead of endogamous couples. The median family incomes of exogamous couples—$18,577 and $18,810—are 28 to 30 percent higher than the median family incomes of endogamous couples—$14,460. The differences between endogamous and exogamous couples are even more dramatic with respect to poverty status. The lower incomes and larger family sizes of endogamous couples have the effect of pushing these husbands and wives below the official poverty threshold. The poverty rate for endogamous couples, 24 percent, is well over twice the rate for exogamous couples. Indian women seem to benefit somewhat more than Indian men from marriage to non-Indians; married couple households with non-Indian husbands had median incomes of $19,005 in 1979, while similar households with non-Indian wives had median incomes of $18,623. Because husbands typically are the primary earners in married couples, these data suggest that the economic disadvantages accruing to Indian men due to their race are not entirely overcome through their marriage to non-Indians, nor are their spouses immune to these disadvantages. From another perspective, Indian women gain more from having a non-Indian husband than non-Indian women gain from having an Indian husband, even though they are likely to marry a relatively successful Indian male.

Although the economic situation of racially exogamous couples is considerably better than the situation of endogamous couples, it is im-

TABLE 5.24

Median Family and Household Incomes and Percentage of Families Below Poverty Level Among Racially Endogamous and Exogamous Married Couples With at least One American Indian or Alaska Native Partner (1979 dollars)

	American Indian Husband and Wife	Indian Husband, Non-Indian Wife	Indian Wife, Non-Indian Husband
Median Family Income	$14,460	$18,577	$18,810
Median Household Income	14,600	18,623	19,005
Percentage of Families Below Poverty Level	24.4	10.0	10.1

SOURCE: Public-Use Microdata Sample, 5 percent A File.

portant to realize that exogamy alone is not responsible for these bene-fits; indeed, racial intermarriage represents a host of complex, interde-pendent conditions related to socioeconomic well-being. American Indians who marry non-Indians very often are younger, better educated, and more likely to live in metropolitan areas than American Indians who marry within their race. These characteristics, particularly educa-tion and metropolitan residence, provide important economic advan-tages. Another consideration that cannot be underestimated is that American Indians who marry non-Indians are very likely more oriented toward the material economic values of American culture, better able to meet the demands of an advanced industrial society, and hence more successful than American Indians committed to traditional native val-ues and lifestyles.

Assimilation and Intermarriage

The extraordinarily high level of racial intermarriage for American Indians provides a good reason to expect that growing numbers of Amer-ican Indians and their descendants will choose non-Indians for spouses and to a greater or lesser degree become absorbed into the dominant culture. Some of these Indians will abandon their cultural heritage al-together, while others may make only minor accommodations as a re-sult of having a non-Indian spouse. This raises a question that is ex-tremely controversial within many quarters of the American Indian community: Are American Indians assimilating so quickly through ra-cial intermarriage that they will eventually, in the not too distant fu-ture, marry themselves out of existence?

For most of this century, anthropologists and other social scientists have been predicting that American Indians as a distinctive ethnic group would vanish in the wake of poverty, disease, and the demands of West-ern civilization.[27] By the mid 1950s many of these same anthropologists began revising their predictions.[28] However, the data on marriage pat-terns raise the prospect that Indians, through their spousal choices, may accomplish what disease, Western civilization, and decades of federal Indian policy failed to achieve.

Predicting the future viability of the Indian population is a risky and difficult, if not inadvisable, venture. However, recently published

[27]Ralph Linton, ed., *Acculturation in Seven American Indian Tribes* (Gloucester, MA: Peter Smith, 1963).

[28]Evon Z. Vogt, "The Acculturation of American Indians," *Annals of the American Academy of Political and Social Science* 311(1957):137–146; Brewton Berry, "The Myth of the Vanishing Indian," *Phylon* 21(1960):51–57.

data from the U.S. Office of Technology Assessment (OTA) provide some interesting insights into the impact of racial exogamy on the Indian population. Recall from Chapter 2 that "blood quantum" is a measure of Indian ancestry in which, for example, a "full-blood" is someone who is entirely descended from American Indians and has no non-Indian ancestors; ½ blood quantum might denote a non-Indian father and a full-blood Indian mother, or one of a large number of other possible combinations. Although it is not necessarily so, persons with, say, ¾ or full-blood quantums are typically less assimilated and more committed to traditional Indian lifestyles than persons of ¹⁄₃₂ or ¹⁄₆₄ blood quantums. With this idea in the background, the OTA published a number of population projections showing the changing distribution of blood quantum within the Indian population through the year 2080.[29]

Some of these projections were based on patently unreasonable assumptions—for instance, that American Indians do not marry non-Indians or that all Indians are full-bloods. However, one projection in particular is interesting because it is based on BIA data for the distribution of blood quantums and takes into account the prevalence of racial intermarriage among Indians based on data from the 1980 census. The results from this OTA projection (referred to as Scenario III in the original report) are limited to the 32 states with reservations served by the IHS, and these data are shown in Table 5.25. These projections predict not surprisingly that in relative numbers the percentages of persons with ½ or more Indian blood quantums will decline throughout this century and the next one, dropping precipitously from 87 to 8 percent in the next 100 years. The proportion of persons with ¼ to ½ Indian blood quantums is predicted to grow from about 10 percent of the Indian population in 1980 to a peak of 40 percent in 2040 and then decline to 33 percent by 2080. However, the proportion of persons with less than ¼ Indian blood quantums is expected to increase from 4 percent to 59 percent by 2080.

The relative percentages for the distribution of blood quantum show that persons with ½ blood quantum or more will shrink, if not disappear, as a significant segment of the American Indian population. Does this mean that persons with predominantly American Indian ancestors are drifting toward numerical extinction? The answer to this question is best answered with absolute, rather than relative, numbers. Viewing these numbers, it is easy to make two conclusions. One is that the OTA projections forecast massive growth in the American Indian population of the 32 states that it covers, from 1,295,450 Indians in 1980 to 15,767,206 in 2080. Over 90 percent of these persons will have a mi-

---

[29]U.S. Office of Technology Assessment (1986).

TABLE 5.25

Office of Technology Assessment
Population Projections by Blood Quantum,
1980–2080, Percentage of Population in Parentheses
(32 states with federal reservations)

Year	Percent Blood Quantum			Total
	50.0 and Above	25.0–49.9	Less Than 25.0	
1980	1,125,746	123,068	46,636	1,295,450
	(86.9)	(9.5)	(3.6)	(100.0)
2000	1,722,116	345,309	146,092	2,213,517
	(77.8)	(15.6)	(6.6)	(100.0)
2020	2,119,717	1,106,343	465,084	3,691,144
	(57.4)	(30.0)	(12.6)	(100.0)
2040	2,188,193	2,418,528	1,454,754	6,061,475
	(36.1)	(39.9)	(24.0)	(100.0)
2060	1,866,738	3,971,782	4,090,935	9,929,455
	(18.8)	(40.3)	(41.2)	(100.0)
2080	1,292,911	5,187,411	9,286,884	15,767,206
	(8.2)	(32.9)	(58.9)	(100.0)

SOURCE: Adapted from U.S. Office of Technology Assessment, *Indian Health Care* (Washington, DC: U.S. Government Printing Office, 1986).

nority of Indian ancestors—less than ½ blood quantum—but the number of persons with ½ or more blood quantum is expected to be 1,292,911 in 2080, almost the same number as the total Indian population of these 32 states in 1980. This is slightly less than the total Indian population, including all blood quantums, residing in reservation states in 1980, 1,295,450 persons. The OTA forecasts predict that the ½ blood quantum group will grow and then decline over the next 100 years. In any event, persons with a majority of Indian ancestors are certainly not expected to disappear according to these predictions.

Racial exogamy is hardly a new phenomenon in the American Indian population, and in all likelihood there is a long history of relations with non-Indians, especially among tribes from the eastern United States, which had very early contact with white immigrants. Among Indians enumerated from the 1910 census, only 56.5 percent reported full-blood quantums. Full-blood Indians were most likely undercounted in this census, for a variety of reasons, yet this statistic indicates a surprising degree of racially mixed parentages at a time when American Indians were still highly isolated from the mainstream of American society.

Definitional differences make strict comparisons between these projections and data collected by the Census Bureau problematic at best.

Census data are based entirely on self-identification and completely disregard blood quantum. Using ½ blood quantum as a criterion for defining who is an Indian provides a considerably more restricted view of the American Indian population, though how much more restricted is difficult to ascertain. Despite these definitional differences, these projections combined with data from the 1980 and earlier censuses suggest very strongly that the much anticipated decline and disappearance of the American Indian population is unlikely to happen in the foreseeable future, even with continuing high rates of intermarriage between Indians and non-Indians.

The blood quantum projections produced by the OTA are perhaps most remarkable because they probably simulate a process that has been occurring within the Indian population throughout this century and, if the OTA is correct, will continue to occur throughout most of the next century. That is, high rates of racial intermarriage between American Indians and non-Indians are producing large numbers of persons who can legitimately claim some amount, no matter how small, of American Indian ancestry. For the overwhelming majority of these persons, American Indian will be only a tiny fraction of their total ancestry. As of 1980 there were already many such individuals in the American population. These individuals could recall the presence of American Indians in their ancestry, but racially they identified more closely with the white or black population than with American Indians. In 1980 there were 5.5 million such individuals, and in Chapter 2 they are described as "Americans of Indian Descent." The OTA projections suggest that this group is likely to become very large in the next 100 years.

In an article written long before the 1980 census, anthropologist Nancy Lurie commented that in American society the slightest trace of black ancestry is regarded as sufficient for membership in the black population.[30] Citing BIA policies requiring ¼ blood quantum, she also noted that attaining membership in the American Indian population requires an ancestral heritage considerably more homogeneous than other racial groups, especially blacks. Lurie speculated that if American Indians were identified in the same way as American blacks, there might have been as many as 10.0 million Indians in the mid 1960s. This ballpark estimate is not very different from the 6.8 million persons claiming American Indian and Alaska Native ancestry in the 1980 census.[31]

[30]Nancy O. Lurie, "The Enduring Indian," *Natural History* 75(1966):10–22.

[31]U.S. Bureau of the Census, "Ancestry of the Population by State, 1980," *1980 Census of Population, Supplementary Report*, PC80-51-10 (Washington DC: U.S. Government Printing Office, 1983).

Racial endogamy among American Indians has been sufficient to reproduce a core population with enough Indian ancestry to make "American Indian" a meaningful category for racial self-identification. Again, if the OTA projections are correct, American Indians as a distinctive racial group also will continue to persist well into the twenty-first century. Although American Indians have remarkably high rates of racial exogamy, the expectation that they are about to marry themselves out of existence is an unlikely prospect, especially for the next 50 to 100 years.

This conclusion is based on the historical record that for a very long time, at least throughout this century, racial exogamy has not been an uncommon phenomenon among American Indians. It also rests heavily on the population projections made by the OTA. However, it would be misleading to suggest that these projections represent a reality that inevitably will come to pass. On the contrary, such estimates are based on scenarios involving large numbers of assumptions that may be incorrect or have a high probability of changing, especially over a period as long as 100 years. For example, racial intermarriage among American Indians could increase during the next 100 years, which would reduce the numbers of persons with more than ½ blood quantums. On the other hand, the OTA projections do not allow for the fact that endogamous couples have more children than exogamous couples, which over time would increase the number of persons with more than ½ blood quantums. In short, the OTA projections in Table 5.25 are at best no more than suggestive of what might happen in the next 100 years. Nevertheless, they offer possible answers to the questions of why there are so many persons who claim American Indian ancestry (as opposed to race) and whether there will be a distinctive Indian population toward the end of the next century.

Concluding Remarks

The findings pertaining to the characteristics of American Indian families and households are relatively straightforward. Most American Indian householders are males, although Indian households have more single female householders than white households and fewer than black households. American Indians also tend to live in larger households than blacks and whites. American Indian households are larger, in part, because of the presence of persons outside the immediate family and because of larger numbers of children in these households, especially in reservation and nonmetropolitan areas. However, apart from this difference the structure of family relationships does not vary according to place of residence. For instance, family roles are distributed no differently in metropolitan than nonmetropolitan locations.

Marital status distribution also is similar among groups regardless of residence, except that divorce is relatively more common among Indians in metropolitan and nonreservation locations. American Indians tend to marry younger than other groups, and they are more likely than blacks to be married but less so than whites. Given that Indian women, like women in general, live somewhat longer than Indian men, one of the major gender differences is that Indian women are more likely to be widowed than Indian men. On the other hand, Indian men are more likely to be single than Indian women. They also are less likely to be divorced, suggesting that remarriage is more common among men than women.

Married couple families represent the most common type of household arrangement in the American Indian population; they are not as common as in the white population, but they are more common than in the black population. The opposite is true for families with single female householders; namely, there are fewer single female householders among American Indians than among blacks but more than among whites. American Indians are somewhat less likely than other racial groups to reside in nonfamily households.

The most dramatic differences in family types are those associated with socioeconomic status. Clearly, single female householders in the American Indian population represent a highly disadvantaged group within an already disadvantaged minority. These women are the most likely to be high school dropouts and the least likely to have completed high school and/or attended college. They are most likely to be out of the labor force, and if they are working it is most likely in clerical and technical jobs or in service work. In view of their concentration in low-paying occupations and marginal attachment to the labor force, it is hardly surprising that American Indian women who are single householders have lower family and household incomes, more poverty, and more dependence on public assistance than any other Indian household type. This level of economic hardship is particularly alarming because these women are more likely than other Indian householders to be caring for children, particularly children aged 6 to 17. Furthermore, the data presented in this chapter clearly show that greater numbers of children are associated with higher levels of economic hardship. This does not imply that children directly result in lower standards of living, but that the number of children ever born is part of a complex process in which poverty is impetus for higher levels of fertility at the same time that large families strain scarce resources and limit economic opportunities. For example, Indian women with low levels of education are less likely to fully understand the implications of unrestricted fertility at the same time that childbearing, especially among very young women, disrupts academic achievement. Consequently, these women generally have more children ever born than their better-educated counterparts. The association between children ever born and socioeconomic well-being is manifest in other ways. American Indian women with large numbers of children ever born are least likely to be in the labor force, are most likely to be living in poverty and dependent on public assistance, and have lower family and household incomes than Indian women with fewer children.

The extremely marginal economic position of American Indian women who are single householders and/or have many children typifies a small, though deeply disadvantaged group within the Indian population. In reality, the childbearing of American Indian women varies considerably with respect to age and geography. One development that may contribute to future improvements in socioeconomic well-being is that in recent years the fertility of American Indian women has declined. Middle-aged American Indian women who reached their peak childbearing years during the "baby boom" era of the 1950s have considerably higher fertility than either older or younger women. Indian women residing in nonmetropolitan and/or reservation locations tend to have more children than Indian women residing in other areas.

From one perspective, racial exogamy can be viewed as an indicator of racial integration and may also reflect a degree of incorporation into mainstream society. According to this view, American Indians who marry non-Indians, particularly white spouses, should be better integrated and less disadvantaged than American Indians in endogamous marriages. There is some merit to this argument because exogamous couples are, in economic terms, well ahead of racially endogamous couples by every indicator: education, labor force participation, and income.

The phenomenally high rate of interracial marriages characteristic of the American Indian population (53 percent of married American Indians are married to non-Indians) also raises the controversial question of whether American Indians are risking extinction, which "experts" have been predicting for decades. The very limited evidence from population projections suggests that the numbers of persons with a plurality of Indian ancestors will continue to increase into the next century. Paralleling this trend, the numbers of persons with minute amounts of American Indian ancestry also will skyrocket in the coming decades. However, this most likely represents the continuation of a long-term process. Racially mixed unions are not a new development in the American Indian population, and already there are several million Americans who claim modest amounts of American Indian ancestry, even though their racial self-identification typically is with groups other than American Indians.

Whether the family and household characteristics described in this chapter bode ill or well for the Native American population in the future, only time will tell. The resilience of American Indians has made possible their physical survival and the preservation of their culture. Much of this resilience can be traced to the central role of the family in their social structure and tribal cultures. In the future, the strength of American Indian family organization undoubtedly will be a crucial factor in the vitality of this population.

6

LANGUAGE AND EDUCATION

S INCE THE early decades of this century, social scientists and policy analysts have grimly recounted the poverty and economic hardships endured by American Indians.[1] The current socioeconomic standing of American Indians merits special concern for its implications about the successes and failures of public policies designed to alleviate Indian poverty and about the overall structure of socioeconomic well-being in American society. In this chapter and the next two chapters the socioeconomic standing of American Indians will be examined in relation to a variety of statistical yardsticks available from the 1980 census. This chapter focuses on two basic dimensions of human capital—language and education—which are typically considered important precursors of successful participation in the labor force.

Language as a determinant of social and economic well-being is usually considered in relation to immigrant groups such as Hispanics and Asians who arrived in this country from societies and cultures distant from English-speaking North Americans. American Indians, in con-

---

[1]See, for example, Institute for Government Research, *The Problem of Indian Administration* [The Meriam Report] (Baltimore: Johns Hopkins University Press, 1928); William A. Brophy and Sophie D. Aberle, *The Indian: America's Unfinished Business* (Norman: University of Oklahoma Press, 1966); Alan L. Sorkin, *American Indians and Federal Aid* (Washington, DC: Brookings Institution, 1971); Sar A. Levitan and Barbara Hetrick, *Big Brother's Indian Programs: With Reservations* (New York: McGraw-Hill, 1971).

trast, are neither immigrants nor far removed (at least in geographic terms) from large English-speaking populations. The fact that American Indians continue to speak an Indian language probably surprises many readers. Certainly, there are relatively few American Indians alive today for whom the English language is completely incomprehensible, but it is equally true that in parts of the United States Indian languages are still a common form of communication.

Along with the ability to speak fluent English, education has been traditionally viewed as a fundamental source of material well-being. The prevailing wisdom in American society is that education is a great equalizer that assists persons of humble social origins to overcome the disadvantages of their backgrounds. For most Americans, educational success bodes economic success in later life. For racial and ethnic minorities, education is an escalator for upward mobility, and lack of education virtually eliminates opportunities for advancement. A vast literature in sociology[2] and economics documents the critical importance of education in mediating socioeconomic success.

Language and Socioeconomic Status

The inability to speak English well is a frequently cited disadvantage which limits the economic opportunities of immigrant groups.[3] If these groups are handicapped by their lack of facility with the English language, then the extent to which American Indians are disadvantaged by their native tongue also is an issue that needs attention.

Very little systematic information exists about the linguistic behavior of American Indians in the late twentieth century. The information available from the 1980 census is at best imprecise and incomplete in detail; nonetheless, it is the best available data for the Indian population as a whole.[4] Linguistic behavior is not precisely defined in census sources but is loosely conceived in terms of the "language spoken at

[2]William H. Sewell and Robert M. Hauser, *Education, Occupation, and Earnings* (New York: Academic Press, 1975); Archibald O. Haller, "Social Psychological Aspects of Schooling and Achievement," in Robert M. Hauser, Archibald O. Haller, David Mechanic, and Taissa S. Hauser, eds., *Social Structure and Behavior* (New York: Academic Press, 1982); Kenneth I. Spenner and David L. Featherman, "Achievement Ambitions," *Annual Review of Sociology* 4(1978):373–420; Jacob Mincer, *Schooling, Experience and Earnings* (New York: National Bureau of Economic Research, 1974).

[3]Marta Tienda and Lisa J. Neidert, "Language, Education, and Socioeconomic Achievement of Hispanic Origin Men," *Social Science Quarterly* 65(1984):519–536; John Mirowsky and Catherine E. Ross, "Language Networks and Social Status among Mexican Americans," *Social Science Quarterly* 65(1984):555–564.

[4]In this case, the total Indian population includes all persons aged 3 and over.

home" and an individual's ability to speak English. Persons are classified according to whether they speak English "very well," "well," "not
well," or "not at all." Combining these pieces of information makes it
possible to discuss language skills in terms of three broad categories of
English fluency: persons who speak only English at home; persons who
speak a language other than English at home but speak English fluently;
and persons who do not speak English at home and cannot speak English fluently.

Two further comments about this classification scheme need to be
made. First, judgments about whether a person speaks English well or
not very well are purely subjective, and they do not necessarily correspond to objective standards for ascertaining linguistic competency. In
short, there is little precision in this approach, and at best these data are
no more than an approximate estimate of language skills. One person
appraised as speaking English "not well" by one judge might be considered as speaking "well" or even "very well" by another. Second, the English-speaking Anglo culture is pervasive enough throughout the United
States that very few American Indians speak no English whatsoever;
only 1 percent of the total Indian population fits into this category. As
a result, data for American Indian language use are most indicative of
bilingualism or native language retention. It is not necessarily a measure of social or cultural isolation stemming from non-English monolingualism, as might be true for some Asian and Hispanic immigrant
groups.

Geographic Distribution of Languages Spoken at Home

Region: Table 6.1 shows the geographic distribution of languages
spoken by American Indians and Alaska Natives. Assuming that language retention is facilitated by the presence of a large and/or concentrated population of native speakers, it might be expected that the largest percentages of persons speaking an Indian language are found in
areas with large populations of American Indians. In fact, there are large
differences between areas in terms of the prevalence of native language
use, and these differences roughly parallel the overall distribution of the
Indian population. That is, areas with small Indian populations such as
the Middle Atlantic and South Atlantic states also have very small percentages of persons speaking Indian languages. As few as 4 percent of
the Indian population in the South Atlantic states speak a native language, which is only 1 percent more than the percentage of Spanish-
speaking persons in this area. On the other hand, the Mountain states
have a very large Indian population, 62 percent of which speak a native

TABLE 6.1

*Percent Distribution of Languages Spoken at Home
by American Indians and Alaska Natives,
by Census Geographic Divisions*

Census Division	Native	Spanish	English	Total
New England	10.0	2.5	87.5	100.0
Mid Atlantic	6.7	7.5	85.8	100.0
E. North Central	5.6	3.3	91.1	100.0
W. North Central	21.0	1.1	77.9	100.0
South Atlantic	3.6	2.9	93.5	100.0
E. South Central	13.9	2.2	83.9	100.0
W. South Central	11.8	3.6	84.6	100.0
Mountain	62.0	3.4	34.6	100.0
Pacific	11.9	7.6	80.5	100.0

SOURCE: Public-Use Microdata Sample, 5 percent A File.

language. This area includes groups such as the Navajo, Hopi, and Pueblo Indians, which have large numbers of persons who use their tribal language.

The correspondence between language use and population size is not perfect. The West North Central states have a relatively large Indian population but only about one fifth speak an Indian language. The most obvious anomaly is evident in the Pacific states. This area has a very large Indian population but relatively few native language speakers. Urbanization has a negative impact on native language use, and Indians in the Pacific states, especially California, are highly urbanized. However, before turning to the data bearing on this assertion, two other observations can be made about Table 6.1. One is that the vast majority of American Indians speak only English at home; in every area of the United States except the Mountain states between 78 and 94 percent of the Indian population regularly use English at home.

The other observation is that Spanish language use among American Indians is almost nonexistent except in the Pacific and Middle Atlantic states. Low levels of Spanish language use are not entirely predictable, particularly for the Mountain division, which includes the southwestern states. Indians in this area have had a long history of contact with Spanish-speaking populations. The Papago reservation, for example, shares a common border with Mexico. Migration by Mexican and American Indians, legal and illegal, also increases contact with Spanish-speaking populations in this area. However, the Indians in this area have a long history of resistance to Spanish-speaking authorities and antagonism toward Spanish-speaking settlers.[5]

Residence: The claim that urban environments reduce the use of native languages rests on two observations. One is that urban Indian populations have a diverse tribal composition.[6] Large urban Indian populations are composed of persons hailing from many different tribes and for whom there is no common language, except English. Even for very large urban Indian populations, the number of persons speaking a specific Indian language is probably very small, especially compared with tribally homogeneous populations in rural and/or reservation locations. Another factor that may lower the use of native languages in metropolitan areas is that urban Indians are simply inundated by the English language—in the media, in schools, at work, and in virtually every other place outside their homes. In short, there is little need and few opportunities for American Indians to use their native language in urban areas.

Table 6.2 shows the distribution of persons speaking an American Indian language within geographic areas and by place of residence. Almost without exception, the largest percentages of native language speakers are found in nonmetropolitan and reservation areas. For example, 76 percent of American Indians residing in nonmetropolitan areas of the Mountain states speak an Indian language at home compared with 35 percent in metropolitan areas. In the same states 68 percent of Indians residing on or near a reservation speak a native language compared with only 12 percent in nonreservation areas. Similar conditions exist in the Pacific states, which include the large and highly urban Indian population of California. In these states only 6 percent of the metropolitan Indian population speak a native language compared with 29 percent of the nonmetropolitan population.

The largest concentration of Indian language speakers lives on or near reservations in the East South Central states. However, this under-

---

[5]Thomas D. Hall, "Incorporation in the World-System: Toward a Critique," *American Sociological Review* 51(1986):390–402.

[6]Stan Steiner, *The New Indians* (New York: Dell, 1968); Alan L. Sorkin, *The Urban American Indian* (Lexington, MA: Heath, 1978); Hazel W. Hertzberg, *The Search for an American Indian Identity: Modern Pan-Indian Movements* (New York: Syracuse University Press, 1980); Russell Lawrence Barsh and James Youngblood Henderson, *The Road: Indian Tribes and Political Liberty* (Berkeley: University of California Press, 1980).

TABLE 6.2

Percent Distribution of the American Indian
and Alaska Native Population Speaking a Native Language

Census Division	Metropolitan	Nonmetro-politan	Off Reservation	On or Near Reservation
New England	6.3	25.2	6.4	17.8
Mid Atlantic	4.9	19.9	3.4	17.5
E. North Central	4.7	8.2	4.5	9.3
W. North Central	13.6	28.9	9.7	31.1
South Atlantic	3.8	3.2	2.5	17.2
E. South Central	4.8	29.2	4.9	90.5
W. South Central	11.6	12.2	12.4	8.0
Mountain	34.6	75.8	11.9	67.5
Pacific	5.5	29.2	6.2	18.0

SOURCE: Public-Use Microdata Sample, 5 percent A File.

scores the observation that Indian language use is not sustained by large populations alone. Although 91 percent of persons residing on or near a reservation in this area speak a native language at home, these individuals are barely more than 1 percent[7] of the total American Indian population who use a native language.

Language Use and Social Characteristics

Tables 6.1 and 6.2 show only whether or not an Indian language is used at home. They do not show the degree of English fluency, and they do not reveal how fluency is related to other population characterstics, particularly the generally poor social and economic conditions of American Indians. The next series of tables provides a few insights into these matters.

Age: The rapid growth of the United States as a highly urbanized and industrialized society very likely has increased contacts between Indians and non-Indians in complex and uncountable ways. Innovations

[7]This estimate is taken from an unreported tabulation.

178

in technology and transportation have been especially important developments that have brought Indians and non-Indians together. The advent of modern telecommunications technology in the second half of this century has brought about the diffusion of cultural practices on an unprecedented scale. Because of satellite technology in particular, virtually no place in the United States is isolated from the mainstream culture. Receiver dishes for satellite signals are not an unusual sight on some reservations.

According to this perspective, as the telecommunications revolution has hastened the spread of American culture, older American Indians, who acquired their language skills before radio and television, should be considerably more likely to speak a native language than younger Indians born after the rise of modern mass communications. One implication of this view is that radio and television are contributing to the acculturation of younger Indians, resulting in declines in native language use.[8]

With these issues in the background, the relationship between age and native language use is especially important. Table 6.3 shows levels of English fluency for different groups aged 11 and over. (We can assume that most persons have consolidated their language behavior by age 10.) As a rough guide, persons aged 30 and under were born after the large-scale spread of radio and television. Persons aged 60 and under were born in a period when radio was widely available. For older persons born during the advent of commercial radio, there is very little difference between them and younger persons of the television generation. About 74 percent of American Indians aged 11–20 speak only English at home compared with about 73 percent of persons aged 50–60. If the use of English is growing, then it is growing very slowly, and indeed it changed very little during the decade of the 1970s. For comparative purposes, in the 1970 census 32 percent of the total Indian population (Alaska Natives excluded) reported an American Indian language as their mother tongue.[9]

To the extent that mass communications have changed language behavior, radio probably has had a larger influence than television. Persons born before radio, and especially persons over age 70, are the most different in their language use; they are least likely to speak only English at home and most likely to speak no English whatsoever. Although there are very few differences in the rate of English monolingualism between older and younger American Indians, a slight shift in language

---

[8]Notably, a story in the *Washington Post* (July 12, 1987, p. A3) reports a resurgence in native language use by American Indian youth.

[9]U.S. Bureau of the Census, *"American Indians," 1970 Census of Housing and Population, Subject Report* (Washington, DC: U.S. Government Printing Office, 1973).

TABLE 6.3

Percent Distribution of Language Use
Among American Indians and Alaska Natives, by Age

Age	Speak Only English		Speak a Native Language and Speak English Fluently		Speak a Native Language and Cannot Speak English Fluently	
	Males	Females	Males	Females	Males	Females
11–20	73.9	73.7	24.4	24.8	1.7	1.4
21–30	73.1	73.9	25.4	24.6	1.5	1.4
31–40	72.8	73.5	25.5	24.4	1.6	2.1
41–50	71.2	71.4	25.4	24.7	3.4	3.9
51–60	72.8	72.5	23.0	23.2	4.2	4.3
61–70	70.8	72.1	23.8	23.4	5.3	4.4
70 and Over	64.1	73.1	28.1	21.9	7.8	4.9

SOURCE: Public-Use Microdata Sample, 5 percent A File.

behavior can be seen in Table 6.3. Instead of abandoning their native language in favor of English, younger American Indians appear more adept with both tongues than their elders. The percentage of native language monolinguals is not large, even among the very old, but it is measurably larger than the percentage of monolinguals under age 30. On the other hand, the percentage of American Indians who speak English fluently yet speak a native language at home is larger among younger persons than older ones. In short, younger Indians are slightly more likely to be bilingual than their elders but very little different in terms of speaking only English.

Education: Observing that younger American Indians appear to have become bilingual instead of English monolingual is particularly interesting because this signals a potentially significant liability in school and the labor market. Table 6.4 displays the relationship between levels of schooling completed and the English fluency of American Indians and Alaska Natives aged 25 and over. Persons who speak only English at home constitute 72.4 percent of the total Indian population aged 25 and over. As the statistics in Table 6.4 show, this group is relatively well educated compared with other segments of the Indian population. Almost two thirds of these individuals have completed 12 or more years of schooling. Bilingual American Indians, 24.6 percent of the population, are somewhat less successful in their school achievements. Slightly more than half of this population have finished 12 or more years of

TABLE 6.4

*Percent Distribution of English Fluency and Schooling
Attained by American Indians and Alaska Natives Aged 25 and Over*

Years of Education	Speak Only English	Speak Native Language and Speak English Fluently	Speak Native Language and Cannot Speak English Fluently
0–8	17.1	29.1	74.1
9–11	19.7	19.4	10.1
12	33.3	28.2	8.7
13–15	20.3	16.4	4.7
16 and Over	9.6	6.9	2.4
Total	100.0	100.0	100.0

SOURCE: Public-Use Microdata Sample, 5 percent A File.

schooling. The lower levels of educational attainment among bilinguals are not due to higher rates of high school dropouts but to higher rates of persons who did not attend school beyond eighth grade. The overwhelming majority of persons who cannot speak English fluently have equally low levels of education; nearly three fourths never reached high school. In light of these findings, it is worth recalling that the vast majority of persons with 8 years or less of schooling are persons aged 50 and over.

Although the data suggest a relationship between education and English fluency, the circumstances linking these characteristics are extremely complex. It should not be presumed that lower levels of English fluency are directly responsible for lower educational achievement or that bilingualism automatically translates into an educational limitation. This might be true in some respects, but there are many other factors involved in this relationship. Indeed, it is not clear whether more schooling results in English monolingualism or whether English monolingualism promotes school success. Age is an important consideration, for example, because older Indians are less educated and more likely to speak a native language than younger Indians. Place of residence also plays a role because persons in rural areas tend to be less educated, older, and more likely to speak a native language than persons residing in urban places.

Labor Force Participation: Besides its impact on educational success, fluency in another language besides English is often cited as a disadvantage in the labor market. English fluency and its association with higher levels of education presumably lead to more success in the labor market. The data in Table 6.5 generally support this expectation. American Indians who speak only English at home, men and women alike, are substantially more likely to be employed than those who speak Indian languages; for example, 62 percent of male English monolinguals are employed compared with 53 and 41 percent of male native language speakers. Not surprisingly, these results must be reversed to describe the relationship between English fluency and being out of the labor force. For women who cannot speak English fluently, 73 percent are not in the labor force compared with only 50 percent of English monolinguals.

The data for unemployment are more difficult to interpret. The differences between monolinguals and fluent bilinguals are small, and the fact that persons who cannot speak English fluently have lower levels or about the same levels of unemployment as fluent persons is an unexpected finding. However, recall that persons who cannot speak English fluently are typically older and that older workers are either employed or drop out of the labor force, so they are not counted as unemployed. This is most apparent in the high percentages of persons who cannot speak English fluently who also are not in the labor force.

TABLE 6.5

Percent Distribution of Language Use and Civilian Labor Force Status of American Indians and Alaska Natives Aged 16 and Over

Labor Force Status	Speak Only English	Speak a Native Language and Speak English Fluently	Speak a Native Language and Cannot Speak English Fluently
Employed			
Males	62.1	52.5	40.7
Females	44.5	40.0	23.1
Unemployed			
Males	9.8	10.2	7.5
Females	5.7	6.3	3.4
Unemployment Rate[a]			
Males	13.6	16.3	15.6
Females	11.4	13.6	12.8
Not in Labor Force			
Males	28.1	37.3	51.8
Females	49.8	53.7	73.3

SOURCE: Public-Use Microdata Sample, 5 percent A File.

[a]Percentage of the civilian labor force unemployed. Other unemployment figures are for all persons in and out of the labor force.

Occupation: The data for labor force participation indicate that attachment to the labor force varies across levels of English fluency. Given this result, occupational differences also should be related to levels of English fluency. However, Table 6.6 shows that the relationship between occupation and English fluency is relatively weak. The occupational distributions for English monolinguals and fluent bilinguals are almost identical, with the exceptions of Service and lower-level white collar occupations (Technical, Sales, and Administrative Support). For these occupations, Indians who speak only English enjoy a small advantage, because they are more likely to be in lower-level white collar occupations while fluent bilingual Indians are more likely to be in Service jobs. In summary, bilingualism appears to be related to factors that discourage labor force participation, but for those bilingual Indians able to secure employment, their language skills do not pose insurmountable handicaps. By the same logic, English-speaking monolingual Indians are more successful than bilinguals in finding employment, but not in relation to the kinds of jobs they hold.

TABLE 6.6

Percent Distribution of Occupation and Language
of Employed American Indians and Alaska Natives Aged 16 and Over

Occupation	Speak Only English	Speak a Native Language and Speak English Fluently	Speak a Native Language and Cannot Speak English Fluently
Managerial and Professional	13.3	14.4	8.9
Technical, Sales, and Administrative Support	23.6	20.3	10.3
Service	21.5	19.6	23.0
Farming, Forestry, and Fishing	4.9	5.3	8.6
Precision Production, Craft, and Repair	13.9	13.5	15.1
Operators, Fabricators, and Laborers	24.7	23.5	35.6
Total	100.0	100.0	100.0

SOURCE: Public-Use Microdata Sample, 5 percent A File.

Predictably, American Indians who cannot speak English fluently are concentrated in blue collar occupations. Over one third are employed in low-skill Operator, Fabricator, and Laborer jobs. In contrast, less than one fifth are employed in white collar occupations, about half of whom are employed in managerial and professional occupations. How persons who cannot speak English fluently can obtain and hold high-level white collar employment may seem puzzling. However, this figure actually represents a relatively small number of persons, many of whom are most likely employed in jobs such as executives in tribal governments.

Income: In terms of how language skills are related to economic well-being, the most literal measures are differences in income across levels of English fluency. Table 6.7 shows median incomes from different sources for each category of English fluency. It is clear that persons who speak only English at home enjoy relatively high incomes while native language speakers receive substantially smaller sums. Persons who speak only English at home have family and household incomes 25 percent higher than the family and household incomes of fluent bilinguals and 75 percent higher than the family incomes of persons who cannot speak English fluently.

TABLE 6.7

English Fluency and Median Income by Source
for American Indians and Alaska Natives Aged 16 and Over
(1979 dollars)

Source	Speak Only English	Speak a Native Language and Speak English Fluently	Speak a Native Language and Cannot Speak English Fluently
Family Income	$16,535	$13,210	$9,470
Household Income	16,010	12,810	9,470
Wages and Salaries	7,005	6,075	5,330
Self-Employment	6,505	5,005	3,005
Farm	3,005	2,505	1,475
Interest, Dividends, and Rents	645	575	805
Social Security	2,525	2,180	2,225
Public Assistance	2,125	1,855	1,805
Other Sources	1,725	1,805	1,655
Total Personal Income	6,210	5,190	3,605

SOURCE: Public-Use Microdata Sample, 5 percent A File.

Differences in median income across levels of English fluency are most pronounced for family and household income, but in almost every instance English monolinguals enjoy markedly higher incomes. Overall, the total personal incomes of English monolinguals are about 20 percent higher than the personal incomes of fluent bilinguals and about 72 percent higher than the incomes of persons who speak English poorly or not at all. Wages and salaries are a major source of income for most American Indians (see Chapter 8). For persons with jobs the income gap between these workers is somewhat smaller. Median wages and salaries are $7,005 for English-speaking monolinguals, 15 percent higher than the wages and salaries of fluent bilinguals and over 30 percent higher than the wages and salaries of persons who speak English poorly. The earnings differentials for self-employment are even larger.

These inequalities are perpetuated into retirement. The Social Security Administration's practice of indexing pension benefits to lifetime earnings means that English monolinguals, who earn the most as workers, also claim higher retirement benefits than persons who speak a native language. The only type of income that is higher for persons who cannot speak English fluently is from interest, rents, and dividends; it is about 25 percent higher than such income received by English monolinguals. This may represent income received by older reservation Indians from royalties accruing from sources such as mineral leases and grazing land rentals; however, it does not amount to a sizable source of wealth.

American Indian Education

Background

Popular stereotypes typically show American Indians leading simple lives, close to nature and distant from the demands of urban society. From this perspective, American Indian education is characterized by an informal tradition of oral teachings passed from one generation to another; formal education is an alien concept. This stereotype makes the exceedingly low level of schooling among American Indians understandable. Like most stereotypes, this image is far removed from reality but contains a few elements of truth.

For many tribes, oral teaching is an integral part of their culture. However, since the beginnings of American society, American Indians have been involved in varying degrees with the educational institutions of this nation. Christian missionaries commonly established schools for the education and "civilization" of Indian children. The original charter of Harvard University, America's oldest institution of higher learning, provided for the education of American Indians as one of its missions. John Ross, the great nineteenth century chief of the Cherokees, attended a private academy in Tennessee. One of the first public school systems established west of the Mississippi River was not created to teach the children of white settlers; it was established by the Cherokee tribe in eastern Oklahoma after the tribe was relocated from its home east of the Mississippi.

In the late nineteenth century, reformers advocated education as a way of hastening the cultural assimilation of American Indians into American society. These reformers hoped that by removing Indians from their home environments, they could be taught to give up their traditional culture and adopt the ways of white society.[10] To carry out this policy schools such as the Hampton Institute[11] in Virginia and Carlisle[12] in Pennsylvania were established. Indian students from areas across the United States were more or less forcibly recruited and brought to these schools by train.

In the wake of the late nineteenth century reforms that established Hampton and Carlisle, the Bureau of Indian Affairs (BIA) also developed an extensive network of boarding schools for Indian youth. Appropriations for Indian schools were first allocated in 1877. These funds initially supported 150 schools for Indian students, including 48 boarding facilities. By 1910 the BIA was expending nearly $3.8 million to support 389 Indian schools, of which 106 were boarding schools with almost 20,000 students in residence—about 61 percent of all students in Indian schools.[13]

Cultural assimilation was the primary mission of these schools. In anticipation of BIA schools, the 1869 report of the Board of Indian Commissions commented:

> By educating the children of these tribes in the English language these differences would have disappeared and civilization would have followed at once. Nothing then would have been left but the anti-

---

[10]Robert M. Utley, *The Indian Frontier of the American West, 1846–1890* (Albuquerque: University of New Mexico Press, 1984).

[11]The Hampton Institute was also assigned the duty of teaching newly freed slaves. Today it is a predominantly black university.

[12]Jim Thorpe, the great Indian athlete, attended Carlisle.

[13]U.S. Bureau of the Census, *The Indian Population in the United States and Alaska, 1910* (Washington, DC: U.S. Government Printing Office, 1915), p. 195.

pathy of race, and that, too, is always softened in the beams of a higher civilization.[14]

The curriculum of BIA schools was confined mostly to teaching basic literacy and vocational skills. Some schools harshly punished students for speaking their native language and forbade other cultural practices, such as participating in traditional ceremonies or using herbal remedies.[15]

Although Hampton and Carlisle are no longer centers for Indian education, and the BIA has closed nearly all of its boarding schools, special measures for Indian education still exist. For example, the BIA and some tribal governments sponsor scholarships for Indian students. Institutions such as Haskell in Lawrence, Kansas, and Bacone in Muskogee, Oklahoma, exist primarily as colleges for Indian students from across the United States. The Navajo Community College primarily meets the needs of the Navajo tribe, and in California the collective efforts of American Indian and Chicano community organizers established D-Q University outside Davis in the 1970s. As this history suggests, formal education for American Indians is not a new development. However, until recently American Indians have had little control over the institutions providing for their education.

The decade of the 1970s was an important period in the history of Indian education as Indian educators gradually gained more control over the curriculum, policies, and administration of Indian education. During this time developments such as the Indian Self-Determination and Educational Assistance Act of 1975 (Public Law 93-638), growing numbers of Indian school boards, tribally operated schools, institutions such as Navajo Community College and D-Q University, and a host of alternative schools in urban and reservation areas marked the first large-scale involvement of Indian people in educational programs.

The 1970s were also important for Indian education because during this period numerous public policies attempted to promote the education of racial and ethnic minorities. Public school systems and institutions of higher education also made concerted efforts to increase the numbers of minority graduates by sponsoring programs such as Upward Bound. In the context of public policy initiatives promoting Indian education, data from the 1980 census are especially meaningful for judging the global impact of these measures on the Indian population at large.

[14]Ibid.
[15]Estelle Fuchs and Robert J. Havighurst, *To Live on This Earth: American Indian Education* (New York: Doubleday, 1972), chap. 11.

Educational Attainments

Secondary Schooling: Figures 6.1–6.3 present several indicators of school achievement for blacks, whites, and American Indians between 1970 and 1980. By every measure blacks and Indians have markedly lower levels of education than whites. For example, Figure 6.2 shows that slightly over one half of all blacks and Indians aged 25 and over have completed high school compared with over two thirds of whites. Similarly, Figure 6.3 shows that 17 percent of whites aged 25 and over have four or more years of college, while only 8 percent of blacks and Indians have a similar education.

Although Indians and blacks lag behind whites in their educational attainments, the 1970s were a period of substantial gains for both of these groups. The largest educational gains made by American Indians in the 1970s are reflected in percentages of high school graduates for 1970 and 1980 (see Figure 6.2). At the beginning of the decade American

FIGURE 6.1

Percentage of Blacks, Whites, and American Indians and Alaska Natives Aged 25 and Over With 5 Years or Less of Schooling Completed

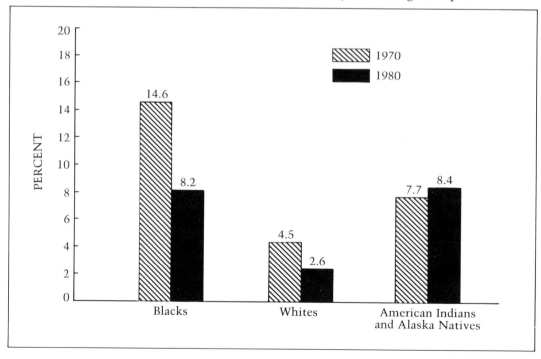

FIGURE 6.2

Percentage of Blacks, Whites, and American Indians and Alaska Natives Aged 25 and Over With 12 Years of Schooling Completed

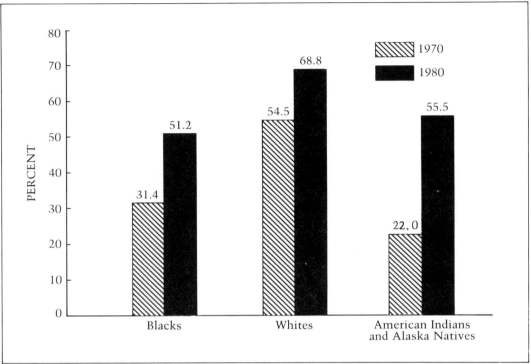

Indians were far behind blacks in terms of high school graduates but moved ahead of them by 1980, growing from 22 percent to 56 percent during this period. As a milestone, the 1970s were a decade in which a majority of Indians and blacks attained a high school diploma.

Postsecondary Schooling: Despite increases in secondary schooling, growing numbers of high school graduates have not produced significant increases in college graduates for Indians or blacks. The percentage of Indians and blacks with four or more years of postsecondary education doubled between 1970 and 1980, but the gap between these groups and the white population increased slightly. For example, the percentage difference between whites and Indians completing four years or more of college was 9.4 points in 1980 compared with 7.5 points in 1970. In other words, the percentage of the American Indian population with advanced education grew during the 1970s, but it expanded less than the percentage of the white population pursuing college educations.

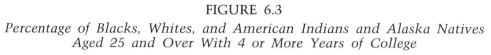

FIGURE 6.3

Percentage of Blacks, Whites, and American Indians and Alaska Natives Aged 25 and Over With 4 or More Years of College

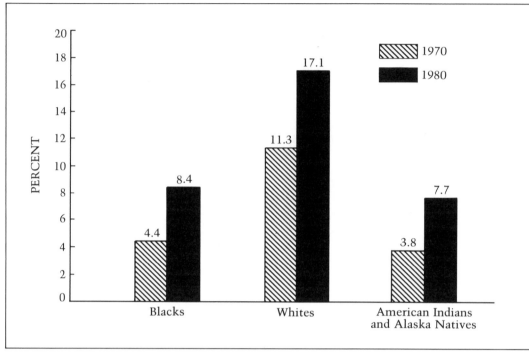

In view of the numerous programs designed to promote college attendance by minority students, Figure 6.3 may be disappointing. However, without such programs it is conceivable that the gap between whites and American Indians (and blacks) might be much larger. Why gains in secondary schooling were not translated into higher rates of postsecondary schooling is not clear.

One way of looking at this problem is simply to compute the crude multiplier by which increases in secondary school completion are converted to postsecondary education. Among whites, a 14.3 pecent increase in high school graduates produced a 5.8 percent increase in four-year college attendance, yielding a multiplier of .406. This means that each 1 percent increase in high school graduates results in an increase of .406 percent in persons with four or more years of college (that is, for every 100 additional whites graduating from high school, an additional 41 will complete four or more years of college). For American Indians, this multiplier is only .116, signifying that for every additional 100 Indians who finish high school, only an additional 12 will complete four or more years of college. If Indians in 1980 attended college in the same multiples as whites, 13.8 percent should have completed at least four years of postsecondary schooling. This means that 6 percentage points, or two thirds of the 9.4 point deficit between whites and Indians, can be accounted for by lower rates of college attendance by American Indians.

Why have American Indians not converted their secondary schooling gains into similar gains at higher levels? One reason is that in spite of public policy initiatives, discrimination and other factors limit opportunities for higher education or otherwise prevent Indian students from completing four years of college. Admitting Indian students to college does not guarantee that they will stay there.

Another reason is that Indian education has traditionally emphasized short-term vocational training instead of academic studies. In the past, BIA boarding schools and other educational assistance programs heavily favored vocational training for Indian students.[16] By the same token, a baccalaureate degree in literature, political science, or other academic pursuits may have little apparent value to Indian youths making their homes on a reservation or in an inner city.[17]

A third, and perhaps most disturbing, reason is that the universality of high school diplomas has forced Indian students to acquire this degree as a minimum requirement for entering the job market, but not for the purpose of continuing their education. The widespread availability of programs to assist Indian high school dropouts with GED examinations also might increase the numbers of persons reporting a high school education, or its equivalent, without improving college attendance or abating the Indian high school dropout rate.

In fact, the 1980 census questionnaire instructed respondents with GEDs to report their schooling as 12 years. Assuming that persons with GED certificates are less likely to attend college than persons completing four years of high school would explain at once the striking increase in high school completion and the dismally low rates of college attendance by American Indians. Unfortunately, this matter cannot be explained further because it is impossible to distinguish in census data persons with GEDs from those with high school diplomas.

School Enrollment

There are indicators in the data from the 1980 census that a relatively large number of Indian youths are curtailing their education before finishing high school. Preliminary evidence of this behavior can be

---

[16]Fuchs and Havighurst (1972), chap. 11.
[17]Fuchs and Havighurst (1972), chap. 11.

seen in the age-specific rates of school enrollment among American Indian and Alaska Native youths in Table 6.8. Not surprisingly, this table shows that very few children under age 5 are enrolled in school, and most likely those enrolled are in private preschool programs or in programs such as Head Start, many of which are tribally sponsored. Tribal involvement in preschool programs may explain why there is no difference in under age 5 school enrollments for reservation and nonreservation areas; Indian children living on a reservation may have about the same access to preschool programs as those living outside reservation boundaries. A more salient comparison can be made with metropolitan and nonmetropolitan areas, because very young Indian children in nonmetropolitan areas are less likely to be in school than those in metropolitan areas.

The data for school enrollment indicate that most Indian and Alaska Native children, as do other children, generally begin school at about age 5 or 6. Table 6.9 also shows that primary school attendance is almost universal for these children. Regardless of residence, the proportion of Indian students aged 7 to 14 enrolled in school is no less than 94 percent. The balance of students not enrolled may be a function of reporting errors, the extreme isolation of students in areas such as Alaska and the Southwest, and a small number of families who withhold their children from school for religious, health, or other reasons.

While primary school attendance is almost universal among Indian children, this is by no means the case for secondary school enrollment. At ages 13 and 14 most Indian students have entered or are about to enter their first year of high school. In many areas age 16 is the earliest

TABLE 6.8

Percentage of American Indian and Alaska Native Youths Aged 19 and Under Enrolled in School

Age	Metropolitan	Nonmetropolitan	Off Reservation	On or Near Reservation
Under 5	15.5	12.5	14.0	14.1
5–6	85.2	83.3	83.7	84.8
7–8	98.3	96.4	98.3	96.5
9–10	98.8	96.5	98.4	97.2
11–12	98.5	96.6	98.8	96.5
13–14	97.9	94.4	98.1	94.7
15–16	88.3	85.9	89.0	85.5
17–18	60.6	57.9	58.7	60.1
19	28.3	30.6	29.7	28.6

SOURCE: Public-Use Microdata Sample, 5 percent A File.

that students may legally withdraw from school; thus, school enroll-ments for 15- and 16-year-olds are significantly lower than those for 13- and 14-year-olds. Another sharp drop appears among students aged 17 and 18. Only about 6 in 10 Indian youths in this age group are enrolled in school. This estimate of nonattendance is as pronounced in urban areas as it is in reservation areas. A further indication of the low levels of postsecondary school attendance is that over two thirds of 19-year-old Indian youths are not enrolled in school.

School Progress

A way of viewing the magnitude of the high school dropout prob-lem among Indians is from the vantage point of school progress. Stu-dents who fall behind in their schooling are more likely to drop out and are less likely to complete postsecondary schooling than students who keep up their studies.

The Census Bureau does not collect information about school prog-ress, but it is possible to estimate it by making certain assumptions about school attendance patterns and then comparing ages with educa-tional levels. The percentages in Table 6.9 are based on the assumption that by age 5 or 6 most Indian children enrolled in school will be in the first grade and thereafter will be promoted one grade each year. By ages 17 and 18, these students should be enrolled in or have completed the twelfth grade. These assumptions are consistent with the school enroll-ment figures of Table 6.8.

According to these assumptions, no children aged 5 or 6 start be-hind in school; they are enrolled in the first or second grade, that is, ahead or on time. However, at each older age group, the percentage of students who are behind in grade grows quickly. For example, in reser-vation and nonmetropolitan areas, the proportion of 7- and 8-year-olds behind in school is about 6 percent. Among children aged 11 and 12 in the same areas about 15 percent appear to be behind in school.

The impact of dropout behavior becomes most obvious at about age 16. Students in nonmetropolitan areas have the most dismal record of progress, with over one quarter of youths aged 15 and 16 and two fifths of those aged 17 and 18 behind in school, showing the impact of drop-outs. At best, in metropolitan and nonreservation locations one third of Indian students who should be juniors or seniors in high school appear to be below this level or have left school altogether; this percentage is higher elsewhere.

Comparing Table 6.9 with Table 6.8 shows how well enrollment figures reflect school achievement. This is most easily seen for the 17-

TABLE 6.9
School Progress of American Indians and Alaska Natives Aged 5–18

Age	Percentage Metropolitan		Percentage Nonmetropolitan		Percentage Off Reservation		Percentage On or Near Reservation	
	Behind	Ahead or On Time	Behind	Ahead or On Time	Behind	Ahead or On Time	Behind	Ahead or On Time
5–6	0.0	100.0	0.0	100.0	0.0	100.0	0.0	100.0
7–8	4.3	95.7	6.4	93.6	4.8	95.2	5.8	94.2
9–10	8.9	91.1	11.0	89.0	9.5	90.5	10.3	89.7
11–12	9.3	90.7	15.7	84.3	10.3	89.7	14.1	85.9
13–14	11.5	88.5	20.1	79.9	12.8	87.2	17.9	82.1
15–16	17.7	82.3	25.7	74.3	18.0	82.0	24.5	75.5
17–18	33.0	67.0	41.0	59.0	33.6	66.4	39.4	60.6

SOURCE: Public-Use Microdata Sample, 5 percent A File.

and 18-year-old age group. In Table 6.8, 60 percent of metropolitan youths are shown enrolled in school. In Table 6.9, 67 percent of these youths are ahead or on time in their school progress. Reconciling these figures means that 7 percent of metropolitan youths not enrolled in school are not behind and probably are early high school graduates. The remaining 33 percent are most likely behind because they are dropouts. Notably, the slippage between school enrollment and normal progress is much lower in reservation and nonmetropolitan locations, suggesting that early graduation and graduation at younger ages is less common in these areas.

Geographic Distribution of Education

The geographic distribution of education is important for understanding where educational gains were made during the 1970s and the extent to which a high school education is truly universal. For example, it is useful to know the location of areas with exceedingly low levels of education, especially those that are otherwise hidden in the statistics showing gains for the nation as a whole. Table 6.10 shows the percentage distribution of adult men and women with 12 years or more of schooling completed.

Among the conclusions that can be drawn from this table, perhaps the most general is that the distribution of high school graduates among American Indian men and women across geographic locations is relatively uniform. Equally evident is that in almost all places a majority of American Indians report that they have completed 12 or more years of schooling. Indian males in nonmetropolitan areas of the South Atlantic states report the lowest rates of high school completion (36.9 percent), but this figure pertains to a relatively small number of individuals. The highest rates of high school completion involve a much larger population of American Indians residing in nonreservation areas of the Mountain states, such as Colorado and New Mexico. About three fourths of the men and women in these areas report 12 or more years of schooling completed.

The most apparent differences are fairly predictable: Populations in nonmetropolitan and reservation areas generally have lower levels of education than populations in other areas. For some areas, such as for Indian men on and off reservations in the Mountain states, the difference can be as large as 20 points. Differences across regions also tend to be small but can be as large as 20 points—comparing metropolitan males in the Pacific and New England states, for instance. Finally, gender differences are the least consistent and smallest across regions. That is, in

TABLE 6.10

Percentage of American Indians and Alaska Natives Aged 25 and Over With 12 or More Years of Schooling Completed, by Census Division

Census Division	Metropolitan		Nonmetropolitan	
	Males	Females	Males	Females
New England	59.9	59.8	45.8	45.9
Mid Atlantic	59.9	61.5	53.9	60.2
E. North Central	62.6	61.9	51.7	48.1
W. North Central	59.8	57.1	52.8	51.3
South Atlantic	63.4	57.9	36.9	39.6
E. South Central	58.4	58.5	49.2	47.3
W. South Central	52.3	60.3	53.9	50.4
Mountain	65.5	62.9	49.2	41.4
Pacific	71.1	67.3	55.4	52.3

SOURCE: Public-Use Microdata Sample, 5 percent A File.

some places more men than women have 12 years or more of schooling, and in other areas the opposite is true. In any case, the difference between men and women rarely exceeds 5 percentage points.

Age Distribution of Education

Table 6.11 shows the distribution of education across age groups instead of regions (as in Table 6.10). Gender differences are not large, but there are consistent differences with regard to residence. Regardless of age or sex, American Indians living in nonmetropolitan or reservation areas have lower levels of education than those residing in other places.

Predictably, educational attainment is closely related to age. Younger American Indians, like other segments of the U.S. population, are better educated than their elders. Except in nonmetropolitan areas, over 75 percent of the Indian population aged 25 to 30 report 12 years or more of schooling completed. In contrast, the proportion of the Indian population aged 70 and over reporting 12 or more years of school completed ranges from 29 percent for metropolitan women to 13 percent for nonmetropolitan men. In metropolitan and nonreservation areas the majority of American Indians aged 50 and younger have a high school education; however, in nonmetropolitan and reservation locations the high school educated majority is younger, aged 40 to 45 and under.

TABLE 6.10 *(continued)*

Census Division	Off Reservation		On or Near Reservation	
	Males	Females	Males	Females
New England	58.0	59.7	56.4	51.5
Mid Atlantic	59.6	62.5	57.9	57.1
E. North Central	62.1	60.9	51.5	50.3
W. North Central	64.9	58.8	49.0	50.3
South Atlantic	51.9	49.0	51.3	50.8
E. South Central	54.9	55.9	55.9	40.9
W. South Central	58.4	55.7	70.6	69.1
Mountain	74.7	72.0	52.2	46.0
Pacific	71.8	66.7	61.5	59.7

Table 6.11 also shows that residential differences between the old and the young are relatively small but become pronounced about ages 40 to 60. This is intriguing because it raises many questions about the impact of education. For example, among younger American Indians the narrow gap between reservation and nonreservation residents may represent similar educational opportunities in these areas or it may indicate that better-educated individuals do not migrate from reservation areas while they are relatively young. However, the large differences among persons over age 40 may represent those who acquired higher (or lower) levels of education by virtue of their residence or better-educated persons who left the reservation for economic opportunities elsewhere.

Opportunities for Postsecondary Education

The next tables highlight in detail the earlier finding that gains in secondary schooling are not translated into gains at the postsecondary level. Table 6.12 shows the probabilities of obtaining four years or more of postsecondary schooling among persons who have completed at least 12 years of schooling.

Regionally, the distribution of educational resources in Table 6.12 generally resembles the data in Table 6.10. Gender differences are not consistent, and residents in metropolitan and nonreservation areas are more likely to attain four or more years of postsecondary schooling than residents of other areas. However, comparing Tables 6.12 and 6.10

TABLE 6.11

Percentage of American Indians and Alaska Natives Aged 25 and Over With 12 or More Years of Education Completed, by Age Group

Age Group	Metropolitan		Nonmetropolitan	
	Males	Females	Males	Females
25–30	78.5	78.8	72.2	70.9
31–35	77.9	75.3	69.3	64.4
36–40	74.9	68.1	58.4	50.1
41–45	64.8	62.7	50.2	40.8
46–50	63.2	56.8	36.6	32.3
51–55	50.2	50.5	27.7	33.1
56–60	48.4	50.1	31.3	31.5
61–65	44.2	45.6	25.8	27.9
66–70	34.2	29.7	23.3	19.0
Over 70	22.5	28.5	12.8	13.5

SOURCE: Public-Use Microdata Sample, 5 percent A File.

shows that the correlation between the percentage of high school graduates and the probability of completing four years or more of college is much less than perfect. Areas with relatively large shares of high school graduates do not necessarily have proportionally large shares of persons with four years of college education. For example, 57.9 percent of males residing on reservations in the Middle Atlantic states have a secondary level education, but only 7 out of 100 have attained four years or more of college, the lowest probability in Table 6.12. In contrast, New England Indian males have the highest probability of completing four years or more of college, although the percentage completing high school is almost identical (58.0) to the Middle Atlantic group.

Table 6.13 parallels Table 6.11 by showing the probabilities of postsecondary education across age groups. Again, the results vary predictably with respect to differences by place and gender. Men are generally more likely to attain four years or more of postsecondary schooling, and the probabilities of this achievement are higher in metropolitan and nonreservation areas than in other locations. However, across age groups, the data in this table reveal a somewhat surprising pattern of results.

Gender and residential differences notwithstanding, the probability of completing four years of college is remarkably small for younger persons, especially individuals under age 30. This reinforces several points already made about American Indian college attendance, but it is surprising in other respects. It is most unexpected because conventional

TABLE 6.11 *(continued)*

Age Group	Off Reservation		On or Near Reservation	
	Males	Females	Males	Females
25–30	76.5	76.4	75.5	75.2
31–35	74.6	72.3	74.9	69.7
36–40	71.4	64.9	65.3	56.7
41–45	61.3	60.2	56.7	46.5
46–50	58.7	53.5	45.8	39.0
51–55	46.9	49.0	34.1	36.5
56–60	46.2	48.4	36.0	34.2
61–65	40.6	39.5	31.2	37.5
66–70	34.6	28.3	23.5	20.4
Over 70	22.4	25.5	13.3	16.9

wisdom presumes that younger people, especially the post-sputnik "baby boom" generation, have had many more opportunities for attending college than their elders. This finding is also surprising in the context of numerous social programs aimed at encouraging higher educational achievements among minority populations in general and American Indians in particular. Have these programs failed and did educational opportunities actually decline in the 1970s? The answer to this question is probably no.

In absolute numbers, the number of Indians with four years or more of college in 1980 exceeded 53,000,[18] more than in any previous census. However, the rise in secondary schooling among younger persons is not, as mentioned, being converted to yet higher levels of education. This is producing a proportionately smaller segment of college-educated persons relative to the number of persons finishing high school. In this respect, the educational opportunities for postsecondary schooling among younger American Indian high school graduates are virtually the lowest in the adult Indian population. This also means that the opportunity to achieve a college degree as a reward for high school graduation is not readily available to the vast majority of young American Indian high school graduates.

For older American Indians, particularly males, Table 6.13 reveals another important and somewhat unexpected result. It appears that the

[18]U.S. Bureau of the Census, *1980 Census of Population, General Social and Economic Characteristics, United States Summary* (Washington, DC: U.S. Government Printing Office, 1983).

TABLE 6.12

Probabilities of Completing Four or More Years of Postsecondary Education for American Indian and Alaska Native High School Graduates Aged 25 and Over, by Census Division

	Metropolitan		Nonmetropolitan	
Census Division	Males	Females	Males	Females
New England	.246	.110	.227	.107
Mid Atlantic	.181	.141	.200	.081
E. North Central	.148	.123	.080	.096
W. North Central	.166	.108	.123	.114
South Atlantic	.223	.155	.171	.154
E. South Central	.224	.128	.167	.125
W. South Central	.211	.164	.160	.111
Mountain	.183	.142	.116	.098
Pacific	.200	.119	.091	.074

SOURCE: Public-Use Microdata Sample, 5 percent A File.

most significant public policies promoting higher education among American Indians were not the initiatives of the 1960s and 1970s but instead were the opportunities made available through the post–World War II GI bill. This legislation made available financial assistance for

TABLE 6.13

Probabilities of Completing Four or More Years of Postsecondary Education for American Indian and Alaska Native High School Graduates Aged 25 and Over, by Age Group

Age Group	Metropolitan		Nonmetropolitan		Off Reservation		On or Near Reservation	
	Males	Females	Males	Females	Males	Females	Males	Females
25–30	.156	.136	.090	.086	.158	.135	.097	.097
31–35	.214	.148	.129	.098	.221	.144	.138	.112
36–40	.192	.130	.144	.103	.200	.122	.141	.123
41–45	.209	.132	.143	.095	.229	.143	.128	.084
46–50	.220	.110	.118	.126	.212	.126	.162	.098
51–55	.245	.121	.125	.143	.247	.133	.150	.115
56–60	.230	.105	.160	.082	.252	.105	.137	.085
61–65	.204	.148	.148	.143	.242	.162	.097	.125
66–70	.186	.124	.148	.138	.200	.118	.123	.149
Over 70	.154	.176	.241	.213	.144	.221	.250	.111

SOURCE: Public-Use Microdata Sample, 5 percent A File.

TABLE 6.12 *(continued)*

Census Division	Off Reservation		On or Near Reservation	
	Males	Females	Males	Females
New England	.250	.136	.229	.039
Mid Atlantic	.219	.152	.070	.068
E. North Central	.141	.129	.097	.067
W. North Central	.180	.100	.108	.121
South Atlantic	.212	.156	.138	.145
E. South Central	.217	.128	.106	.111
W. South Central	.202	.150	.170	.149
Mountain	.245	.129	.125	.115
Pacific	.211	.127	.131	.088

higher education on an unprecedented scale to tens of thousands of re-turning veterans, among them American Indian GIs. The best evidence for this claim appears in the probabilities of advanced schooling for In-dian males residing in metropolitan locations. In 1980 Indian veterans who were aged 20 to 30 in 1945 were aged 55 to 65. This age group overlaps the 56- to 60-year-olds who have the second highest probability of college attendance for high school graduates. The high school gradu-ates with the highest probability of having an advanced education are men now residing in metropolitan areas and those who reached their eighteenth birthday between 1942 and 1947, that is, men who were aged 51 to 55 in 1980.

The likely impact of the GI bill on American Indian men is visible though less pronounced in other areas. Urban Indians with GI bill assis-tance may have had more opportunities to pursue their educations, and by the same token reservation or nonmetropolitan Indians may have migrated and remained in urban areas for the purpose of getting an ed-ucation and taking advantage of job opportunities. Indian women, most of whom were not veterans, do not have the same age-specific variations as Indian men, lending further evidence of the GI bill's impact on Indian education.

Finally, the over-70 age group also has relatively high rates of com-pleting four years of college. However, this age group also has a very low rate of high school graduation. The figures in Table 6.13 most likely reflect the attainments of a small group of extraordinary individuals who, once overcoming the barriers to finishing high school, were able

TABLE 6.14

Educational Attainments of American Indians Aged 25 and Over Residing on the 16 Largest Reservations in 1980

	1970		
Reservation	High School Graduates %	College Graduates %	Attending Tribal or BIA School[a] %
Navajo[c] (AZ, NM, UT)	17.4	0.8	28.6
Pine Ridge (SD)	22.8	1.6	59.1
Gila River (AZ)	20.9	1.5	19.6
Papago (AZ)	12.5	0.4	45.8
Fort Apache (AZ)	14.9	1.9	15.5
Hopi[c] (AZ)	27.5	2.2	56.1
Zuni Pueblo (NM)	18.5	0.2	5.2
San Carlos (AZ)	13.5	0.0	11.7
Rosebud (SD)	23.4	0.4	18.5
Blackfeet (MT)	26.9	1.3	2.9
Yakima (WA)	32.1	1.0	6.1
Eastern Cherokee (NC)	20.7	0.4	73.1
Standing Rock (ND, SD)	28.5	0.3	24.4
Osage[d] (OK)	*	*	0.4
Fort Peck (MT)	23.1	0.6	3.3
Wind River (WY)	35.8	1.7	20.5

SOURCES: *1980 Census of Population, General Social and Economic Characteristics, United States Summary;* "American Indians, Eskimos, and Aleuts on Identified Reservations and in the Historic Areas of Oklahoma," *1980 Census of Population, Subject Report;* and "American Indians," *1970 Census of Population, Subject Report.*

[a]Includes only persons aged 5 to 19.
[b]Includes only persons aged 16 to 19 not enrolled in school and not graduated from high school.
[c]Navajo and Hopi reservation data are not strictly comparable because of administration changes in Navajo-Hopi joint use areas in the 1970s.
[d]Osage reservation data are not available for 1970.

also to acquire additional years of schooling. Ironically, the conditional probability of attending four years or more of college by high school graduates is considerably higher for this age group than for Indians under age 30.

Reservation Education

Table 6.14 shows the schooling of American Indians residing on the 16 largest reservations in 1980. The statistics are interesting mainly for

TABLE 6.14 *(continued)*

Reservation	1980		
	High School Dropouts[b] %	High School Graduates %	College Graduates %
Navajo[c] (AZ, NM, UT)	29.6	34.6	3.2
Pine Ridge (SD)	29.8	42.3	5.1
Gila River (AZ)	47.2	37.2	2.8
Papago (AZ)	25.3	38.7	2.1
Fort Apache (AZ)	44.0	38.0	2.0
Hopi[c] (AZ)	30.4	40.3	2.5
Zuni Pueblo (NM)	28.8	37.3	2.1
San Carlos (AZ)	32.1	43.6	0.9
Rosebud (SD)	19.7	49.7	6.5
Blackfeet (MT)	26.9	57.2	5.3
Yakima (WA)	21.3	57.0	5.1
Eastern Cherokee (NC)	34.4	42.4	2.9
Standing Rock (ND, SD)	41.9	46.0	4.0
Osage[d] (OK)	20.0	62.7	8.1
Fort Peck (MT)	49.8	56.6	3.2
Wind River (WY)	39.4	53.1	2.2

their geographic detail; the numbers are consistent with the comments already made about Indian education. For example, the proportion of high school graduates increased sharply in places such as the Navajo reservation, where it rose from 17.4 to 34.6 percent. Similarly, the proportion of college graduates increased in this decade but remains very small, ranging from 0.9 to 6.5 percent of the population aged 25 and over in 1980. Despite this progress, the dropout rates remain very high in these areas.

Apart from confirming the existence of national trends in specific reservations, the data in Table 6.14 also show the relative importance of BIA schools and tribal schools in these localities. As these figures indicate, there is a wide range of dependence on these organizations. The Osage tribe in northeastern Oklahoma relies mostly on the local public school system, and only 0.4 percent of their children attend BIA or tribal school programs. In contrast, 73.1 percent of the children of the Eastern Cherokee reservation attend such programs. Overall, BIA and tribal school programs continue to provide education to a significant proportion of the children in these places.

Concluding Remarks

This chapter has outlined patterns of language use and the distribution of education in the American Indian and Alaska Native population. As indicators of human capital, these characteristics play a central role in the material well-being of American Indians. American Indians lacking a strong command of English are distinctly disadvantaged in the labor market; schooling provides skills and abilities that can be parlayed into material benefits.

The relationship between language use and material well-being is extremely complex and poorly understood. Nevertheless, the existence of this relationship is apparent among American Indians. Persons who speak only English at home are more likely to be better educated, be active members of the labor force, and enjoy higher incomes than persons who speak an Indian language. Occupations are an exception to this rule; for Indians who overcome the barriers associated with their language and gain fluency in English, speaking a native language poses only a small disadvantage.

In spite of its relationship to social and economic characteristics, the use of native languages does not explain the poverty and economic hardships experienced by American Indians. The reason is that English is almost universally understood in the Indian population, and most Indians speak only English at home. However, it is noteworthy that among Indians who speak a language other than English at home, almost all speak an Indian language; very few speak Spanish at home.

While a large majority of American Indians are fluent in English, there are of course exceptions, and some Indians in some areas are more likely than others to speak a native language. The Mountain states, for example, are an important exception. Not only does this area have a large number of Indians, but the majority also speak a native language at home. Other areas have considerably smaller percentages of native speakers. Nevertheless, in all areas persons who regularly use a native language are more likely to be older and reside in nonmetropolitan and/or reservation locations.

For understanding the socioeconomic status of American Indians with regard to education, this chapter has tried to emphasize several points that are not widely known. One is that exposure to educational institutions is not a new development among American Indians. However, mass education for American Indians is relatively new. Between 1900 and 1930 school attendance by American Indians aged 5 to 20 increased from 40 to 60 percent.[19] By 1980 this figure exceeded 90 percent.

[19]U.S. Bureau of the Census (1937).

Furthermore, Indian control over Indian schools is a recent development, which spread most rapidly during the 1970s. Another important point is that American Indians have made significant strides in secondary schooling. Comparing 1980 with 1970 statistics shows a remarkable increase in the numbers of Indians reporting a high school education. On the other hand, younger American Indians are highly prone to drop out of high school and are not inclined to attend college, even if they complete high school. The rise in secondary school completion may be due to growing numbers of American Indians acquiring GED diplomas.

In relative terms opportunities for attaining four years of college are lowest for American Indians under age 30. Some of these individuals will undoubtedly complete additional years of higher education. But in the absence of substantial numbers of college students over age 30, the proportion of high school graduates attaining four or more years of college is at an alarmingly low post–World War II level among younger Indians. In an economy demanding ever-higher levels of knowledge from workers, this development is an ominous sign for the future.

From the viewpoint of economic well-being, language use and education are important prerequisites, but they hardly tell the full story. Cognitive skills have little economic value unless they can be translated into concrete gains in the labor market. In the next chapter the labor market experiences of American Indians and Alaska Natives are examined.

7

LABOR FORCE PARTICIPATION

T HE WORK PEOPLE do and the money they receive for it are basic
yardsticks for judging economic success in American society.
This chapter deals with the labor market participation of
American Indians as a reflection of how well they have fared in the U.S.
economy.

In the preceding chapter the human capital resources of the American Indian and Alaska Native population were inventoried. Although
preeminently important, these resources do not automatically translate
into economic benefits. Labor force participation is a central concern
because the value of human capital, in economic terms, stems from its
worth in the labor market. Well-educated workers are highly valued and
well rewarded by employers. Likewise, poorly educated workers are not
highly valued and are more likely to be jobless than their better-educated counterparts. By the same token, the value of education is considerably lessened if employment opportunities do not exist for workers,
regardless of their educational qualifications.

Educational credentials aside, high levels of unemployment or low
levels of labor force participation bespeak economic hardship. In this
connection labor force participation reflects the outcome of low educational attainments and at the same time mirrors opportunities for
American Indians to exchange their educational qualifications for economic benefits. The successes and failures of American Indians in ac-

quiring educational resources and their successes and failures in the conversion of these credentials have far-reaching economic consequences.

Estimating Labor Force Participation

Data from the Census Bureau and from the Bureau of Indian Affairs (BIA) are widely used sources of information about labor force participation. This chapter does not use data from the BIA because comparing BIA and Census Bureau estimates usually reveals substantial discrepancies, and in general these figures are not comparable for several reasons.

First, BIA estimates are based on populations residing within or near reservations, while census data are based on the nation as a whole. There are substantial differences in labor force participation between reservation and nonreservation areas. Second, census figures are based on survey data from household respondents, while BIA estimates are derived from sources other than surveys. The BIA explains that its figures

> are labeled "estimates" because they are not based to any major extent on actual surveys. The local Agency offices of the Bureau of Indian Affairs estimated the data using whatever information was available. Accuracy varies from place to place; it is relatively high at small, isolated locations where everyone's activity is common knowledge. Generally, [large areas] . . . are considered the least accurate and most difficult to estimate.[1]

Third, the BIA and the Census Bureau use different definitions of labor force participation, particularly unemployment. The Census Bureau uses the standard Department of Labor definition, which considers all persons currently employed or unemployed and actively seeking work as members of the labor force. Unemployed members of the labor force are persons aged 16 and over without employment who were available for employment and who had been seeking a job during the four weeks previous to the survey. In contrast, the BIA definition specifies unemployed persons as individuals aged 16 and over who are without jobs and seeking employment. The BIA definition is similar to that used by the Labor Department, but it is problematic because of its vagueness about what constitutes employment-seeking behavior.

[1]U.S. Bureau of Indian Affairs, *Local Estimates of Resident Indian Population and Labor Force Status, December 1981* (Washington, DC: mimeographed, 1982), p. 1.

As a result of methodological differences, the estimates of unemployment made by the BIA are ordinarily much higher than the estimates of the Census Bureau. For example, the census estimate of unemployment for American Indians is less than 20 percent for April 1980, while the BIA estimate is 31 percent for December 1981.[2] One reason why census estimates of unemployment are lower than BIA figures is that census procedures exclude persons who have become "discouraged workers" and are no longer actively seeking jobs—specifically, persons who have not sought employment within four weeks. In contrast, BIA estimates are based on a less stringent definition and are more likely to include a larger number of long-term unemployed workers.

The practice of estimating unemployment in different months also is consequential for producing discrepancies in BIA and Census Bureau statistics. December BIA unemployment figures reflect a traditionally sluggish season for the U.S. economy as a whole while April, the month when the census is taken, is a time when job opportunities, especially in outdoor activities such as construction, are in an upswing. For some applications, BIA figures may be preferable, but in most cases where survey methodology, national coverage, and data comparable to other populations are desirable, census estimates are more useful.

Unemployment in census data also can be described from two different, yet complementary perspectives. One view of unemployment is provided by the percentage of *persons aged 16 and over* without work ("percent unemployed"). This statistic indexes the prevalence of unemployment throughout the adult population in relation to employed persons and persons not in the labor force. A second, more familiar statistic is the "unemployment rate," which is the percentage of *the civilian labor force* without work, excluding from consideration persons not in the labor force. This statistic is the most widely publicized estimate of unemployment in the U.S. economy, and it measures the success of persons active in the labor force in finding employment. Differences in labor force participation rates and other factors can make the numerical estimates of unemployment rates and the percent unemployed substantially different.

Labor Force Status

Regardless of which data are used, American Indians have historically had exceedingly low rates of labor force participation. Writing

[2]U.S. Bureau of Indian Affairs (1982), p. 1.

about the Indian labor force, Jacobsen[3] notes that unlike many other ethnic groups the major contribution of American Indians to the national economy has been made in the form of natural resources from tribal lands and not from the residential labor force occupying these areas. Some of the oldest published figures for Indian labor force participation are available in the 1910 special census report on American Indians. Between 1900 and 1910 the percentage of Indians aged 10 and over in "gainful occupations" increased from 36.7 to 39.2 percent. As of 1910, 61.3 percent of Indian males over age 10 were in gainful occupations compared with only 16.0 percent of Indian females.[4] Although school attendance for American Indians increased rapidly throughout this century, as late as the 1960s and 1970s writers were commenting on the low rates of labor force participation by American Indians.[5]

To update earlier published statistics, Figures 7.1 and 7.2 and Table 7.1 show total and age-specific unemployment and labor force participation for blacks, whites, and American Indians. In 1970 American Indians were decidedly the most unemployed and the least active in the labor force. Ten years later small gains by American Indians combined with deteriorating conditions among blacks erased the earlier differences that separated these groups. The privileged position of whites, particularly white males, is clearly evident in the low unemployment and high labor force participation rates that changed relatively little during the 1970s. The unemployment rate of Indians is nearly three times that of whites. The gap is smaller among women, but the unemployment rate among Indian women is still about twice as high as among white women. Ironically, Figures 7.1 and 7.2 suggest that increasing labor force participation by American Indian men and women between 1970 and 1980 was translated into nearly proportional increases in their unemployment.

Age is a well-known factor in labor force participation. Younger workers, for example, have less experience and more difficulty in securing employment. By the same token, low rates of labor force participa-

---

[3]Cardell K. Jacobsen, "Internal Colonialism and Native Americans: Indian Labor in the United States from 1871 to World War II," *Social Science Quarterly* 65(1984):158–171

[4]U.S. Bureau of the Census, *The Indian Population in the United States and Alaska, 1930* (Washington, DC: U.S. Government Printing Office, 1937), p. 250. These figures are probably overestimates because Indians most assimilated also were most easily enumerated. Less assimilated Indians were in all likelihood grossly underrepresented in early censuses, and they were unlikely to be in "gainful occupations."

[5]William A. Brophy and Sophie D. Aberle, *The Indian: America's Unfinished Business* (Norman: University of Oklahoma Press, 1966); Alan L. Sorkin, *American Indians and Federal Aid* (Washington, DC: Brookings Institution, 1971); Sar A. Levitan and Barbara Hetrick, *Big Brother's Indian Programs: With Reservations* (New York: McGraw-Hill, 1971).

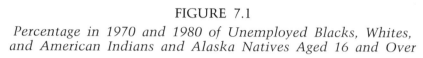

FIGURE 7.1

*Percentage in 1970 and 1980 of Unemployed Blacks, Whites,
and American Indians and Alaska Natives Aged 16 and Over*

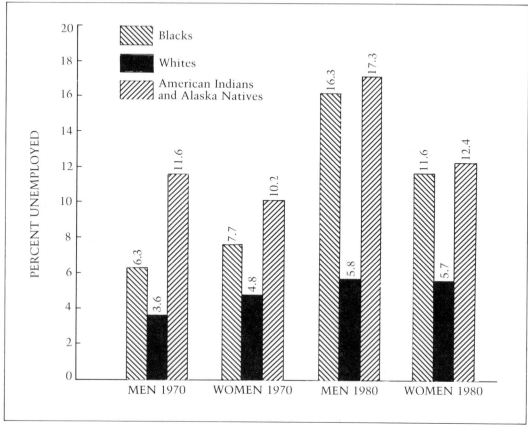

tion by younger persons are indicative of scarce opportunities and barriers to labor market entry. Such conditions retard work experience and
pose severe limits on future opportunities. Table 7.1 shows patterns of
labor force participation within age groups corresponding to important
periods in the careers of many workers.

Among low-income youths, including a sizable number of American Indians and blacks, employment is especially important as a way of
augmenting personal and family income. However, black and American
Indian teenagers are considerably more likely than their white counterparts to be either unemployed or out of the labor force. Joblessness
among black teenagers is a serious problem that periodically receives

FIGURE 7.2

Percentage in 1970 and 1980 of Blacks, Whites, and American Indians and Alaska Natives Aged 16 and Over Not in the Labor Force

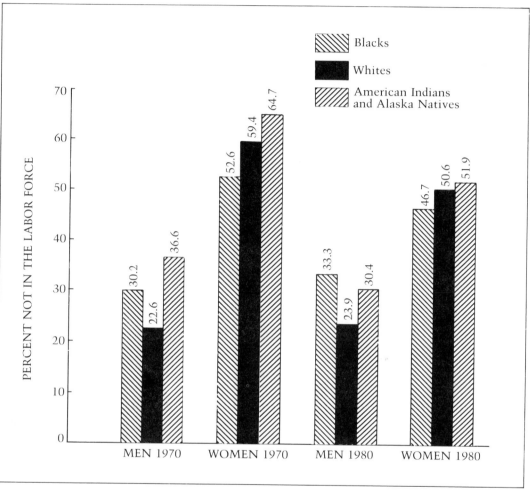

attention in public forums; it is an equally serious problem for American Indian youths.

Ages 20 to 24 are a crucial employment period with long-range implications. Persons in this age group are most likely completing their education and seeking their first full-time job in the labor market. Success or failure at this career stage presage lifelong labor market experiences. Labor force participation is higher and unemployment is lower

TABLE 7.1

*Percent Distribution of Age-Specific Labor Force Participation
for Blacks, Whites, American Indians and Alaska Natives Aged 16 and Over, 1980*

Age and Labor Force Status	Blacks		Whites		American Indians	
	Males	Females	Males	Females	Males	Females
16–19						
Unemployed	27.6	27.9	14.0	11.6	25.1	22.5
NILF*	63.5	69.7	44.5	51.0	55.9	65.0
20–24						
Unemployed	20.3	18.7	10.2	7.1	19.5	15.5
NILF*	26.5	38.6	15.7	30.5	23.1	44.2
25–54						
Unemployed	9.8	8.7	4.5	4.7	11.8	9.9
NILF*	16.3	31.0	6.2	37.4	16.8	42.2
55–64						
Unemployed	6.3	5.1	3.8	4.1	8.7	6.7
NILF*	37.7	55.9	27.8	58.6	43.8	65.9
65 and Over						
Unemployed	7.1	6.5	4.9	5.5	9.5	9.5
NILF*	82.3	89.6	80.6	92.0	83.9	92.0

SOURCE: *1980 Census of Population, General Social and Economic Characteristics, United States Summary.*

*NILF = Not In Labor Force.

for this age group than for teenagers. However, the transition from the school to the workplace is not smooth for many American Indians and blacks. These groups appear to suffer from many of the same disadvantages, which is reflected in similar high rates of unemployment and low rates of labor force participation, especially compared with whites of the same ages. Almost half of all Indian women in this age group are out of the labor force, perhaps because of lack of job opportunities, child care responsibilities, or both.

Ages 25 to 54 are often referred to as "prime working years" because workers in this age group are frequently considered most desirable for their experience and productivity by employers. Not surprisingly, these individuals have higher labor force participation and lower unemployment rates than any other age group. Again, American Indians and blacks have similar rates of unemployment and labor force participation, except that Indian women are much less attached to the labor force than are black women. Compared with men, white women also have a low attachment to the labor force; however, this may represent a trade-off between labor and leisure, because in many other respects their economic situation is relatively good compared with black and American Indian women. The low attachment of Indian women more likely results from the absence of job opportunities. The incomes of Indian women, which are discussed in the next chapter, are sufficiently low that a trade-off between labor and leisure is an unlikely possibility.

In the decade before retirement, ages 55 to 64, labor force participation declines sharply in all three racial groups, while unemployment is remarkably low. Persons in this age group may choose to leave the labor force rather than incur the costs of a job search. Predictably, white workers in this age group retain their advantage, while older Indian and black workers face similar disadvantages in terms of unemployment rates. Social Security, pension benefits, and mandatory retirement rules are most likely responsible for the fact that blacks, whites, and Indians have similar rates of labor force participation, although Indians and blacks are more likely than whites to be unemployed beyond the normal age of retirement.

Residence and Labor Force Participation

The geography of labor force participation is variable because of differences in local economic conditions. American Indians fortunate enough to reside in areas with thriving economies are more likely to be in the labor force than Indians living in economically depressed areas. The data in Tables 7.2, 7.3, and 7.4 show that, like other Americans, Indians benefit from residing in places with healthy regional and local economies. As a rule, metropolitan localities with highly developed economies provide more opportunities for employment than less developed nonmetropolitan areas.

As the data in Table 7.2 show, in metropolitan areas male and female unemployment averages 9.7 and 5.9 percent, respectively, compared with 12.1 and 6.6 percent in nonmetropolitan areas. Similar differences exist in labor force attachment. Although Indian women are less likely than Indian men to be unemployed, they also are less likely to be in the labor force. Among Indian women, 48.7 percent in metropolitan areas and 55.4 percent in nonmetropolitan areas are not in the labor force, compared with 26.7 and 34.6 percent, respectively, of men residing in metropolitan and nonmetropolitan places. It also is interesting to note that residential differences in unemployment and labor force attachment are greater for men than for women.

TABLE 7.2

Percent Distribution of Civilian Labor Force Status of American Indians and Alaska Natives Aged 16 and Over, by Place of Residence, 1980

| Census Division | Metropolitan | | | | | |
| | Employed | | Unemployed[a] | | Not in Labor Force | |
	Males	Females	Males	Females	Males	Females
New England	65.2	48.5	9.7	6.1	25.2	45.3
Mid Atlantic	61.2	44.5	10.3	7.1	28.5	48.3
E. North Central	63.2	41.9	14.7	7.3	22.2	50.7
W. North Central	52.6	44.6	14.7	5.1	32.7	50.3
South Atlantic	70.3	47.1	6.8	5.8	22.8	47.0
E. South Central	70.0	43.5	6.4	6.2	23.7	50.3
W. South Central	66.1	45.7	6.4	3.6	27.6	50.7
Mountain	60.4	45.1	8.9	5.4	30.7	49.5
Pacific	64.3	47.1	9.2	6.5	26.5	46.5

SOURCE: Public-Use Microdata Sample, 5 percent A File.

[a]These percentages are the proportion of the adult population (i.e., aged 16 and over) in the labor force but without employment. This *is not* the unemployment rate, which is the percentage of the civilian labor force without a job. The civilian labor force is the sum of employed and unemployed persons, excluding persons not in the labor force.

The distribution of labor force participation between reservation and nonreservation places in Table 7.3 closely parallels the data in Table 7.2. For example, gender differences are equally prevalent regardless of residence. However, residential differences are slightly less pronounced in Table 7.3 and Table 7.2, probably because some reservations are in close proximity to metropolitan areas and have access to well-developed economies outside reservation boundaries.

In all of these tables differences attributable to variations in regional economies also are observable. American Indians residing in the upper midwestern states of the North Central region almost consistently suffer the highest unemployment and the lowest attachment to the labor market. For example, male unemployment rates in this area hover around 20 percent (see Table 7.4). In contrast, the Sunbelt prosperity of the 1980s provided American Indians residing in these areas

TABLE 7.2 *(continued)*

| Census Division | Nonmetropolitan | | | | | |
| | Employed | | Unemployed[a] | | Not in Labor Force | |
	Males	Females	Males	Females	Males	Females
New England	49.3	45.8	17.3	6.0	33.3	48.2
Mid Atlantic	54.0	29.9	16.1	8.3	29.9	61.8
E. North Central	54.2	35.1	14.9	8.1	30.8	56.8
W. North Central	49.4	38.6	11.1	8.0	39.5	53.4
South Atlantic	62.2	47.6	7.3	4.7	30.5	47.7
E. South Central	58.1	36.3	11.9	10.0	30.0	53.7
W. South Central	56.9	37.6	6.3	3.4	36.8	59.0
Mountain	49.9	34.2	9.2	5.4	40.8	60.4
Pacific	45.9	36.3	14.7	5.7	39.4	57.9

with lower unemployment rates and higher labor force participation than their counterparts in other areas. About 70 percent of metropolitan Indian males aged 16 and over residing in the South Atlantic and East South Central states were employed in 1980 (see Table 7.3). This employment figure is equaled by no other area.

Time at Work

One of the problems with labor force statistics such as those in the preceding tables is that they portray labor force participation as an all or nothing proposition. That is, they create an image of employment as a full-time, year-round condition and unemployment or out of the labor force as perpetual idleness. In reality, many individuals frequently change their labor force status during the course of a year. Some persons enter and exit the labor force, others lose or change jobs, and still others work less or more than 40 hours per week. To gain a better understand-

TABLE 7.3

Percent Distribution of Civilian Labor Force Status of American Indians and Alaska Natives Aged 16 and Over, by Place of Residence, 1980

| Census Division | Off Reservation | | | | | |
| | Employed | | Unemployed[a] | | Not in Labor Force | |
	Males	Females	Males	Females	Males	Females
New England	61.8	48.3	11.6	5.2	26.6	46.6
Mid Atlantic	61.7	43.7	10.3	7.6	28.0	48.7
E. North Central	64.0	42.3	14.6	7.2	21.4	50.5
W. North Central	58.1	42.8	12.5	6.2	29.4	51.0
South Atlantic	67.3	48.1	6.9	5.0	25.8	47.0
E. South Central	65.8	40.6	8.5	7.8	25.8	51.6
W. South Central	62.2	42.5	6.7	3.7	31.1	53.7
Mountain	66.4	47.8	7.0	5.5	26.5	46.7
Pacific	66.8	48.0	9.0	6.3	24.3	45.7

SOURCE: Public-Use Microdata Sample, 5 percent A File.

[a]These percentages are the proportion of the adult population (i.e., aged 16 and over) in the labor force but without employment. This *is not* the unemployment rate, which is the percentage of the civilian labor force without a job. The civilian labor force is the sum of employed and unemployed persons, excluding persons not in the labor force.

ing of this behavior, the temporal dimension of labor force participation is shown in Table 7.5.

Table 7.5 displays the percentages of persons working half of a year or less, working 30 hours a week or less, or unemployed 15 weeks or more annually. As in Tables 7.2, 7.3, and 7.4, the figures in Table 7.5 exhibit striking differences related to gender and residence. For instance, the proportion of women residing on or near reservations who work 26 weeks or less is nearly twice that of Indian men living in nonreservation locations, 39.3 and 20.3 percent, respectively. Even within areas, Indian men spend considerably more time at work than Indian women.

Without question, Indian men are more strongly attached to the labor force than Indian women, and consequently Indian men are also more likely to spend more time unemployed. Paradoxically, the percentages of American Indians working half the year or less in part-time jobs are relatively small. For American Indian men and women aged 16 and over, the median work week is 40 hours, regardless of residence.

TABLE 7.3 *(continued)*

Census Division	On or Near Reservation					
	Employed		Unemployed[a]		Not in Labor Force	
	Males	Females	Males	Females	Males	Females
New England	62.7	47.4	10.2	8.1	27.1	44.4
Mid Atlantic	55.8	39.6	13.4	6.2	30.9	54.2
E. North Central	49.4	32.9	15.1	8.8	35.5	58.3
W. North Central	44.9	40.8	13.4	6.7	41.7	52.5
South Atlantic	57.8	38.9	8.7	9.1	33.5	52.0
E. South Central	65.1	41.9	7.0	6.5	27.9	51.6
W. South Central	71.3	48.2	4.1	2.3	24.6	49.5
Mountain	51.9	36.8	9.3	5.4	38.7	57.8
Pacific	51.0	40.1	12.6	6.3	36.4	53.7

Nevertheless, substantial percentages of Indians spent 15 weeks or more unemployed in 1979—in the range of 36 to 45 percent. This suggests that while American Indians are not unwilling workers, they are exposed to a large measure of job insecurity resulting from quits, firings, and layoffs. Seasonal employment also may be responsible for this pattern of labor force participation.

Correlates of Labor Force Participation

In painstaking studies, labor economists and sociologists have identified a number of factors related to labor force participation in the United States.[6] Replicating these studies for the Indian population is beyond the scope of this discussion. However, Tables 7.6–7.10 show

[6]William G. Bowen and T. Aldrich Finegan, *The Economics of Labor Force Participation* (Princeton, NJ: Princeton University Press, 1969); C. Matthew Snipp and Gary D. Sandefur, "Earnings of American Indians and Alaska Natives: The Effects of Residence and Migration," *Social Forces* 66(1988): 994–1008, have looked at the impact of migration on labor force participation and earnings.

TABLE 7.4

Distribution of Unemployment Rates[a] for American Indians and Alaska Natives Aged 16 and Over, by Place of Residence, 1980

Census Division	Metropolitan		Nonmetropolitan	
	Males	Females	Males	Females
New England	13.0	11.2	26.0	11.6
Mid Atlantic	14.4	13.8	23.0	21.7
E. North Central	18.9	14.8	21.6	18.8
W. North Central	21.8	10.3	18.4	17.2
South Atlantic	8.8	11.0	10.5	9.0
E. South Central	8.4	12.5	17.0	21.6
W. South Central	8.8	7.5	10.0	8.3
Mountain	12.8	10.7	15.6	13.6
Pacific	12.5	12.1	24.3	13.6

SOURCE: Public-Use Microdata Sample, 5 percent A File.

[a]Unemployment rate, defined as the percentage of the civilian labor force without work.

TABLE 7.5

Percent Distribution of Time at Work and Weeks of Unemployment in 1979 for American Indians and Alaska Natives Aged 16 and Over

Residence and Sex	Worked 26 Weeks or Less	Worked 30 Hours or Less per Week	Unemployed 15 or More Weeks
Metropolitan			
Male	21.2	12.3	40.2
Female	31.3	24.4	36.0
Nonmetropolitan			
Male	29.3	11.1	45.2
Female	35.3	22.7	39.2
Off Reservation			
Male	20.3	12.5	40.4
Female	30.6	24.4	36.2
On or Near Reservation			
Male	29.6	10.9	44.1
Female	39.3	23.0	38.3

SOURCE: Public-Use Microdata Sample, 5 percent A File.

TABLE 7.4 *(continued)*

Census Division	Off Reservation		On or Near Reservation	
	Males	Females	Males	Females
New England	15.8	9.7	14.0	14.6
Mid Atlantic	14.3	14.8	19.4	13.5
E. North Central	18.6	14.6	23.4	21.1
W. North Central	17.7	12.7	23.0	14.1
South Atlantic	9.3	9.4	13.1	19.0
E. South Central	11.4	16.1	9.7	13.4
W. South Central	9.7	8.0	5.4	4.6
Mountain	9.5	10.3	15.2	12.8
Pacific	11.9	11.6	19.8	13.6

how American Indian labor force participation is influenced by various conditions. For the sake of clarity, these conditions are discussed separately. Yet it is important to remember that the effects of these conditions on labor force participation do not operate independently. Labor force participation is a complex process subject to many interdependent and offsetting contingencies.

For example, the bivariate relationship showing that women have lower labor force participation than men is true, but well-educated women may be equally if not more likely to be in the labor force than poorly educated men. Furthermore, young, unmarried, well-educated women in metropolitan areas may be vastly more likely to be in the labor force than older, uneducated men living in rural localities. While simple bivariate relationships (for example, gender and labor force participation) are informative, they are not independent of other mitigating factors.

Age and Labor Force Status

Gender, residence, and age are well-known determinants of labor force participation. American Indians, as previous tables show, are no less immune to these conditions than the rest of American society.

Gender and residence are consistently related differences in labor force participation. The effect of age also has been discussed, but without much detail. Table 7.6 shows labor force participation rates for Indian men and women by age groups. The patterns parallel the findings from Table 7.1, and there is no need to belabor these details.

However, a detailed age breakdown offers further insights into the influence of age on Indian work force experience. One is that like other women in the 1980s Indian women did not exit the labor force en masse during their peak childbearing years. Indian women under age 20 are concentrated outside the labor force, but labor force attachment sharply increases for older female cohorts. Between ages 26 and 40 about 60 percent of these women are employed or seeking employment. Indeed, the first substantial increase in the percentage of women not in the labor force is after age 45, beyond the peak childbearing years. For reasons most likely related to economic need, younger Indian women are not departing the labor force to spend extended periods at home raising their children.

TABLE 7.6

Percent Distribution of the Civilian Labor Force Status of American Indians and Alaska Natives Aged 16 and Over, by Age and Sex, 1980

Age	Employed		Unemployed[a]		Not in Labor Force		Unemployment Rate	
	Male	Female	Male	Female	Male	Female	Male	Female
16–20	35.0	31.0	12.0	8.5	53.0	60.5	25.5	21.5
21–25	64.2	48.6	14.3	8.2	21.5	43.3	18.2	14.4
26–30	70.1	52.8	12.5	7.4	17.4	39.8	15.1	12.3
31–35	74.9	55.1	10.0	5.5	15.1	39.4	11.8	9.1
36–40	76.6	55.0	8.7	5.0	14.7	40.0	10.2	8.3
41–45	75.1	52.6	7.9	5.0	17.0	42.4	9.5	8.7
46–50	71.5	45.0	8.2	4.0	20.3	51.0	10.3	8.2
51–55	66.2	42.6	6.9	3.7	27.0	53.6	9.4	8.0
56–60	57.7	33.3	5.5	2.8	36.8	63.9	8.7	7.8
61–65	36.2	22.7	3.7	1.5	60.1	75.8	9.3	6.2
66–70	18.3	11.5	2.2	1.2	79.5	87.4	10.7	9.4
Over 70	9.3	4.4	1.2	0.5	89.4	95.1	11.4	10.2

SOURCE: Public-Use Microdata Sample, 5 percent A File.

[a]These percentages are the proportion of the adult population (i.e., aged 16 and over) in the labor force but without employment. This *is not* the unemployment rate, which is the percentage of the civilian labor force without a job. The civilian labor force is the sum of employed and unemployed persons, excluding persons not in the labor force.

Another finding worth noting is that the peak working years for American Indians are not very different from those of other racial groups. Employment is highest and unemployment lowest for Indian men and women between the ages 30 and 45. However, for American Indians over age 25 the proportion of the civilian labor force without work—that is, the unemployment rate—is relatively constant and hovers around 9 to 11 percent for men and 8 to 10 percent for women. In 1980 the unemployment rate for blacks and whites was 12 and 6 percent, respectively. This table also suggests that the value of work experience for labor force participation peaks around ages 36 to 40 for men and ages 31 to 40 for women.

Education and Labor Force Status

One of the reasons that younger American Indians, particularly those about age 30, enjoy relatively high rates of labor force participation is that they are relatively well educated. The discussion of education in Chapter 6 showed that older American Indians have relatively low levels of postsecondary schooling. Although younger Indians (especially those under age 30) are more likely to complete high school, they are unlikely to acquire advanced educations. Table 7.7 shows the rela-

TABLE 7.7

Percent Distribution of the Civilian Labor Force Status of American Indians and Alaska Natives Aged 16 and Over, by Education and Sex, 1980

Education	Employed		Unemployed[a]		Not in Labor Force		Unemployment Rate	
	Male	Female	Male	Female	Male	Female	Male	Female
0–8	40.6	19.7	7.3	3.2	52.1	77.1	15.2	14.0
9–11	46.8	30.8	12.8	6.5	40.4	62.7	21.5	17.4
12	66.8	50.3	10.9	6.6	22.3	43.1	14.0	11.6
13–15	70.0	58.4	8.9	6.2	21.1	35.4	11.3	9.6
16 and Over	81.3	66.4	3.9	3.7	14.8	29.9	4.6	5.3

SOURCE: Public-Use Microdata Sample, 5 percent A File.

[a]These percentages are the proportion of the adult population (i.e., aged 16 and over) in the labor force but without employment. This *is not* the unemployment rate, which is the percentage of the civilian labor force without a job. The civilian labor force is the sum of employed and unemployed persons, excluding persons not in the labor force.

tionship between years of schooling and labor force participation for the American Indian and Alaska Native population aged 16 and over.

While other factors such as age and family circumstances are also implicated in these figures, the effect of education on American Indian labor force participation differs considerably with respect to gender and type of participation. Although men are more likely than women to be employed, the effect of education on employment appears to be about the same for both sexes. Successively higher levels of education correspond to successively higher levels of employment by about the same amounts for men and women alike. Predictably, Indian men with the most education (16 years or more) are twice as likely to be employed as men with the least education (8 years or less), while highly educated women are three times more likely to be employed than poorly educated females.

The effect of education on unemployment and labor force attachment is considerably more complex. American Indians with eighth grade educations or less have relatively low unemployment, 7.3 and 3.2 percent for men and women, respectively. However, these figures mean that poorly educated American Indians experience little unemployment mostly because they are outside the labor force; they are neither employed nor seeking work and therefore are not unemployed. For example, over three fourths of women with 8 years or less of schooling are not in the labor force. It also is worth remembering that many individuals with less than an eighth grade education are older persons either in retirement or nearing the end of their careers—this also contributes to low levels of labor force participation and low unemployment. On the other hand, the disadvantages accruing to the lack of schooling are most apparent in the civilian labor force—15 percent of men and 14 percent of women with 8 years of schooling or less are jobless.

Consistently higher levels of education are related to consistently higher levels of labor force attachment for men and for women. The smallest percentages of men and women not in the labor force are for persons with 16 years of schooling and over. For employment, a high school diploma appears to be a critical asset. Persons with more than 8 years and less than 12 years of schooling are likely to be young enough and sufficiently schooled to participate in the labor force but without much success. This group has the highest unemployment rate for the entire Indian population over age 16. A high school education and/or some college reduces the likelihood of unemployment, but without question a college degree produces the greatest reduction of this prospect. The high levels of secondary school dropouts and low levels of advanced education among younger Indians are problematic signs for the future of American Indian labor force participation.

Marital Status and Labor Force Participation

Family obligations are often mentioned as important influences on labor force participation in the population at large. Among many American Indians familial duties weigh heavily, and individuals are expected to take responsibility for the well-being of other family members. Marital status reflects one dimension of family obligations that may motivate labor force participation; parental responsibilities may be another. Table 7.8 shows the relationship between labor force participation and marital status.

Single American Indians are usually younger, have less work experience, and probably have fewer family obligations than married persons. Not surprisingly, like other Americans single American Indians are less likely to be employed and more likely to be unemployed or out of the labor force than married persons. In this regard, gender differences play an important role. Single Indian women, for example, are apparently more likely than Indian men to withdraw from the labor force than remain unemployed. In percentages, more single men than women are unemployed, but more women than men are not in the labor force. Among single Indians, slightly more men than women are employed, but more interesting is that single women are more likely than married women to be employed. In contrast, marriage is more conducive to employment for Indian men. This probably reflects a traditional division of labor in which Indian women withdraw from the labor force to assume domestic responsibilities, while Indian men are responsible for the live-

TABLE 7.8

Percent Distribution of the Marital and Labor Force Status of American Indian and Alaska Native Householders Aged 25–54, 1980

Marital Status	Employed		Unemployed[a]		Not in Labor Force		Unemployment Rate	
	Male	Female	Male	Female	Male	Female	Male	Female
Married	81.4	58.4	8.0	5.2	10.6	36.4	8.9	8.2
Widowed	77.0	42.3	2.7	6.9	20.3	50.8	3.4	14.0
Divorced or Separated	74.6	62.4	10.3	7.2	15.1	30.4	12.1	10.3
Single	69.2	66.1	12.6	5.7	18.2	28.2	15.4	7.9

SOURCE: Public-Use Microdata Sample, 5 percent A File.

[a]These percentages are the percent of the adult population (i.e., aged 16 and over) in the labor force but without employment. This *is not* the unemployment rate, which is the percentage of the civilian labor force without a job. The civilian labor force is the sum of employed and unemployed persons, excluding persons not in the labor force.

lihood of their families. This suggests that economic necessity is probably the main motivation for the labor force participation of single Indian women.

Widowhood and divorce are two important types of marital disruption that also affect labor force participation. Widows and widowers are usually older individuals, which is reflected in low rates of labor force participation for this group. The fact that 50 percent of women who have outlived their husbands are out of the labor force supports this contention. Although widows do not participate extensively in the work force, widowed Indian women in the civilian labor force have relatively high unemployment rates, especially compared with Indian men (14.0 and 3.4 percent, respectively). Higher rates of unemployment among American Indian widows may reflect the difficulties experienced by these women who, most likely out of economic necessity, are unsuccessfully seeking employment after the death of their husbands.

Divorced and separated persons experience another type of marital trauma typically very different in terms of its origins, duration, and economic consequences, and usually at a younger age than widows and widowers. Divorced and separated Indian men experience relatively high rates of unemployment, almost as high as never-married men. However, divorced and separated Indian women, probably because they tend to be younger and more employable, have less joblessness and substantially more employment than widowed women. These women also have less unemployment than divorced and separated American Indian men.

Presence of Children and Labor Force Status

The presence of children creates additional financial pressures for labor force participation, but also creates domestic demands that discourage job holding. Table 7.9 shows the labor force participation of men and women in relation to the presence and age of children in the household. For Indian men the presence of children, at any age, has very little impact on labor force participation. Indian men with children under age 6 at home are slightly less likely to be out of the labor force and slightly more likely to be unemployed. This may reflect increased financial responsibility, but the differences between these and other men are very small. The slight increase in labor force participation for these men also may be due to the fact that they, like most other men with young children, are themselves young and therefore more susceptible to unemployment.

The presence and age of children has a direct bearing on the labor force participation of Indian women. Table 7.9 shows that the presence

TABLE 7.9

Percent Distribution of Households with Children
and the Labor Force Status of American Indian and Alaska Native Householders
Aged 25–54

Presence and Age of Children	Employed		Unemployed[a]		Not in Labor Force		Unemployment Rate	
	Male	Female	Male	Female	Male	Female	Male	Female
Children Under 6 Years in Home, No Children 6–17	80.5	51.5	10.1	5.8	9.4	42.7	11.1	10.1
Children Under 6 Years and Children 6–17 Years in Home	80.8	39.4	8.2	7.4	11.0	53.2	9.2	15.8
Children 6–17 Years in Home, No Children Under 6 Years	81.6	59.9	7.4	7.7	11.0	32.4	8.3	11.4
No Children in Home	80.5	63.1	7.9	5.8	11.6	31.1	8.9	8.4

SOURCE: Public-Use Microdata Sample, 5 percent A File.

[a]These percentages are the proportion of the adult population (i.e., aged 16 and over) in the labor force but without employment. This *is not* the unemployment rate, which is the percentage of the civilian labor force without a job. The civilian labor force is the sum of employed and unemployed persons, excluding persons not in the labor force.

of children under age 6 appears to be the most critical influence. The labor force participation of female householders with children aged 6 to 17 is about the same as that of female householders with no children—32 and 31 percent, respectively. However, almost 43 percent of women with children under age 6 are not in the labor force. Interestingly, children aged 6 to 17 seem to have little influence on the decision not to work; but given the presence of young children, the presence of older children gives a further incentive to remain out of the labor force. Women with younger and older children are the most likely to be out of the labor force; 53 percent are in this category.

In relation to children, women's employment patterns mirror their status outside the labor force, and there is relatively little variation in the percentage of American Indian women unemployed. The major impact of children on female labor force participation is in relation to the decision to remain in or out of the labor force. However, Indian women who elect to participate in the labor force do not appear especially successful—Indian women with school age children have unemployment rates higher than their male counterparts, reaching as high as 16 percent.

TABLE 7.10

Percent Distribution of the Labor Force Participation of American Indians Aged 16 and Over Residing on the 16 Largest Reservations in 1980

Reservation	1970		1980		
	In Labor Force %	Unemployment Rate %	In Labor Force %	Unemployment Rate %	In Traditional Occupations %
Navaho[a] (AZ, UT, NM)	32.9	12.0	58.3	23.7	4.5
Pine Ridge (SD)	45.6	16.2	61.8	35.8	1.5
Gila River (AZ)	35.5	13.0	61.5	29.5	1.4
Papago (AZ)	29.8	15.7	58.6	20.4	4.3
Fort Apache (AZ)	36.1	13.8	64.1	20.3	1.4
Hopi[a] (AZ)	36.4	13.7	54.7	20.5	6.3
Zuni Pueblo (NM)	30.2	14.9	79.7	23.2	26.6
San Carlos (AZ)	33.5	13.1	59.1	21.1	1.3
Rosebud (SD)	41.1	25.6	65.0	28.7	0.3
Blackfeet (MT)	41.3	27.5	72.2	37.0	1.7
Yakima (WA)	38.1	13.8	70.1	32.5	1.8
Eastern Cherokee (NC)	50.3	13.5	73.7	21.1	1.8
Standing Rock (ND, SD)	46.7	29.1	65.8	36.0	0.7
Osage[b] (OK)	—	—	65.9	14.2	1.1
Fort Peck (MT)	45.0	25.7	75.7	39.3	1.5
Wind River (WY)	42.1	25.8	68.2	30.2	3.3

SOURCES: "American Indians, Eskimos, and Aleuts on Identified Reservations and in the Historic Areas of Oklahoma," *1980 Census of Population, Subject Report;* and "American Indians," *1970 Census of Population, Subject Report.*

[a]Navajo and Hopi reservations not strictly comparable because of administrative changes in the 1970s.
[b]Osage reservation data not available for 1970.

Reservation Labor Force Participation

Table 7.10 shows rates of unemployment and labor force participation for the 16 largest reservations. Between 1970 and 1980 labor force participation on these reservations increased sharply. However, this appears to have resulted in equally large increases in unemployment, which lends credence to critics who argue that job training and other programs designed to increase labor force participation have failed because they did not match growing labor force participation with growing job opportunities. Unemployment rates in these areas are extraordinarily high and in general higher than most of the statistics reported in previous tables. One reason is that these reservations, unlike many smaller reservations in proximity to urban areas, are located in remote locations distant from economic centers, and their residents indeed suffer from dire unemployment problems.

Perusing this table, one can see that unemployment ranges from 14 percent for the Osage reservation to nearly 40 percent for the Fort Peck reservation in Montana. Notably, the Osage tribe has extensive oil drilling on its reservation and is about 70 miles from Tulsa, Oklahoma—a major metropolitan area. In contrast, reservations such as Fort Peck, Pine Ridge, and Standing Rock are relatively undeveloped and are located in truly remote locations. Table 7.10 also shows the percentage of the labor force in "traditional occupations." The meaning of this term will be discussed in the next chapter, but briefly it includes persons in occupations such as rug weaving or jewelry making, or in certain agricultural jobs. Even on large reservations, relatively few persons are involved in these activities. With 27 percent of the labor force in traditional occupations, the Zuni pueblo is clearly an exception. This percentage probably reflects the activities of Zuni silversmiths, internationally acclaimed for their fine silver inlaid jewelry.

Concluding Remarks

The purpose of this chapter has been to chart the position of American Indians and Alaska Natives in the U.S. labor force. It is hardly surprising that they have not fared particularly well. Historically, American Indians have not widely participated in the industrial labor force that created urban America—especially in the twentieth century. As an overwhelming rural population for most of this century, American Indians have resided in remote areas distant from urban centers of economic activity. In the late nineteenth century, legislation such as the

Dawes Act was intended to encourage Indians to join the agricultural labor force as a way of hastening their assimilation. However, only in the second half of this century has there been serious concern about the lack of American Indian participation in the industrial work force. Gradually, as American Indians have become increasingly urbanized, they also have increased their presence in the labor market.

In many respects, the labor force participation of contemporary American Indians is not particularly different from the rest of the American working age population. Unemployment tends to be higher and participation lower among Indians than among other groups, specifically whites, and certainly these are significant differences. Yet, Indians are subject to many of the same influences and contingencies that influence other segments of American society. Age, place of residence, and gender play a critical role in determining the labor force participation of Indians and non-Indians alike. Similarly, American Indians are not immune to the constraints imposed by education, marital status, and the responsibilities of child care—just as most Americans are constrained. With regard to these factors, Indian women are especially subject to their influence: pushed into the labor force by economic need and pulled away by family obligations. Indian women with very young children are relatively unlikely to be in the labor force, while younger Indian women in their peak childbearing years are more likely to be in the labor force than older women.

Perhaps most significant is that among American Indians unemployment (however measured) is high and labor force attachment is weak. In an economy in which work determines the conditions of existence, and a society in which work defines social position, the disadvantaged status of American Indians is undeniable. The statistics in this chapter bear witness to the fact that economic hardship is virtually unavoidable for many American Indians. The economic consequences of the marginal position of American Indians in the work force are spelled out in the next chapter.

8

OCCUPATION AND INCOME

AMONG AMERICAN Indians fortunate enough to be gainfully employed, occupation is a preeminent indicator of economic and social standing. More than any other characteristic, occupations indicate the kinds of activities that dominate a major portion of workers' lives. For example, white collar professional or managerial occupations are safer, more pleasant, and less physically demanding than blue collar occupations, such as unskilled labor. Sociologists are especially interested in occupations because the work done by individuals is an important reflection of their social position. Persons in high-status occupations such as doctors and lawyers enjoy economic benefits and other privileges not granted to persons on the lower rungs of the socioeconomic ladder.

Although occupation is an important measure of social position, the most direct measure of economic standing is wealth. However, such information is notoriously difficult to obtain. Few individuals, Indians and non-Indians alike, know the actual value of their personal belongings ranging from clothes and jewelry to vehicles, real estate, financial investments, and savings accounts. Among the few persons who know their wealth, fewer would willingly divulge this information. In its absence, income is the most direct and publicly available measure of economic standing.

American Indian Occupations

Manual and Nonmanual Occupations

Like other employed Americans, American Indians and Alaska Natives are engaged in what amounts to an indescribable variety of jobs. For this reason, it is necessary to discuss the types of employment held by Indians in terms of broad categories of occupation. Although such categories may appear simple and straightforward, they are regularly the subject of serious disputes and controversy among sociologists and economists.[1]

[1]Occupational information evolves from a question on the 1980 census form: "What kind of work was this person doing?" According to Census Bureau sources, occupations "should be classified on the basis of work performed." The occupational data published by the Census Bureau are represented in 503 detailed categories that are usually sorted into 13 major occupation groups, which, in turn, are grouped into six summary categories. For the sake of convenience, this discussion uses the six summary categories rather than the more detailed and cumbersome groupings. These categories also can be easily compared with other census publications.

The six categories include *Managerial and Professional* occupations, jobs requiring relatively high levels of skill and/or formal education and entailing a substantial amount of responsibility and/or authority in the workplace: managers and engineers, health professionals such as nurses and pharmacists, and, of course, physicians and attorneys. The *Technical, Sales, and Administrative Support* category includes nonmanual jobs which also require a significant amount of formal training but less than required for Managerial and Professional jobs. These jobs ordinarily involve less workplace authority and responsibility. Technical occupations include x-ray technicians, dental hygienists, paralegal workers, draftspersons, and lab workers. Administrative Support involves a wide range of workers in clerical jobs ranging from payroll clerks to stenographers. Sales occupations are self-explanatory. The category designated as *Service* includes all types of service employment, ranging from protective service workers such as police and fire department employees to maids, janitors, and hairdressers.

The remaining three categories consist of jobs primarily requiring manual labor and considerably less formal training than the first two categories. *Farming, Forestry, and Fishing* occupations include farmers and farm laborers, and laborers on fishing boats are not distinguished from fishing boat owners, provided that the latter also are engaged in fishing activities. *Operators, Fabricators, and Laborers* are probably the least skilled occupations and include assembly line workers, stock handlers, dock loaders, and truck and tractor drivers. In contrast, *Precision Production, Craft, and Repair* occupations include many of the most highly skilled types of blue collar jobs. These occupations include auto mechanics; skilled crafts workers such as carpenters, plumbers, and electricians; as well as machinists and jewelers.

This chapter also presents data for class of worker distribution. "Class of worker" is defined by the Census Bureau in relation to the type of ownership of the employing organization. Workers can be categorized into one of five different groups. *Private Wage and Salary* workers are employed in privately owned establishments. *Employee of Own Company* workers own all or most of the stock in the privately owned establishment where they are employed. *Government* workers are employed by federal, state, and local units of government. *Self-Employed* workers own unincorporated businesses; this category also includes physicians and attorneys in private practice, along with other persons in privately owned organizations without legal charter. Finally, *Unpaid Family* workers work without pay in an establishment owned by a family member; such individuals are frequently the spouses or children of the owner. For American Indians, "class of worker" is especially interesting because it shows the degree to which they are dependent on units of federal and tribal government as sources of employment.

An additional complication is that the occupational classification system used by the Census Bureau was completely revamped between 1970 and 1980, which makes it difficult to compare these years. However, simple comparisons can be made for 1970 and 1980 because it is still possible to distinguish occupations consisting mainly of physical labor from those consisting mainly of mental or verbal tasks—so-called blue collar and white collar jobs—although there is no guarantee that these comparisons will be exact.

Table 8.1 shows changes in the distribution of manual and nonmanual occupations between 1970 and 1980 for blacks, whites, and American Indians. This table confirms the dramatic transformation of the American economy during the 1970s in terms of declines in traditional blue collar jobs such as factory work. All three groups experienced decreases in the percentage of workers in manual occupations and corre-

TABLE 8.1

Percent Distribution of Blacks, Whites, and American Indians Aged 16 and Over Employed in Manual and Nonmanual Occupations, 1970–1980

	1970		1980	
	Males	Females	Males	Females
Blacks				
Manual	81.5	64.7	73.1	48.3
Nonmanual	18.5	35.3	26.9	51.7
Total	100.0	100.0	100.0	100.0
Gender Gap		34.7		26.0
Whites				
Manual	58.7	35.6	55.5	30.3
Nonmanual	41.3	64.4	44.5	69.7
Total	100.0	100.0	100.0	100.0
Gender Gap		25.6		24.9
American Indians				
Manual	77.6	57.4	72.1	43.6
Nonmanual	22.4	42.6	27.9	56.4
Total	100.0	100.0	100.0	100.0
Gender Gap		22.7		29.1

SOURCES: *1980 Census of Population, General Social and Economic Characteristics, United States Summary; 1970 Census of Population, Characteristics of the Population, United States Summary;* and "American Indians," *1970 Census of Population, Subject Report.*

sponding increases in nonmanual occupations. However, there was considerable variation in the magnitude of these changes.

In 1970 whites in nonmanual occupations vastly outnumbered blacks and American Indians in similar types of employment. For example, the percentage of white males in nonmanual occupations in 1970 was twice that of Indians and blacks in these jobs. However, increases in the percentages of Indian and black males in white collar jobs were larger during the 1970s than the more modest increase for white males. By 1980 white men were still heavily concentrated in nonmanual jobs, but the gap between them and Indian and black men narrowed slightly. Women were more likely than men to be employed in nonmanual occupations, probably because of the large numbers of women in clerical work.

The gap between white workers and black and Indian workers is not much different for women than for men. In 1970 white women in nonmanual employment outnumbered Indians and blacks by over 20 percentage points. Gains during the 1970s by Indian women exceeded gains by blacks, but by 1980 Indian women still lagged behind white women in nonmanual jobs by over 13 points. Even with structural changes in the economy and public policies to increase employment opportunities, such as Affirmative Action, American Indians and blacks were considerably more likely than whites to earn their livelihoods in less desirable, physically demanding manual occupations.

In Table 8.1 the entry labeled "Gender Gap" measures the segregation of men and women into manual and nonmanual occupations. The gender gap measure is based on the index of dissimilarity, a widely used and easily computed measure of segregation.[2] This measure is equal to 100.0 when there is complete occupational segregation—for instance, if there are no women in blue collar occupations. It is equal to 0.0 when there is no segregation. It also represents the percentage of cases that would have to be reallocated to achieve an equal distribution of men and women in manual and nonmanual occupations. In 1970 American Indians were the least gender-segregated of the three races. However, over the decade a surge in nonmanual employment among American Indian women substantially increased gender segregation in this population. Consequently, in 1980 gender segregation was considerably more prevalent among American Indians than among other racial groups. Ironically, this happened during a period of stable or declining gender segregation among whites and blacks.

[2]The index of dissimilarity (Δ) is computed as $\frac{\Sigma |P_{i1} - P_{i2}|}{I} = \Delta$. Critics point to a number of technical flaws in this measure, but it continues to be a well-known and widely used measure. The estimates of Δ in Table 8.9 are based on percentages not reported in this table.

Occupational Differences

Table 8.2 presents occupational data for 1980 using the six Census Bureau summary categories. The data in this table parallel most of the observations already made about the occupations of blacks, whites, and American Indians and contain several other details worth noting. With regard to white collar occupations, blacks and American Indians differ by only a few percentage points. For example, 15 percent of employed black men are in Technical, Sales, and Administrative Support occupations compared with 13 percent of Indian men. Likewise, about 17 percent of black women are in Managerial and Professional jobs compared with 18 percent of Indian women. There are larger differences among blacks and Indians in blue collar jobs than in white collar jobs. For instance, Indians are decidedly less likely than blacks to be in Service occupations but more likely than whites to be in these jobs. Although the differences are very small, finding that American Indians are most likely to be in Farming, Forestry, and Fishing occupations is fully consistent with the relatively large concentrations of Indians who reside in rural areas.

The most significant differences between blacks and Indians are in relation to their distribution within skilled and semiskilled or unskilled

TABLE 8.2

*Percent Distribution of Employed Blacks, Whites,
and American Indians and Alaska Natives in Selected Occupations, 1980*

Occupation	Blacks		Whites		American Indians	
	Males	Females	Males	Females	Males	Females
Managerial and Professional	11.7	16.5	25.0	22.4	14.8	17.8
Technical, Sales, and Administrative Support	15.2	35.2	19.5	47.3	13.1	38.6
Service	17.0	29.3	8.3	16.3	12.6	25.1
Farming, Forestry, and Fishing	3.4	0.5	4.2	0.9	5.6	1.2
Precision Production, Craft, and Repair	15.5	2.3	21.4	2.3	24.1	3.2
Operators, Fabricators, and Laborers	37.2	16.2	21.6	10.8	29.8	14.1
Total	100.0	100.0	100.0	100.0	100.0	100.0

SOURCE: *1980 Census of Population, General Social and Economic Characteristics, United States Summary.*

TABLE 8.3

Percent Distribution of Occupations of Employed American Indians and Alaska Natives Aged 16 and Over, by Census Division

Census Division	Managerial and Professional		Technical, Sales, and Administrative Support		Service	
	Males	Females	Males	Females	Males	Females
New England	18.0	15.4	11.1	34.3	15.6	23.2
Mid Atlantic	13.9	14.1	12.2	39.8	17.3	24.4
E. North Central	10.3	13.8	9.3	30.8	14.4	29.5
W. North Central	12.6	13.0	10.0	33.0	16.8	31.9
South Atlantic	11.8	12.3	9.8	29.1	10.5	22.2
E. South Central	13.8	13.9	10.9	30.6	10.7	25.2
W. South Central	12.6	13.7	11.7	37.2	10.0	28.1
Mountain	12.3	16.2	9.0	34.1	16.5	30.8
Pacific	13.4	14.8	13.2	40.1	13.5	26.4

SOURCE: Public-Use Microdata Sample, 5 pecent A File.

occupations. Among men, and women to a lesser degree, American Indians are much more likely than blacks to be employed in a skilled manual occupation. Conversely, black men are considerably more likely than Indian men to be employed in semiskilled or unskilled occupations. Not surprisingly, both blacks and Indians have higher percentages in these blue collar occupations than whites.

This difference between blacks and Indians is notable because it may stem from educational programs, especially employment and training programs, for American Indians that stress (critics say overstress) vocational training in the skilled trades.[3] From this perspective, blacks and Indians suffer equal disadvantages acquiring the skills they need for high-status white collar jobs, which is reflected in the percentages of their number in nonmanual employment. However, by virtue of vocational training in BIA schools, relocation and employment assistance

[3]See the comments of Estelle Fuchs and Robert J. Havighurst, *To Live on This Earth: American Indian Education* (NY: Doubleday, 1972), pp. 219–221.

TABLE 8.3 *(continued)*

Census Division	Farming, Forestry, and Fishing		Precision Production, Craft, and Repair		Operators, Fabricators, and Laborers	
	Males	Females	Males	Females	Males	Females
New England	5.7	1.3	22.4	3.3	27.2	22.5
Mid Atlantic	3.0	1.3	22.0	3.1	31.6	17.3
E. North Central	4.8	1.3	20.6	2.5	40.6	22.1
W. North Central	8.6	2.0	20.7	4.0	31.3	16.1
South Atlantic	8.8	4.2	27.4	2.6	31.7	29.6
E. South Central	6.8	2.5	24.7	4.6	33.1	23.2
W. South Central	6.3	1.7	26.2	3.3	33.2	16.0
Mountain	7.9	2.1	23.0	3.5	31.3	13.2
Pacific	9.1	2.7	21.2	3.3	29.6	12.7

programs, and other job training programs, American Indians have special opportunities for entering skilled occupations not afforded to the black labor force.

Occupation and Residence

Tables 8.3 and 8.4 display the geographic distribution of American Indians within occupational categories. Regional variations in the occupational structure of American Indians are due mainly to differences in regional economies, particularly in the types of economic activity in which Indians are employed. As Table 8.3 shows, there is relatively little variation in American Indian occupational distributions across areas of the United States. For example, employment in Farming, Forestry, and Fishing occupations are least common in the highly urbanized areas of the Middle Atlantic states, and only 3 percent of the male labor force is in this type of work. In the Pacific states, which include Washington, Oregon, and Alaska, logging and fishing are important, and about 9 percent of the male Indian labor force is employed in these occupations.

This area includes many tribes for which fishing is not only an important livelihood but also guaranteed by treaty agreements and prolonged court battles. In Washington state, for example, the Lummi tribe derives a major part of its income from a tribally owned and operated fishery. Nevertheless, jobs in these activities constitute a relatively small share of the area's total employment, and it is much smaller in other areas.

Other instances of regional differences also exist. The highly industrialized East North Central states of Illinois, Michigan, Indiana, and Ohio have the largest concentration of Indian men employed in factory jobs, represented by the category of Operators, Fabricators, and Laborers. Similarly, textile factories are a major source of employment in the South Atlantic states. Nearly 44 percent of all nondurable manufacturing jobs held by Indians in the South are in the textile industry.[4] Work in the textile industry ordinarily involves semiskilled or unskilled labor, and many of these jobs are filled by women. Consequently, finding that nearly 30 percent of Indian women in the South Atlantic area are employed as Operators, Fabricators, and Laborers is not surprising. Of course, not all of these women work in textile mills because such occupations are characteristic of many industries, particularly light manufacturing, which is also prevalent in the South. However, this figure is particularly interesting because it represents one of the largest concentrations of Indian women in blue collar occupations.

There are two reasons for presenting the data shown in Table 8.3. One is to show that regional variations are not large, but those that are visible are consistent with the kinds of economic activity commonly associated with particular areas—textiles in the South, for example. Another reason is that the types of work in which Indians are employed are preeminently the result of the sorts of job opportunities available in local economies. The occupations of most American Indians transcend tribal and cultural predispositions and depend heavily on opportunities in the local labor market. Needless to say, there are exceptions to this general statement. Tribes such as the Lummi in Washington state promote economic development projects compatible with tribal lifestyles—for example, fishing—but in spite of these efforts most Indians adopt vocations in response to local economic conditions.

Underscoring these points, Table 8.4 shows the relationship between place of residence and the occupations of employed Indians. In view of the substantial differences related to place of residence already documented, there is a marked absence of occupational differences for

[4]U.S. Bureau of the Census, *1980 Census of Population, General Social and Economic Characteristics, United States Summary*, PC80-1-C1, Table 206 (Washington, DC: U.S. Government Printing Office, 1983).

TABLE 8.4

Percent Distribution of Occupations of American Indians and Alaska Natives
Aged 16 and Over, by Place of Residence

Occupation	Metropolitan		Nonmetropolitan		Off Reservation		On or Near Reservation	
	Males	Females	Males	Females	Males	Females	Males	Females
Managerial and Professional	13.7	14.6	10.9	14.0	13.0	13.7	12.2	15.4
Technical, Sales, and Administrative								
Support	12.9	38.7	7.9	30.2	12.3	36.5	9.2	34.4
Service	13.2	26.1	14.9	30.9	12.4	26.0	15.7	30.4
Farming, Forestry, and Fishing	5.3	1.7	11.4	3.3	5.4	2.0	10.5	2.6
Precision Production, Craft, and Repair	23.5	3.4	22.2	3.2	24.4	3.3	21.1	3.3
Operators, Fabricators, and Laborers	31.4	15.5	32.7	18.4	32.5	18.5	31.3	13.9
Total	100.0	100.0	100.0	100.0	100.0	100.0	100.0	100.0

SOURCE: Public-Use Microdata Sample, 5 percent A File.

237

these places. Among Indians who have successfully obtained employment, the occupational structure in which they participate is about the same, regardless of where they live. The few noticeable differences apparent in Table 8.4 are small but predictable. For example, jobs in Farming, Forestry, and Fishing are more common in nonmetropolitan and reservation areas. On the other hand, white collar jobs are slightly more common in metropolitan and nonreservation locations.

Class of Worker

Given that metropolitan areas ordinarily have much larger concentrations of white collar workers than nonmetropolitan locations, the small differences apparent among Indian workers are puzzling. However, the class of worker distribution provides a helpful clue. Although the occupations of American Indians are not dramatically different from other workers, the American Indian population is unique in its dependence on the federal government for employment. This is amply evident from the class of worker distributions for blacks, whites, and Indians in Table 8.5.

American Indians rely heavily on government agencies for employ-

TABLE 8.5

Percent Distribution of Class of Worker
of Employed Blacks, Whites, and American Indians, 1970–1980

Class	Blacks		Whites		American Indians	
	1970	1980	1970	1980	1970	1980
Private Wage and Salary Worker	80.7	70.2	75.0	76.0	70.0	66.3
Federal and State Government Worker	8.4	14.2	8.1	7.7	15.6	16.9
Local Government Worker	6.8	13.1	7.2	8.2	8.8	11.6
Self-Employed Worker	3.8	2.4	9.0	7.5	5.1	4.8
Unpaid Family Worker	0.3	0.1	0.7	0.6	0.5	0.4
Total	100.0	100.0	100.0	100.0	100.0	100.0

SOURCES: *1980 Census of Population, General Social and Economic Characteristics, United States Summary; 1970 Census of Population, Characteristics of the Population, United States Summary;* and "American Indians," *1970 Census of Population, Subject Report.*

ment, particularly federal and tribal government jobs; this is especially true in reservation areas. In typically depressed reservation economies, there are relatively few private-sector jobs. Agencies such as the Bureau of Indian Affairs and the local tribal government are an important source of what are often considered the "best" jobs on the reservation. Along with the Post Office, they are sometimes the only source of white collar employment. These jobs are usually filled by Indians for a number of reasons, but a particularly important factor is that the BIA and tribal governments use an "Indian preference" criterion similar to the federal government's veteran preference in hiring decisions. Furthermore, during the 1970s tribal governments were a major source of low-wage jobs requiring few skills as a result of CETA[5] public works and job training programs. Consequently, large concentrations of Indians are in public-sector jobs. The Indian preference system and the prevalence of government programs on or near reservations seem to account for the small rural-urban differences in white collar employment.

The claim that reservations have high concentrations of government workers cannot be directly substantiated with the figures in Table 8.5. However, the data in Table 8.6 clearly support this statement. American Indians residing on or near reservations are more likely than those living in other places to be employed in a federal or local government agency. State governments typically exercise little authority over reservation affairs, so it is not surprising that a relatively small percentage of the Indian labor force is employed in state agencies. About 32 percent of Indian men and 37 percent of Indian women living on or near a reservation are employed by federal and local government authorities, compared with 16 percent of men and 17 percent of women residing in nonreservation areas. Because most reservations are in nonmetropolitan locales, there are substantial metropolitan-nonmetropolitan differences in public-sector employment as well, but these differences are slightly smaller than those between reservation and nonreservation areas.

Traditional Occupations

The dependence of American Indians on government as a source of employment is probably surprising to anyone without a close knowledge of reservation life. The idea that many employed Indians work as bureaucrats, clerks, and other types of officials probably does not fit most stereotypes of Indians. Widely held beliefs about Indian employ-

---

[5]Comprehensive Employment and Training Act (CETA) was federally sponsored and operated under contract by tribal governments or consortiums of tribes.

TABLE 8.6

Percent Distribution of Class of Worker of Employed American Indians and Alaska Natives Aged 16 and Over

Class	Metropolitan		Nonmetropolitan		Off Reservation		On or Near Reservation	
	Males	Females	Males	Females	Males	Females	Males	Females
Private Wage and Salary Worker	69.4	70.8	57.7	52.9	71.9	73.6	55.7	51.8
Federal Government Worker	11.9	9.3	13.7	16.3	9.4	6.8	16.9	18.6
State Government Worker	3.8	5.6	7.0	8.9	3.8	5.7	6.6	8.2
Local Government Worker	7.8	10.6	14.0	17.9	6.8	9.7	14.6	18.0
Self-Employed Worker	6.7	3.2	7.2	3.2	7.6	3.4	5.9	2.9
Unpaid Family Worker	0.4	0.5	0.4	0.8	0.5	0.8	0.3	0.5
Total	100.0	100.0	100.0	100.0	100.0	100.0	100.0	100.0

SOURCE: Public-Use Microdata Sample, 5 percent A File.

ment tend to portray Indians as rug weavers, shepherds, hunters and trappers, guides, jewelry makers, and, of course, Indian "chiefs." Like most stereotypes, these images contain a small element of truth, and no discussion of American Indian occupations would be complete without at least briefly looking at how well these stereotypes fit with reality.

Based on the content of its detailed occupational titles, the Census Bureau has identified certain occupations as the kind that might be regarded as "traditional" Indian occupations. The complete list of occupations recognized as "traditional" by the Census Bureau is shown in Appendix 5 and includes such occupations as jewelers, dancers, and craftsmen, which reflect activities that are traditional in American Indian culture. For example, silversmith is an occupation that, when practiced by most southwestern Indians, represents an important tradition in southwestern Indian culture. Needless to say, there is a large measure of slippage in identifying traditional occupations; for example, some, or maybe many, Indian silversmiths are not practicing an art form that is traditional among their people. On the other hand, the list of census titles also may inadvertently omit a few occupations that might legitimately be regarded as "traditional."

Table 8.7 shows the distribution of American Indians employed in "traditional" occupations across areas of the United States by place of residence. The most obvious conclusion to be drawn from these data is that traditional occupations do not constitute a major source of employment for the American Indian labor force. Although Indians appear dependent on region-specific economic activity and on the public sector for employment, they do not rely heavily on economic activities closely related to their cultural heritage. It is most likely that many traditional occupations for American Indians, such as traditional crafts (especially those purchased mainly by other Indians), provide a livelihood insufficient for survival and consequently may be practiced as an avocation and not as a principal source of income.

The distribution of employed workers in traditional occupations clearly shows that most are situated in nonmetropolitan and/or reservation locations. This is probably the result of two factors: (1) American Indians engaged in traditional lifestyles are more likely to reside in rural and/or reservation locations, and (2) a number of the occupations classified as traditional are related to agriculture (shepherd for instance), and these occupations are most often practiced outside metropolitan areas. This may also explain why women are significantly less represented in traditional occupations than men, since they tend not to be employed in agricultural occupations. This is somewhat unexpected, considering that some tribal traditions assign women responsibility for agricultural production.

TABLE 8.7

Percent Distribution of American Indians and Alaska Natives Aged 16 and Over in Traditional Occupations, 1980

Census Division	Metropolitan		Nonmetropolitan		Off Reservation		On or Near Reservation	
	Males	Females	Males	Females	Males	Females	Males	Females
New England	7.8	9.3	14.5	1.2	8.0	6.2	11.4	11.0
Mid Atlantic	7.7	4.5	7.3	2.8	8.0	4.8	6.7	2.9
E. North Central	8.8	6.3	10.8	7.9	9.3	6.9	9.4	6.0
W. North Central	8.1	6.2	10.3	4.0	7.4	5.5	10.7	4.9
South Atlantic	7.4	3.9	10.5	7.4	8.5	5.6	12.3	5.7
E. South Central	9.4	4.6	11.0	3.5	9.1	4.3	18.6	3.2
W. South Central	7.3	5.4	8.1	3.3	7.4	4.7	8.1	5.3
Mountain	9.6	5.2	7.9	3.9	9.7	5.9	8.4	4.2
Pacific	9.5	5.9	16.5	5.6	9.3	6.0	13.6	5.6

SOURCE: Public-Use Microdata Sample, 5 percent A File.

Occupation and Age

Tables 8.8 and 8.9 describe the relationship between occupation and other social characteristics—namely, age and education. Age has an impact on occupational choice or placement in two ways. As workers grow older, they may acquire more schooling, more training, and, especially, additional years of work experience. Training and experience are an important source of opportunities for workers to improve their skills and occupational standing. However, studies[6] suggest that the benefits of age quickly diminish, and older workers may even experience an erosion of their position in the workplace.

Table 8.8 shows the age-specific occupational structures for American Indian men and women aged 16 and over. These data are noteworthy because they reflect the aggregate career experiences of American Indian workers and especially because they are suggestive about the stages by which Indian workers become concentrated in certain types of occupations. As the data indicate, Indian men are concentrated in blue collar occupations and Indian women in lower-status white collar jobs. It also is apparent that younger Indian workers typically do not begin their careers in occupations requiring many skills.

Each of the age categories in Table 8.8 can be viewed, very roughly, as corresponding to different phases in the careers of workers. At ages 16–20, most young American Indian men and women have relatively few job skills and almost no work experience compared with older Indian workers. The opportunities for workers of this age are limited to what are probably low-skill, low-wage jobs. This is especially true for young men, 60 percent of whom are employed in Service or Operator, Fabricator, and Laborer occupations. Only 14 percent of men under age 20 are employed in nonmanual jobs. In contrast, 72 percent of Indian women of this age group are employed in Service or Technical, Sales, and Administrative Support occupations, probably engaged in work such as clerk-typist, retail sales, receptionist, waitress, and motel maid jobs.

At ages 21 to 30 Indian workers have completed most or all of their formal schooling and are in the early stages of their working lives. For men and women in this age group, employment in Service occupations is less important than it is for teen workers; this is similar to non-Indian workers. However, Indian men show a marked propensity for skilled Precision Production, Craft, and Repair occupations. In contrast, female workers are more highly concentrated in nonmanual occupations than

---

[6]Jacob Mincer, *Schooling, Experience and Earnings* (New York: National Bureau of Economic Research, 1974); David L. Featherman and Robert M. Hauser, *Opportunity and Change* (New York: Academic Press, 1978).

TABLE 8.8

Percent Distribution of Age and Occupations of Employed American Indians and Alaska Natives Aged 16 and Over, by Age and Sex

Age and Sex	Managerial and Professional	Technical, Sales, and Administrative Support	Service	Farming, Forestry, and Fishing	Precision Production, Craft, and Repair	Operators, Fabricators, and Laborers
16–20						
Male	3.9	9.5	23.1	11.3	14.8	37.3
Female	5.8	39.1	33.3	4.2	2.8	14.8
21–30						
Male	9.8	11.9	12.6	6.4	24.6	34.7
Female	13.1	42.0	23.5	1.6	3.1	16.7
31–40						
Male	17.2	11.4	10.8	5.4	25.5	29.7
Female	18.0	34.1	25.4	1.7	3.6	17.1
41–50						
Male	17.5	11.2	10.9	7.4	23.1	29.9
Female	18.8	28.0	29.8	2.3	3.6	17.5
51–60						
Male	16.8	9.8	12.9	7.3	24.6	28.6
Female	17.6	26.7	32.4	2.1	3.9	17.3
61–65						
Male	13.0	9.1	15.4	11.0	25.4	26.1
Female	18.7	21.6	38.8	3.0	3.0	14.9
66 and Over						
Male	13.0	10.4	20.6	18.0	18.9	19.1
Female	15.9	21.2	40.8	4.7	3.4	14.0

SOURCE: Public-Use Microdata Sample, 5 percent A File.

men of the same age or younger women. In view of these differences between age groups, it is also noteworthy that the percentage of American Indians in semiskilled or unskilled occupations—Operators, Fabricators, and Laborers—is about the same for both age groups.

Between ages 31 and 60 the occupational distributions are similar for each age group. This is not surprising because this age range roughly corresponds to the peak years in the working lives of most individuals. By age 30 or shortly thereafter many if not most persons have settled into an occupation for the duration of their tenure in the labor force. As a result, there are relatively few major differences among these age groups. Women aged 31 to 60 are slightly more concentrated in Managerial and Professional occupations than younger women and, surprisingly, the percentage of these women in other white collar occupations is substantially smaller. The percentage of women in Technical, Sales, and Administrative Support occupations drops sharply at ages 31 to 40 and becomes smaller for each older age group. In contrast, the percentage of women in Service occupations is successively larger for each age group over 30. The occupational structures in which Indian men participate are highly stable regardless of age.

Occupation and Education

The importance of educational qualifications for occupational entry is clearly apparent in Table 8.9. This table contains the occupational distribution of Indian workers for given levels of education. As these figures show, the lack of a high school diploma virtually eliminates opportunities for white collar employment, especially for men. Women lacking a high school diploma are more successful than men in gaining nonmanual employment, but most likely these are jobs in retail sales or menial clerical work. Apart from these jobs, poorly educated women are most often employed in Service occupations (about 40 percent). Operator, Fabricator, and Laborer occupations are the next most likely sources of employment for these women. For Indian men with less than 12 years of schooling, Operators, Fabricators, and Laborers are the most common occupations, followed by Precision Production, Craft, and Repair and Service.

Completing 12 or more years of schooling greatly improves job opportunities, somewhat more for Indian women than for Indian men. Specifically, a high school diploma makes available to Indian women a wide range of opportunities in clerical and sales that are eschewed by

TABLE 8.9

Percent Distribution of Occupations of Employed American Indians and Alaska Natives Aged 16 and Over, by Years of Schooling and Sex, 1980

Years of Schooling and Sex	Managerial and Professional	Technical, Sales, and Administrative Support	Service	Farming, Forestry, and Fishing	Precision Production, Craft, and Repair	Operators, Fabricators, and Laborers	Total
0–8							
Male	4.8	4.6	14.1	14.5	23.2	38.8	100.0
Female	7.7	11.8	42.6	4.8	4.6	28.5	100.0
9–11							
Male	4.4	5.4	17.7	9.9	23.5	39.1	100.0
Female	6.1	22.3	40.2	3.4	4.4	23.6	100.0
12							
Male	8.0	11.0	12.5	6.3	26.5	35.7	100.0
Female	9.9	42.4	25.8	1.8	3.4	16.7	100.0
13–15							
Male	16.5	18.8	14.3	4.7	22.7	23.0	100.0
Female	18.7	50.3	19.0	1.3	2.2	8.5	100.0
16 and Over							
Male	54.9	17.6	7.6	2.3	8.6	9.0	100.0
Female	58.8	28.4	7.9	0.7	1.2	3.0	100.0

SOURCE: Public-Use Microdata Sample, 5 percent A File.

Indian men. Over 40 percent of women with 12 years of schooling are employed in Technical, Sales, and Administrative Support occupations. These women also are considerably less likely than their less educated counterparts to be employed in Service work. On the other hand, comparing Indian men who have 12 years of schooling with Indian men who have less schooling shows that the former benefit only slightly by being somewhat more likely to be in skilled Precision Production, Craft, and Repair occupations and slightly less likely to be in semiskilled or unskilled occupations.

However, there is little doubt that completing 16 or more years of schooling, the equivalent of a college degree, yields significant advantages in the labor market. Among men with 16 or more years of schooling, the likelihood that they are employed in white collar occupations is considerably higher compared with men with less education. About 73 percent of these men are in white collar jobs compared with 25 percent of male college dropouts and technical training graduates. For women, 16 or more years of schooling also increases the likelihood of nonmanual employment, but the increase is not as great as it is for men. This is because the major shift into white collar employment among Indian women occurs at high school graduation, the usual minimum qualification for clerical jobs. Nevertheless, advanced education beyond high school is a boon for Indian women because there is a decided tendency for these women to have Managerial and Professional occupations, and they are less likely to be employed in Technical, Sales, and Administrative Support jobs.

American Indian Incomes

The process of income generation is extremely complex, and though intensely studied it is not well understood.[7] Almost everything that is known about income generation is related to personal earnings. Although the income that people receive from their jobs is extremely important, there are other sources of income besides work. Unfortunately, even less is known about these types of income than about personal earnings. This chapter will describe the sources of income received by

[7]Christopher Jencks, Marshall Smith, Henry Acland, Mary Jo Bane, David Cohen, Herbert Gintis, Barbara Heyns, and Stephan Michelson, *Inequality: A Reassessment of the Effect of Family and Schooling in America* (New York: Harper & Row, 1972).

American Indians, the amounts received, and the social characteristics of the recipients.[8]

Another way of viewing American Indian income is from the standpoint of poverty thresholds. The official poverty threshold used by the Census Bureau is based on notions about the minimum income necessary to procure the essentials of food, shelter, clothing, and transportation. The dollar figure corresponding to the poverty threshold is variable, depending on family size and composition. For income received in 1979, the poverty threshold for single persons under age 65 and living

[8]Income information collected by the Census Bureau is ordinarily reported in connection with three different types of recipient. *Personal income* refers to the money received from various sources by individuals. The wages and salaries paid to individual workers by their employers is a good example of personal income. *Family income* is distinct from personal income, and it includes money income received by all members of the same family residing in the same household. *Household income* is the money received by all persons in a household, regardless of their family relationship. Typically, family incomes are highest because of multiple earners in family units. Household income is slightly lower because this figure includes individuals living alone. Personal income, because it represents only one earner, is usually the lowest of the three types of reported income. Incidentally, income is reported for 1979 and not 1980 because the census was taken early in 1980, and most persons are unable to accurately estimate their full-year incomes in advance.

Income data reported by the Census Bureau are typically classified as originating from one of seven possible sources. *Wage and salary income* is defined by the Census Bureau as the "money earnings received for work performed as an employee at any time during the calendar year. . . . It includes wages, salary, pay from Armed Forces, commissions, tips, piece-rate payments, and cash bonuses earned. Sick leave pay is included." See U.S. Bureau of the Census, *Public Use Microdata Samples Technical Documentation* (Washington, DC: U.S. Bureau of the Census, 1983), p. K-23. For most persons, wages and salaries constitute the largest and most important source of income. *Nonfarm self-employment income* is defined as gross receipts minus business expenses which individuals receive from a business or professional enterprise in which they are engaged for their own benefit. This includes the so-called salaries which proprietors and professionals in private practice pay themselves. For many Americans this is another important source of income, but for American Indians it is less important because relatively few are self-employed. *Farm self-employment* is similar to other kinds of self-employment income except that it specifically originates with the proceeds of agricultural production. All three sources of income are broadly defined as earnings. *Interest, dividend, and rent income* represents money from diverse sources, such as deposits in interest-bearing accounts, payments from stocks and bonds, copyright fees, royalties from oil and gas leases, and the rental of real estate. For some American Indians, oil and gas royalties and land rentals are a significant source of income. Some tribes retain control over large amounts of natural resources, such as energy minerals and grazing. *Social Security income* is money paid in survivors', disability, and old-age benefits. This income is obviously very important for retirement age American Indians. *Public assistance income* is received from a host of local, state, and federal programs and is frequently labeled as "welfare" benefits. These payments include traditional welfare sources such as Aid to Families with Dependent children (AFDC), but they also represent many other sources of assistance, including categorical aid for the elderly, blind, and disabled not covered by Social Security benefits. Because it includes AFDC, this source of income is prominent in the households of single mothers with young children. Finally, *income from all other sources* is a residual category for money received from sources other than one of the preceding six types.

alone was $3,774. A husband, wife, and their two children under age 18, in contrast, were considered living below the poverty line if their total family income was below $7,356. Poverty figures also vary depending on whether the data are for persons, households, or families.

Comparisons with Blacks and Whites

The first set of statistics pertaining to the income and poverty level of American Indians is shown in Table 8.10. If we compare American Indians with blacks and whites over time, it is clear that American Indians have enjoyed the largest increases in family and household incomes and the largest reductions in families living in poverty. In 1969 the Indian median family income was 96 percent of black median family income and only 59 percent of white median family income. During the 1970s Indian median family income increased by 19 percent, pushing it ahead of black family income, which increased by less than 5 percent. By 1980 the median family income of blacks was 92 percent of the median family income of Indians. However, the economic position of American Indians remains far behind whites. Even with the gains of the 1970s, Indian family incomes are only 66 percent of white family in-

TABLE 8.10

Median Incomes and Families with Incomes Below Poverty Line for Blacks, Whites, and American Indians, 1969–1979 (1979 dollars)

	Median Family Income	Median Household Income	Percentage of Families Below Poverty Line
Blacks			
1969	$12,013	$ 9,215	29.8
1979	12,598	10,943	26.5
Whites			
1969	19,723	16,058	8.6
1979	20,835	17,680	7.0
American Indians			
1969	11,547	[a]	33.0
1979	13,724	12,256	23.7

SOURCES: *1980 Census of Population, General Social and Economic Characteristics, United States Summary; 1970 Census of Population, Characteristics of the Population, United States Summary;* and "American Indians," *1970 Census of Population, Subject Report.*

[a]Not available.

comes. The changes in American Indian income predictably correspond to declines in poverty, and the changes in poverty closely parallel the changes in family income.

Geographic Distribution of Income

Region: The geographic distribution of economic resources is an important issue that has been examined several times in connection with other indicators of socioeconomic conditions. Regional variations in education, labor force participation, and occupation were clearly evident in the preceding text, but they are not especially large or dramatic. As a result, it is not surprising to find that wage and salary incomes, which are most closely related to education, labor force participation, and occupation also do not vary greatly from one area to another (see Table 8.11). Significantly, there is no area of the United States in which Indian incomes reach or exceed white incomes as a whole.

The lowest wage and salary income, $5,610, is found in the West North Central states, which include places with significant numbers of Indians, such as Minnesota and the Dakotas. In comparison, the Middle Atlantic states are highly urbanized and have small Indian populations. Yet Indians in this area have a higher median wage and salary income ($8,225) than Indians anywhere else in the United States. In absolute terms the gap between the highest and lowest Indian wages and salaries is about $2,600. In relative terms the lowest wage and salary incomes are 68 percent of the highest.

TABLE 8.11

Median Incomes of American Indians and Alaska Natives and Percentage With Incomes Below Poverty Line, by Census Division (1979 dollars)

Census Division	Family Income	Household Income	Wage and Salary Income	Percentage Below Poverty Line
New England	$13,988	$13,210	$7,005	27.3
Mid Atlantic	16,005	15,005	8,225	20.2
E. North Central	17,230	16,488	7,945	19.3
W. North Central	13,530	12,725	5,610	31.2
South Atlantic	14,465	13,870	6,925	21.0
E. South Central	13,010	12,452	6,005	27.0
W. South Central	15,010	13,755	7,005	21.1
Mountain	13,005	12,340	6,005	36.2
Pacific	17,775	16,820	7,805	18.4

SOURCE: Public-Use Microdata Sample, 5 percent A File.

Compared with wages and salaries, the absolute differences in family and household income are larger, and the areas with the highest and lowest incomes are also different. The lowest family and household incomes, $13,005 and $12,340, are found in the Mountain states, followed closely by the East South Central states; the latter do not have a large Indian population, but the former do. Notably, Indians in the Mountain states also have the second lowest wage and salary incomes compared with the entire American Indian labor force.

On the other hand, a large Indian population resides in the Pacific states, and Indians residing in this area report the highest family and household incomes. In this regard, it is worth noting that the Pacific states include Alaska, which is known for extraordinarily high incomes and an equally high cost of living. For this reason, the incomes of Alaska Natives, particularly Aleuts, are considerably higher than the incomes of Indians in the lower 48 states.[9] However, this does not betoken a markedly higher standard of living for this group.

In relative terms the gap between both the highest and lowest median family income and household income is 73 percent, which is only slightly smaller than the gap between high and low wages and salaries. This suggests that although regional differences in family and household incomes involve larger amounts of money, these differences are similar to variations in wages and salaries. Not surprisingly, the geographic distribution of persons living in poverty is consistent with these patterns, ranging from a low of 18 percent in the Pacific states to a high of 36 percent in the Mountain states.

Residence: Place of residence is another important dimension of geography associated with differences in socioeconomic conditions. Table 8.12 provides a highly detailed view of income differences for places of residence by listing median incomes according to source. For family and household income, the results are predictable. American Indians residing in metropolitan and nonreservation places have the highest incomes, and the largest differentials are between metropolitan and nonmetropolitan areas, with median family incomes ranging from $12,465 to $15,818. Both types of income are over 25 percent higher in metropolitan places than in nonmetropolitan places.

Except for farm income, which is higher in nonmetropolitan areas, American Indians in metropolitan areas consistently receive higher incomes regardless of source. Overall, total personal income is about 31 percent higher ($6,565 versus $5,005) in metropolitan areas than in nonmetropolitan areas. Wages and salaries constitute the largest source of

[9]In 1979 Eskimo and Aleut median family incomes were $13,829 and $20,313, respectively, compared with $13,678 for American Indians.

TABLE 8.12

*Median Incomes and Percentage of American Indians and Alaska Natives
With Incomes Below Poverty Line, by Source (1979 dollars)*

Source	Metropolitan	Nonmetropolitan	Off Reservation	On or Near Reservation
Family Income	$16,660	$13,055	$16,410	$14,010
Household Income	15,818	12,465	15,145	13,350
Wages and Salaries	7,505	6,005	7,405	6,005
Self-Employment	6,780	5,005	6,255	5,270
Farm	2,605	2,775	2,770	2,505
Interest, Dividends, and Rents	625	605	695	555
Social Security	2,806	2,195	2,505	2,305
Public Assistance	2,205	1,805	2,155	1,865
Other Sources	1,805	1,605	1,780	1,705
Total	6,565	5,005	6,495	5,105
Percentage Below Poverty Line	20.0	31.8	19.9	30.6

SOURCE: Public-Use Microdata Sample, 5 percent A File.

American Indian income ($7,505 and $6,005), followed closely by income from self-employment ($6,780 and $5,005). Interestingly, American Indian entrepreneurs in metropolitan areas enjoy substantial rewards, with incomes over 35 percent higher than incomes of their nonmetropolitan counterparts. These sources of income are higher than total personal income because the figures for total personal income include welfare recipients, retired persons, and the disabled who do not work and depend on income from sources other than gainful employment and who receive incomes substantially below the incomes of employed persons. This implies that a considerable incentive exists for labor force participation instead of relying on nonemployment income sources.

Finally, in view of the large land holdings and natural resources frequently ascribed to reservation Indians,[10] it might be expected that they would receive significant amounts of income from sources such as farm operations and payments from interest, dividends, and rents. This might be true for a handful of tribes, but for the vast majority of American Indians living on reservations these sources of income amount to a paltry sum. In fact, farm income and money from interest, dividends, and rents are lower for Indians residing on or near reservations than for Indians residing in any other place. There are many reasons why this is the case, but in short most farmland belonging to Indians is leased by non-Indians for relatively small amounts of money, and large-scale natural resource development has benefited only a very small minority of the total American Indian population.[11]

Total Income and Gender

The income data in Tables 8.10–8.12 are revealing, but they are also somewhat misleading for two reasons. First, they do not distinguish between male and female income recipients, even though men have higher incomes than women. Second, the figures in these tables are based on persons who reported receiving a particular type of income in 1979. It is impossible to determine from these tables the relative contribution that each income source makes to the *total* personal income and overall economic well-being of the Indian population as a whole.

One view of the relative importance of different sources of income for American Indians is provided by the data in Table 8.13; the means are adjusted by the numbers of persons receiving a particular type of income so they will reflect the relative contribution that different income sources make to the mean total personal income of American Indians. In terms of differences for gender and place of residence, this table offers a slightly different perspective but does not alter any conclusions already made.

For American Indian men and women alike, wages and salaries constitute the largest and most important source of income. Wages and salaries contribute from 81 to 84 percent of total income for men and 74 to 77 percent for women. Men also receive significantly larger amounts

[10]D. Stanley Eitzen, *Social Problems* (Boston: Allyn & Bacon, 1983).

[11]Sar A. Levitan and Barbara Hetrick, *Big Brother's Indian Programs: With Reservations* (New York: McGraw-Hill, 1971); Sar A. Levitan and William B. Johnston, *Indian Giving: Federal Programs for Native Americans* (Baltimore: Johns Hopkins University Press, 1975).

TABLE 8.13

Adjusted Mean Per Capita Sources and Percentage of Total Personal Income for American Indians and Alaska Natives (1979 dollars)

	Metropolitan		Nonmetropolitan		Off Reservation		On or Near Reservation	
	Males	Females	Males	Females	Males	Females	Males	Females
Wages and Salaries	$7,424 83.6%	3,859 77.2	5,843 80.6	2,998 74.2	7,243 82.8	3,592 76.5	6,275 82.4	3,305 75.8
Nonfarm Self-Employment	480 5.4	130 2.6	451 6.2	76 1.9	514 5.9	119 2.5	406 5.3	92 2.1
Farm Self-Employment	49 0.6	11 0.2	116 1.6	23 0.6	84 1.0	18 0.4	60 0.8	10 0.2
Interest, Dividends, and Rents	160 1.8	117 2.3	94 1.3	101 2.5	156 1.8	118 2.5	107 1.4	96 2.2
Social Security	241 2.7	273 5.5	251 3.5	288 7.1	249 2.8	284 6.0	239 3.1	259 5.9
Public Assistance	93 1.0	329 6.6	123 1.7	306 7.6	87 1.0	297 6.3	128 1.7	340 7.8
All Other Sources	435 4.9	277 5.6	371 5.1	247 6.1	416 4.7	416 5.8	403 5.3	256 6.0
Income Total	8,882 100.0	4,996 100.0	7,249 100.0	4,039 100.0	8,749 100.0	4,844 100.0	7,618 100.0	4,358 100.0

SOURCE: Public-Use Microdata Sample, 5 percent A File.

from other employment-related sources of income, although they are much less important in relative terms.

These gender-specific differences are consistent with other data. However, one further observation about gender differences should be mentioned. While men receive higher incomes for employment-related activities, Social Security and public assistance make up a larger part of female incomes. Indian women live longer than Indian men, making Social Security a more significant source of income. Indian women are more likely than Indian men to be solely responsible for the care of young children and, as a result, are more reliant on public assistance programs such as AFDC for support. This means that the total income of women is less than the total income of men, not only because they are paid less for their work, but also because they are more likely than men to depend on the limited benefits of Social Security and public assistance programs.

Differences by place of residence are more modest than gender differences and do not display significant departures from the other data. However, one interesting finding related to residence is the small contribution—only about 2 percent of the average total personal income—that money from farming and from interest, rents, and dividends makes to the total personal income of Indians residing on or near reservations. The number of Indians receiving farm self-employment income, for example, is so small, and the amount they receive is so little, that this source of income has little impact on the economic well-being of the Indian population as a whole. From this perspective, American Indians residing on or near reservations benefit little from the wealth of natural resources that is ascribed to them by some analysts and public commentators.

Social Characteristics of Wage and Salary Earners

Age: Tables 8.14–8.16 display the relationship between wages and salaries and antecedent social characteristics such as age, education, and occupation. This discussion focuses on wages and salaries because of their importance to the total incomes received by American Indians and because wages and salaries reflect the relative importance of certain social characteristics by their value in the market. As noted in Chapter 7, the value of age in the labor market is curvilinear for most workers, and the American Indian work force is not an exception. This is clearly evident in the data shown in Table 8.14.

Youths with little work experience are obviously not highly valued. American Indians aged 20 and under have smaller wages and salaries

TABLE 8.14

Median Wage and Salary Income and Poverty Status
of American Indians and Alaska Natives Aged 16 and Over
(1979 dollars)

Age	Median Wages and Salaries		Percentage Below Poverty Line	
	Males	Females	Males	Females
16–20	$ 2,265	$1,707	30.3	34.9
21–30	8,005	5,005	20.3	26.7
31–40	12,510	6,213	16.7	23.7
41–50	13,005	6,005	17.5	23.4
51–60	10,537	4,723	19.4	25.6
61–70	5,688	3,115	23.9	31.2
71 and Over	3,760	3,010	32.3	35.8

SOURCE: Public-Use Microdata Sample, 5 percent A File.

than those in any other age group. However, as workers begin to reach their prime working years in their mid 20s, their wages and salaries appear to increase substantially. The wages of Indian males aged 21 to 30 are over 3.5 times higher than the wages of younger workers. Although the income differentials between age groups become smaller, wages and salaries are higher for each successive age group up to ages 41 to 50 for men and 31 to 40 for women. Wages are also consistently smaller for every age group of women; the wage differential between men and women is smallest among youth aged 16 to 20 and becomes larger at each higher age bracket until retirement ages. This probably means that a mutual dependence on nonemployment retirement incomes is a great equalizer of the incomes received by American Indian men and women. It is also not surprising that the relationship between poverty and age inversely follows the relationship between wages and salaries and age.

Education: For many reasons education has a decisive influence on the wages and salaries of workers. According to some theories, increasing education raises worker productivity, which is translated into higher earnings.[12] Other theories claim that educational credentials confer special entitlements that provide access to higher paying jobs.[13] Regardless of which theory is correct, American Indians reap significant economic

[12]Gary Becker, *Human Capital* (New York: National Bureau of Economic Research, 1964).
[13]Randall Collins, *The Credential Society* (New York: Academic Press, 1979).

TABLE 8.15

*Levels of Education and Median Wage and Salary Income
of American Indians and Alaska Natives (1979 dollars)*

Years of Education	Males	Females
0–8	$ 7,205	$4,005
9–11	4,885	3,005
12	9,305	5,395
13–15	11,005	6,005
16 and Over	15,505	9,495

SOURCE: Public-Use Microdata Sample, 5 percent A File.

rewards from educational achievements.[14] This is evident in Table 8.15. The earnings gap between the most educated and least educated American Indian men amounts to an absolute difference of $8,300, and in relative numbers the annual earnings of the most educated men are 215 percent greater than the annual earnings of the least educated men. Among American Indian women, who normally earn less than men in any case, the absolute differences in wages and salaries between the most educated and the least educated are smaller than the gap between men. Yet in relative terms the gap is slightly larger for women than for men. The earnings of the most educated Indian women are 237 percent higher than the earnings of their least educated counterparts.

A somewhat unexpected finding in Table 8.15 is that American Indian men and women with the least education do not have the lowest wages and salaries. This dubious distinction is reserved for Indian high school dropouts who have completed more than an eighth grade education, with median incomes of $5,885 and $3,005 for men and women, respectively. Although education is a critical factor in determining earnings, other factors are important—work experience, for example, which is closely related to age. American Indians with the lowest levels of education, eighth grade or less, do not have the lowest earnings because most likely they are older and have sufficient work experience to com-

[14]This is consistent with studies by James D. Gwartney and James E. Long, "The Relative Earnings of Blacks and Other Minorities," *Industrial and Labor Relations Review* 31(1978):336–346; Ronald L. Trosper, "Earnings and Labor Supply: A Microeconomic Comparison of American Indians and Alaskan Natives to American Whites and Blacks," Social Welfare Research Institute, Publication no. 55 (Boston: Boston College, 1980); and Gary D. Sandefur and Wilbur J. Scott, "Minority Group Status and the Wages of Indian and Black Males," *Social Science Research* 12(1983):44–68. Trosper claims that Indians benefit less from education than blacks or whites, while Sandefur and Scott argue that the opposite is true.

pensate for their lack of schooling. On the other hand, high school drop-outs tend to be younger and, having neither education nor experience, they are the least valued and most poorly paid of all Indian workers.

Occupation: The salutary impact of education on earnings does not mean that well-educated persons are automatically well paid, regardless of their employment. On the contrary, highly educated persons enjoy high earnings because they are more likely than poorly educated persons to work in high paying jobs. This is evident in statistics showing the median wages and salaries paid in specific occupations (Table 8.16). A comparison of the data in Table 8.16 with the data for educational levels and occupations in Table 8.9 will show that the relationship between education and earnings exists by virtue of the fact that higher education leads to employment in higher paid occupations.

Predictably, there is a large gap between the highest paid and lowest paid occupations. For Indian men, the highest paid jobs are in Manage-rial and Professional occupations, with median earnings exceeding $14,000. The lowest paid jobs are in Farming, Forestry, and Fishing oc-cupations. Given that these are the highest and lowest paid occupations, it is worth noting that they do not include a sizable percentage of the American Indian labor force compared with other skilled and semi-skilled occupations.

An especially striking characteristic of Table 8.16 is that American Indian men earn from 1.6 to 1.9 times more than Indian women in the

TABLE 8.16

Occupations and Median Wage and Salary Income of American Indians and Alaska Natives (1979 dollars)

Occupation	Males	Females
Managerial and Professional	$14,045	$8,805
Technical, Sales, and Administrative Support	10,805	6,005
Service	5,425	3,005
Farming, Forestry, and Fishing	4,005	1,395
Precision Production, Craft, and Repair	11,005	6,005
Operators, Fabricators, and Laborers	8,005	4,975

SOURCE: Public-Use Microdata Sample, 5 percent A File.

same occupation. Furthermore, the relative earnings gap is larger among female workers than among male workers. The highest paid Indian men earn 3.5 times more than the lowest paid, but for women the gap is much larger. Managerial and Professional occupations provide the highest earnings for women, with a median of $8,805. However, this figure is 6.3 times more than the earnings of women in Farming, Forestry, and Fishing jobs, who earn a median $1,395 annually. Again, these occupations involve a relatively small share of Indian women in the labor force, meaning that most American Indians, men and women alike, are not concentrated in either the highest or lowest paid occupations.

Reservation Income

Table 8.17 shows family income and families in poverty on the 16 most populated reservations in 1980. Excluding the Osage, from one third to over one half of all Indian families residing on these reservations had incomes below the official poverty line. While these numbers indicate economic hardship on a depression-like scale, they are nonetheless better than the poverty rates for 1969. In 1969 the proportion of families living in poverty ranged from 42.0 percent on the Wind River reservation to a phenomenal 78.1 percent on the Papago reservation. Between 1970 and 1980 these reservations experienced reductions in poverty ranging from 19.5 percent for the Eastern Cherokee to virtually no change at the Pine Ridge reservation, with most reservations in the middle of this range.

Given that most reservations witnessed reductions in family poverty during the 1970s, it might be reasonable to expect that this would be matched by substantial increases in family income. However, reductions in poverty did not necessarily result from higher real family income. This is evident by comparing changes in median family income with changes in poverty. For example, family poverty declined at the Zuni pueblo from 56.7 to 44.6 percent during the 1970s. Yet, during the same period real family income at the Zuni pueblo did not increase, and in fact it actually dipped slightly, from $10,476 to $10,354, a 1 percent decrease. The Zuni notwithstanding, the other reservations in Table 8.17 experienced income gains that might be expected with lower poverty, but in several cases the gain involved only a few hundred dollars. On the other hand, reservations such as the Navajo, Papago, and Blackfeet added more than $2,000 to their median family incomes.

The Osage are clearly an anomaly in Table 8.17, for no other reason than their extraordinarily high family incomes compared with other reservations. There are several possible explanations for this finding: (1)

TABLE 8.17
Median Family Incomes and Families With Incomes Below Poverty Levels for American Indians Residing on the 16 Largest Reservations in 1980 (1979 dollars)

Reservation	1969			1979		
	Median Family Income	Percentage of Families Below Poverty Line		Median Family Income	Percentage of Families Below Poverty Line	Percentage of Families Receiving BIA Assistance
Navajo[a] (AZ, UT, NM)	$ 6,106	62.1		$ 8,397	50.5	7.0
Pine Ridge (SD)	7,745	54.3		7,942	54.7	10.2
Gila River (AZ)	6,766	58.6		7,955	50.7	8.8
Papago (AZ)	4,950	78.1		7,003	56.2	8.3
Fort Apache (AZ)	8,599	53.3		9,273	47.6	2.5
Hopi[a] (AZ)	6,839	61.8		8,197	50.9	6.3
Zuni Pueblo (NM)	10,476	56.7		10,354	44.6	1.1
San Carlos (AZ)	7,932	62.3		7,986	53.6	3.1
Rosebud (SD)	6,795	62.9		8,868	47.7	9.2
Blackfeet (MT)	8,430	47.8		10,576	33.7	5.9
Yakima (WA)	10,231	45.5		11,324	34.2	9.4
Eastern Cherokee (NC)	8,168	52.2		9,774	32.7	2.3
Standing Rock (ND, SD)	7,231	58.3		8,107	51.3	14.2
Osage[b] (OK)	NA	NA		16,095	13.9	5.4
Fort Peck (MT)	10,111	46.7		10,864	38.4	20.5
Wind River (WY)	9,241	42.0		10,816	36.0	3.0

SOURCES: *1980 Census of Population*, "American Indians, Eskimos, and Aleuts on Identified Reservations and in the Historic Areas of Oklahoma," *1980 Census of Population, Subject Report*; and "American Indians," *1970 Census of Population, Subject Report*.
[a]Navajo and Hopi reservations are not strictly comparable because of administrative changes in the 1970s.
[b]Osage reservation data are not available for 1970.

Osage reservation residents are relatively well educated and have relatively high rates of labor force participation; (2) the reservation is located within commuting distance of the metropolitan Tulsa labor market, which experienced a major expansion with the Sunbelt growth of the 1970s; (3) a number of Osage families are the recipients of royalties from oil leases on their reservation. High oil prices during the 1970s stimulated oil production on leases that in earlier years had been too unprofitable to operate. Which of these factors was most important in raising Osage family incomes to their high level in 1979 is impossible to identify, but all three probably played a role.

The last column in Table 8.17 shows the percentage of families receiving BIA public assistance, which is similar to the welfare relief provided by many county and city governments under the title of general assistance. It is not the same as AFDC, and it usually involves smaller benefits with fewer restrictions than AFDC.[15] Considering the relatively high poverty rates and low family incomes, the level of BIA public assistance on these reservations is surprisingly low; except for two areas, 10 percent or less of reservation families receive BIA assistance. Indian families may be receiving aid from other programs such as AFDC or food stamps, but clearly they are not heavily reliant on this type of BIA assistance. Other programs may be taking up the slack, but it also may be true that some Indian families are loathe to avail themselves of BIA assistance for reasons of pride and a distaste for encounters with the BIA bureaucracy.

Concluding Remarks

The discussion in this chapter employed the six basic occupation categories developed by the Census Bureau. These categories are extremely broad, but they are useful because they facilitate comparisons with other published information and because they are easily described. Admittedly, however, they lack detail, and in some instances they obscure useful information. Nevertheless, their advantages outweigh their limitations.

One of the most striking findings uncovered in this research is that there are substantial differences in the occupations of American Indian men and women. American Indian men are most heavily concentrated in blue collar jobs requiring manual labor. The expansion of white collar

[15]Theodore W. Taylor, *The Bureau of Indian Affairs* (Boulder, CO: Westview Press, 1984).

jobs that occurred throughout the 1970s benefited Indian men only slightly. In contrast, the percentage of Indian women in white collar occupations increased substantially between 1970 and 1980. This does not mean that Indian women made significant inroads into high-level managerial and professional positions. On the contrary, clerical and para-professional jobs are probably typical white collar occupations for American Indian women. A similar pattern exists for black workers, except that American Indians, men and women alike, were slightly more likely to have nonmanual employment.

The fact that American Indian men did not benefit from growing numbers of nonmanual jobs does not mean that Indian men, or women, are completely isolated from the mainstream economy. Viewing the regional differences in American Indian occupations shows that Indians, like other American workers, usually hold jobs that are common in an area. In places where textiles or other types of manufacturing are dominant, Indians appear well represented in occupations associated with factory work. Place of residence also makes a large difference in the kinds of work done by American Indians; the most important distinction is between metropolitan and nonmetropolitan locations. Not surprisingly, Indians in nonmetropolitan places are more likely to be in manual occupations, especially in jobs related to agriculture, forestry, and fishing. Reservation residence has less of an impact on the types of jobs held by Indians, except to the extent that reservations are more likely to be outside metropolitan areas.

If Indian workers are not unique in their dependence on regional and local economies, they also are not unique in their occupations; the percentage of the American Indian labor force in "traditional" occupations—such as jewelry making and crafts—is very small. This is true even in areas such as reservations that should have relatively large numbers of workers in these occupations. There are important exceptions to this rule, of course, such as the Zuni pueblo, where a tradition of fine silverwork and other crafts exists.

American Indians also are not very different from other workers in terms of the requirements and rewards of occupational careers. Younger American Indians tend to start their working lives in low-wage, low-skill jobs such as service occupations and with age and experience move into other kinds of work. For the small share of Indian youths who pursue a college education, higher levels of schooling are associated with more opportunities for entering white collar occupations. Likewise, white collar occupations are identified with higher levels of economic benefits. However, Indian women should regard themselves as doubly disadvantaged because they are generally better educated and more poorly paid than Indian men in the same occupations.

While Indian workers have characteristics in common with other segments of the U.S. labor force, especially blacks, are there characteristics that make American Indian workers unique and different from other U.S. workers? Indeed, in at least one very important way American Indian workers differ from the rest of the labor force, and that is in the level of dependence on public-sector employment. In particular, from the inception of reservations the federal government has had a continual presence on reservation lands. As such, the federal government has been an employer of first and last resort for a vast number of Indians residing in areas nearly bereft of other forms of economic activity. With the reorganization of tribal governments in 1934, and the Indian Self-Determination Act of 1975, which enlarged their responsibilities, tribal governments also provide a significant source of employment. More than most other groups, American Indians depend on public-sector largess for job opportunities, and they suffer disproportionately from fiscal austerity.

American Indian dependency on public-sector job opportunities may partially explain why American Indian incomes increased substantially between 1970 and 1980, in the wake of public-sector expansion lasting into the early 1970s. Although some observers[16] have argued that the economic position of minority populations was diminished in the 1970s, blaming antipoverty programs for the damage, it would be hard to defend this position in regard to American Indians. At the time of the 1970 census, American Indians were unquestionably the poorest, most poverty-stricken group in the United States, with incomes well below those of the black population. By 1980 poverty among American Indians declined and real incomes rose to levels exceeding the real incomes of blacks. The causes and circumstances surrounding these gains may never be identified beyond doubt, but something undoubtedly happened in the years between 1970 and 1980 to affect the economic position of the Indian population.[17] Although Indians were slightly ahead of blacks in 1980, both groups have incomes that are still well below the incomes of whites.

The fact that the American Indian labor force relies heavily on the public sector for jobs does not imply an equally heavy reliance on the public sector for income unrelated to employment. For American Indians, cash transfers in the form of public assistance payments do not

[16]Charles Murray, *Losing Ground: American Social Policy, 1950–1980* (New York: Basic Books, 1984).

[17]Changes in the composition of the American Indian population due to changes in self-identification probably played a role in this process. However, even areas where changes in racial identification were negligible, for example, reservations, experienced significant increases in incomes.

represent a significant source of income. These payments are relatively small compared with income from other sources and contribute a very small percentage of the total personal income for the Indian population. In short, American Indians are not heavily dependent on the public purse for unearned income, and the amounts they receive are hardly generous. On the contrary, earnings, primarily as wages and salaries, represent the largest and most important source of income for the vast majority of American Indians.

In view of the large holdings of reservation real estate, and the natural resources that are sometimes found on this land, the observation that wages and salaries provide the lion's share of income for most American Indians might be surprising to some readers. Yet nearly half the Indian population resides in a metropolitan area, and a large majority do not live within reservation boundaries, though they may be able to claim rights to reservation land. Even for persons residing on or near reservation land, the income they receive for mineral royalties, energy and timber leases, and grazing rents, for example, is negligible. It is true that a few tribes receive, or have received in the past, sizable amounts of money from the development of their land and natural resources, but they are exceptions.

Finally, regional differences in income are visible, but they are not especially large or predictable. Southern states, for example, are frequently associated with lower incomes than the rest of the country. However, Indians in the South do not have particularly low incomes. In fact, areas with especially low American Indian family and household incomes include the Mountain and West North Central states, in which there are large numbers of American Indian residents. Larger income differences are related to places of residence. However, these gaps are smaller than the differences due to gender. For example, Indian men in metropolitan areas earn more than Indian men in nonmetropolitan places, but the difference in the earnings of these men is smaller than the differences in male and female earnings in metropolitan or nonmetropolitan areas.

Since the beginning of this century, the American Indian population has grown in size, become more urbanized, and in many important ways accommodated the demands of contemporary industrial society. American Indians today are better educated, better employed, and have better incomes than they did even 10 years ago.

Does this mean that American Indians have disappeared into the melting pot of Anglo society? The answer to this question is an unqualified no. American Indians still bear the markings of a population outside the economic mainstream. By the standards of white Americans, American Indians are not well educated; they are marginally attached to the labor force; they do work that is not highly valued; and the consequences of these liabilities are poverty and economic hardship. Furthermore, there are great differences between Indians in urban and rural places. The fate of American Indians in the next century may depend on their success in passing along their culture at the same time that they learn to cope with the demands of postindustrial American society. In this regard, whether American Indians choose to remain isolated from Anglo society or instead migrate to urban centers of economic activity may eventually be decisive in their future.

9

MIGRATION

B Y TRADITION and circumstance, American Indians have often moved from one location to another. Until the mid nineteenth century, many tribes regularly traveled long distances in accordance with the seasons for hunting, trapping, gathering, and trade. As the non-Indian population grew larger in this country, Indians frequently had little choice except to move from one territory to another. Although traditional nomadic lifestyles have all but disappeared among American Indians, the geographic mobility of this population has not been curtailed. On the contrary, American Indians continue to be a highly mobile segment of American society.[1]

Historical Background

Understanding the causes and consequences of migration is important because it provides insights into the processes by which popula-

[1]Joan Ablon, "Relocated American Indians in the San Francisco Bay Area: Social Interactions and Indian Identity," *Human Organization* 23(1964):296–304; Calvin L. Beale, "Migration Patterns of Minorities in the United States," *American Journal of Agricultural Economics* 55(1973):938–946; James H. Gundlach and Alden E. Roberts, "Native American Indian Migration and Relocation: Success or Failure," *Pacific Sociological Review* 12(1978):117–128; Robert A. Hackenberg and C. Roderick Wilson, "Reluctant Emigrants: The Role of Migration in Papago Indian Adaptation," *Human Organization* 31(1972): 171–186; Arthur Margon, "Indians and Immigrants: A Comparison of Groups New to the City," *Journal of Ethnic Studies* 4(1976):17–28; John A. Price, "The Migration and Adaptation of American Indians to Los Angeles," *Human Organization* 27(1968):168–175.

tions are geographically distributed. In Chapter 3 the distribution of the Indian population was discussed in the context of historic events affecting the shape of this distribution in contemporary times. A brief review of the historical context of Indian migration is useful for developing a perspective on contemporary migration.

Migration Before 1800

American Indians have been a more or less migratory population since long before the arrival of Columbus. In fact, migration is the most commonly invoked explanation for the origins of the American Indian population.[2] Anthropologists believe that the ancestors of modern American Indians migrated to North America from Asia across a land bridge that is now the Bering Strait. Because this land bridge (Beringia) has existed several times in recent geological history, there are numerous estimates of when American Indians might have migrated to this continent. According to Thornton, the weight of opinion suggests that the Indian population first migrated to the North American continent about 25,000 years ago.[3] However, some estimates suggest that this migration occurred as early as 40,000 years ago. Commenting on this debate, Thornton notes that "they could have arrived earlier [than 25,000 years ago], and probably did; they could have arrived later but probably did not."[4] He also points out that the ancestors of modern Alaska Natives, Eskimos and Aleuts, migrated to this area much later than the forerunners of the Indian population in the lower 48 states. The ancestors of Alaska Natives probably settled in this area 10,000 to 14,000 years ago.[5]

Continued migration further dispersed the Indian population throughout North America and into South America. One estimate suggests that the descendants of the Beringia migrants reached the Gulf of Mexico within 350 years and that the entire hemisphere from Canada to the southernmost end of South America was populated within 1,000

---

[2]Russell Thornton, *American Indian Holocaust and Survival: A Population History Since 1492* (Norman: University of Oklahoma Press, 1987), provides an excellent overview of anthropological theories about migration across the Bering Strait. It should be noted, however, that many Indians, particularly spiritual leaders, consider these theories implausible at best and offensive at worst.

[3]Thornton (1987).

[4]Thornton (1987).

[5]Thornton (1987) also points out that American Indians and Alaska Natives are genetically distinct; the latter are genetically closer to present-day Siberians. In his words, "They are *Native Americans* but not *American Indians*" (unpublished manuscript, p. 18).

years.[6] This estimate is speculative, but it is clear from archaeological evidence that American Indians inhabited the area that is now Chile about 13,000 years ago and reached Tierra del Fuego about 10,000 years ago.

In the thousands of years after they arrived and dispersed on this continent, changing environmental and ecological conditions undoubtedly were an impetus for periodic redistributions of the indigenous population. Very little is known about these redistributions but, without question, one of the most historically important occurred in the decades following the arrival of Columbus. In their voyages to the New World, Columbus and subsequent explorers brought with them a host of infectious diseases. These diseases, unknown among the native populations of the Western Hemisphere, had a devastating impact on the indigenous populations, causing deaths numbering in the millions (see Chapter 1 for a detailed discussion).

One of the consequences of the sixteenth century epidemics and the massive depopulation of the continent was a large-scale redistribution of the native population. Exact details about the full impact of disease epidemics on population redistribution are not known. Dobyns, for example, argues that the lives lost due to disease were massive in number,[7] which would have led to an equally staggering realignment of the population as survivors fled infected areas and as new groups came to reside in the areas once occupied by disease victims. By his own admission, Dobyns's estimates of the mortality caused by disease are controversially high, and by extension more moderate estimates of disease-related mortality render a somewhat less dramatic view of American Indian population redistribution in the sixteenth century.

Regardless of the exact magnitude of redistribution, the arrival of Europeans brought about a major upheaval in the spatial organization of the Indian population. An equally important though less appreciated fact is that maps showing "original" territories of tribal cultures circa 1700 actually reflect the outcomes of a long-term process and large-scale upheavals in the preceding 200 years. There are many reasons to believe that the boundaries of tribal cultural areas remained in a more or less constant flux depending on migration, population growth and decline, and changing environmental conditions.

[6]Martin (1973), quoted in Thornton (1987).
[7]Henry F. Dobyns, *Their Number Become Thinned: Native American Population Dynamics in Eastern North America* (Knoxville: University of Tennessee Press, 1983).

Migration After 1800

The next major upheaval in the distribution of the Indian population was not due to biological agents. Instead, it grew out of the continuing surge of European immigrants and culminated in a series of political actions taken by the young government of the United States. Under the administration of Andrew Jackson, legislation was passed that initiated the removal of eastern tribes to locations west of the Mississippi River, primarily in Oklahoma. This legislation signaled the beginning of an era lasting over 60 years, during which almost the entire Indian population was relocated and settled on reservation lands or in the Indian territory in Oklahoma (see Chapter 3). The goal of this legislation was to settle the Indian population in places distant from the mainstream of American society.

In recent history, relocation policies have tried to achieve precisely the opposite goals pursued by nineteenth century removal legislation. Since 1950 various relocation programs have used benign means to encourage American Indians to leave their reservation homes and take up residence in urban locales. Under the auspices of the Bureau of Indian Affairs, the Direct Relocation Program (later called the Employment Assistance Program) assisted hundreds of families and thousands of individuals to move to cities such as Los Angeles and Seattle. The Commissioner of Indian Affairs reported that in fiscal 1954, for example, 2,163 Indians participated in the BIA relocation program.[8] Sorkin reports that between 1952 and 1972 about 100,000 Indians participated in this program.[9] In the years of its existence BIA relocation efforts varied in scope and in magnitude, but they continued unabated until the program was terminated by the Reagan administration. In any given year the number of individuals participating in the BIA relocation program represented a very small share of the total Indian population, but some observers believe that the cumulative effect of this program, spanning three decades, played a very large role in urbanizing the Indian population during the 1950s, 1960s, and 1970s.[10]

Thus, the spatial distributions of the contemporary Indian population have been shaped by historical events coinciding with long-term patterns in migration. Even more important is that the migratory behav-

[8]Cited in Russell Thornton, Gary D. Sandefur, and Harold G. Grasmick, *The Urbanization of American Indians* (Bloomington: Indiana University Press, 1982).

[9]Alan L. Sorkin, *American Indians and Federal Aid* (Washington, DC: Brookings Institution, 1971).

[10]Price (1968); Sorkin (1978); Donald L. Fixico, *Termination and Relocation: Federal Indian Policy, 1945–1960* (Albuquerque: University of New Mexico Press, 1986).

ior of the contemporary population will influence the geographic distribution of future generations of American Indians.

Concepts of Migration

Migration is ordinarily defined as a permanent relocation from one geographic area to another.[11] In the simplest terms migration occurs when individuals, families, or households decide to abandon their home in one place and establish a new home somewhere else. Because "home" is an ambiguous and difficult-to-define concept, the Census Bureau defines migration as a change in "the usual place of residence," letting individual respondents decide where they usually reside.

Defining migration in this way is somewhat problematic for the Indian population. Many American Indians belong to extensive kin networks with whom they may frequently share a residence for brief or extended periods. Until recently, urban relocation programs also made possible frequent changes of address. Participation in relocation programs was not restricted to lifelong reservation residents, nor did participation once in the program automatically exclude subsequent participation. Critics of the relocation programs frequently charged, perhaps correctly, that these efforts were nothing more than a revolving door to the reservation.[12]

The upshot of having extensive kin networks and/or receiving financial assistance for relocation is that some segments of the Indian population are sufficiently mobile that the question of "usual" place of residence cannot be answered easily or with a single address. Unfortunately, migration data from the 1980 census do not contain information about the frequency of migration, so it is not possible to identify individuals or subpopulations for whom "usual residence" might be problematic to define. To use these data requires the presumption, rightly or wrongly, that all persons are able to report a single location as their place of usual residence.[13]

Besides simply describing the relative numbers of persons entering or leaving a location, another more detailed way of describing Indian

[11]Henry S. Shryock and Jacob S. Siegel, *The Methods and Materials of Demography* (Washington, DC: U.S. Government Printing Office, 1971), provide a discussion of the methodology of migration research. Michael J. Greenwood, "Research on Internal Migration in the United States: A Survey," *Journal of Economic Literature* 13(1975):397–433, provides a discussion of research findings.

[12]Sorkin (1978).

[13]This is a problem not only for American Indians but also for gypsies, migrant farm workers, and other highly mobile populations.

mobility is in terms of migration status, which describes whether a person has changed residences and, if so, approximately how distant the new residence is from the old residence. The Census Bureau reports several categories of migration status, and each implies successively greater distances in migration. These categories are published as "same house" (that is, no migration), "different house, same county" (migration within the boundaries of a specified county), "different county, same state" (migration to or from another county in the same state), "different state" (migration to or from another state), and "abroad" (migration from outside the United States).

Although these categories imply an order of increasing distance, this is not necessarily true. For example, it is conceivable that a household residing adjacent to a state or county boundary could move a few yards and appear to have moved a greater distance than another household moving several miles in the same county.

A third way of describing migration behavior is in terms of "migration streams." This chapter presents data for migration streams between metropolitan and nonmetropolitan areas and between nonreservation areas and areas on or near reservations. Metropolitan and reservation emigration are flows to nonmetropolitan and nonreservation places. Metropolitan and reservation immigration are streams moving in the opposite direction. In the context of this discussion, "stayers" (reservation stayers, for example) are persons who either have not changed their residence *or* have not changed the type of area in which they reside. For instance, metropolitan to metropolitan migrants are classified as metropolitan stayers.

The most widely used source of migration data published by the Census Bureau is based on residential changes for the five years preceding the 1980 census. Persons classified as migrants by this criterion are individuals who in 1980 did not inhabit the same residence that they had occupied in 1975. For many purposes, this definition is preferable because all persons over age 5 have the same length of time to migrate, and the 1975 to 1980 period designates a fixed, specific time in history.

Spatial Characteristics of American Indian Migration

Migration Rates

This discussion of American Indian migration begins by showing the crude rates of inmigration and outmigration for different areas of the United States; bear in mind that the size of the Indian population varies considerably across these areas. Table 9.1 displays the national distri-

TABLE 9.1

Migration Rates for American Indians and Alaska Natives
Between Areas of 1975 and 1980 Residences (in percentages)

Census Division	Inmigration	Outmigration	Net Inmigration
New England	10.9	15.7	−4.8
Mid Atlantic	11.1	12.2	−1.1
East North Central	8.5	9.8	−1.3
West North Central	9.4	9.4	0.0
South Atlantic	12.4	9.0	3.4
East South Central	21.7	21.4	0.3
West South Central	7.7	6.0	1.6
Mountain	7.1	5.4	1.7
Pacific	18.4	7.9	10.5

SOURCE: Public-Use Microdata Sample, 5 percent A File.

bution of inmigration, outmigration, and net migration among American Indians and Alaska Natives. The figures show that the propensity to migrate varies considerably from one area to another. Areas with relatively small Indian populations tend to have fairly high rates of inmigration and outmigration—for example, New England and especially the East South Central states, which recirculated over one fifth of their Indian population between 1975 and 1980. In contrast, the Mountain and West South Central states have very large Indian populations but very small migration rates, ranging from 5.4 percent for Mountain outmigration to 7.7 percent for West South Central inmigration.

These variations in migration rates are partially due to the large differences in the population sizes of these areas. One person migrating into or out of a small population makes a larger contribution to the overall migration rate than another person migrating into or out of a large population. Nevertheless, it is clear that areas such as New England and the East South Central United States have relatively mobile populations compared with other areas.

Net inmigration shown in Table 9.1 offers a slightly different view of Indian mobility. Although mobility varies considerably in terms of inmigration and outmigration, high rates of migration do not necessarily reflect a massive redistribution of the population. Perhaps the most interesting finding is that patterns in American Indian net migration parallel well-known patterns in the total population. Like other segments of the U.S. population, American Indians have tended to move away from the "Rustbowl" states. The New England, Middle Atlantic, and East North Central states lost American Indians because of migration, while the American Indian population in the Sunbelt states of the South and the West grew from migration. The West North Central and the East South Central states gained about the same number of Indian in-migrants as they lost in outmigration, making their net migration rates near zero.

The Pacific states deserve special attention because they experienced massive inmigration on a scale unlike any other part of the United States. As of 1980 over 18 percent of the American Indian population in the Pacific states moved there between 1975 and 1980. This influx of migrants was not offset by outmigration, which stood at only about 8 percent. A closer look at the data for this area shows that, not surprisingly, 68 percent moved to California, 20 percent to Washington, 6 percent to Oregon, 4 percent to Alaska, and the remaining 2 percent to Hawaii. Given the large urban Indian population in California, it is plausible to assume that most of the migration to California was probably directed at cities such as Los Angeles, San Francisco, and Sacramento.

Flow Rates

A somewhat different and considerably more detailed view of American Indian migration is presented in Table 9.2, which shows the geographic origins and destinations of American Indian migrants. The entries in Table 9.2 are inflow and outflow coefficients based on the population leaving or entering an area. As a result, they have a slightly different meaning than migration rates shown in Table 9.1. In New England, for example, 34.0 percent of all persons moving into this area between 1975 and 1980 had previously resided in the Middle Atlantic area. New England also received a relatively large number of inmigrants from the Pacific (22.0 percent) and the South Atlantic (20.0 percent) states. Among persons who resided in New England during 1975 and moved before 1980, 24.7 percent moved into the South Atlantic states, 21.3 percent moved to the West South Central states, and 22.5 percent moved to the Pacific states, probably California.

In the broadest sense, the detailed patterns of migration in Table 9.2 mirror the crude rates of migration in Table 9.1. As a destination point, the Pacific states are consistently popular among migrants from all other regions. Within any given location, anywhere from 17 to 53 percent have resettled in the Pacific states area. The Mountain states have the largest proportion of Indian migrants moving west. This is especially significant because of this area's large number of Indians and reservations. Not surprisingly, the Sunbelt states of the West South

TABLE 9.2

*Percent Distribution of Migration Between 1975 and 1980 Residences
of American Indians and Alaska Natives*

1975 Residence	1980 Residence				
	New England	Mid Atlantic	E. North Central	W. North Central	South Atlantic
New England					
In	–	10.4	0.5	0.7	6.6
Out	–	11.2	1.1	2.3	24.7
Mid Atlantic					
In	34.0	–	13.2	3.2	17.0
Out	9.7	–	15.3	5.1	32.4
E. North Central					
In	8.0	10.4	–	11.2	18.5
Out	1.5	3.6	–	11.7	22.7
W. North Central					
In	2.0	7.3	17.6	–	7.2
Out	0.3	2.3	11.7	–	7.8
South Atlantic					
In	20.0	35.4	17.2	8.7	–
Out	3.6	12.2	12.5	9.0	–
E. South Central					
In	2.0	6.2	5.9	4.2	10.1
Out	0.8	4.7	9.3	9.4	26.6
W. South Central					
In	8.0	6.3	12.3	26.3	17.0
Out	1.2	1.8	7.3	21.9	16.7
Mountain					
In	4.0	4.2	10.8	23.9	8.1
Out	0.5	0.9	5.1	15.7	6.2
Pacific					
In	22.0	19.8	22.5	21.8	15.5
Out	1.9	3.3	8.1	10.8	9.1

SOURCE: Public-Use Microdata Sample, 5 percent A File.

Central and, to a lesser degree, the South Atlantic states also are consistently popular with migrants from other places. In general, the figures in Table 9.2 further demonstrate that the American Indians, like the rest of U.S. residents, are moving in westward and southward directions. As further evidence of this pattern, the South Atlantic is a popular destination for Indians in the East but not in the West. As a destination, the South Atlantic receives from 23 to 32 percent of outmigrants from the New England, Middle Atlantic, East North Central, and East South Central states. In comparison, the South Atlantic is a destination for

TABLE 9.2 *(continued)*

1975 Residence	1980 Residence			
	E. South Central	W. South Central	Mountain	Pacific
New England				
In	7.4	4.8	1.1	3.4
Out	10.2	21.3	6.7	22.5
Mid Atlantic				
In	2.5	3.5	2.7	6.0
Out	1.7	8.0	8.0	19.9
E. North Central				
In	33.1	10.4	7.4	7.7
Out	14.7	15.0	14.3	16.5
W. North Central				
In	8.3	16.4	16.7	13.3
Out	3.2	21.0	28.5	25.2
South Atlantic				
In	21.5	12.6	5.9	11.6
Out	9.3	17.9	11.1	24.4
E. South Central				
In	–	7.3	0.9	4.9
Out	–	22.6	3.9	22.7
W. South Central				
In	9.8	–	15.4	14.0
Out	3.5	–	23.7	23.9
Mountain				
In	2.5	19.7	–	39.1
Out	0.7	18.0	–	42.9
Pacific				
In	14.9	25.3	49.9	–
Out	3.2	17.5	46.1	–

less than 17 percent of outmigrants from the West South Central states and as little as 6 percent from the Mountain states.

These observations about the direction of migration do not mean that the Indian population is experiencing a large-scale redistribution. On the contrary, there appears to be a high degree of circulatory mobility within the Indian population. American Indians allegedly participate in circular migration patterns.[14] Whether this is true is impossible to ascertain from census data. However, it is clear that just as the Pacific states are an important destination point, they are an equally important

[14]Hackenberg and Wilson (1972).

point of origin. Migrants from the Pacific account for 15 to 50 percent of the incoming Indian population in every other part of the United States. It is significant that while 53 percent of outmigrating American Indians in the Mountain states are destined for the Pacific, about 50 percent of Mountain state inmigrants have arrived from the Pacific.

The high rate of exchange between the Mountain and Pacific states is undoubtedly influenced by the apparent attractiveness of the West Coast and by the proximity of these areas to areas with large Indian populations. The effects of proximity in promoting migration are evident in places other than the Mountain and Pacific states. For example, migration rates are relatively high between adjacent areas such as West North Central and West South Central states and along the eastern seaboard linking New England with the Middle Atlantic and South Atlantic states. A third example of relatively localized migration patterns is the exchanges between the West North Central, West South Central, and Mountain states, areas with relatively large Indian populations.

Migration Status

Tables 9.3 and 9.4 show the geographic distribution of American Indian and Alaska Native migrants in terms of migration status. The previous tables presented migration in terms of movement between relatively large geographic areas and as a result overlooked mobility within areas such as states or counties: moves which are more common though less dramatic. Table 9.3 shows the distribution of migration status for areas of the United States. Given the foregoing discussion, the information in Table 9.3 is fairly predictable: American Indians and Alaska Natives are a highly mobile population. With the exception of the Mountain states, less than 50 percent of American Indians in every area of the United States resided in the same house between 1975 and 1980. While there are minor variations in the distribution of migration status, most of the areas are not very different from one another.

There are, however, a few interesting differences. For example, Indians in the Mountain states, despite their predisposition to move west, appear to be one of the most sedentary Indian groups in the nation. Nearly 60 percent of this population resided in the same house in 1975 and 1980 (the highest in the United States). Compared with other areas, they were least likely to move within state, and they have one of the lowest proportions of out-of-state inmigrants; 11.6 percent. Indians in the East South Central states represent the other extreme. Not only is this a very small population compared with the Mountain states, but it is a very mobile population as well. Only about one third of the East

TABLE 9.3

Percent Distribution of Migration Between 1975 and 1980 Residences of American Indians and Alaska Natives, by Census Division

Census Division	Same House	Different House, Same County	Different County, Same State	Different State	Total
New England	48.1	27.5	9.9	14.5	100.0
Mid Atlantic	48.3	28.9	10.7	12.1	100.0
E. North Central	44.2	33.2	11.8	10.8	100.0
W. North Central	41.8	30.6	14.5	13.1	100.0
South Atlantic	44.6	28.6	10.0	16.8	100.0
E. South Central	37.0	28.1	9.2	25.7	100.0
W. South Central	45.7	28.4	14.4	11.5	100.0
Mountain	59.5	20.1	8.8	11.6	100.0
Pacific	40.7	34.4	13.2	11.7	100.0

SOURCE: Public-Use Microdata Sample, 5 percent A File.

South Central Indian population maintained the same residence between 1975 and 1980, while more than one quarter made short-distance, within-county moves, and one quarter moved into this area from out of state. Finally, it is not surprising that Indians in the Pacific states were highly mobile, but the data showing that the preponderance of migration is within county and not from out of state are somewhat unexpected, particularly in view of the popularity of this area among Indians in other parts of the country. Despite the high rates of inmigration for this area, in the context of a very large resident population, persons moving into this area from out of state constituted a relatively small part of the total number.

In regard to place of residence and migration status, American Indians in metropolitan and off-reservation areas are very similar, as are those in nonmetropolitan and reservation areas. Nevertheless, there are sizable differences associated with place of residence. As might be expected, American Indians who resided in metropolitan and off-reservation places were decidedly more mobile than Indians living in rural and/or reservation areas. One possible reason for this difference is that Indian communities in nonmetropolitan and/or reservation areas repre-

TABLE 9.4

Percent Distribution of American Indians and Alaska Natives,
by Place of Residence and Migration Between 1975 and 1980 Residences

Place of Residence	Same House	Different House, Same County	Different County, Same State	Different State	Total
Metropolitan	40.9	31.3	6.8	21.0	100.0
Nonmetropolitan	54.6	25.4	10.9	9.1	100.0
Off Reservation	41.4	31.0	12.7	14.9	100.0
On or Near Reservation	52.5	26.3	11.4	9.8	100.0

SOURCE: Public-Use Microdata Sample, 5 percent A File.

sent the long-term established homes of many American Indians, while urban areas are populated by a sizable number of Indians who are new residents of these places. As a result, metropolitan Indians are less likely than nonmetropolitan Indians to be established, long-term residents— only 41 percent of metropolitan Indians had resided in the same house between 1975 and 1980 compared with 55 percent of nonmetropolitan Indians.

Reservation Migration

Despite their similarities, metropolitan residents differ from off-reservation residents in at least one significant way. Persons living away from reservations are more likely than metropolitan residents to have migrated from one county to another in the same state. On the other hand, metropolitan residents are more likely than any other group to have made an interstate move between 1975 and 1980, implying that Indians living in urban areas probably have moved long distances prior to settling in a metropolitan environment. This would be particularly true for American Indians moving from reservations in the Mountain states into urban areas of the Pacific, such as Los Angeles, San Francisco, and Seattle. To complete this picture, Table 9.5 offers a detailed view of the distribution of migrants and nonmigrants on the 16 largest reservations, most of which are located in the Mountain states. This table shows that these reservations vary considerably with respect to the magnitude as well as the timing of inmigration.

With the exception of the Osage reservation, the proportion of Indians who have always lived on their home reservation ranges from a

TABLE 9.5

*Percent Distribution of Inmigration by Year
on the 16 Largest Reservations in 1980, American Indians Aged 1 and Over*

	Year Moved onto Reservation				
Reservation	Always Lived on Reservation	1979 or 1980	1975 to 1978	1974 or earlier	Total
Navajo[a] (AZ, NM, UT)	89.7	2.8	2.2	5.3	100.0
Pine Ridge (SD)	81.3	4.9	6.5	7.3	100.0
Gila River (AZ)	79.8	7.7	4.3	8.2	100.0
Papago (AZ)	80.2	4.9	5.2	9.7	100.0
Fort Apache (AZ)	90.2	4.1	2.4	3.3	100.0
Hopi[a] (AZ)	91.2	3.4	2.2	3.2	100.0
Zuni Pueblo (NM)	89.7	2.2	3.0	5.1	100.0
San Carlos (AZ)	84.4	6.0	3.9	5.7	100.0
Rosebud (SD)	76.1	7.4	7.4	9.1	100.0
Blackfeet (MT)	83.2	4.1	5.5	7.2	100.0
Yakima (WA)	69.4	6.2	8.8	15.6	100.0
Eastern Cherokee (NC)	79.7	3.1	5.4	11.8	100.0
Standing Rock (ND, SD)	71.3	10.2	6.9	11.6	100.0
Osage (OK)	44.4	14.8	16.5	24.3	100.0
Fort Peck (MT)	66.4	8.4	9.9	15.3	100.0
Wind River (WY)	77.3	7.6	7.4	7.7	100.0

SOURCE: "American Indians, Eskimos, and Aleuts on Identified Reservations and in the Historic Areas of Oklahoma," *1980 Census of Population, Subject Report.*

[a]Navajo and Hopi reservation data are not strictly comparable because of administrative changes in Navajo-Hopi joint use in the 1970s.

low of 66 percent for the Fort Peck reservation in Montana to a high of 90 percent for the Navajo and Fort Apache reservations and the Zuni pueblo. Inmigration on these reservations in some instances exceeds and in other cases falls below the levels of inmigration in Table 9.1 for much larger areas. Another notable characteristic is that for most of these places, the majority of inmigrants have moved into these areas between 1975 and 1980. For example, 15 percent of the residents of the Rosebud and Wind River reservations moved into these places between 1975 and 1980, compared with 9 and 8 percent, respectively, who moved into them before 1975. Not all of these reservations have disproportionate numbers of recent inmigrants. On the Eastern Cherokee reservation pre-1975 inmigrants outnumber inmigrants in subsequent years by a margin of 12 to 9 percent. Likewise, on the Navajo and Yakima reservations about equal percentages of the population moved onto these reservations before and after 1975, though the Navajo reservation had a lower percentage of inmigrants than the Yakima reservation.

An especially significant finding in Table 9.5 is the massive rate of inmigration for the Osage reservation. In 1970 the Osage reservation was so small that the Census Bureau reported almost no information for it because of the bureau's policies for protecting the confidentiality of census data. Yet between 1970 and 1980 the Osage reservation grew from less than 2,300 (the minimum size for which data for reservations were reported) to over 4,700 (see Chapter 3). The information necessary for decomposing this population growth into exact components due to fertility, mortality, and net migration is unavailable. Nevertheless, it should be amply clear that inmigration was a major factor in the growth of this reservation during the 1970s. The cause of this increase is difficult to determine with certainty, but one possible reason is that the reservation enjoyed an upsurge of development in its petroleum reserves during the rise of oil and gas prices in the mid- to late 1970s. The economic activity stimulated by this development very likely increased economic opportunities, which, in turn, attracted inmigrants to the reservation.

The Causes and Consequences of Migration

The census data available for American Indians ordinarily are for a single point in time. For the purposes of identifying the causes and consequences of migration, it is necessary to have data for two or more periods. The information presented next shows the relationship between migration status and other selected characteristics known to be linked with residential mobility. In most instances it is possible only to show how migration between 1975 and 1980 is related to some other characteristics such as marital status in 1980. In this example, it is important to realize that simply because migration and marital status are statistically related does not necessarily mean that one must be the direct cause of the other. The causal relationships in a number of the following tables are not perfectly clear; they are nonetheless suggestive about the circumstances likely to precipitate or result from migration in the American Indian population.

Racial Differences in Migration Status

Racial differences in migration status are shown for blacks, whites, and American Indians in Table 9.6. American Indians are more mobile in most respects than blacks and whites. Only 47 percent of the Indian population resided in the same house in 1975 and 1980 compared with

TABLE 9.6

Percent Distribution of Migration Between 1975 and 1980 Residences
of Blacks, Whites, and American Indians and Alaska Natives
Aged 5 and Over

	Blacks	Whites	American Indians and Alaska Natives
Same House	56.8	53.9	47.1
Different House, Same County	29.4	24.3	28.8
Different County, Same State	5.6	10.4	11.6
Different State	7.0	10.1	11.4
Outside U.S.	1.2	1.3	1.1
Total	100.0	100.0	100.0

SOURCE: *1980 Census of Population, General Social and Economic Characteristics, United States Summary.*

54 percent of whites and 57 percent of blacks. Blacks are more mobile than whites in terms of short-distance residential mobility but only slightly more mobile than Indians. In contrast, Indians are noticeably more likely than blacks and, to a lesser degree, whites to be movers across state or county boundaries. A somewhat surprising finding is that almost the same percentage of Indians were living outside the United States in 1975 as were blacks and whites.

Antecedents of Migration

Activity in 1975: Table 9.7 offers a slightly different perspective on the relationship between kinds of activities and migration status subsequent to 1975. From this perspective the activities listed should be viewed as factors that might "push" persons into changing their residence. Although the percentage of the American Indian population attending college or serving in the military is very small, the impact of these activities is unmistakable. As Table 9.7 shows, college and military service are not primary reasons for migration among the Indian population at large; few Indians are in college or in the military. Nevertheless, for American Indians who do participate in these activities, a

TABLE 9.7

Percent Distribution of Migration Between 1975 and 1980 Residences of American Indians and Alaska Natives Aged 21 and Over, by Activity in 1975

Activity in 1975	Same House	Different House, Same County	Different County, Same State	Different State	Total
In Armed Forces	14.4	17.9	15.6	52.1	100.0
Attending College	24.1	28.3	19.6	28.0	100.0
Working Part Time	35.2	33.2	15.4	16.2	100.0
Working Full Time	43.4	31.6	12.8	12.2	100.0
Other	53.9	25.9	10.2	10.0	100.0

SOURCE: Public-Use Microdata Sample, 5 percent A File.

change in residence is virtually assured. Not surprisingly, military service has a larger impact on migration than any other activity; only 14 percent of American Indians in the military in 1975 continued to live in the same house until 1980, while 52 percent were residing in another state by 1980.

Compared with the military, college has less of an impact on migration and is less likely to result in moves across state lines. As a group, persons attending college are relatively diverse in terms of their migration experiences; 24 percent of Indian college students in 1975 remained in the same house until 1980, while 28 percent moved within the same county and 28 percent moved across state boundaries. The balance of 20 percent remained within state boundaries while changing their county of residence. Compared with college or the military, employment is most clearly related to residential stability. Persons working part time in 1975 were less likely to move than students or military personnel. Persons working full time in 1975 were even less likely candidates for migration; 32 percent of American Indians employed full time in 1975 subsequently moved within their county of residence; fewer moved across county or state boundaries—13 and 12 percent, respectively. Persons in the "other" category are the least mobile, and from unreported tabulations this group includes a sizable number of retirees and other persons not in the labor force.

Labor Force Participation: To find that persons least likely to migrate are either employed or out of the labor force is significant for two

282

TABLE 9.8

Percent Distribution of Labor Force Status in 1975 and 1980,
and Migration Status of American Indians and Alaska Natives
Aged 21 and Over Between 1975 and 1980 Residences

	Same House	Different House, Same County	Different County, Same State	Different State	Total
In Labor Force 1975 and 1980	42.6	32.4	12.5	12.5	100.0
In Labor Force 1975, Out of Labor Force 1980	39.4	29.1	16.6	14.9	100.0
Out of Labor Force 1975, In Labor Force 1980	37.3	29.2	13.3	20.2	100.0
Out of Labor Force 1975 and 1980	58.5	23.8	9.5	8.2	100.0

SOURCE: Public-Use Microdata Sample, 5 percent A File.

reasons. One is that theory and research dealing with migration show that job opportunities are frequently a motive for changing residences—people often move in search of employment.[15] The other reason is that BIA relocation programs were explicitly designed to help Indians move for the purpose of joining the labor force.[16]

The data in Table 9.8 are consistent with this reasoning, and they are consistent with the findings in Table 9.7. Among the Indian population aged 21 and over living in the same residence in 1975 and 1980, nearly 43 percent were in the labor force in these years, while 59 percent were out of the labor force in 1975 and 1980. Entry into the labor force appears to be the most common reason for moving across state lines. About 20 percent of persons who were in the labor force in 1980 but not in 1975 moved across state lines in this period. Exiting the labor force also promotes interstate migration; 15 percent of persons who dropped out of the labor force also moved across state lines. Significantly, persons outside the labor force are least represented in the categories of migrant status. Slightly over 8 percent of migrants moving across state lines were out of the labor force in 1975 and 1980.

Age: Changes in labor force participation and migration behavior are closely tied to events taking place at various points in a person's lifetime. As people pass through various stages in their life, such as col-

[15]Greenwood (1975).
[16]Sorkin (1971); Fixico (1986).

TABLE 9.9

Percent Distribution of Age and Migration Status
Between 1975 and 1980 Residences for American Indians and Alaska Natives

Age	Same House	Different House, Same County	Different County, Same State	Different State	Total
5–20	48.4	28.1	11.5	12.0	100.0
21–30	26.4	37.5	16.8	19.3	100.0
31–40	41.9	30.2	12.9	15.0	100.0
41–50	58.3	23.7	10.1	7.9	100.0
51–60	65.9	20.9	7.1	6.1	100.0
61–70	73.6	17.0	5.6	3.8	100.0
Over 70	72.5	19.8	5.2	2.5	100.0

SOURCE: Public-Use Microdata Sample, 5 percent A File.

lege, military service, work, marriage, child-rearing, and retirement, they become more or less likely to migrate than others. Table 9.9 displays patterns of migration for American Indians of different ages. These distributions reveal significant similarities between Indians and non-Indians; migration, for example, tends to be among younger American Indians. The median age of American Indians residing in the same house in 1975 and 1980 was 28 years compared with 23 years for persons moving across state boundaries between 1975 and 1980.

Another way of looking at these distributions is to focus on changes in the age distribution, especially above ages 31 to 40. At ages 21 to 30 residence in the same house between 1975 and 1980 is least common and interstate migration is most common; almost 20 percent of this age group moved. However, over age 30 the likelihood of migration decreases steadily and reaches its lowest point among American Indians over age 70. Among this oldest group of Indians, only 3 percent moved across state boundaries, and 73 percent did not change residences.

Indian youths, like other youths, do not remain in the homes of their parents (or other guardians such as grandparents) as they reach the end of their teen years. Approximately 52 percent of persons under age 20 in 1980 changed residences between 1975 and 1980, 28 percent moving locally. However, 74 percent of those aged 21–30 changed residence between 1975 and 1980, 38 percent moving locally. These findings are most interesting in light of American Indian values about the importance of family and the importance of maintaining kin networks.[17] Evi-

[17]Jamake Highwater, *The Primal Mind: Vision and Reality in Indian America* (New York: Harper & Row, 1981).

TABLE 9.10

Percent Distribution of Marital Status in 1980,
and Migration Between 1975 and 1980 Residences
for American Indians and Alaska Natives Aged 21 and Over

Marital Status in 1980	Same House	Different House, Same County	Different County, Same State	Different State	Total
Married	48.6	27.4	11.7	12.3	100.0
Widowed	64.9	22.9	7.3	4.9	100.0
Divorced	33.2	37.1	14.7	15.0	100.0
Separated	34.0	34.4	16.0	15.6	100.0
Single	41.1	30.6	12.9	15.4	100.0

SOURCE: Public-Use Microdata Sample, 5 percent A File.

dently, younger Indians contemplating a change in residence are most likely to move locally, but next most likely to relocate out of state.

Marriage and Children: Family circumstances may be a critical consideration in deciding whether and where to move. The next tables show the family composition of different classes of American Indian migrants. The percentage distribution of married and unmarried persons across each type of migrant class is shown in Table 9.10. It is important to remember that family status and age are closely related, and Tables 9.9 and 9.10 provide insights into the complex events that trigger geographic mobility.[18]

Married and single persons were more likely to be residing in the same house between 1975 and 1980 than were divorced or separated persons, by a margin of about 15 percent for married persons and 7–8 percent for single persons. Among separated and divorced persons, about the same percentages remained in the same house or moved locally, and the interstate mobility of these individuals equaled the interstate mobility of single persons. Finally, widowed persons were least likely to be interstate migrants and most heavily represented among nonmigrants, about 5 and 65 percent, respectively. In large measure, this is probably due to the fact that younger persons are more likely than older persons to migrate and less likely to be widowed.

Along with marital status, the presence and age of children affect decisions to migrate. Moving with children before they reach school age

[18]Margaret Mooney Marini, "Age and Sequencing Norms in the Transition to Adulthood," *Social Forces* 63(1984):229–244; Margaret Mooney Marini, "The Order of Events in the Transition to Adulthood," *Sociology of Education* 57(1984):63–84; Gail Sheehy, *Passages: Predictable Crises of Adult Life* (New York: Bantam Books, 1974).

TABLE 9.11

Percent Distribution of Migration Status Between 1975 and 1980 Residences of American Indians and Alaska Natives Aged 21 and Over, by the Age and Presence of Children

Household Type	Same House	Different House, Same County	Different County, Same State	Different State	Total
Families with Children Under Age 6	32.3	32.8	16.3	18.6	100.0
Families with Children Aged 6–17	54.1	25.2	10.0	10.7	100.0
Families with Children Under Age 6 and Aged 6–17	41.8	31.5	13.6	13.1	100.0
Families WIthout Children	58.3	24.1	8.6	9.0	100.0
Nonfamily Households	32.3	32.8	16.3	18.6	100.0

SOURCE: Public-Use Microdata Sample, 5 percent A File.

is less disruptive than moving after they have entered school and established relationships with friends and teachers. Families with young children may also be more likely to migrate simply by virtue of the parents' youth and their need to seek employment, go to school, serve in the military, and establish a home outside their parents' residence. Table 9.11 shows how the composition of migrant groups reflects these contingencies. Among persons who remained in the same residence, families with young children were the least common (excepting nonfamily households). In contrast, families with children under age 6 were as likely to be interstate migrants as families without children. Families with older children and families without children were most likely to have remained in the same residence between 1975 and 1980. Families without children were most sedentary probably because they are composed of married couples with an "empty nest"—that is, their children have moved out of the household.

Socioeconomic Profiles of Migrants

Besides family circumstances, economic conditions are frequently cited as reasons for migration. Relocation to take advantage of job or educational opportunities is an obvious reason for migration. Migration that leads to a higher education or better job may mean higher earnings and a better standard of living—obvious consequences of geographic mobility. In the next tables the social and economic profiles of migrants and nonmigrants are presented.

Education: For American Indians, especially those residing in remote reservation and/or nonmetropolitan areas, migration is a virtual necessity for acquiring a higher education. Similarly, a dearth of job opportunities in these areas may be a reason for better-educated American Indians to move to areas where opportunities are more abundant. The educational profiles of American Indian movers and stayers are shown in Table 9.12. Persons with the equivalent of a high school education are about equally distributed in all four groups. At most, persons who move across state lines are only a little more likely to have 12 years of schooling than persons who do not change residence; again, this reflects the fact that interstate migrants are younger than nonmigrants. Apart from this similarity, there are substantial differences among these groups with respect to educational attainment.

The most visible difference among these groups stems from the fact that migrants are better educated than nonmigrants, and interstate migrants are better educated than persons migrating within the same county. For example, nearly 51 percent of nonmigrants had less than 12 years of schooling and only about 6 percent had completed four or more years of college. These findings suggest that geographic mobility provides opportunities for higher education, but it is equally plausible that well-educated American Indians must relocate to areas where opportu-

TABLE 9.12

*Percent Distribution of Education and Migration Status
of American Indians and Alaska Natives Aged 25 and Over
Between 1975 and 1980 Residences*

Years of Education	Same House	Different House, Same County	Different County, Same State	Different State
0–8	31.5	17.7	12.4	11.6
9–11	19.1	20.0	20.7	13.4
12	28.6	32.9	31.0	32.7
13–15	14.5	21.2	22.8	26.3
16 and Over	6.3	8.2	13.1	16.0
Total	100.0	100.0	100.0	100.0

SOURCE: Public-Use Microdata Sample, 5 percent A File.

nities to exploit their training are more abundant. One possible scenario is that Indian high school and college graduates from the Mountain states, upper Midwest, and Northeast are joining migration streams to the South and the West, especially to urban areas in California.

Occupation: From the standpoint of occupations, the differences among the groups in Table 9.13 are very small for any given occupational category, in most instances not more than 1 or 2 percentage points. The largest benefits accruing to migration can be observed by comparing the two most different groups, interstate migrants and nonmigrants, in relation to blue and white collar occupations. This comparison indicates that interstate migrants are slightly ahead of migrants who did not change residence between 1975 and 1980. About 41 percent of the former group were employed in white collar jobs compared with 36 percent of the latter.

Finding that American Indian migrants and nonmigrants vary so little with respect to occupation is somewhat surprising, but it reveals a possible motivation behind geographic mobility, that taking a job or seeking employment is a motive for migration. Recall from Table 9.8 that the percentage of interstate migrants entering the labor force between 1975 and 1980 was twice as large as that of nonmigrants. How-

TABLE 9.13

*Percent Distribution of American Indians and Alaska Natives
Aged 21 and Over in Occupational Categories,
by Migration Status Between 1975 and 1980 Residences*

Occupation	Same House	Different House, Same County	Different County, Same State	Different State
Managerial and Professional	15.4	13.8	15.9	17.4
Technical, Sales, and Administrative Support	20.4	23.2	24.2	23.7
Service	19.1	18.8	18.8	18.2
Farming, Forestry, and Fishing	5.7	3.6	3.6	3.7
Precision Production, Craft, and Repair	14.5	14.6	14.5	14.4
Operators, Fabricators, and Laborers	24.9	26.0	23.0	22.6
Total	100.0	100.0	100.0	100.0

SOURCE: Public-Use Microdata Sample, 5 percent A File.

TABLE 9.14

Percent Distribution of Wage and Salary Income
for American Indians and Alaska Natives Aged 21 and Over,
and Percentage Changing Residences Between 1975 and 1980

Wages and Salaries	Same House	Different House, Same County	Different County	Different State
Under $2,500	16.4	15.9	18.7	16.7
2,500–4,999	13.4	14.0	13.7	15.7
5,000–7,499	15.2	15.3	16.1	18.5
7,500–9,999	12.7	12.6	12.7	12.3
10,000–12,499	11.5	12.0	11.0	11.4
12,500–14,999	6.7	7.3	6.1	6.6
15,000–17,499	6.6	7.2	6.3	5.4
17,500–19,999	4.8	4.6	3.9	3.7
Over 20,000	12.7	11.1	11.5	9.7
Total	100.0	100.0	100.0	100.0

SOURCE: Public-Use Microdata Sample, 5 percent A File.

ever, the jobs being taken or sought by persons migrating long distances apparently are not markedly better than the jobs held by nonmigrants or persons changing residence locally. While American Indians may move to gain employment, there is little evidence that they move to take better jobs.

Wages and Salaries: The small differences in the occupational characteristics of American Indian migrants and nonmigrants foreshadow equally small differences in their wages and salaries (see Table 9.14). Not only are these differences small, but there is evidence that geographic mobility may be a modest liability. American Indian workers who did not change residence between 1975 and 1980 had a median wage and salary income of $8,503 in 1979 compared with $7,378 for interstate migrants. Another way of viewing this difference is that nearly 31 percent of nonmigrant Indian workers received wages and salaries exceeding $12,500 in 1979 compared with 25 percent of interstate migrants.

Despite the apparent lack of occupational benefits and the possible costs of migration, it is important to underscore several points before reaching conclusions about these results. Migrants, particularly interstate migrants, on the average tend to be younger. Thus, while these younger people may migrate after finishing school for the purpose of taking employment, they seldom have the work experience to realize significant economic benefits from their mobility. Alternatively, sedentary American Indians are usually older and have more work experience; and although they are typically less educated, their age, experience, and geographic stability seem to offset this disadvantage.

Another key point is that this discussion deals with migration during a five-year period. While there may be few immediate benefits, in the long run migration may indeed yield significant benefits. Over the course of a lifetime, migration may provide access to opportunities that would not be otherwise available. From this perspective, it might be impossible to observe the positive economic consequences accruing to migration within the relatively short span of five years.

Characteristics of Migration Streams

The balance of this chapter is devoted to the characteristics of different groups classified according to whether they were movers or stayers between 1975 and 1980, particularly in terms of place of origin and place of destination for movers and place of residence for stayers. This information is important because migration streams reveal characteristics of persons participating in the redistribution of the Indian population across reservations, cities, and other areas.

Migration Incentives

Activity in 1975: Table 9.15 summarizes the 1975 activities preceding the geographic mobility (or immobility) reported by American Indians in 1980. One finding underscores an earlier discussion about how military service promotes migration while employment discourages mobility. However, the data in Table 9.15 show that persons in military service in 1975 were substantially more likely than civilians to have become metropolitan immigrants between 1975 and 1980. About 20 percent of all persons serving in the military in 1975 moved from a nonmetropolitan to a metropolitan place compared with about 5 percent of all American Indian civilians working full time in 1975. From this standpoint, military service appears to have a powerful role in the urbanization of American Indians. In contrast, full- or part-time employment has a decidedly stabilizing influence on persons in metropolitan and nonmetropolitan areas and seems to have little bearing on whether American Indians move to or from metropolitan places.

290

TABLE 9.15

Percent Distribution of Activity in 1975
and Migration Streams of American Indians and Alaska Natives Aged 21 and Over
Changing Places of Residence Between 1975 and 1980

Migration Stream	In Armed Forces	Attending College	Working Part Time	Working Full Time	Other
Metropolitan Stayers	49.2	56.8	56.8	59.3	48.1
Metropolitan Immigrants	20.4	11.2	5.6	4.9	4.5
Metropolitan Emigrants	8.8	8.1	5.2	3.9	3.0
Nonmetropolitan Stayers	21.6	23.9	32.4	31.9	44.4
Total	100.0	100.0	100.0	100.0	100.0
Off Reservation Stayers	57.7	51.5	55.9	58.5	48.0
Reservation Emigrants	8.5	6.5	4.9	2.9	2.8
Reservation Immigrants	22.9	24.0	20.7	23.0	32.9
Reservation Stayers	10.9	18.0	18.5	15.6	16.3
Total	100.0	100.0	100.0	100.0	100.0

SOURCE: Public-Use Microdata Sample, 5 percent A File.

Comparing the percentage distributions for metropolitan- and reservation-related migration streams shows that the streams between these areas are very different. Among Indians working full time in 1975, about the same proportion who stayed in metropolitan areas between 1975 and 1980 also stayed in nonreservation areas: 59.3 and 58.5 percent, respectively. Similarly, the percentage of persons immigrating to metropolitan places is only slightly higher than that of persons emigrating from reservations: 4.9 percent and 2.9 percent, respectively. The percentage of persons moving to reservations is relatively large compared with persons leaving metropolitan areas, and the percentage of persons staying on reservations is consistently smaller than the percentage of persons staying in nonmetropolitan areas.

There are several possible reasons for these differences. One is that reservation- and metropolitan-related migration streams are not mutually exclusive. Migration to a metropolitan residence does not per-

TABLE 9.16

Percent Distribution of Labor Force Status in 1975 and 1980,
and Migration Streams of American Indians and Alaska Natives Aged 21 and Over

Migration Stream	In Labor Force 1975 and 1980	In Labor Force 1975, Out of Labor Force 1980	Out of Labor Force 1975, In Labor Force 1980	Out of Labor Force 1975 and 1980
Metropolitan Stayers	60.1	53.5	48.4	48.7
Metropolitan Immigrants	4.9	5.4	8.9	3.5
Metropolitan Emigrants	3.4	7.1	5.2	2.5
Nonmetropolitan Stayers	31.6	34.0	37.5	45.3
Total	100.0	100.0	100.0	100.0
Off Reservation Stayers	59.4	51.7	48.4	48.6
Reservation Emigrants	3.0	4.6	4.6	2.4
Reservation Immigrants	15.5	18.4	19.8	14.7
Reservation Stayers	22.1	25.3	27.2	34.3
Total	100.0	100.0	100.0	100.0

SOURCE: Public-Use Microdata Sample, 5 percent A File.

force imply giving up a residence on or near a reservation. Another possible explanation is more speculative but considerably more intriguing. This is the possibility that the migration data in the two bottom rows of Table 9.15 are indicative of the high rates of migration between reservations and other places, particularly urban areas, that are frequently reported in case studies.[19] Partial support for this idea appears in the exceedingly heavy migration flows between the large reservation populations in the Mountain states and the equally large urban populations in the Pacific states, especially California (see Table 9.2).

Labor Force Participation: Migration streams can also be viewed in terms of their relationship to changes in labor force participation. Labor force participation is a powerful influence on decisions to migrate, but as the data in Table 9.16 show, it also might be regarded as a major

[19]Hackenberg and Wilson (1972); Price (1968).

consideration in decisions not to migrate, especially in metropolitan areas where 60 percent of persons active in the labor force in 1975 and 1980 were also metropolitan residents in these years. Not surprisingly, this is about the same percentage of persons in the labor force in 1975 and 1980 who did not live on or near a reservation.

Age: These migration streams do not have similar age distributions. The median age of all American Indians over age 5 is about 25 years.[20] Predictably, the median ages for different types of migrants and nonmigrants are below and above the figure for the total Indian population. Nonmigrants living in metropolitan and/or nonreservation areas have the highest median age of about 27 years. The Indian population residing in nonmetropolitan places, moving to and from nonmetropolitan areas, and moving into areas on or near a reservation are somewhat younger, with a median age of 24 years. The populations of long-term (1975–1980) reservation residents and persons moving away from reservation lands have a median age of 23 years. The youthful age of persons remaining on or near reservation lands is due to the relatively large numbers of children in these areas. The age distributions of American Indians in and out of migration streams are not very different from other segments of the U.S. population, except that the Indian population is somewhat younger than other racial groups.

Marital Status: The data in Table 9.17 display systematic differences connected with the direction of migration and place of residence. Predictably, among married persons the majority are metropolitan stayers, followed by nonmetropolitan stayers. Married persons also are about as likely to be moving toward metropolitan areas as they are toward nonmetropolitan areas. Widowed American Indians are least mobile and most concentrated in nonmetropolitan areas. However, other single persons are much more likely to be mobile, especially divorced or separated persons. Marital disruptions have a distinctly urban quality because the majority of divorced or separated persons reside in metropolitan areas or moved in that direction between 1975 and 1980. Except for widowed American Indians, single persons were much more likely than married persons to remain in or relocate to metropolitan areas.

The figures for persons migrating to and from reservation areas are not very different from those for metropolitan and nonmetropolitan places, but several interesting comparisons can be made. For example, widowed persons are more likely than any other group to be returning to the reservation, suggesting that the death of a spouse is a strong in-

---

[20]U.S. Bureau of the Census, *1980 Census of Population, General Social and Economic Characteristics, United States Summary* (Washington, DC: U.S. Government Printing Office, 1983).

TABLE 9.17

*Percent Distribution of Marital Status in 1980,
and Migration Streams of American Indians and Alaska Natives Aged 21 and Over*

Migration Stream	Married	Widowed	Divorced	Separated	Single
Metropolitan Stayers	53.1	52.1	61.0	59.0	52.6
Metropolitan Immigrants	4.7	2.1	6.7	6.9	7.0
Metropolitan Emigrants	3.9	1.8	4.3	4.2	3.8
Nonmetropolitan Stayers	38.3	44.0	28.0	29.9	36.6
Total	100.0	100.0	100.0	100.0	100.0
Off Reservation Stayers	54.1	53.3	57.0	58.7	48.4
Reservation Emigrants	2.9	1.9	4.0	5.0	4.1
Reservation Immigrants	27.4	33.4	20.4	21.0	28.1
Reservation Stayers	15.6	11.4	18.6	15.3	19.4
Total	100.0	100.0	100.0	100.0	100.0

SOURCE: Public-Use Microdata Sample, 5 percent A File.

centive to return to the reservation, especially for older American Indians. Perhaps owing to the lack of jobs, single persons are relatively unlikely to remain in or migrate to areas on or near reservations. Married persons, in contrast, are more likely to move to a place on or near a reservation but, like single persons, they are unlikely to have been long-time residents. In fact, never-married single persons are more likely than any other group to have been on or near a reservation in 1975 and 1980. However, such persons tend to be young and have had neither the time nor the opportunity to migrate.

Children: The figures in Table 9.18 complement these observations by showing the presence and age of children in the families of migrants and nonmigrants. Needless to say, families without children or with young children are more mobile than families with school-age children. Persons in nonfamily households or families with young children are slightly more likely to be metropolitan immigrants—between 8 and 9 percent, respectively. On the other hand, families with older children are about as likely to be moving out of cities as they are to be moving into them; about 4 percent of persons in families with children aged 6 to 17 moved out of metropolitan areas between 1975 and 1980 while about 3 percent moved into them. One interpretation of these data is that young families caring for children below school age are more inclined than families with older children to move to metropolitan locations, perhaps in search of employment. As their children grow older, these families become more sedentary, possibly because they are more reluctant to move their children from one school to another or because the perceived benefits of migration, especially in economic terms, are not sufficient to outweigh the costs of moving an entire family.

The data for reservation-related migration streams highlight the role of children in migration decisions and the direction of migration.

TABLE 9.18

Percent Distribution of Age and Presence of Children in Household, and Migration Streams of American Indians and Alaska Natives Changing Places of Residence Between 1975 and 1980

Migration Stream	Families with Children Under Age 6	Families with Children Aged 6–17	Families with Children Under Age 6 and Aged 6–17	Families Without Children	Nonfamily Households
Metropolitan Stayers	48.6	53.0	43.3	57.0	61.5
Metropolitan Immigrants	9.3	3.2	5.6	3.6	8.4
Metropolitan Emigrants	5.0	3.8	5.0	2.5	4.6
Nonmetropolitan Stayers	37.1	40.0	46.1	36.9	25.5
Total	100.0	100.0	100.0	100.0	100.0
Off Reservation Stayers	49.5	53.0	43.5	56.1	60.1
Reservation Emigrants	4.6	2.7	3.1	2.0	5.4
Reservation Immigrants	18.1	30.4	31.3	29.4	18.8
Reservation Stayers	27.8	13.9	22.1	12.5	15.7
Total	100.0	100.0	100.0	100.0	100.0

SOURCE: Public-Use Microdata sample, 5 percent A File.

Persons in nonfamily households or in families with young children are slightly more inclined to move away from reservation areas than are persons in other types of households. Persons in nonfamily households also were most likely to have been away from reservation areas between 1975 and 1980, while persons in families with older children were least likely to have been away from reservation areas in this period. Perhaps most interesting is that persons in families with older children were least likely to have been long-term reservation residents, but they were most likely to be among those persons moving to areas on or near reservation lands.

In sum, the data in Table 9.18 reveal a unique pattern of migration for American Indians: Metropolitan areas are attractive to families with young children and, as a corollary, persons in such families are fewer in number among migrants moving into the proximity of reservation lands. Among families with older, school-age children, the opposite is true. Older children are associated with migration into reservation areas but not away from metropolitan places. Needless to say, such children also are an important factor in decisions not to migrate. Nevertheless, among migrants there is a pattern that suggests that metropolitan areas are not highly attractive to families with school-age children, while reservation locales represent an appealing alternative.

For many American Indians, metropolitan areas are alien environments distant from family, friends, and traditional lifestyles. The potential economic benefits of urban residence may offset these unattractive qualities in the short term, particularly among younger persons with new families. In the long term, however, as children begin to reach school age, the liabilities of city life multiply and make residence in less urban areas, particularly in proximity to reservation lifestyles, a motive for migration. Whether this is true cannot be ascertained from census data, but case studies of urban Indian migrants suggest that this is a plausible scenario.[21]

Socioeconomic Profiles of Migration Streams

Education: American Indians residing in metropolitan areas in 1975 and 1980 were better educated than nonmigrants outside metropolitan areas (see Table 9.19): 33 and 17 percent, respectively, having completed more than 12 years of schooling. Perhaps attesting to their younger age, American Indians moving into metropolitan areas were better educated

[21]Ablon (1964); Jack O. Waddell and O. Michael Watson, eds., *The American Indian in Urban Society* (Boston: Little, Brown, 1971).

TABLE 9.19

*Percent Distribution of Education and Migration Streams
of American Indians and Alaska Natives
Changing Places of Residence Between 1975 and 1980*

Migration Stream	Years of Education					
	0–8	9–11	12	13–15	16 and Over	Total
Metropolitan Stayers	17.5	18.2	31.6	22.0	10.7	100.0
Metropolitan Immigrants	13.2	14.1	32.5	25.2	15.0	100.0
Metropolitan Emigrants	12.0	20.2	34.3	21.8	11.7	100.0
Nonmetropolitan Stayers	34.5	20.1	28.2	12.4	4.8	100.0
Off Reservation Stayers	20.1	19.5	30.9	19.3	10.2	100.0
Reservation Emigrants	11.3	15.8	31.0	25.7	16.2	100.0
Reservation Immigrants	16.9	19.5	33.4	22.7	7.5	100.0
Reservation Stayers	33.7	17.7	28.3	14.5	5.8	100.0

SOURCE: Public-Use Microdata Sample, 5 percent A File.

than either group of nonmigrants. Just over 40 percent of metropolitan immigrants completed more than 12 years of schooling. In contrast, metropolitan emigrants are educated no better than the nonmigrants they leave behind.

There are two possible reasons why metropolitan immigrants are especially well educated, besides their youth. One reason is that metropolitan immigration includes a sizable number of persons moving to metropolitan areas in pursuit of education beyond high school. Another reason is that there are more opportunities for better-educated workers in metropolitan areas, which is a likely stimulant of migration among better-educated Indians in nonmetropolitan areas.

In many respects, the data for reservations represent a potentially serious problem in the form of a reservation "brain drain." A frequently cited problem in generating economic activity on reservations is the absence of highly trained, well-educated workers. However, these data also reveal the presence of a "Catch-22," in which reservations are depleted of their best-educated population in favor of metropolitan places where jobs are more abundant. This means that economic development on reservations is handicapped by the outmigration of better-educated workers, who are forced to migrate owing to the lack of economic opportunities.

Occupation: The possibility that better-educated American Indians leave or never move into reservation areas because of the lack of job opportunities raises the question of what kinds of jobs are held by these migrants. Given their higher education, are reservation emigrants or metropolitan immigrants obtaining jobs that might be difficult to find in nonmetropolitan or reservation locations, especially white collar jobs? Table 9.20 displays the occupational distributions for each type of migrant and nonmigrant.

Metropolitan labor markets are frequently presumed to have more abundant opportunities than nonmetropolitan markets, and the data in Table 9.20 do not dispute this idea. American Indians residing in metropolitan areas, migrants and nonmigrants alike, are distinctly more likely than Indians in nonmetropolitan areas to be working in a white collar occupation. In fact, the percentage of metropolitan stayers in white collar jobs is slightly higher than the percentage of metropolitan immigrants in similar employment—42 and 40 percent, respectively. On the other hand, Indians leaving metropolitan areas are measurably less likely to have nonmanual occupations than Indians in metropolitan areas but more likely than Indians who did not reside in metropolitan areas in 1975 or 1980.

Given the overlap between reservation and nonmetropolitan areas, the finding that the lowest percentage of white collar workers reside on or near reservation lands is not surprising. However, it is remarkable that the largest percentage of white collar workers is found among American Indians who moved away from a reservation area; nearly 44 percent of such persons were in nonmanual employment in 1980, although most of these persons were in lower-skill white collar jobs and not in professional or managerial positions. This finding highlights the apparent positive outcomes stemming from reservation emigration.

However, the apparent benefits reaped by reservation emigrants may be misleading. One reason is that migration is highly selective of certain types of individuals. While some Indians may enjoy more opportunities simply by moving away from reservation lands, it is equally if not more likely that well-qualified individuals have no choice except to leave the areas on or near reservation lands to take advantage of better economic opportunities elsewhere. One study, for example, found that well-qualified American Indians benefited from being in urban areas, but migration alone was insufficient to produce noticeable economic gains for individuals lacking basic qualifications such as education and

TABLE 9.20

Percent Distribution of Occupations and Migration Streams of American Indians and Alaska Natives Aged 21 and Over Changing Places of Residence Between 1975 and 1980

Migration Stream	Managerial and Professional	Technical, Sales, and Administrative Support	Service	Farming and Forestry, Fishing	Precision Production, Craft, and Repair	Operators, Fabricators, and Laborers	Total
Metropolitan Stayers	16.4	25.8	17.1	2.8	14.6	23.3	100.0
Metropolitan Immigrants	16.4	23.9	16.6	3.4	13.2	26.5	100.0
Metropolitan Emigrants	13.5	20.7	23.2	4.6	15.2	22.8	100.0
Nonmetropolitan Stayers	13.5	17.4	21.1	7.2	14.3	26.5	100.0
Off Reservation Stayers	15.0	23.2	17.1	3.3	15.2	26.2	100.0
Reservation Emigrants	16.7	27.0	16.5	3.0	14.2	22.6	100.0
Reservation Immigrants	14.8	22.7	21.6	5.5	13.5	21.9	100.0
Reservation Stayers	15.8	19.0	21.0	6.7	13.9	23.6	100.0

SOURCE: Public-Use Microdata Sample, 5 percent A File.

experience.[22] In other words, finding that American Indians who leave reservation areas realize significant benefits most likely reflects the "pull" of more abundant opportunities outside the reservation combined with the "push" that well-qualified Indians may feel to take advantage of opportunities away from reservation lands.

Wages and Salaries: The ultimate test of the economic benefits accruing to migrants and nonmigrants is manifest in wage and salary differentials. Presumably, an important reason for moving to metropolitan areas and away from reservation and/or nonmetropolitan places is the belief that migration will improve not only access to jobs but also access to better-paying jobs. The empirical evidence bearing on this idea appears in Table 9.21, which shows the wage and salary incomes for different types of American Indian and Alaska Native migrants and nonmigrants. The large percentage of American Indians who leave areas on or near reservations and have white collar jobs was especially striking because of its implications about the possible economic outcomes of reservation outmigration.

However, the data in Table 9.21 show that these same individuals are not realizing significant income gains, despite their employment situation. Only about 9 percent of reservation emigrants have wage and salary incomes above $20,000, which is virtually no different from reservation stayers, 10 percent of whom had wages and salaries above $20,000. Almost equal percentages of reservation stayers and leavers had incomes below $2,500. In fact, reservation emigrants had a median wage and salary income of $7,250, which is slightly lower than that of reservation stayers ($7,537) and markedly lower than that of Indians who did not reside on or near reservation lands in 1975 or 1980.

The modest wage and salary incomes of reservation emigrants are unexpected because a relatively large percentage of these Indians have white collar occupations, which are usually associated with higher pay than blue collar occupations. However, a number of mitigating factors might account for this anomaly. One factor is that reservation emigrants are relatively young and inexperienced. Youthful reservation outmigrants lacking work experience are virtually certain to receive lower wages and salaries than more experienced workers. Another factor is that reservation emigrants do not have the highest paying white collar jobs. Clearly, these migrants are not disproportionately represented in managerial and professional occupations. A third factor is that reservation emigrants have spottier labor force participation histories because of the recency of their migration. These considerations help explain why there is no necessary linkage between occupation and income.

[22]C. Matthew Snipp and Gary D. Sandefur, "Earnings of American Indians and Alaska Natives: The Effects of Residence and Migration," *Social Forces* 66(1988):994–1008.

TABLE 9.21

Percent Distribution of Wage and Salary Incomes and Migration Streams of American Indians and Alaska Natives Aged 21 and Over Changing Places of Residence Between 1975 and 1980

Migration Stream	Under $2,500	$2,500 to 4,999	$5,000 to 7,499	$7,500 to 9,999	$10,000 to 12,499	$12,500 to 14,999	$15,000 to 17,499	$17,500 to 19,999	Over $20,000	Total
				Percentage with Wages and Salaries						
Metropolitan Stayers	14.0	12.5	13.6	12.0	12.3	7.6	7.7	5.4	14.9	100.0
Metropolitan Immigrants	16.4	15.1	19.4	13.9	12.2	5.7	5.9	4.3	7.0	100.0
Metropolitan Emigrants	20.0	16.5	15.4	16.2	11.0	4.6	4.8	2.5	9.1	100.0
Nonmetropolitan Stayers	19.8	15.2	18.3	13.2	10.7	6.1	5.4	3.2	8.1	100.0
Off Reservation Stayers	14.5	13.3	15.3	12.7	11.9	7.3	6.9	5.0	13.3	100.0
Reservation Emigrants	19.2	16.4	16.0	12.3	12.7	7.5	5.1	2.4	8.5	100.0
Reservation Immigrants	19.7	15.1	16.5	11.8	11.0	6.0	6.6	4.1	9.3	100.0
Reservation Stayers	18.9	14.3	16.6	13.0	11.2	6.2	6.2	3.8	9.9	100.0

SOURCE: Public-Use Microdata Sample, 5 percent A File.

The figures in Table 9.21 also underscore the point that there is no necessary linkage between migration and income, particularly for metropolitan-related mobility. American Indians residing in metropolitan places in 1975 and 1980 enjoyed considerably higher wages than other groups. Metropolitan stayers had the smallest proportion of workers with wages and salaries under $2,500 (14 percent), the largest proportion of workers with incomes over $20,000 (15 percent), and the highest median wage and salary incomes ($9,562). Metropolitan inmigrants appear to have benefited somewhat from their place of residence, but their median income of $7,384 is well below that of longer-term metropolitan Indians. Former metropolitan residents and long-term nonmetropolitan residents have even lower wages, but they do not trail far behind the migrants to metropolitan areas. The median wage and salary incomes for metropolitan emigrants and nonmetropolitan stayers in 1979 were $7,191 and $7,048, respectively.

Concluding Remarks

This chapter has dealt with the geographic mobility of American Indians, beginning with an overview of its earliest occurrences. Anthropologists believe that American Indians became the first inhabitants of this land by migrating from Siberia across the Bering land bridge about 25,000 years ago. Little is known about the migration behavior of these early Indians. Perhaps in search of more favorable climates and more abundant environments for hunting and gathering, these people moved slowly eastward and southward. After 10,000 to 15,000 years the ancestors of the Bering immigrants had succeeded in settling the entire Western Hemisphere, from the Arctic Circle to Tierra del Fuego.

Considerably more is known about American Indian migration since Columbus's arrival, particularly in response to European contact. Contact with Europeans brought about two historically significant periods of massive migration, one early and unplanned and the other resulting from the implementation of public policy. The first of these periods resulted from the transmission of epidemic diseases brought to the New World by Spanish, English, and French explorers. These diseases decimated the American Indian population, leaving the survivors to redistribute themselves into smaller, more sparsely populated settlements. The second period stemmed from massive increases in the non-Indian population along the East Coast, creating intense pressures for land occupied by East Coast tribes. Eventually, the political response to these pressures was legislation mandating the removal of these Indians to territories west of the Mississippi River. A period of continuing hostilities between Indians and non-Indians finally led to the development of the federal reservation system, in which nearly the entire American Indian population was resettled on reservation land or in the Indian territory of Oklahoma.

In more recent times public policy also has played a role in American Indian migration, though in a more benign manner. After World War II the American Indian population rapidly increased in urban areas. This process was undoubtedly hastened by relocation programs sponsored by the BIA that encouraged American Indians to migrate from remote reservations with few economic opportunities to the economic mainstream of urban America. Although the success of these programs in upgrading the economic opportunities of American Indians or in hastening their assimilation is debatable, they are credited with helping thousands of American Indians relocate to urban environments—some permanently and others temporarily.[23]

The geography of American Indian migration can be described in terms of broad shifts and local flows. The broad shifts follow patterns characteristic of the U.S. population at large. The available data indicate that the Indian population, like the rest of American society, is slowly gravitating to locations in the West and the South. However, it should be noted that the so-called Sunbelt migration streams out of the industrial Northeast involve relatively small numbers of Indians. Local flows are migration streams which make possible the broad westward and southward movements. Perhaps the most important of these flows is the conduit between the Mountain and Pacific states. This flow is especially important because it links a large urban Indian population on the West Coast with an equally large Indian population situated mainly on reservation land. There are traces of other flows apparent in the data. For example, there is one along the East Coast linking Indians in New England and the Middle Atlantic and South Atlantic states; another stream is based on flows between the West North and West South Central states.

The data for American Indian migration also reveal some possible causes and consequences of migration as reflected in the characteristics of American Indian movers and stayers. Overall, American Indian migrants tend to be younger than nonmigrants and single. Their motives for migration include seeking employment, attending college, or serving in the armed forces. They also tend to be better educated. A particularly interesting finding is that young children not yet in school do not impede migration. In comparison, older children apparently limit migration, and migration decisions distinctly favor movement out of metropolitan areas and toward locations on or near reservation lands.

[23]Fixico (1986).

Although American Indian migrants are better educated, they do not necessarily fare better than nonmigrants in the labor market. Occupationally, migrants are not disproportionately represented in the ranks of white collar workers. The possible exceptions to this rule are individuals who leave areas on or near reservations and find employment in nonprofessional white collar occupations. Financially, American Indian migrants do not reap immediate gains for their mobility; their wages and salaries are typically below those received by nonmigrants, particularly in metropolitan areas. However, this may be due to the youth and lack of job experience among Indian migrants. While the short-term outlook does not promise sizable rewards for mobility, the conclusion that long-term gains do not accrue to migration is not necessarily true.

The direction of movement is another way of viewing migration, especially in relation to metropolitan and reservation origins and destinations. The direction of migration is important because it highlights basic processes in population redistribution, such as urbanization among American Indians, and is associated with particular types of movers and stayers. For example, American Indians moving to metropolitan areas tend to be single and younger and better educated than nonmigrants or persons moving away from these areas. On the other hand, persons leaving or staying in metropolitan areas include a sizable percentage of older persons, many with older children. A particularly noteworthy finding is that the highest divorce figures are found among the residents and former residents of metropolitan places. Divorce is lowest among nonmetropolitan American Indians.

Decisions to stay or leave an area appear to hinge on different kinds of contingencies involving an extremely complex interaction of individual characteristics and the characteristics of the place in which they reside. Metropolitan areas do not seem as attractive to older Indians with school-age children as they do to younger Indians seeking employment. In this regard, military service and job opportunities are particularly salient motives for metropolitan migration; and among steadily employed Indians, a large percentage do not readily migrate away from metropolitan residences. In fact, employment has a stabilizing influence on migration decisions. In part this may be due to the relatively large economic benefits received by long-term (longer than five years) metropolitan residents. These Indians have wages and salaries considerably higher than those of metropolitan newcomers even though both groups have similar occupational profiles. Nevertheless, both groups enjoy better occupational and monetary situations than Indians in nonmetropolitan areas. Perhaps most ironic is that Indians who leave reservation areas do not make much progress in upgrading their incomes; again, perhaps this is due to their youth.

Comparing metropolitan- and reservation-related migration streams also provides a number of interesting similarities and differences. The similarities between these areas are not coincidental because of the overlap between them; this overlap makes the differences that exist especially interesting. There is a high degree of similarity in the characteristics of persons moving away from reservations and persons moving into cities. Likewise, off-reservation stayers bear a striking resemblance to metropolitan stayers. However, persons moving out of metropolitan places and persons moving on or near a reservation appear to involve different groups of individuals with different characteristics. Indians who are long-term nonmetropolitan residents are not necessarily the same as long-term reservation residents.

In American society the commonplace nature of migration is sometimes attributed to the fact that the United States is a nation founded by restless immigrants, and to this day their descendants have continued to move in search of opportunities elsewhere. If this is true, then it is equally true that American Indians are not only the first inhabitants of this land but its first immigrants as well. Despite past attempts to immobilize them, American Indians have been highly mobile throughout their history and continue to be so today.

10

AMERICAN INDIANS
TODAY AND TOMORROW

I N THE not-so-distant past, experts solemnly forecast the extinction of
American Indians. Resting on five centuries of history, this prediction was considered as certain as the passing of the seasons; and like
the seasons, American Indians would pass into history, never to return.
Of course, this prediction has yet to be fulfilled. And if there is a lesson
here, it might be that past history may be the best guide to future behavior, but it is not infallible, especially in the long term. With this
lesson in mind, a chapter with "tomorrow" in its title may seem a trifle
reckless. However, the predictions that follow are modest.

These predictions rest on two rather simple though profoundly important facts: The American Indian population has been growing, and it
is extremely diverse in many ways. Extrapolating these simple facts produces two equally simple predictions: In the future the American Indian
population is certain to be larger, and it is certain to be more diverse.[1]

The balance of this discussion reviews what past changes and present conditions may hold for American Indians in the future. An especially important matter concerns the forces behind the growing diversity of the American Indian population.

[1]Population growth does not perforce imply greater diversity. However, the purpose
of this chapter is to suggest ways in which future growth in the American Indian population will be accompanied by changes in its composition.

Population Loss and Revitalization

No one truly knows the magnitude of native population losses following 1492 because no one knows with certainty the size of the indigenous population at the time that Columbus made landfall in the Caribbean. There have been, of course, many informed guesses. The original inhabitants of this land were probably larger in number than the 1 million once believed to exist, but probably less than the 18 million proposed in recent estimates.[2] In the absence of revolutionary new knowledge, these guesses are likely to become better informed in the future, but they will remain guesses nevertheless.

Despite the uncertainty of our knowledge, we do know that 500 years ago the Western Hemisphere was populated by a number of complex civilizations that never reached maturity. The most highly developed of these cultures were located in Central America and South America, and our knowledge of them comes from the legacy of their artifacts—artwork, housewares, and architecture. In the area of what is now the United States, smaller and somewhat less complex societies were prevalent. Their remains are scattered throughout the nation, especially in the Southwest and Midwest. These remnants are evidence that once-vigorous societies occupied this land and gave it up only lately to the newcomers from Europe. The land may not have been thickly settled, but neither was it the virgin territory of popular mythology.

After the arrival of Europeans, the descendants of the original Americans did not prosper. The importation of lethal diseases, extended periods of warfare, and episodes of genocide very nearly extinguished what is now the American Indian population. In a period of 400 years a once-thriving population that hosted a polyglot of cultures was almost driven to extinction.[3] At the end of the nineteenth century fewer than 250,000 American Indians were alive. In the aftermath of this destruction the survivors coped in different ways.

For some American Indians in the late nineteenth century, the holocaust was dealt with in revitalization movements, such as the Ghost Dance, spreading through tribes in the Plains and the Southwest.[4] The Ghost Dancers believed that their dance would bring their ancestors to life and drive the white settlers from their lands. The official response to this movement was brutal repression that culminated in the Wounded Knee massacre of 1890.

[2]Henry F. Dobyns, *Their Number Become Thinned: Native American Population Dynamics in Eastern North America* (Knoxville: University of Tennessee Press, 1983).
[3]Russell Thornton, *American Indian Holocaust and Survival: A Population History Since 1492* (Norman: University of Oklahoma Press, 1987).
[4]Russell Thornton, *We Shall Live Again: The 1870 and 1890 Ghost Dance Movements as Demographic Revitalization* (New York: Cambridge University Press, 1986).

Other American Indians coped with their situation by adopting the ways of the white settlers. Some tribes, such as the Cherokee, intermingled white ways with tribal customs and came to be known as "civilized." In other instances, some American Indians made individual efforts to abandon their heritage and merge themselves with the dominant culture. To encourage this behavior, federal authorities passed further legislation to hasten the erosion of tribal culture. The Allotment Acts[5] of the 1890s, for example, tried without much success to make yeoman farmers out of nomadic hunters in the plains.

Finally, other American Indians, believing, as Geronimo did, that the end of their civilization was near, retired to the reservations to live in peace among their kinsmen. Toward these Indians the official response was benign neglect. At best, the reservations of the late nineteenth and early twentieth centuries were viewed by many observers as the final resting places for ancient cultures that would soon give way to modern industrial society.[6] In anticipation of this, a virtual army of social scientists descended upon these communities to document their lifestyles for posterity.[7]

The purpose of recounting this small bit of history is that it underscores the profound significance of American Indian population growth during this century. Since 1890 the American Indian population has grown almost continually, with the largest increase occurring between the 1970 and 1980 censuses. To be sure, the largest measure of this increase was due to changes in ethnic identity, though the actual percentage is impossible to determine. Nevertheless, that so many persons now identify themselves as American Indians reflects a profound shift in recent history, in what it means to be American Indian, and perhaps in American society as well.

American Indian Identity

A Shifting Ground

Until recently, to identify as an American Indian was to acknowledge a stigma. The ideology of the "melting pot," racial discrimination, and a wide variety of negative stereotypes provided few incentives to

---

[5]Leonard A. Carlson, *Indians, Bureaucrats, and Land: The Dawes Act and the Decline of Indian Farming* (Westport, CT: Greenwood Press, 1981).

[6]Francis Paul Prucha, *The Great Father: The United States Government and the American Indians*, vol. 1 (Lincoln: University of Nebraska Press, 1984), chap. 22.

[7]The Smithsonian's Bureau of Ethnology dispatched anthropologists throughout the United States who produced voluminous accounts of American Indian culture.

American Indians to take pride in their heritage. On the contrary, being able to "pass" into white society was a great inducement to do so.[8] In some tribes bitter divisions developed between full-bloods and mixed-bloods, with distinctions between the assimilated ("progressive") mixed-bloods and the traditional ("blanket-ass") full-bloods.

In this environment it is hardly surprising that for many individuals their American Indian heritage was of little value. To be an American Indian often meant that one had not developed the requisite skills to avoid being identified as such. This may be why the Census Bureau historically has been least successful in counting American Indians in areas such as large cities with traditionally small Indian populations.[9] In such areas Indians were more likely to avoid detection because enumerators were more likely to confuse them with European ethnics, such as those from the Mediterranean.

Events in the 1960s and 1970s, such as the civil rights movement, deeply influenced American society, and American Indians were no less affected. In these decades much of the stigma attached to being American Indian was lifted. This brought a surge of ethnic pride and doubtless encouraged many persons to renew their interest in their cultural heritage and to rethink their racial identification. In this period many tribes actively promoted their traditional cultures through cultural awareness programs and other activities. For example, the Cherokee tribe developed a curriculum to promote Cherokee-speaking among children and refresh the language skills of adults.

Another important development of the 1960s and 1970s was that the federal government curtailed its heretofore tireless efforts to promote the assimilation of American Indians. During this period the development of tribal organization and autonomy was promoted through legislation such as the Indian Self-Determination and Education Act of 1975. Numerous land claims and treaty rights cases also were settled in this period. In recognizing the legitimacy of Indian rights, the federal government also recognized the symbolic importance of American Indian identity. In the 1980 census tribal governments, urban Indian organizations, and the Census Bureau made unprecedented efforts to encourage American Indians to identify themselves as such, with

[8]From personal experience, for American Indians to have records or documents incorrectly showing a family member as white or some other race is not an uncommon anecdote.

[9]U.S. Bureau of the Census, *Special Reports: Nonwhite Population by Race* (Washington, DC: U.S. Government Printing Office, 1953), p. 3B-5. In this document the authors point out that the most inaccurate enumerations of American Indians in the 1940 census were found in places where the American Indian population was sparse, in urban areas, for example.

remarkable results. The American Indian population increased by an astonishing 72 percent.

The 1980 census was remarkable because of what it revealed not only about the changing fortunes of American Indians, but also about their assimilation. Through decades of assimilation, and particularly as a result of extraordinarily high rates of marriage with non-Indians, large numbers of persons *do not* strongly identify with their American Indian heritage and *do not* resemble the socioeconomic profile of most American Indians, yet they are able to recall some small amount of Indian ancestry. There are nearly 6 million such individuals, compared with the 1.4 million persons who better resemble conventional ideas about who is an American Indian.

These numbers are most remarkable in connection with some thoughts about American Indians presented by Nancy Lurie 20 years ago.[10] Lurie observed that for blacks the slightest amount of black ancestry is sufficient for membership in the black population. Noting the high rates of intermarriage with non-Indians and years of assimilationist policy, Lurie surmised that if membership in the Indian population were defined in the same way that it is for blacks, the Indian population would be much larger than prevailing estimates. Specifically, Lurie guessed that "upward of 10,000,000" Americans could claim some small amount of Indian ancestry.[11] From the 1980 census, this estimate appears too high, but it is certainly not bad as a ballpark guess.

American Indians and Americans of Indian Descent

With an ongoing process of assimilation and intermarriage, what appears to be taking place is the creation of two somewhat distinct populations of persons with American Indian background. One is a core population of individuals strongly connected to their American Indian heritage. In terms of their residence, lifestyle, socioeconomic characteristics, and even appearance, this group constitutes a population easily identifiable as American Indian. Members of this group are most likely to speak a native language, live on a reservation, have knowledge of their traditional culture, and participate in a community that identifies itself as American Indian and has a special set of relations with the federal government. A second population consists of persons who can recall, legitimately, some amount of Indian ancestry but have little knowledge of Indian culture and in most respects do not resemble the core population of American Indians.

[10]Nancy O. Lurie, "The Enduring Indian," *Natural History* 75(1966):10–22.
[11]Lurie (1966), p. 10.

Projections from the Office of Technology Assessment[12] and the 1980 census suggest, very clearly, that the first group is much smaller than the second. Furthermore, although both groups will continue to grow in the foreseeable future, the second group is likely to grow at a much faster rate than the first group. The implications of this growth for the future are twofold.

The boundaries separating these populations with American Indian ancestry are not well defined. Persons who change their racial identification, for example, are in an important sense moving from one group to another because, as Barth contends, self-identification is the essence of ethnic group membership.[13] Equally true is that changes in self-identification also betray changes in ethnic group membership. Following this reasoning, persons most likely to change their self-identification are most likely at the "margins" or the "gray areas" of groups that more strongly or weakly identify with their American Indian ancestry.

Implications for Population Growth

For these reasons future growth in the American Indian population, net of natural processes, is extremely difficult to predict. Growing conservatism, intolerance of minority rights, increases in discrimination, or a decline in the popularity of a minority identification might cause some individuals to "outmigrate" from the American Indian population into the non-Indian population. This would lead to a decline or a smaller than expected growth in the Indian population. On the other hand, growing tribal autonomy, continuing ethnic pride, and sustained recognition of minority civil rights might consolidate the gains of the 1960s and 1970s. This would lead to expected or greater than expected growth in the Indian population. How changes in the political climate of the 1980s have affected persons with American Indian ancestry is a fascinating subject awaiting the results of the 1990 census and subsequent censuses.

A second implication of these developments, especially rapid growth in the numbers of persons with small amounts of Indian ancestry, is that this is likely to further complicate the ambiguity over who is and is not an American Indian. This is a matter with serious legal and political ramifications, particularly from the standpoint of apportioning legal entitlements.

[12]U.S. Office of Technology Assessment, *Indian Health Care* (Washington, DC: U.S. Government Printing Office, 1986); also see the discussion in Chapter 5.
[13]Fredrik Barth, "Introduction," in Fredrik Barth, ed., *Ethnic Groups and Boundaries* (Boston: Little, Brown, 1969).

Unlike membership in other minority groups, membership in the American Indian population confers certain rights and privileges. These range from the right to vote in tribal elections and to participate in community events to eligibility for health and scholarship services. Needless to say, the criteria for determining who is an Indian are considerably more stringent in connection with scarce resources, such as health and education benefits, than they are for other activities. Furthermore, these criteria are not consistent among the federal agencies serving Indian populations. And the tribes themselves are not of one mind about who can be a tribal member and thereby eligible for tribal services.

Many tribes depend upon a minimum level of ancestry as determined by blood quantum for tribal membership. Some tribes in Oklahoma, for example, require as little as $\frac{1}{16}$ blood quantum for membership, while other tribes in the Southwest require as much as $\frac{1}{2}$ blood quantum. The federal government often uses a $\frac{1}{4}$ blood quantum rule. One outcome of these inconsistencies is that tribes that use less than $\frac{1}{4}$ blood quantum for membership may have a significant number of their people ineligible for federal assistance, and thereby exclusively dependent on nonfederal tribal services—to the extent that such services as day care, housing, and educational assistance are needed. In other areas some Indians are eligible for federal services but are not entitled to membership in the tribe of their ancestry. The dilemma facing all tribes using a blood quantum criterion for tribal membership is that lowering this requirement invariably enlarges the population needing assistance from a scarce and very limited pool of resources. Restricting or maintaining current blood quantum requirements, on the other hand, means that some of the children or grandchildren of bona fide tribal members inevitably will be disinherited.

The prevalence of intermarriage among Indians and non-Indians, though not a new phenomenon, is clearly extensive, which means that blood quantum rules are likely to come under harsher scrutiny in the future. An additional problem is that among Indians who marry members of different tribes, the blood quantum of their children is further diluted. In areas where intertribal marriage is extensive, Oklahoma, for example, it is possible, albeit unusual, for a single person to be descended solely from American Indian ancestry, perhaps from 10 different tribes, but ineligible by blood quantum rules for membership in any one of the tribes.

A second, even more vexing problem entails groups of American Indians who have never been recognized by the federal government. Around the country there are a number of groups and organizations that claim they are legitimate American Indian tribal entities. Some of these claims may be dubious, but many of these groups can make a credible claim to legitimate tribal status. The Wisconsin Winnebago tribe was not acknowledged until the early 1960s, for instance, because the federal government insisted that all of the Winnebago had been relocated to a Nebraska reservation; ergo, there were no longer any Wisconsin Winnebago. However, the Wisconsin Winnebago are the descendants of tribal members who successfully resisted relocation to Nebraska. They were recognized eventually, but as of 1985 over 100 groups were being considered for official recognition by the Bureau of Indian Affairs Branch of Acknowledgment and Research. Periodically, the BIA creates a "new," formerly unrecognized tribe through its acknowledgment proceedings.

The upshot of these developments is that through the processes of mate selection—Indians who marry non-Indians or Indians from other tribes—or through bureaucratic fiat a new and different Indian population is emerging. Just as today's Indians are different from those of several generations ago, tomorrow's Indians are likely to be different from those of today. Blood quantum will likely become an increasingly unworkable indicator, and the gap between population estimates based on blood quantum and the number of self-identified American Indians appearing in surveys such as the census is likely to grow very large.

Migration and Urbanization

Migration contributes to social heterogeneity by moving and redistributing otherwise homogeneous populations, increasing contacts between people of different cultures, and amalgamating old forms of social organization to create new types of human communities. Clearly, the American Indian population of today reflects a history of upheavals in its geographic distribution.

Historically, migration has been an exceedingly important force in the diversification of the American Indian population. And the impetus for mobility has arisen from human actions and natural causes. Before the appearance of Europeans, American Indians most likely moved in response to environmental changes, the availability of sustenance, and conflicts over hunting and fishing grounds. After the arrival of Europeans, American Indian migration increasingly responded to the course of human events; the spread of infectious diseases and subsequent massive population losses were undoubtedly a major influence on migration for several centuries. Later, public policy became a driving force behind migration.

Removal

It is no accident that most American Indians today reside west of the Mississippi River. Federal legislation in the early nineteenth century forced the removal of thousands of American Indians from their homes in the eastern United States—many were moved to the Indian territory of modern-day Oklahoma. In the wake of this policy, small bands of Indians escaped removal and were left behind in their native lands. The descendants of these Indians continue to live in small communities in the East. The largest eastern Indian populations are located in New York and in North Carolina. In New York, tribes such as the Oneida and Mahican escaped removal to Wisconsin. North Carolina is home for the eastern Cherokee who escaped a deadly march to Oklahoma.

As a result of this history, the modern Oklahoma Indian population is a unique admixture of native Plains tribes (for example, Cheyenne, Kiowa, Osage) and relocated Woodlands tribes. Over time, however, these tribes have developed a distinctive identity by dint of their history and their close proximity to one another. Oklahoma Choctaw, for example, are distinctively different from those descendants of the Choctaw who escaped removal and now reside in central Mississippi. Similarly, the southern Cheyenne of Oklahoma have a distinctly different community from the northern Cheyenne of Montana, though both are descendants of the Plains Cheyenne tribe. The differences between the Oklahoma tribes and their brethren elsewhere can be at once subtle and striking; it can involve differences such as nuances and pronunciation in native languages, styles in art and craftwork, folklore, and community organization, to mention only a few. The social experiment that created the Indian territory produced a remarkably diverse American Indian population within a relatively small area. At the same time, this further diversified the American Indian population nationwide by creating branches such as the "eastern" and "western" Cherokee.[14]

Relocation

More recently, urban migration, particularly that sponsored by the BIA, helped set in motion a process that is almost certain to reshape the American Indian population—in many respects this process is well under way. The urban relocation programs of the 1950s and 1960s were

[14]Branched tribes such as the eastern (North Carolina) and western (Oklahoma) Cherokee are completely autonomous. The eastern and western Cherokee did not fully acknowledge the existence of one another until a formal reunion was held in Tennessee in 1984—almost 150 years after the Cherokee removal.

314

expected to improve the economic situation of American Indians by hastening their assimilation into the mainstream of the industrial work force. The impact of these programs on the material well-being of American Indians is debatable, but without question these programs were an important part of the rapid urbanization of American Indians after World War II.

The American Indian population remains one of the least urbanized in American society. Slightly more than half of the Indian population lived outside metropolitan areas in 1980. The urban Indian population is concentrated in a handful of cities; a number of these cities are located on the West Coast, particularly California. Whether the rural-urban distribution of the American Indian population will, in the future, remain the same or become more or less urbanized is difficult to predict. Historical experience would predict more urbanization, but there are no longer relocation programs hastening this process. Furthermore, many reservations and communities are actively seeking to stem the urban flow by various means such as reservation development programs. Economic development can stem migration and even promote return migration; the Osage reservation is an extreme example (see Chapters 3 and 9), but the success of many reservation development programs has been mixed.

Migration and Pan-Indian Identity

The outlook for the near future is that the American Indian population is unlikely to become dramatically de-urbanized, which has significant implications for its composition in the future. Perhaps most important is that rural-urban residence has been and will continue to be a major bifurcation in the Indian population.

Rural Indians, particularly those on reservations, tend to be strongly linked to their tribe because tribal affairs play a much larger role in their lives than they do for their urban counterparts. These Indians also tend to be more traditional, be poorer, and have a vastly different relationship with the federal government. Urban Indians do not receive assistance from agencies such as the Bureau of Indian Affairs or Indian Health Service, and they are distant from tribal business and the day-to-day activities of tribal life. Urban Indians are perhaps unique because of the prevalence of pan-Indianism among them.

Pan-Indianism entails a global political, economic, and social agenda that tends to discount the importance of tribal organization and emphasizes priorities that are often very different from the local agendas of individual tribes. Pan-Indianism stresses the importance of *Indian* identity over *tribal* identity; that is, tribal allegiances are subsidiary to matters that affect the American Indian population as a whole. This perspective places a very different emphasis on issues affecting the American Indian population, including the criteria for who are entitled to call themselves American Indian and, by implication, entitled to certain rights and benefits.

Migration that enlarges the urban Indian population will most likely increase the prevalence of pan-Indianism. One outcome of this development will be a gradual shift in the meaning of American Indian identity, especially in the way in which American Indian identity is defined.[15] Pan-Indian ideas about who is an Indian are in many ways more open-ended and ambiguous than the criteria applied by tribal organizations and the federal government. A surge in pan-Indian activities in the 1960s and 1970s undoubtedly fueled the massive growth in the Indian population due to shifts in ethnic identification. Underscoring this point, most dramatic growth in the American Indian population occurred in urban areas. A large and growing urban Indian population strongly committed to pan-Indian philosophies and ideals could render the self-identified status of American Indians even more ambiguous in the future than it has been in past censuses. At the least, the very existence of large numbers of urban Indians adds an important dimension of heterogeneity to the American Indian population.

Social and Economic Conditions

American Indians have in common the dubious distinction of being one of the poorest groups in American society. Despite this status, all American Indians are not in the grip of desperate poverty. In fact, rural-urban migration and residence are closely linked to significant social and economic divisions within the Indian population.

Despite popular and misleading stereotypes of their benefiting from the discovery of oil or other minerals on their land, American Indians have been a historically poor people. Even before the arrival of Columbus, the indigenous populations of North America did not succeed in developing societies with vast amounts of accumulated wealth. There were, however, extensive trading networks based on barter—not very different from Europe in the early Middle Ages.

---

[15]Joane Nagel, "The Roots of Red Power: Demographic and Organizational Bases of Indian Activism, 1950–1980," paper presented at the annual meeting of the American Sociological Association, Atlanta, 1988.

With the arrival of Europeans, American Indians found a new group of trading partners. However, Europeans also introduced business practices, ethics, and values that frequently were not well understood by American Indians and often worked to their disadvantage. Concepts such as private property and other legal instruments, credit, and personal profit-making, for example, were utterly foreign. In the early history of white-Indian relations, misunderstandings over trade often led to hostilities and sometimes violent conflict. Over time, the ascendancy of European society and the formation of the United States gradually resulted in the economic subordination of American Indians. This has entailed a long history of exploitation ranging from the trading post system of the nineteenth and early twentieth centuries to contemporary disputes over the terms of lease agreements for reservation lands and allegations of resource mismanagement by the BIA.

American Indians have never been well integrated into the economic mainstream of American society. In part this has been the result of geographic isolation. However, as some observers have noted, American Indians also have been reluctant to adopt values and lifestyles that would promote acquisitiveness and reward avarice. For many American Indians in the 1980s, great wealth and material possessions are not a matter of overwhelming importance.

This does not mean that American Indians care nothing about having their families comfortably housed, healthy, clothed, and well nourished. It also does not mean that American Indians will not avail themselves of economic opportunities. It does mean that economic resources are commonly viewed as at best a means to an end but seldom an end in themselves. Acquiring wealth for the sake of wealth is a difficult concept for many American Indians to comprehend, especially those from traditional cultural backgrounds. In this context, there have been important changes in the Indian population.

Despite their depressed economic position, American Indians are wealthier today than they have been at any point in the past. This is true for Indians living on rural reservations and in cities. During the 1970s American Indians across the nation enjoyed significantly improved economic conditions. By 1980 they were better housed, better educated, more employed, and healthier than they had been even a decade before. These improvements, combined with deteriorating conditions in the black population, meant that by 1980 American Indians had reached economic parity with blacks. Yet, it hardly needs to be said that both of these groups are substantially below the high standard of living enjoyed by whites.

One reason for this rise in the standard of living for American Indians might be that a number of relatively well off persons switched their racial self-identification from, say, white to Indian between 1970 and 1980. However, there were significant increases in economic well-being even in places where population growth was moderate and hence less subject to change due to shifts in self-identification.

The plethora of social programs designed to alleviate poverty and improve economic opportunities was very likely an important source of the gains made in the 1970s. There were improvements in the housing of American Indians, for example. The data are not beyond dispute, but public housing programs sponsored by the Department of Housing and Urban Development and the BIA probably played a major role in these improvements. Programs to help students complete high school or obtain a GED increased the education and employability of some American Indians who would be less educated and jobless otherwise. More American Indians found work in the 1970s, and this was no doubt aided by public employment and job training programs. In the wake of federal cutbacks of these programs, reservation unemployment rates (BIA estimates) increased from 27 percent in 1979 to 39 percent in 1983. In the same years unemployment on the Navajo reservation jumped from 20 to 45 percent.

Some of the rise in the standard of living for American Indians also might have been the result of tribal efforts to develop reservation economies. Some reservations exploited their energy resources, others tried to attract light manufacturing, and still others experimented with tribally owned enterprises. In recent years duty-free outlets for tobacco and gaming operations have been highly lucrative though controversial income sources. Some of these tribal business ventures have been more successful than others, some have been outright failures, and, in any case, few offer significant benefits for urban American Indians living in locations distant from their reservations.

As American Indians become more expert in managing their affairs, as more opportunities develop in Indian communities, and as more Indians become better educated, the outlook for continued economic gains appears promising. However, there are signs on the horizon that call for a less sanguine forecast. Most troubling is that some American Indians will enjoy a prosperous future while others, perhaps many, will remain at the bottom of the socioeconomic ladder—creating yet another division within the American Indian population based on social class.

A number of factors caution against too rosy an outlook. The dependency of many tribes on federal support makes American Indians highly vulnerable to shifting political commitments. Funding cutbacks have had an adverse impact on many Indian communities, and in the future calls for fiscal austerity and a mounting federal deficit make it unlikely that the federal government can be seen as a reliable source of assistance. The shrinking role of the federal government is particularly problematic because it represents the decline of a significant source of opportunities for employment and educational advancement.

Declining educational opportunities for American Indians is an especially serious threat to their future economic well-being. Data from the 1970 and 1980 censuses suggest that while more American Indians are attaining a high school diploma, the relative number going beyond this level is very small; at the same time more whites are attending college. This development is most problematic because of recent changes in the American economy.

In an information-based service economy, American Indians lacking postsecondary education are certain to be shuffled into low-wage, insecure jobs with few fringe benefits—assuming even that such jobs are available. Studies have found that most of the income gap between whites and Indians is due to the competitive advantages enjoyed by whites because they have more education and experience.[16] The existing data give no reason to expect that American Indians are about to become significantly more competitive in the labor market without external intervention—that is, federal educational assistance—and this, too, is not on the horizon.

Another threat to economic well-being is that American Indian fertility is relatively high, especially in nonmetropolitan areas where most reservations are located. While Indian fertility has declined, and younger women appear to be having fewer children than older women, it continues to be substantially higher than white fertility. This is problematic from at least three perspectives.

High rates of fertility are an obvious problem because large families are a financial burden. For workers with large families, already limited resources must be stretched to meet the needs of family members. The upshot is a greatly diminished standard of living for these families.

High fertility is also troublesome from the standpoint of apportioning public goods. To assure a minimum level of well-being, much less to break the cycle of poverty, American Indian children especially need provisions for adequate health care and disease prevention, nutrition, and educational assistance. Resources for these public goods are limited at the federal level and exceedingly so for tribal governments. Nonethe-

---

[16]Gary D. Sandefur and Wilbur J. Scott, "Minority Group Status and the Wages of Indian and Black Males," *Social Science Research* 12(1983):44–68; James D. Gwartney and James E. Long, "The Relative Earnings of Blacks and Other Minorities," *Industrial and Labor Relations Review* 31(1978):336–346; C. Matthew Snipp, "On the Cost of Being American Indian: Ethnic Identity and Economic Opportunity," in James Johnson and Melvin Oliver, eds., *Proceedings of the Conference on Comparative Ethnicity* (Los Angeles: Institute for Social Science Research, University of California, 1988).

less, high fertility means a greater demand for public services; and in the absence of an expanding resource base, it will be necessary to allocate fewer resources for each child in the future.

Finally, high fertility is likely to become increasingly problematic for reservations with fixed land bases; it already has been a problem in some areas. For American Indians desiring a reservation home, high fertility means greater competition for existing land, more densely populated settlement areas, and less land for grazing and agriculture. For example, the Navajo reservation is a large reservation with a large population, and the land is arid and easily overgrazed. Over the years Navajo herdsmen settled in lands disputed with the Hopi reservation. In the mid 1980s this situation erupted into an intense and sometimes violent conflict that required federal intervention. It eventually resulted in a massive relocation of Navajo families to other parts of the reservation or outside the reservation entirely. This is an extreme example, but one that is instructive about what high fertility will mean for many reservations in the next century.

The economic future of the Indian population is neither hopeful nor hopeless. One possible outcome, given these mixed indicators, is that there will be greater economic divisions among future generations of American Indians, not unlike divisions in the black population suggested by Wilson.[17] Some American Indians, including those who took advantage of opportunities more widely available in the 1960s and 1970s, will attain educations and occupations sufficient to provide middle- and upper-middle-income standards of living. Presumably, some of these advantages will be passed along to the children of these Indians. Many other American Indians lacking education and job opportunities will find themselves in a position familiar to the Indian population: among the poorest of the poor.

The economic divisions in the American Indian population are likely to follow other predictable and closely interrelated divisions. American Indians in rural areas may very likely remain poorer than their urban counterparts. Rural Indians are less educated and face many more disadvantages than urban Indians. As urban Indians take advantage of opportunities and the economic growth in America's cities, there is reason to expect that growing differences in the standards of living will add to other differences between rural and urban Indians.[18]

[17]William Julius Wilson, *The Declining Significance of Race* (Chicago: University of Chicago Press, 1978).

[18]The solution to this problem is not to move rural American Indians into cities; that has been tried already. Migration in general and relocation programs in particular do not have much impact on the economic well-being of American Indians. See C. Matthew Snipp and Gary D. Sandefur, "Earning of American Indians and Alaska Natives," The Effects of Residence and Migration," *Social Forces* 66(1988):994–1008.

Assimilation is another dimension of diversity within the American Indian population. Some Indians are more assimilated than others, and their economic circumstances are ordinarily better than those of less assimilated Indians. High rates of intermarriage and the projected growth of the American Indian population into the next century will very likely produce a large number of relatively assimilated persons with an American Indian background, along with a smaller, less assimilated population of American Indians. Assuming that members of the more assimilated group nonetheless retain their Indian identity, the social distance between these groups is likely to become even greater, not only in cultural terms but in economic terms as well. This means that in the future economic inequality within the American Indian population, as mirrored in the gap between the richest and poorest American Indians, is likely to increase. The economic differences between American Indians and Americans of Indian Descent (see Chapter 2) are an indication of what the future may hold.

Does this mean that American Indians, especially those living on reservations, should don suits and move to the city in search of business careers? The answer to this question is no, not exactly, because this is not an option for many American Indians, and it does not assure the vitality of the Indian population. Instead, some tribes are pursuing a middle-ground strategy, and this is another source of growing diversity among American Indians. Namely, American Indians in growing numbers, individually and tribally, are involved in various types of business enterprises.

Some of these businesses are consonant with cultural traditions, such as the Lummi fishing industry, and others are not, such as manufacturing and retail shops. More important, some of these activities have been exceptionally successful while others have failed. Within a tribe, successful business development creates job opportunities and higher standards of living. Profits from tribally operated ventures also subsidize public services for tribal members. However, between tribes the emergence of successful business development among a few tribes and not among others contributes to greater economic inequality within the American Indian population as a whole.

Concluding Remarks

American Indians have been an enduring part of the American social mosaic, literally since the founding of this society. In fact, it is perhaps more accurate to say that the social institutions of the European immigrants developed around and eventually engulfed the societies of the first Americans. Regardless, the descendants of the first Americans have proved to be nothing if not resilient and adaptable; they have survived and managed to sustain a distinctive ethnic identity.

The resiliency of the American Indian population is probably its most essential characteristic. It is the reason why American Indians are here today and why they will be here tomorrow. American Indians changed when it was necessary for their survival, but they have adjusted in ways that have allowed them to preserve their most valued traditions and lifestyles. The American Indian population of tomorrow will, most likely, be very different from the one living today, just as those living today are different from their ancestors. This is a sign of a vital dynamic culture. If American Indians had not changed their culture, their survival into this century would have been doubtful.

That American Indians no longer wander the plains on horseback in search of wild game does not mean that there are no longer any "real" Indians. It means only that American Indians have not contented themselves with becoming museum relics of an era in past history; they are no different from most Americans, who would not seriously wish for the return of covered wagons and sod huts. On the other hand, American Indians have not opted for all that American society can offer, at some cost. Most of these costs have been in various forms of economic hardship and deprivation.

Despite these hardships, the future of the American Indian population is in some ways brighter today than it has been for a very long time. Whether this will continue in the future is impossible to predict, but the 1990 census will provide many important clues. Looking beyond the census into the next century, it can only be hoped that with the passage of time the first of this land will not be the last to share in its wealth.

APPENDIX 1

TRIBAL POPULATION
ESTIMATES

TABLE A1.1

Tribal Population Estimates from the 1980 Census
for American Indian Tribes and Alaska Native Villages
(estimates based on tabulation from sample data)

Tribe	Population
Abenaki	829
Alabama Coushatta[a]	1,058
Alaska Native (n.e.c.)	587
Alaska Native	491
Sealaska	96
Alaskan Athabaskans	10,136
Alaskan Athabaskan	9,499
Doyon	329
Tanaina	293
Other Alaskan Athabaskan Tribes	15
Aleut and Eskimo	661
Akutan	36
Aleut	193
Calista	86
Chugach	153
Eskimo	91
Kotzebue Sound	32
Other Aleut and Eskimo Tribes	70
Algonquian (n.e.c.)	1,709
Apache	35,861
Apache (n.e.c.)	23,896
Chiricahua	475
Fort Sill Apache	211
Jicarilla Apache	1,591
Kiowa Apache	258
Mescalero Apache	1,989
Payson Apache	45
San Carlos Apache	3,880
White Mountain Apache	3,508
Other Apache Tribes	8
Arapaho	4,423
Arikara	1,536
Assiniboine	3,986
Bannock	490
Blackfeet[a]	21,964
Brotherton	173
Caddo	1,733

n.e.c.: not elsewhere classified

SOURCE: U.S. Bureau of the Census, unpublished tabulations.

[a]Reporting and/or processing problems may have affected the data for this tribe.
[b]Any Mohawk entry of "Ganieka" would have been coded Wailaki.
[c]Any entry with the spelling "Micmac" would have been coded Cheyenne River Sioux.

TABLE A1.1 *(continued)*

Tribe	Population
Cahuilla	1,240
Cahuilla	917
Soboba	219
Torres-Martinez	42
Other Cahuilla Tribes	62
California Tribes (n.e.c.)	586
Cahto	13
Digger	52
Mattole	49
Morongo	191
Wappo	76
Yuki	96
Other California Tribes	109
Canadian and Latin American	7,804
Catawba	1,500
Cayuse	157
Chehalis	259
Chemakuan	480
Hoh	95
Quileute	385
Chemehuevi	467
Cherokee	232,080
Cherokee	230,792
Eastern Cherokee	1,013
Etowah Cherokee	43
Tuscola	78
United Keetoowah	55
Western Cherokee	78
Other Cherokee Tribes	21
Cheyenne	9,918
Cheyenne	7,071
Northern Cheyenne	2,724
Southern Cheyenne	123
Chickahominy	838
Chickasaw	10,317
Chinook	1,396
Chinook	1,315
Clatsop	39
Columbia River Chinook	37
Other Chinook Tribes	5
Chippewa	73,602
Bad River	237
Bay Mills Chippewa	345
Bois Forte	73
Chippewa	69,064
Lac Courte Oreilles	260
Lac du Flambeau	37

TABLE A1.1 *(continued)*

Tribe	Population
Lake Superior	66
Leech Lake	55
Leelanau	46
Mille Lac	70
Minnesota Chippewa	779
Ontonagon	99
Red Cliff Chippewa	65
Red Lake Chippewa	226
Saginaw Chippewa	344
St. Croix Chippewa	16
Sault Ste. Marie Chippewa	798
Sokoagon Chippewa	131
Turtle Mountain	432
White Earth	397
Other Chippewa Tribes	62
Chitimacha	346
Choctaw	50,220
Choctaw	49,954
Clifton Choctaw	266
Chumash[a]	1,458
Chumash	1,453
Other Chumash Tribes	5
Clallam	893
Clallam	606
Lower Elwah	43
Port Gamble Clallam	237
Other Clallam Tribes	7
Coeur d'Alene	684
Coharie	508
Colorado River	954
Colville	5,456
Comanche	9,037
Coos	128
Costanoan	506
Cowlitz	949
Cree	6,611
Creek	28,278
Creek	27,893
Eastern Creek	86
Lower Muskogee	184
Muskogee	34
Thlopthlocco	61
Other Creek Tribes	20
Croatan	187
Crow	7,074
Cupeno	287
Agua Caliente	63
Cupeno	224

TABLE A1.1 *(continued)*

Tribe	Population
Delaware	5,381
Delaware	4,686
Munsee	130
Sand Hill	565
Diegueno	1,394
Diegueno	1,157
Manzanita	31
San Pascual	123
Santa Ysabel	47
Other Diegueno Tribes	36
Eastern Tribes (n.e.c.)	2,637
Moor	85
Nansemond	32
Natchez	53
Nipmuc	70
Southeastern Indians	2,303
Tunica	51
Other Eastern Tribes	43
Flathead	4,948
Fort Hall	450
Gabrieleno	1,810
Gros Ventres	2,121
Atsina	64
Gros Ventres	2,057
Haida	1,434
Haliwa	2,087
Hidatsa	1,549
Hitchiti	22
Hoopa	1,984
Houma	2,600
Iowa	947
Iroquois	38,218
Cayuga	796
Iroquois	4,068
Mohawk[b]	13,455
Oneida	8,132
Onondaga	864
Seneca	7,220
Seneca	6,923
Seneca Nation	97
Tonawanda Seneca	200
Seneca-Cayuga	437
Tuscarora	2,155
Wyandot	1,091
Kalispel	181
Karok	1,959
Kaw	677
Kickapoo	2,355

TABLE A1.1 *(continued)*

Tribe	Population
Kiowa	7,386
Klamath	2,107
Konkow	337
Kootenai	386
Long Island	304
Matinecock	144
Montauk	122
Poosepatuck	27
Other Long Island Tribes	11
Luiseno	1,237
LaJolla	39
Luiseno	901
Pala	148
Pauma	36
Pechanga	113
Lumbee	28,631
Lummi	4,100
Maidu	1,177
Makah	1,040
Maliseet	527
Mandan	1,013
Mattaponi	136
Menominee	6,044
Miami	2,330
Miccosukee[a]	62
Micmac[c]	1,143
Mission Indians	2,497
Miwok	2,142
Modoc	763
Mohegan	521
Mono	1,378
Nanticoke	983
Narragansett	2,072
Navajo	158,633
Nez Perce[a]	2,222
Nomalaki	228
Northwest Tribes	276
Columbia Wenatchee	51
Kalapuya	65
Tillamook	82
Other Northwest Tribes	78
Omaha	3,090
Oregon Athabaskan	633
Osage	6,884
Oto	1,510
Ottawa	6,500
Paiute[a]	9,253
Burns Paiute	67

TABLE A1.1 *(continued)*

Tribe	Population
Northern Paiute	57
Paiute	9,158
Pyramid Lake	20
Southern Paiute	110
Walker River	34
Other Paiute Tribes	77
Pamunkey	335
Papago	13,297
Papago	13,272
Other Papago Tribes	25
Pawnee	2,454
Penobscot	1,390
Peoria	645
Pequot	435
Pima	11,722
Piscataway	478
Pit River	1,276
Pomo	3,154
Eastern Pomo	72
Kashaya	50
Northern Pomo	52
Pomo	2,945
Other Pomo Tribes	35
Ponca	2,056
Potawatomi	9,715
Citizen Band	484
Forest County	37
Huron Potawatomi	127
Potawatomi	8,630
Prairie Band	421
Other Potawatomi Tribes	16
Powhatan	320
Pueblo[a]	42,552
Acoma	3,017
Arizona Tewa	326
Cochiti	832
Hopi	8,930
Isleta	2,544
Jemez	1,425
Keres (n.e.c.)	688
Laguna	4,041
Nambe	263
Picuris	26
Pojoaque	37
Pueblo (n.e.c.)	2,617
Sandia	741
San Felipe	1,707
San Ildefonso	232

TABLE A1.1 *(continued)*

Tribe	Population
San Juan	425
Santa Ana	354
Santa Clara[a]	446
Santo Domingo	2,512
Taos	1,396
Tesuque	199
Tewa	2,109
Tigua	561
Zia	694
Zuni	6,430
Puget Sound Salish	6,591
Duwamish	123
Muckleshoot	551
Nisqually	204
Nooksack	537
Puget Sound Salish	58
Puyallup	618
Samish	115
Sauk-Suiattle	142
Skokomish	491
Skykomish	57
Snohomish	491
Snoqualmie	238
Squaxin Island	313
Steilacoom	142
Stillaguamish	72
Suquamish	373
Swinomish	459
Tulalip	1,183
Upper Skagit	424
Quapaw	929
Quinault	1,659
Rappanhannock	266
Sac and Fox-Mesquakie	3,381
Salinan	284
Schaghticoke	199
Seminole[a]	10,363
Seminole	9,893
Seminole Nation of Oklahoma	73
Seminole Tribe of Florida	391
Other Seminole Tribes	6
Serrano	206
Shasta	330
Shawnee	4,343
Absentee Shawnee	359
Shawnee	3,984
Shinnecock	1,040

TABLE A1.1 *(continued)*

Tribe	Population
Shoshone	9,830
Goshute	130
Shoshone	9,343
Te-Moak Western Shoshone[a]	116
Yomba[a]	123
Other Shoshone Tribes	118
Siletz	704
Sioux	78,608
Blackfeet Sioux	304
Brule Sioux	144
Cheyenne River Sioux[c]	3,570
Crow Creek Sioux	1,230
Dakota Sioux	1,416
Devil's Lake Sioux	123
Flandreau Santee	87
Fort Peck	128
Lower Brule Sioux	733
Mdewakanton Sioux	136
Oglala Sioux	12,582
Pine Ridge Sioux	89
Prior Lake Sioux	149
Rosebud Sioux	5,764
Santee Sioux	1,261
Sioux	45,319
Sisseton Sioux	1,039
Standing Rock Sioux	1,845
Teton Sioux	522
Wahpeton Sioux	54
Yankton Sioux	1,912
Yanktonai Sioux	112
Other Sioux Tribes	89
Sinuslaw	351
Spokane	1,753
Stockbridge	1,547
Tlingit	9,509
Tolowa	396
Tsimshian	1,587
Umatilla	965
Ute	5,821
Uintah Ute	36
Ute	5,079
Ute Mountain Ute	696
Other Ute Tribes	10
Wailaki[b]	583
Walla-Walla	262
Wampanoag	1,415
Warm Springs	1,336

TABLE A1.1 *(continued)*

Tribe	Population
Washo	1,414
Washo	1,377
Other Washo Tribes	37
Wichita	707
Winnebago	5,165
Wintu	2,044
Wiyot	243
Yakima	6,506
Yaqui	5,197
Barrio Libre	471
Yaqui	4,721
Other Yaqui Tribes	5
Yavapai Apache	149
Yokuts	1,764
Chuckhansi	539
Tachi	267
Tule River	398
Yokuts	560
Yuchi	245
Yuman	6,611
Cocopah	758
Havasupai	527
Hualapai	1,046
Maricopa	752
Mohave	1,514
Quechan	1,237
Yavapai	777
Yurok	2,994
Other Specified Tribes	459
Fort Berthold	23
Gila River	34
Grande Rhonde	60
Los Coyotes	44
Round Valley	31
Scotts Valley	65
Shoalwater	142
Tribe Not Specified	34,529
Tribe Not Reported	304,455

APPENDIX 2

TRIBAL POPULATION
ESTIMATES BY STATE

TABLE A2.1

Tribes With 400 or More American Indians, by State, 1980

Alabama	
Total	9,239
Cherokee	2,033
Choctaw	934
Creek	1,315
Ail other	958
Not reported	3,999
Alaska	
Total	22,631
Alaskan Athabaskan	8,744
Cherokee	707
Haida	994
Tlingit	6,764
Tsimshian	1,168
All other	2,321
Not reported	1,933
Arizona	
Total	154,175
Apache	
Total	13,867
Apache (n.e.c.)	6,744
San Carlos Apache	3,767
White Mountain Apache	3,293
Cherokee	2,713
Chippewa	458
Choctaw	727
Colorado River	919
Navajo	76,642
Papago	11,509
Pima	9,957
Pueblo[a]	
Total	8,690
Hopi	6,969
Sioux	1,052
Yaqui	3,494
Yuman	

n.e.c.: not elsewhere classified.
SOURCE: U.S. Bureau of the Census, unpublished tabulations.

[a]Reporting and/or processing problems may have affected the data for this tribe.
[b]Any Mohawk entry of "Ganienka" would have been coded Wailaki.
[c]Miscoding of entries of "Lummee," "Lummi," "Lumbee," or "Lumbi" may have affected the data for this tribe.
[d]Any entry with the spelling "Micmac" would have been coded Cheyenne River Sioux.

TABLE A2.1 *(continued)*

Total	3,898
Cocopah	579
Hualapai	843
Maricopa	634
Mohave	840
Yavapai	683
All other	5,860
Not reported	14,389
Arkansas	
Total	12,713
Cherokee	6,385
Choctaw	1,064
All other	2,360
Not reported	2,904
California	
Total	227,757
Apache	7,012
Arapaho	415
Blackeet[a]	4,990
Cahuilla	1,100
California Tribes (n.e.c.)	444
Canadian and Latin American	2,437
Cherokee	51,360
Cheyenne	697
Chickasaw	1,523
Chippewa	3,879
Choctaw	7,973
Chumash[a]	1,298
Comanche	1,383
Costanoan	453
Cree	544
Creek	3,038
Crow	723
Delaware	516
Diegueno	1,276
Gabrieleno	1,702
Hoopa	1,798
Iroquois	
Total	3,294
Iroquois (n.e.c.)	908
Mohawk[b]	1,006
Seneca	591
Karok	1,511
Kiowa	700
Luiseno	1,136

TABLE A2.1 (continued)

Maidu	1,011
Mission Indians	2,213
Miwok	1,984
Mono	1,192
Navajo	6,030
Nez Perce[a]	407
Osage	1,185
Paiute[a]	3,679
Papago	980
Pima	1,036
Pit River	1,149
Pomo	2,817
Potawatomi	1,146
Pueblo[a]	
Total	3,340
Hopi	888
Pueblo (n.e.c.)	1,004
Seminole[a]	1,306
Shawnee	566
Shoshone	1,482
Sioux	6,587
Ute	500
Wailaki[b]	449
Washo	493
Wintu	1,619
Yaqui	1,269
Yokuts	
Total	1,571
Chuckhansi	492
Yokuts	437
Yuman	
Total	1,847
Mohave	515
Quechan	843
Yurok	2,422
All other	20,609
Not reported	58,815
Colorado	
Total	20,682
Apache	716
Cherokee	3,780
Chippewa	528
Choctaw	431
Navajo	2,086
Pueblo[a]	487

TABLE A2.1 *(continued)*

Sioux	1,862
Ute	
Total	1,889
Ute	1,323
Ute Mountain Ute	556
All other	4,451
Not reported	4,452
Connecticut	
Total	4,822
Cherokee	699
All other	2,816
Not reported	1,307
Delaware	
Total	1,380
Not reported	516
District of Columbia	
Total	986
Not reported	590
Florida	
Total	24,714
Blackfeet[a]	489
Cherokee	5,042
Creek	2,193
Iroquois	469
Seminole[a]	1,026
All other	3,764
Not reported	11,731
Georgia	
Total	9,876
Cherokee	2,855
All other	1,832
Not reported	5,189
Hawaii	
Total	2,833
Cherokee	691
All other	1,470
Not reported	672

TABLE A2.1 *(continued)*

Idaho	
Total	10,405
Cherokee	1,088
Navajo	419
Nez Perce[a]	420
Shoshone	2,274
Sioux	409
All other	3,199
Not reported	2,596
Illinois	
Total	19,118
Blackfeet[a]	494
Cherokee	4,182
Chippewa	1,533
Choctaw	669
Iroquois	
Total	836
Oneida	542
Menominee	434
Sioux	750
All other	3,910
Not reported	6,310
Indiana	
Total	9,495
Cherokee	3,265
Miami	1,089
All other	2,563
Not reported	2,578
Iowa	
Total	6,311
Cherokee	973
Sac and Fox-Mesquakie	870
Sioux	1,077
All other	1,784
Not reported	1,607
Kansas	
Total	17,829
Apache	400
Cherokee	4,760
Choctaw	625
Creek	594
Kickapoo	658
Navajo	465

TABLE A2.1 *(continued)*

Potawatomi	1,634
Sioux	569
All other	4,831
Not reported	3,293
Kentucky	
Total	4,497
Cherokee	1,801
All other	1,258
Not reported	1,438
Louisiana	
Total	12,841
Cherokee	1,631
Choctaw	1,221
Houma	2,271
All other	1,951
Not reported	5,767
Maine	
Total	4,360
Maliseet	446
Passamaquoddy	1,240
Penobscot	752
All other	1,367
Not reported	555
Maryland	
Total	8,946
Cherokee	1,852
Lumbee[c]	571
Piscataway	470
All other	1,974
Not reported	4,079
Massachusetts	
Total	8,996
Cherokee	1,105
Iroquois	
Total	929
Mohawk[b]	574
Micmac[d]	452
Sioux	424
Wampanoag	988
All other	2,924
Not reported	2,174

TABLE A2.1 *(continued)*

Michigan	
Total	44,712
Apache	746
Blackfeet[a]	832
Canadian and Latin American	469
Cherokee	7,972
Chippewa	
Total	12,881
Chippewa	11,720
Sault Ste. Marie Chippewa	566
Iroquois	
Total	1,803
Mohawk[b]	895
Ottawa	5,052
Potawatomi	1,620
Sioux	727
All other	4,196
Not reported	8,414
Minnesota	
Total	36,527
Cherokee	842
Chippewa	
Total	24,125
Chippewa	22,749
Minnesota Chippewa	645
Sioux	2,938
All other	2,915
Not reported	5,707
Mississippi	
Total	6,836
Cherokee	703
Choctaw	3,000
All other	658
Not reported	2,475
Missouri	
Total	14,820
Blackfeet[a]	456
Cherokee	5,857
Choctaw	401
Sioux	438
All other	3,843
Not reported	3,825

TABLE A2.1 *(continued)*

Montana	
Total	37,623
Assiniboine	2,889
Blackfeet[a]	4,571
Cherokee	858
Cheyenne	
Total	2,661
Cheyenne	425
Northern Cheyenne	2,222
Chippewa	2,578
Cree	3,661
Crow	4,846
Flathead	3,177
Gros Ventres	1,245
Sioux	3,255
All other	2,157
Not reported	5,725
Nebraska	
Total	9,059
Cherokee	475
Omaha	2,118
Sioux	
Total	2,701
Oglala Sioux	445
Santee Sioux	443
Sioux	1,461
Winnebago	1,065
All other	1,224
Not reported	1,476
Nevada	
Total	14,256
Cherokee	1,309
Paiute[a]	3,648
Shoshone	2,330
Washo	765
All other	3,574
Not reported	2,630
New Hampshire	
Total	1,342
New Jersey	
Total	10,028
Blackfeet[a]	430

TABLE A2.1 *(continued)*

Cherokee	2,053
Delaware	740
Iroquois	599
Nanticoke	453
All other	2,696
Not reported	3,057
New Mexico	
Total	106,585
Apache	
Total	3,734
Apache	702
Jicarilla Apache	1,517
Mescalero Apache	1,478
Cherokee	1,200
Navajo	57,919
Pueblo[a]	
Total	26,849
Acoma	2,588
Cochiti	752
Isleta	2,254
Jemez	1,235
Keres (n.e.c.)	648
Laguna	3,298
Pueblo (n.e.c.)	485
San Felipe	1,693
Santo Domingo	2,366
Taos	1,055
Tewa	1,465
Zia	617
Zuni	5,880
All other	5,007
Not reported	11,876
New York	
Total	43,508
Algonquian	405
Apache	505
Blackfeet[a]	775
Canadian and Latin American	446
Cherokee	4,587
Chippewa	505
Delaware	438
Iroquois	
Total	16,265
Cayuga	548

TABLE A2.1 *(continued)*

Iroquois (n.e.c.)	897
Mohawk[b]	7,919
Oneida	865
Onondaga	687
Seneca	4,507
Tuscarora	826
Shinnecock	781
Sioux	598
All other	5,327
Not reported	12,876
North Carolina	
Total	65,808
Cherokee	
Total	7,688
Cherokee	6,815
Eastern Cherokee	845
Coharie	491
Eastern tribes (n.e.c.)	
Total	1,440
Southeastern Indians	1,412
Haliwa	1,637
Iroquois	
Total	999
Tuscarora	824
Lumbee[c]	26,447
Lummi[c]	1,677
All other	3,521
Not reported	21,908
North Dakota	
Total	19,905
Arikara	880
Chippewa	9,201
Hidatsa	1,169
Mandan	400
Sioux	4,749
All other	1,145
Not reported	2,361
Ohio	
Total	15,300
Blackfeet[a]	605
Cherokee	5,667
Iroquois	438

TABLE A2.1 *(continued)*

Sioux	515
All other	3,726
Not reported	4,349
Oklahoma	
Total	171,092
Apache	1,097
Arapaho	886
Caddo	1,231
Cherokee	59,270
Cheyenne	3,364
Chickasaw	6,027
Choctaw	24,162
Comanche	4,244
Creek	15,421
Delaware	1,689
Iroquois	
Total	1,258
Seneca	436
Kickapoo	953
Kiowa	5,004
Navajo	890
Osage	3,029
Oto	1,013
Pawnee	1,269
Ponca	1,424
Potawatomi	2,296
Sac and Fox-Mesquakie	1,272
Seminole[a]	5,037
Shawnee	1,876
Sioux	1,024
Wichita	405
All other	6,510
Not reported	20,441
Oregon	
Total	29,783
Apache	516
Blackfeet[a]	757
Cherokee	4,864
Chinook	788
Chippewa	1,365
Choctaw	488
Klamath	1,500
Navajo	411
Paiute[a]	536

TABLE A2.1 *(continued)*

Silete	574
Sioux	1,348
Umatilla	660
Warm Springs	1,000
Yakima	648
All other	8,545
Not reported	5,783
Pennsylvania	
Total	10,928
Blackfeet[a]	533
Cherokee	2,808
Iroquois	845
All other	3,472
Not reported	3,270
Rhode Island	
Total	3,186
Narragansett	1,512
All other	952
Not reported	722
South Carolina	
Total	6,655
Catawba	1,116
Cherokee	1,092
All other	1,285
Not reported	3,162
South Dakota	
Total	45,525
Sioux	
Total	38,417
Cheyenne River Sioux[d]	2,765
Crow Creek Sioux	1,123
Dakota Sioux	889
Lower Brule Sioux	693
Oglala Sioux	10,335
Rosebud Sioux	5,179
Sioux	13,084
Sisseton Sioux	715
Standing Rock Sioux	1,533
Yankton Sioux	1,427
All other	2,855
Not reported	4,253

TABLE A2.1 *(continued)*

Tennessee	
Total	6,946
Cherokee	2,318
All other	1,337
Not reported	3,291
Texas	
Total	50,296
Alabama Coushatta[a]	813
Apache	1,517
Blackfeet[a]	675
Canadian and Latin American	513
Cherokee	13,911
Chickasaw	1,074
Chippewa	542
Choctaw	4,634
Comanche	1,019
Creek	1,374
Iroquois	507
Navajo	837
Potawatomi	430
Pueblo[a]	510
Sioux	1,259
All other	6,438
Not reported	14,243
Utah	
Total	19,994
Cherokee	955
Navajo	9,178
Paiute[a]	702
Pueblo[a]	472
Shoshone	494
Sioux	477
Ute	2,626
All other	2,885
Not reported	2,205
Vermont	
Total	1,041
Virginia	
Total	9,867
Cherokee	1,836
Chickahominy	547
All other	2,663
Not reported	4,821

TABLE A2.1 *(continued)*

Washington	
Total	61,233
Apache	598
Blackfeet[a]	1,950
Canadian and Latin American	617
Cherokee	5,201
Chemakuan	466
Chippewa	2,334
Choctaw	617
Clallam	743
Colville	4,832
Cowlitz	735
Cree	566
Flathead	837
Iroquois	419
Lummi[c]	2,115
Makah	970
Navajo	485
Nez Perce[a]	644
Puget Sound Salish	
Total	5,623
Muckleshoot	472
Nooksack	501
Puyallup	525
Swinomish	423
Tulalip	1,078
Quinault	1,419
Sioux	2,148
Spokane	1,557
Tlingit	1,415
Yakima	5,060
All other	9,822
Not reported	10,060
West Virginia	
Total	2,317
Cherokee	579
All other	579
Not reported	1,159
Wisconsin	
Total	30,553
Cherokee	940
Chippewa	8,370
Iroquois	
Total	5,028
Oneida	4,961

TABLE A2.1 *(continued)*

Menominee	4,772
Potawatomi	671
Stockbridge	934
Winnebago	2,068
All other	2,789
Not reported	4,981
Wyoming	
Total	8,192
Arapaho	2,149
Cherokee	639
Shoshone	1,289
Sioux	709
All other	1,562
Not reported	1,844

APPENDIX 3

CHARACTERISTICS OF AMERICAN INDIAN MORTALITY

TABLE A3.1

*Age-Specific Mortality Rates Among American Indians
and Alaska Natives and All Races, 1982–1984
(per 100,000 population)*

Age	American Indians	All Races
Under 1	1,231.4	1,107.3
1–4	89.7	55.9
5–14	28.1	26.9
15–24	176.6	96.0
25–34	284.4	121.4
35–44	363.6	201.9
45–54	668.2	535.7
55–64	1,279.1	1,299.5
65–74	2,407.0	2,874.3
75–84	5,014.3	6,441.5
85 and Over	10,532.9	15,168.0

SOURCE: Indian Health Service Chart Book Series, April 1987.

TABLE A3.2

*Age-Adjusted Mortality Rates for Selected Causes
Among American Indians and Alaska Natives and All Races, 1984
(per 100,000 population)*

Cause of Death	American Indians	All Races
Cardiovascular Disease	173.1	228.4
Malignant Neoplasms	88.4	133.5
Accidents	81.3	35.0
Auto	42.0	19.1
Other	39.3	15.9
Liver Disease and Cirrhosis	30.7	10.0
Diabetes	20.6	9.5
Pneumonia and Influenza	18.4	12.2
Homicide	14.5	8.4
Suicide	12.9	11.6
Tuberculosis	1.8	0.5

SOURCE: Indian Health Service Chart Book Series, April 1987.

TABLE A3.3

Mortality Rates for Leading Causes of Death
Among American Indian and Alaska Native
Men and Women, 1982–1984
(per 100,00 population)

Cause of Death	Males	Females
Heart Disease	129.3	89.6
Accidents	120.6	40.9
Auto	62.2	24.7
Other	58.4	16.2
Malignant Neoplasms	66.3	59.8
Liver Disease and Cirrhosis	25.6	19.3
Suicide	23.1	—
Cerebrovascular Diseases	22.7	23.7
Homicide	21.5	7.7
Diabetes	12.9	17.5

SOURCE: Indian Health Service Chart Book Series, April 1987.

TABLE A3.4

Leading Causes of Infant Deaths,
American Indians and Alaska Natives and All Races, 1982–1984
(per 1,000 live births)

Cause	American Indians	All Races
Sudden Infant Death Syndrome	2.2	1.5
Congenital Anomalies	1.8	2.4
Respiratory Distress Syndrome	0.6	1.0
Prematurity and Low Birthweight	0.5	0.9
Accidents	0.4	0.3
Pneumonia and Influenza	0.4	0.2

SOURCE: Indian Health Service Chart Book Series, April 1987.

FIGURE A3.1

*Infant Mortality Rates for American Indians
and Alaska Natives and All Races, 1970–1983
(per 100,000 live births)*

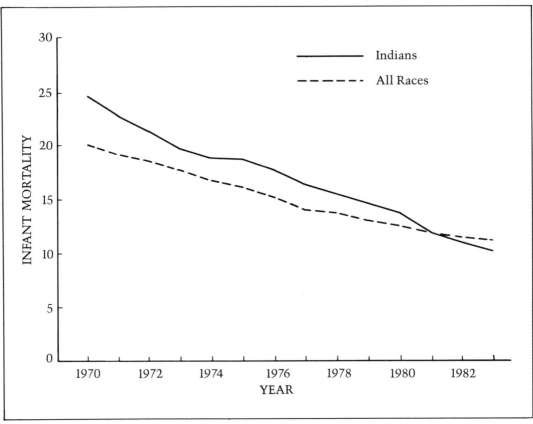

SOURCE: Indian Health Service Chart Book Series, April 1987.

FIGURE A3.2

*Age-Adjusted Accident Death Rates for American Indians
and Alaska Natives and All Races, 1970–1983
(per 100,000 population)*

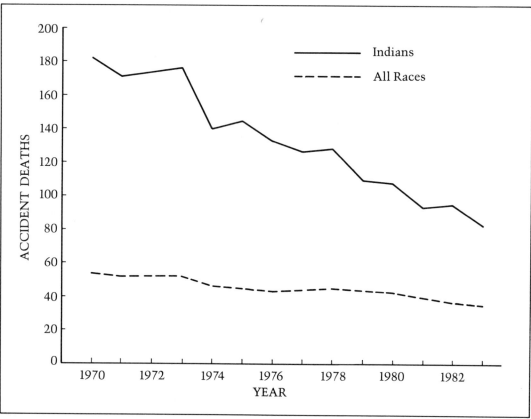

SOURCE: Indian Health Service Chart Book Series, April 1987.

FIGURE A3.3

*Age-Adjusted Suicide Death Rates for American Indians
and Alaska Natives and All Races, 1970–1983
(per 100,000 population)*

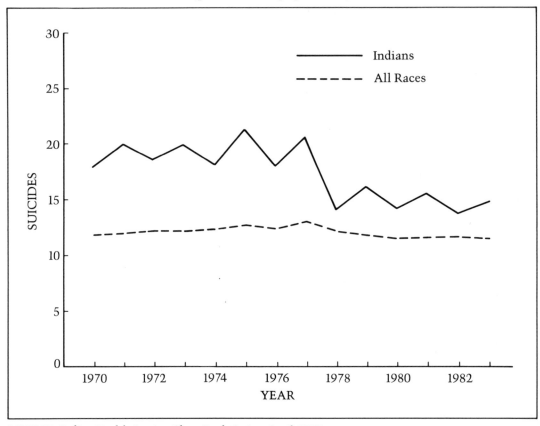

SOURCE: Indian Health Service Chart Book Series, April 1987.

FIGURE A3.4

*Age-Adjusted Homicide Death Rates for American Indians
and Alaska Natives and All Races, 1970–1983
(per 100,000 population)*

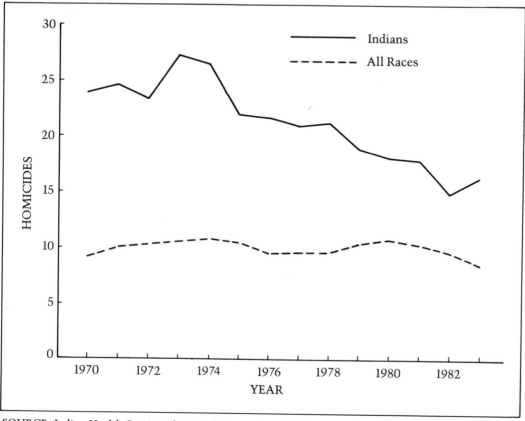

SOURCE: Indian Health Service Chart Book Series, April 1987.

FIGURE A3.5

*Age-Adjusted Alcoholism-Related Death Rates for American Indians
and Alaska Natives and All Races, 1970–1983
(per 100,000 population)*

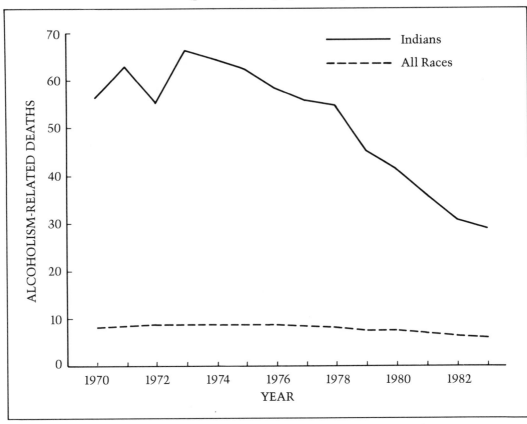

SOURCE: Indian Health Service Chart Book Series, April 1987.

FIGURE A3.6

Age-Adjusted Malignant Neoplasm Death Rates for American Indians and Alaska Natives and All Races, 1970–1983 (per 100,000 population)

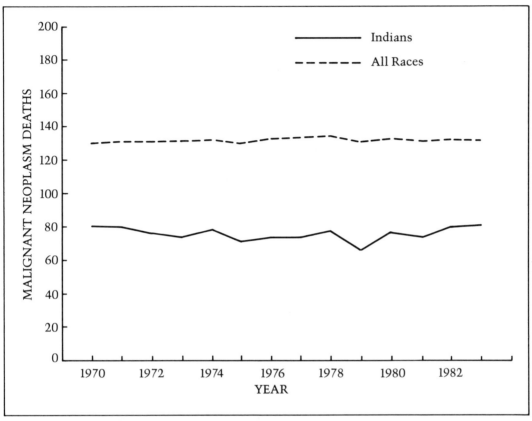

SOURCE: Indian Health Service Chart Book Series, April 1987.

FIGURE A3.7

*Age-Adjusted Tuberculosis Death Rates for American Indians
and Alaska Natives and All Races, 1970–1983
(per 100,000 population)*

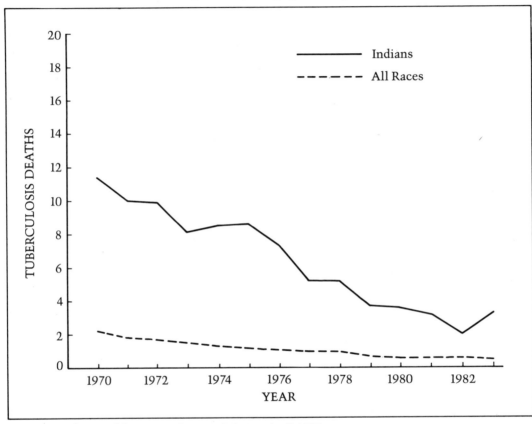

SOURCE: Indian Health Service Chart Book Series, April 1987.

FIGURE A3.8

*Age-Adjusted Diabetes Mellitus Death Rates for American Indians
and Alaska Natives and All Races, 1970–1983
(per 100,000 population)*

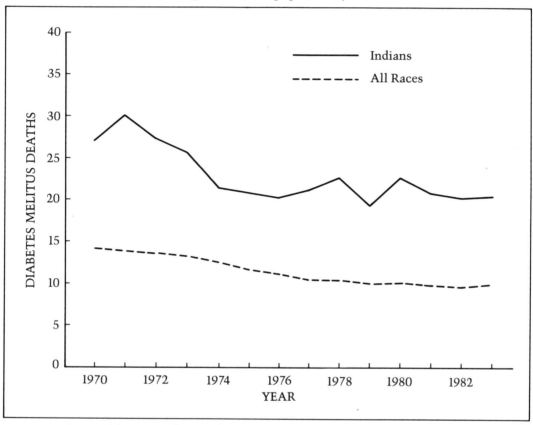

SOURCE: Indian Health Service Chart Book Series, April 1987.

APPENDIX 4

BLOOD QUANTUM REQUIREMENTS OF FEDERALLY RECOGNIZED AMERICAN INDIAN TRIBES

TABLE A4.1

*Federally Recognized[a] American Indian Tribes
and Approximate Enrollments,[b] by Blood Quantum Requirements[c]*

Tribe	Approximate Enrollment
½ Blood Quantum Required	
Big Valley Rancheria: Pomos/Pit River	200
Duck Water Shoshone—Nevada	325
Hannahville Community	399
Havasupai Tribe—Arizona	533
Hopi Tribe	5,063
Jamul Indian Village—California	62
Miccosukee Tribe—Florida	275
Mississippi Band of Choctaws	3,790
Northern Cheyenne—Montana	5,416
Omaha Tribe—Nebraska	3,876
Pueblo—Isleta	3,224
Shoshone-Bannock Tribe: Ft. Hall	3,100
St. Croix Chippewa—Wisconsin	543
Ute Mountain Tribe	1,528
Yavapai-Apache Camp Verde	11,000
Yomba: Shoshone	95
Quinault Tribe	546
⅜ Blood Quantum Required	
Jicarilla Apache Tribe	2,308
¼ Blood Quantum Required	
Absentee—Shawnee	1,971
Ak Chin	495
Alturas Rancheria	21
Apache—Oklahoma	833
Assiniboine—Sioux	8,318
Bay Mills—Sault Ste. Marie	840
Blackfeet Tribe—Montana	12,879
Bridgeport Paiute	70
Burns Paiute	205
Cabazon Band	38

SOURCE: Unpublished tabulations from the Indian Health Service.

[a]Federally recognized tribes are the designated tribal authorities officially recognized by federal agencies such as the Bureau of Indian Affairs. They do not necessarily correspond to the tribal names by which individuals identified themselves in the 1980 census, though in most cases they are closely related.

[b]Enrollments are approximate and based on records maintained by tribal authorities and supplied upon request to the Indian Health Service. There is no necessary connection between the numbers of persons officially enrolled in a tribe as a tribal member and the number of persons who identify a tribal affiliation in the census.

[c]Blood quantum requirements reflect degrees of ancestry necessary to qualify tribal membership. Rules for documenting ancestry are complex and vary from tribe to tribe.

TABLE A4.1 *(continued)*

Tribe	Approximate Enrollment
Campo Band	78
Cheyenne—Arapaho	7,677
Cheyenne River Sioux	9,361
Coast Indian—Yurok	35
Cocopah—Arizona	800
Coeur D'Alene	1,200
Colorado River	2,707
Comanche—Oklahoma	7,413
Confederated Salish & Kootenai	6,210
Confederated—Chehalis	377
Confederated—Colville—Washington	6,636
Confederated—Umatilla—Oregon	1,342
Confederated—Warm Spring—Oregon	2,400
Cortina—Wintun—California	101
Crow Tribe—Montana	6,961
Crow Creek—Sioux South Dakota	3,075
Devil Lake Sioux North Dakota	3,300
Ely Colony—Nevada	312
Flandreau Santee—Sioux	504
Forest County Potawatomi—Wisconsin	683
Fort Belnap Community	4,608
Fort Bidwell Community	199
Fort McDermitt Paiute—Shoohone	529
Fort McDowell Mohave—Apache	520
Fort Mojave	788
Gila River Pima—Maricopa	11,000
Grindstone Rancheria	87
Hoh—Washington	101
Hoopa Valley—California	1,598
Hualapai	1,375
Iowa—Oklahoma	286
Jamestown Band Clallam—Washington	150
Kaibab Band Paiute	250
Kalispel Community	185
Keweenaw Bay Indians Community	3,135
Kickapoo—Kansas	1,198
Kickapoo—Oklahoma	7,948
Kootenai	65
Lac Courte Oreilles of Lake Superior—Chippewa	3,500
Lac du Flambeau Band Lake Superior Chippewa	1,972
Las Vegas—Paiute	105
Lovelock Paiute	163
Lower Brule Sioux	2,643
Lower Elwha Community	403
Lummi	1,225

TABLE A4.1 *(continued)*

Tribe	Approximate Enrollment
Menominee—Wisconsin	6,263
Minnesota Chippewa Tribe (6 reservations)	33,745
Moapa Band of Paiute	380
Navajo	175,893
Nez Perce	2,560
Nisqually—Washington	175
Nooksack—Washington	425
Oneida—Wisconsin	8,844
Otoe-Missouria—Oklahoma	1,450
Paiute—Utah	543
Paiute-Shoshone: Fallon	1,200
Pauma Band—Luiseno Mission	91
Pawnee—Oklahoma	2,249
Pit River: X-L Ranch	3,031
Ponca	2,022
Prairie Band—Potawatomi	3,289
Laguna—Pueblo	6,406
Quechan—Ft. Yuma	2,182
Quinault	1,800
Red Lake Band of Chippewa	8,104
Reno-Sparks	507
Robinson Rancheria	183
Rosebud Sioux—South Dakota	15,438
Sac & Fox—Oklahoma	2,145
Saginaw Chippewa—Michigan	891
Salt River: Pima-Maricopa	4,143
San Carlos Apache	9,800
Santa Rosa—Santa Rosa Rancheria	209
Sauk-Suiattle—Washington	220
Seminole—Florida	1,218
Shappee Mdewakanton Sioux—Prior Lake	86
Shoewood Valley Rancheria	231
Shoalwater Bay	101
Shoshone-Paiute—Duck Valley	1,635
Skokomish Washington	501
Southern Ute	1,096
Spokane—Washington	1,938
Standing Rock Sioux	9,613
Stockbridge—Munsee: Mohican—Wisconsin	1,346
Summit Lake Paiute	66
Susanville Rancheria	175
Te-Moak Band Western Shoshone	1,726
Three Affiliated—Fort Berthold	7,341
Tonto Apache	63
Tuolumne Band: Miwok	102
Turtle Mountain Band Chippewa	24,000

TABLE A4.1 *(continued)*

Tribe	Approximate Enrollment
Twenty-Nine Palms Band—Luiseno Ranch	13
Walker River Paiute	1,100
Washoe Nev./California	2,332
White Mountain Apache	8,841
Wichita—Oklahoma	996
Winnebago—Nebraska	2,923
Winnemucca Indian Colony—Nevada	30
Wisconsin Winnebago	3,347
Yankton Sioux Tribe—South Dakota	5,260
Yavapai—Prescott	110
Verington Paiute—Campbell Ranch	363
Kiowa	7,948
⅛ Blood Quantum Required	
Aqua Caliente Band of Cahuilla	218
Caddo	2,031
Capitan Grande Band	451
Citizen Band of Potawatomi	11,071
Confederated—Siletz	1,550
Delaware—W. Oklahoma	955
Elem Indian Colony Pomos	152
Fort Sill Apache—Oklahoma	272
La Jolla Band—Luiseno Mission	420
Mesa Grande Band	286
Muckleshoot—Washington	408
Rincon Band—Luiseno Mission	500
Sac & Fox of Missouri: Kansas/Nebraska	243
San Manual—Serrano Mission	40
San Pasqual Band—Diegueno	278
Sisseton—Wahpeton Sioux	8,000
Squaxin Island	290
Suquamish—Port Madison	583
Sycuan Band—Diegueno Mission	55
Upper Skagit	215
1/16 Blood Quantum Required	
Chitimacha—Louisiana	260
Confederated—Grande Ronde	1,100
Fort Independence Paiute—California	65
Manzanita Band—Dieugeno Mission	50
Pala Band-Luiseno: California	475
Shingle Spring Band—Miwok	75
Stillaguamish	153
United Keetoowah	7,500
Ute: Untahi Ouray	1,720
Wyandotte—Oklahoma	3,347
Osage—Oklahoma	8,768

APPENDIX 5

TRADITIONAL OCCUPATIONS RECOGNIZED BY THE CENSUS BUREAU

TABLE A5.1

Occupations Recognized in the 1980 Census
as "Traditional" Livelihoods for American Indians and Alaska Natives

Tribal Government Occupations
    Officials and administrators: includes tribal chairpersons, governors,
        lieutenant governors, presidents, principal chiefs, representatives,
        spokespersons, and village chiefs
    Legislators: includes tribal council persons
    Judicial administrators: includes tribal judges

Artist and Performer Occupations
    Dancers: includes buckskin, fancy, hoop, kachina, shawl, straight, team, and
        traditional dancers
    Drummers and singers: includes drummers, northern, southern, stomp
        dance, and peyote singers
    Painters: includes sand and any other specified painters
    Potters: includes clay and any other specified potters

Handworking Occupations
    Basket makers: includes cedar, bark, reed, and any other specified basket
        makers
    Beaders: includes hand, loom, and any other specified beaders
    Bustle makers: includes feather and any other specified bustle makers
    Carvers: includes ivory, soapstone, wood, and any other specified carvers
    Fan makers: includes feather and any other specified fan makers
    Moccasin makers: includes buckskin, leather, fur, and any other specified
        moccasin makers
    Quilters: includes star and any other specified quilters
    Rattle makers: includes gourd, peyote, and any other specified rattle makers
    Weavers: includes belts, blankets, handbags, rugs, and any other specified
        weavers
    Doll makers: includes corn husk, crown dancer, kachina, and any other
        specified doll makers
    Drum makers: includes group, hand, and any other specified drum makers
    Quill workers: includes porcupine quills and any other specified quill
        workers
    Roach makers: includes persons who use porcupine hair and any other
        specified roach makers
    Tanners: includes buckskin and any other specified tanners

Other Occupations
    Native healers: includes medicine persons, shamans, and spiritual healers
    Sheep workers: includes persons who herd sheep

APPENDIX 6

MAPS OF CENSUS
REGIONS AND DIVISIONS
AND OF OKLAHOMA
HISTORIC AREAS

MAP A6.1

*Geographic Regions and Divisions of the United States,
Designated by the U.S. Bureau of the Census*

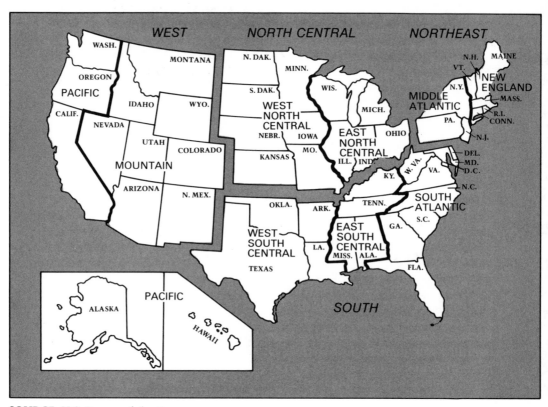

SOURCE: U.S. Bureau of the Census.

MAP A6.2

Identified Historic Areas of Oklahoma (excluding urbanized areas), 1980, and "Indian Territory," Circa 1830–1900

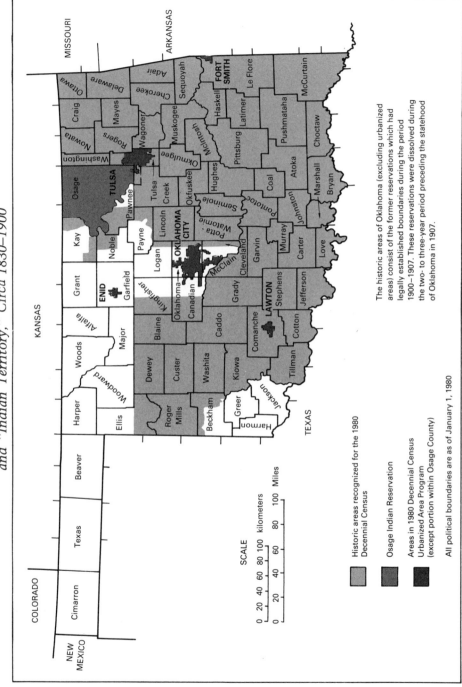

The historic areas of Oklahoma (excluding urbanized areas) consist of the former reservations which had legally established boundaries during the period 1900–1907. These reservations were dissolved during the two- to three-year period preceding the statehood of Oklahoma in 1907.

Historic areas recognized for the 1980 Decennial Census

Osage Indian Reservation

Areas in 1980 Decennial Census Urbanized Area Program (except portion within Osage County)

All political boundaries are as of January 1, 1980

SCALE

0 20 40 60 80 100 kilometers

0 20 40 60 80 100 Miles

SOURCE: U.S. Bureau of the Census.

Bibliography

Ablon, Joan "Relocated American Indians in the San Francisco Bay Area: Social Interactions and Indian Identity." *Human Organization* 23 (1964):296–304.

American Indian Policy Review Commission (AIPRC) *Final Report of the American Indian Policy Review Commission.* Washington, DC: U.S. Government Printing Office, 1977.

Aschmann, Homer *The Central Desert of Baja California: Demography and Ecology.* Riverside, CA: Manessier, 1967 (1959)

Barsh, Russell Lawrence, and James Youngblood Henderson *The Road: Indian Tribes and Political Liberty.* Berkeley: University of California Press, 1980.

Barth, Fredrik "Introduction." In Fredrik Barth, ed. *Ethnic Groups and Boundaries.* Boston: Little, Brown, 1969.

Beale, Calvin L. "Migration Patterns of Minorities in the United States." *American Journal of Agricultural Economics* 55 (1973):938–946.

Bean, Frank D., and John P. Marcum "Differential Fertility and the Minority Group Status Hypothesis: An Assessment and Review." In Frank D. Bean and W. Parker Frisbie, eds. *The Demography of Racial and Ethnic Groups.* New York: Academic Press, 1978.

Becker, Gary *Human Capital.* New York: National Bureau of Economic Research, 1964.

Berkhofer, Robert F., Jr. *The White Man's Indian.* New York: Vintage Books, 1978.

Berry, Brewton "The Myth of the Vanishing Indian." *Phylon* 21 (1960):51–57.

Bianchi, Suzanne M., and Daphne Spain *American Women in Transition.* New York: Russell Sage Foundation, 1986.

Bieder, Robert E. "Scientific Attitudes Toward Indian Mixed-Bloods in Early Nineteenth Century America." *Journal of Ethnic Studies* 8 (1980):17–30.

Borah, Woodrow W. "The Historical Demography of Aboriginal and Colonial America: An Attempt at Perspective." In William M. Denevan, ed. *The Native Population of the Americas in 1492.* Madison: University of Wisconsin Press, 1976.

Bowen, William G., and T. Aldrich Finegan *The Economics of Labor Force Participation.* Princeton, NJ: Princeton University Press, 1969.

Brophy, William A., and Sophie D. Aberle *The Indian: America's Unfinished Business.* Norman: University of Oklahoma Press, 1966.

Browman, David L. *Early Native Americans: Prehistoric Demography, Economy, and Technology.* The Hague: Mouton, 1980.

Bumpass, Larry L., and Charles F. Westoff *The Later Years of Childbearing.* Princeton, NJ: Princeton University Press, 1970.

Butz, William, and Michael Ward "The Emergence of Countercyclical U.S. Fertility." *American Economic Review* 69 (1979):318–327.

Collins, Randall *The Credential Society.* New York: Academic Press, 1979.

Cook, Sherburne F., and Woodrow W. Borah *Essays in Population History: Mexico and the Caribbean,* vols. 1 and 2. Berkeley: University of California Press, 1971 and 1974.

Crosby, Alfred W., Jr. *The Columbian Exchange: Biological and Cultural Consequences of 1492.* Westport, CT: Greenwood, 1972.

Denevan, William M., ed. *The Native Population of the Americas in 1492.* Madison: University of Wisconsin Press, 1976.

DeRosier, Arthur H. *The Removal of the Choctaw Indians.* Knoxville: University of Tennessee Press, 1970.

De Vos, George "Ethnic Pluralism: Conflict and Accommodation." In George De Vos and Lola Romanucci-Ross, eds. *Ethnic Identity: Cultural Continuities and Change.* Palo Alto, CA: Mayfield, 1975.

Dobyns, Henry F. "Estimating Aboriginal American Population: An Appraisal of Techniques with a New Hemispheric Estimate." *Current Anthropology* 7 (1966):395–416.

—————— "Reply." *Current Anthropology* 7 (1966):440–444.

—————— *Native American Historical Demography: A Critical Bibliography.* Bloomington: Indiana University Press, 1976.

—————— *Their Number Become Thinned: Native American Population Dynamics in Eastern North America.* Knoxville: University of Tennessee Press, 1983.

Driver, Harold E. *Indians of North America.* Chicago and London: University of Chicago Press, 1969.

Easterlin, Richard A. *Birth and Fortune.* New York: Basic Books, 1980.

Eitzen, D. Stanley *Social Problems.* Boston: Allyn & Bacon, 1983.

Fey, Harold E., and D'Arcy McNickle *Indians and Other Americans: Two Ways of Life Meet.* New York: Harper & Brothers, 1959.

Fixico, Donald L. *Termination and Relocation: Federal Indian Policy, 1945–1960.* Albuquerque: University of New Mexico Press, 1986.

Foreman, Grant *Indian Removal.* Norman: University of Oklahoma Press, 1932.

Fuchs, Estelle, and Robert J. Havighurst *To Live on This Earth: American Indian Education.* Garden City, NY: Doubleday, 1972.

Goldsby, Richard A. *Race and Races.* New York: Macmillan, 1971.

Goldscheider, Calvin, and Peter R. Uhlenberg "Minority Group Status and Fertility." *American Journal of Sociology* 74 (1969):361–372.

Greenwood, Michael J. "Research on Internal Migration in the United States: A Survey." *Journal of Economic Literature* 13 (1975):397–433.

Gundlach, James H., and Alden E. Roberts "Native American Indian Migration and Relocation: Success or Failure." *Pacific Sociological Review* 12 (1978):117–128.

Gwartney, James D., and James E. Long "The Relative Earnings of Blacks and Other Minorities." *Industrial and Labor Relations Review* 31 (1978):336–346.

Hackenberg, Robert A., and C. Roderick Wilson "Reluctant Emigrants: The Role of Migration in Papago Indian Adaptation." *Human Organization* 31 (1972):171–186.

Hall, Robert L. "An Interpretation of the Two-Climax Model of Illinois Prehistory." In David L. Browman, ed. *Early Native Americans.* The Hague: Mouton, 1980.

Hall, Thomas D. "Incorporation in the World-System: Toward a Critique." *American Sociological Review* 51 (1986):390–402.

Haller, Archibald O. "Social Psychological Aspects of Schooling and Achievement." In Robert M. Hauser, Archibald O. Haller, David Mechanic, and

Taissa S. Hauser, eds. *Social Structure and Behavior.* New York: Academic Press, 1982.

Hertzberg, Hazel W. *The Search for an American Indian Identity: Modern Pan-Indian Movements.* New York: Syracuse University Press, 1980.

Highwater, Jamake *The Primal Mind: Vision and Reality in Indian America.* New York: Harper & Row, 1981.

Hodge, William H. "Navajo Urban Migration: An Analysis from the Perspective of the Family." In Jack O. Waddell and O. Michael Watson, eds. *The American Indian in Urban Society.* Boston: Little, Brown, 1971.

Hogan, Dennis P. "The Variable Order of Events in the Life Course." *American Sociological Review* 43 (1978):573–586.

Indian Health Service. Chart Book Series. Washington, DC: U.S. Department of Health and Human Services, April 1987.

Institute for Government Research *The Problem of Indian Administration* [The Meriam Report]. Baltimore: Johns Hopkins University Press, 1928.

Jacobsen, Cardell K. "Internal Colonialism and Native Americans: Indian Labor in the United States from 1871 to World War II." *Social Science Quarterly* 65 (1984):158–171.

Jencks, Christopher; Marshall Smith; Henry Acland; Mary Jo Bane; David Cohen; Herbert Gintis; Barbara Heyns; and Stephan Michelson *Inequality: A Reassessment of the Effect of Family and Schooling in America.* New York: Harper & Row, 1972.

Kroeber, Alfred L. "Native American Population." *American Anthropologist* 36 (1934):1–25.

———— "Cultural and Natural Areas of Native North America." American Archaeology and Ethnology no. 38. Berkeley: University of California Press, 1939.

Levitan, Sar A., and Barbara Hetrick *Big Brother's Indian Programs: With Reservations.* New York: McGraw-Hill, 1971.

Levitan, Sar A., and William B. Johnston *Indian Giving: Federal Programs for Native Americans.* Baltimore: Johns Hopkins University Press, 1975.

Linton, Ralph, ed. *Acculturation in Seven American Indian Tribes.* Gloucester, MA: Peter Smith, 1963.

Lurie, Nancy O. "The Enduring Indian." *Natural History* 75 (1966):10–22.

MacLeod, William C. *The American Indian Frontier.* New York: Knopf, 1928.

Margon, Arthur "Indians and Immigrants: A Comparison of Groups New to the City." *Journal of Ethnic Studies* 4 (1976):17–28.

Marini, Margaret Mooney "Age and Sequencing Norms in the Transition to Adulthood." *Social Forces* 63 (1984):229–244.

———— "The Order of Events in the Transition to Adulthood." *Sociology of Education* 57 (1984):63–84.

Mincer, Jacob *Schooling, Experience and Earnings.* New York: National Bureau of Economic Research, 1974.

Mirowsky, John, and Catherine E. Ross "Language Networks and Social Status among Mexican Americans." *Social Science Quarterly* 65 (1984):555–564.

Momeni, Jamshid A. *Demography of Racial and Ethnic Minorities in the United States: An Annotated Bibliography with a Review Essay.* Westport, CT: Greenwood Press, 1984.

Montagu, M. F. Ashley *An Introduction to Physical Anthropology,* 3rd ed. New York: Columbia University Press, 1960.

Mooney, James *The Aboriginal Population of America North of Mexico.* Smithsonian Miscellaneous Collections, vol. 80, no. 7. Washington, DC: Smithsonian Institution, 1928.

Murray, Charles *Losing Ground: American Social Policy, 1950–1980.* New York: Basic Books, 1984.

Nagel, Joane "The Roots of Red Power: Demographic and Organizational Bases of Indian Activism, 1950–1980." Paper presented at the annual meeting of the American Sociological Association, Atlanta, 1988.

Officer, James E. "The American Indian and Federal Policy." In Jack O. Waddell and O. Michael Watson, eds. *The American Indian in Urban Society.* Boston: Little, Brown, 1971.

Passel, Jeffrey S. "Provisional Evaluation of the 1970 Census Count of American Indians." *Demography* 13 (1976):397–409.

Passel, Jeffrey S., and Patricia A. Berman "Quality of 1980 Census Data for American Indians." *Social Biology* 33 (1986):163–182.

Pearce, Diana "Women in Poverty." In Arthur Blaustein, ed. *The American Promise: Equal Justice and Economic Opportunity.* New Brunswick, NJ: Transaction Books, 1982.

Petersen, William "Concepts of Ethnicity." In Stephan Thernstrom, ed. *Harvard Encyclopedia of American Ethnic Groups.* Cambridge, MA: Harvard University Press, 1980.

Price, John A. "The Migration and Adaptation of American Indians to Los Angeles." *Human Organization* 27 (1968):168–175.

Retherford, Robert D., and Lee-Jay Cho "Age-Parity-Specific Birth Rates and Birth Probabilities from Census or Survey Data on Own Children." *Population Studies* 32 (1978):567–581.

Rindfuss, Ronald R.; Larry L. Bumpass; and Craig St. John "Education and Fertility: Implications for the Roles Women Occupy." *American Sociological Review* 45 (1980):431–437.

Rindfuss, Ronald R., and James A. Sweet *Postwar Fertility Trends and Differentials in the United States.* New York: Academic Press, 1977.

Ruffing, Lorraine Turner "Navajo Economic Development: A Dual Perspective." In Sam Stanley, ed. *American Indian Economic Development.* The Hague: Mouton, 1978.

Sandefur, Gary D., and Wilbur J. Scott "Minority Group Status and the Wages of Indian and Black Males." *Social Science Research* 12 (1983):44–68.

Sewell, William H., and Robert M. Hauser *Education, Occupation, and Earnings.* New York: Academic Press, 1975.

Sheehy, Gail *Passages: Predictable Crises of Adult Life.* New York: Bantam Books, 1974.

Shryock, Henry S., and Jacob S. Siegel *The Methods and Materials of Demography.* Washington, DC: U.S. Government Printing Office, 1971.

Simpson, George Eaton, and J. Milton Yinger *Racial and Cultural Minorities,* 3rd ed. New York: Harper & Row, 1965.

Smith-Lovin, Lynne, and Ann R. Tickamyer "Nonrecursive Models of Labor Force Participation, Fertility Behavior, and Sex Role Attitudes." *American Sociological Review* 43 (1978):541–556.

Snipp, C. Matthew "On the Cost of Being American Indian: Ethnic Identity and Economic Opportunity." In James Johnson and Melvin Oliver, eds. *Proceedings of the Conference on Comparative Ethnicity.* Los Angeles: Institute for Social Science Research, University of California, 1988.

Snipp, C. Matthew, and Gary D. Sandefur "Earnings of American Indians and

Alaska Natives: The Effects of Residence and Migration." *Social Forces* 66 (1988):994–1008.

Snipp, C. Matthew, and Alan L. Sorkin "American Indian Housing: An Overview of Conditions and Public Policy." In Jamshid A. Momeni, ed. *Race, Ethnicity, and Housing in the United States.* Westport, CT: Greenwood Press, 1986.

Sorkin, Alan L. *American Indians and Federal Aid.* Washington, DC: Brookings Institution, 1971.

—————— *The Urban American Indian.* Lexington, MA: Heath, 1978.

Spenner, Kenneth I., and David L. Featherman "Achievement Ambitions." *Annual Review of Sociology* 4 (1978):373–420.

Stanley, Sam, and Robert K. Thomas "Current Demographic and Social Trends Among North American Indians." *Annals* 436 (1978):111–120.

Staples, Robert, and Alfredo Mirande "Racial and Cultural Variations Among American Families: A Decennial Review of the Literature on Minority Families." *Journal of Marriage and the Family* 42 (1980):887–903.

Steiner, Stan *The New Indians.* New York: Dell, 1968.

Steward, Julian H. "Theory and Application in a Social Science." *Ethnology* 2 (1955):292–302.

Sturtevant, William C., ed. *Handbook of North American Indians.* Washington, DC: Smithsonian Institution, U.S. Government Printing Office, 1981.

Sweet, James A. "Components of Change in the Number of Households, 1970–1980." *Demography* 21 (1984):129–140.

Tax, Sol "The Impact of Urbanization on American Indians." *Annals* 436 (1978):121–135.

Taylor, Theodore W. *The Bureau of Indian Affairs.* Boulder, CO: Westview Press, 1984.

Terrell, John Upton *American Indian Almanac.* New York and Cleveland: World, 1971.

Thernstrom, Stephan; Ann Orlov; and Oscar Handlin "Introduction." In Stephan Thernstrom, ed. *Harvard Encyclopedia of American Ethnic Groups.* Cambridge, MA: Harvard University Press, 1980.

Thornton, Russell "But How Thick Were They?" *Contemporary Sociology* 31 (1984):149–150.

—————— *American Indian Holocaust and Survival: A Population History Since 1492.* Norman: University of Oklahoma Press, 1987.

Thornton, Russell; Gary D. Sandefur; and Harold G. Grasmick *The Urbanization of American Indians.* Bloomington: Indiana University Press, 1982.

Thornton, Russell, and Joan Marsh-Thornton "Estimating Prehistoric American Indian Population Size for United States Area: Implications of the Nineteenth Century Population Decline and Nadir." *American Journal of Physical Anthropology* 55 (1981):47–53.

Tienda, Marta, and Lisa J. Neidert "Language, Education, and the Socioeconomic Achievement of Hispanic Origin Men." *Social Science Quarterly* 65 (1984):519–536.

Trosper, Ronald L. "Earnings and Labor Supply: A Microeconomic Comparison of American Indians and Alaskan Natives to American Whites and Blacks." Social Welfare Research Institute. Publication no. 55. Boston: Boston College, 1980.

Trovato, Frank "A Macrosociological Analysis of Native Indian Fertility in Canada: 1961, 1971, 1981," *Social Forces* 66 (1987):463–485.

Ubelaker, Douglas H. "The Sources and Methodology for Mooney's Estimates of North American Indian Populations." In William M. Denevan, ed. *The Native Population of the Americas in 1492.* Madison: University of Wisconsin Press, 1976.

Uhlmann, Julie M. "The Impact of Modernization of Papago Indian Fertility." *Human Organization* 31 (1972):149–161.

U.S. Bureau of the Census "Marital Characteristics," *1980 Census of Population, Subject Report,* PC80-2-4C. Washington, DC: U.S. Government Printing Office, 1985.

—————— "American Indians, Eskimos, and Aleuts on Identified Reservations and in the Historic Areas of Oklahoma (Excluding Urbanized Areas)," *1980 Census of Population, Subject Report,* PC80-2-1D. Washington, DC: U.S. Government Printing Office, 1985.

—————— *Statistical Abstract of the United States: 1985.* Washington, DC: U.S. Government Printing Office, 1985.

—————— "Ancestry of the Population by State, 1980." *1980 Census of Population, Supplementary Report,* PC80-51-10. Washington, DC: U.S. Government Printing Office, 1983.

—————— *1980 Census of Population, General Social and Economic Characteristics, United States Summary,* PC80-1-C1. Washington, DC: U.S. Government Printing Office, 1983.

—————— *Public-Use Microdata Samples Technical Documentation.* Washington, DC: U.S. Department of Commerce, 1983.

—————— *Twenty Censuses: Population and Housing Questions, 1790–1980.* Washington, DC: U.S. Government Printing Office, 1979.

—————— "American Indians." *1970 Census of Housing and Population, Subject Report,* PC(2)-1F. Washington, DC: U.S. Government Printing Office, 1973.

—————— *Special Reports: Nonwhite Population by Race.* Washington, DC: U.S. Government Printing Office, 1953.

—————— *Vital Statistics Rates in the United States, 1900–1940.* Washington, DC: U.S. Government Printing Office, 1943.

—————— *The Indian Population in the United States and Alaska, 1930.* Washington, DC: U.S. Government Printing Office, 1937.

—————— *The Indian Population in the United States and Alaska, 1910.* Washington, DC: U.S. Government Printing Office, 1915.

U.S. Bureau of Indian Affairs *Local Estimates of Resident Indian Population and Labor Force Status, December 1981.* Washington, DC: mimeographed, 1982.

U.S. Office of Technology Assessment *Indian Health Care.* Washington, DC: U.S. Government Printing Office, 1986.

Utley, Robert M. *The Indian Frontier of the American West, 1846–1890.* Albuquerque: University of New Mexico Press, 1984.

Vogt, Evon Z. "The Acculturation of American Indians." *Annals of the American Academy of Political and Social Science* 311 (1957):137–146.

Waddell, Jack O., and O. Michael Watson, eds. *The American Indian in Urban Society.* Boston: Little, Brown, 1971.

Waite, Linda J., and Kirstin A. Moore "The Impact of Early First Birth on Young Women's Educational Attainment." *Social Forces* 56 (1978):845–865.

Waite, Linda J., and Glenna D. Spitze "Young Women's Transition to Marriage." *Demography* 18 (1976):681–694.

Waite, Linda J., and Ross M. Stolzenberg "Intended Childbearing and Labor

Force Participation of Young Women: Insights from Nonrecursive Models." *American Sociological Review* 41 (1976):235–252.

Weller, Robert H. "The Employment of Wives, Role Incompatibility and Fertility." *Milbank Memorial Fund Quarterly* 46 (1967):507–526.

Westoff, Charles F., and Norman B. Ryder "Contraceptive Practice Among Urban Blacks in the United States, 1965." *Milbank Memorial Fund Quarterly* 48 (1970):215–233.

—— *The Contraceptive Revolution.* Princeton, NJ: Princeton University Press, 1977.

Willcox, Walter F. "Increase in the Population of the Earth and of the Continents since 1650." In Walter F. Willcox, ed. *International Migrations*, vol. 2. New York: National Bureau of Economic Research, 1931.

Willey, Gordon R. *An Introduction to American Archaeology.* Englewood Cliffs, NJ: Prentice-Hall, 1966.

Yinger, J. Milton, and George Eaton Simpson "The Integration of Americans of Indian Descent." *Annals* 436 (1978):137–151.

Name Index

A

Aberle, Sophie D., 97n, 98n, 103n, 173n, 209n
Ablon, Joan, 3n, 266n, 296n
Acland, Henry, 247n
American Indian Policy Review Commission (AIPRC), 27, 62n
Aschmann, Homer, 8n, 10

B

Bane, Mary Jo, 247n
Barsh, Russell Lawrence, 177n
Barth, Fredrik, 37, 38, 311n
Beale, Calvin L., 266n
Bean, Frank D., 141n, 147n
Becker, Gary, 256n
Berkhofer, Robert F., Jr., 3n, 29, 30n, 32n
Berman, Patricia A., 58n, 70–72
Berry, Brewton, 165n
Bianchi, Suzanne M., 144n, 152n, 154n
Bieder, Robert E., 32n, 33n
Blumenfeld, Ruth, 38n
Board of Indian Commissioners, 186–187
Borah, Woodrow Wilson, 6n, 15n, 16
Bowen, William G., 217n
Breen, Nancy, 142
Brophy, William A., 97n, 98n, 103n, 173n, 209n
Browman, David L., 17n
Bumpass, Larry L., 153n, 154n
Bureau of Ethnology, Smithsonian Institution, 23, 308n
Butz, William, 154n

C

Carlson, Leonard A., 308n
Chadwick, Bruce A., 40n

Chaudhuri, Joyotpaul, 5n
Cho, Lee-Jay, 142n
Cohen, David, n
Collins, Randall, 256n
Cook, Sherburne F., 6n
Crosby, Alfred W., Jr., 6n, 15, 19n, 20n

D

Deloria, Vine, Jr., 5n
Denevan, William M., 8n, 9, 10, 15n, 16n
DeRosier, Arthur H., 74n
De Vos, George, 37, 38
Dobyns, Henry F., 3n, 6–12, 10, 13, 14, 15n, 16, 18, 19n, 20n, 21n, 22–24, 30n, 268, 307n
Driver, Harold E., 8–9, 10, 13, 31n, 40, 42, 97n

E

Easterlin, Richard A., 154n, 155n
Eitzen, D. Stanley, 253n

F

Featherman, David L., 174n, 243n
Fey, Harold E., 36n
Finegan, T. Aldrich, 217n
Fixico, Donald L., 269n, 283n
Foreman, Grant, 74n
Frisbie, W. Parker, 141n
Fuchs, Estelle, 80n, 82n, 187n, 191n, 234n

G

Geronimo, 1, 308
Gintis, Herbert, 247n
Goldsby, Richard A., 28, 30n, 31n
Goldscheider, Calvin, 148n
Grant, Ulysses S., 66

Subject Index

Boldface numbers refer to figures and tables.

A

Abenaki tribe: total population size, **324**

accident mortality rates, **350, 351, 353**

administrative definitions of race, 28–29, 32–37

administrative support occupations: age distribution of, **244,** 245; defined, 230*n;* and educational attainment, **246,** 247; and language use, 183, **183;** and migration status, **288;** and migration streams, **299;** racial distribution of, **233;** regional distribution of, **234;** residential distribution of, **237;** wage and salary income from, **258**

Affirmative Action, 232

African ancestry, **49,** 50, **52**

age: children ever born by, **146,** 146–151, **149, 150, 151, 152, 153, 156;** of children residing in households by family type, **137,** 137–138; of children residing in households by migration status, 285–286, **286;** and educational attainment, 192–193, **194,** 195–202, **198–199, 200;** at first marriage, **131,** 150–151, **151,** 153; of housing structure, 109–111, **110, 112,** 116, **118,** 118–119; and labor force participation, 209–213, **212,** 219–221, **220;** and language use, 179–180, **180;** and migration status, 283–285, **284;** and migration streams, 293; and occupational distribution, 243, **244,** 245; and population distribution, 88–91, **89, 90, 91, 92, 94, 95;** and school enrollment, **192,** 192–193; and school progress, 193, **194,** 195; specific fertility,

141–144, **143;** wage and salary distribution by, 255–256, **256**

Aid to Families with Dependent Children (AFDC), 248*n,* 261

air conditioning, **114,** 115, **115,** 116, **117**

Alabama: sixteenth century tribes of area now occupied by, **43;** tribes with 400 or more members in, **334**

Alabama Coushatta tribe: population size in Texas, **346;** total population size, **324**

Alaska: migration to, 273; population growth in, **77;** sixteenth century tribes of area now occupied by, **43;** tribes with 400 or more members in, **334**

Alaskan Athabaskan tribes: population size in Alaska, **334;** total population size, **324**

Alaska Native Claims Settlement Act, 86

Alaska native demography, *see* demography

Alaska Native villages, 86, **86;** total population size, **324**

Albuquerque, New Mexico: population growth in, 80–81, **81;** population size of, **81**

alcoholism-related mortality rates, **356**

Aleut tribes: demography of, *see* demography; total population size, **324**

Algonquian tribe: population size in New York, **342;** total population size, **324**

Allotment Acts of 1887, 36, 308

amenities, housing, 112–116, **114, 115, 117**

American Indian demography, *see* demography

American Indian females: age at first marriage of, 131, **131,** 150–151, **151;** age-